A SOURCE BOOK OF GESTALT PSYCHOLOGY

A SOURCE BOOK OF GESTALT PSYCHOLOGY

Prepared by
WILLIS D. ELLIS
ASST. PROFESSOR OF PSYCHOLOGY
UNIVERSITY OF ARIZONA

With an Introduction by
PROFESSOR K. KOFFKA

LONDON
ROUTLEDGE & KEGAN PAUL LTD
BROADWAY HOUSE, 68-74 CARTER LANE E.C.4

First published 1938
Second impression 1950
Third impression 1967
Fourth impression 1969

Published by
Routledge & Kegan Paul Ltd
Broadway House, 68-74 Carter Lane
London, E.C.4

SBN 7100 6115 3

Printed in Great Britain by
Lowe & Brydone (Printers) Ltd., London

CONTENTS

PREFACE

The war, differences of tongue, sentiment, and background all contributed towards making it difficult for English-speaking readers to welcome *for what they were* the experimental methods and results of certain German psychologists. The gap thus created was not bridged until very recent times: notably by the publication in 1935 of Professor K. Koffka's *Principles of Gestalt Psychology.* Even this important work, however, does not wholly effect the necessary transition from the German psychology of 1912 to the present day, and Professor Koffka himself mentions this in a Preface footnote of his book. The present volume is offered in the hope that it may play a part in completing the structure. Too often it has been said by English and American authors that the *Gestalttheorie* was all—or nearly all—*Theorie.* It is possible that judgments of this sort were not formed on the basis of an extensive reading of the sources.

Why is it that one now hears such condemnations less frequently than formerly? The answer is that by now a number of experimental reports have been written in English and the force of the theory's meaning has thus begun to be apparent. But a real anomaly still remains. This *Source Book of Gestalt Psychology* may be looked upon as a kind of album whose purpose is to put the reader in touch with "the years between". From it he may gain some knowledge of what underlies the Gestalt theory both in fundamental findings and, *above all*, in manner of thinking, of addressing oneself to problems, and in the utilization of results. The results obtained in one part of a research programme should prove helpful in furthering subsequent inquiry. They do this best if all are integrated in a clearly conceived plan. The *way* Gestalt psychologists think is something every thinking person should find exhilarating to observe. None of the summaries given in this volume fails to exhibit this trait, this manner of approaching problems. To me one of the most delightful phases of preparing these abstracts has been the effort to reproduce faithfully the *thought processes* of my authors. If readers of the book catch this feature in its pages, I feel sure they too will experience the thrill one has at seeing a neat logical or mathematical demonstration. The arguments are oft-times closely reasoned and the reader's progress may not always be swift, but the reward is never disappointing.

The book is a series of abstracts or summaries of thirty-four articles and one book published in Germany between 1915 and 1929 by the leading exponents of Gestalt psychology and their students. Reference is given in each case to the original publication, and marginal page indications show the source of every statement. Direct translation was intentionally kept at a minimum. This has its advantages as well as its disadvantages. The original material was approximately ten times as long as the summaries. If the gist of that original has been retained, I shall be glad, for I have striven diligently to accomplish this. Wherever I have failed the interested reader will have no trouble in finding the debated passage, since the marginal page references are given as guide. In all cases these page numbers serve also to indicate the fullness of treatment. When several such marginal numbers follow one another in close succession, one sees that only a little has been taken from each of the indicated pages; when they are more widely spaced, this shows that more was being used and thus the text at such points more nearly approaches actual translation. The disadvantages of this procedure are, of course, that the author's intent may not always be clearly represented. For all such occurrences I offer sincere apologies both to the reader and to the original author, for on no occasion was such distortion intended. My sole aim is and has been to present a faithful picture of this Source material. Very few of those who may find use for this book would have cared to read all of the material, even in translation, which it condenses. If an abstract of that material is of value, losses occasioned by the abstracting process itself may not be too damaging.

I have many debts. The Institute for International Education made it possible for me to study in Germany and thus collect the material necessary for this work. Assistance from the Alexander von Humboldt Stiftung was also of great value in prolonging my residence there. Counsel and encouragement came from many whom I wish now to thank. But no other assistance could have helped very much had it not been for the invaluable aid of Professor Koffka who has read and criticized the entire manuscript. The book's defects spring from shortcomings of my own and difficulties inherent in the method of its composition, but its merits are due to Professor Koffka's wise guidance.

To my colleague, Professor O. A. Simley, and to my wife I am indebted for their painstaking work in correcting the proofs.

For permission to reproduce in its present form the materials of this book I am grateful to the authors and their German publishers.

W. D. E.

University of Arizona,
Tucson, Arizona.
January, 1938.

INTRODUCTION

A book like this needs no recommendation. Those who are interested in the earlier work of the gestalt school of psychologists will turn to it without a special invitation, and those who have no such interest will give it a wide berth. Moreover, whatever had to be said about the plan and purpose of the book has been said by its author.

That I add my name to his in these brief passages has purely personal reasons; on the one hand I have acquired a rather personal interest in the book itself through the many hours in which I helped the author in giving it its final shape; and on the other hand the table of contents naturally reminds me of an earlier period in my own life, that period in which my scientific work had just found its direction and received its first strong impetus.

I remember the publications of every one of the articles and books which form the substance of the following pages, and my own reaction to them. The collection of these many and varied papers must by its very nature fail to reproduce the historical situation when the addition of one paper meant the increase of the existing gestalt literature by 100 per cent, when practically each new paper opened up a new field to the kind of approach that seemed so new and fruitful to the few enthusiasts who then carried the work and bore the responsibility. The reader who looks at the table of contents and rearranges it in chronological order with this idea in his mind may catch a glimpse of the exciting times we had in those early days; he will also see how the range of the work spread continually like a spider's web. The material of this book shows the spreading movement chiefly within one field, the psychology of perception, although the reader will find also contributions to other parts, the psychology of thought and action. I think I may truly assert that this expansion of the field of gestalt psychology has progressed at an accelerated rate since 1929, the date of the last paper included in these pages.

My connection with this book goes back to the spring of 1933. At that time Dr. Ellis, newly returned from Europe, passed through Northampton and told me of his enterprise. I was then in the midst of writing my own book on gestalt psychology and therefore predisposed to see the advantages of Dr. Ellis's plan for the English speaking student of psychology. So I promised my full support, and when in the autumn of that year Dr. Ellis came for two years to Amherst, we embarked together on the painstaking task of revising his first drafts.

When we started, the main part of the work was done ; with a very few exceptions all the articles now contained in this volume had been transcribed from the German. But nobody who has not undertaken a similar kind of work can judge of the difficulties inherent in it. Two problems, neither of them easy, have to be solved : condensation and translation. Condensation was necessary in order to unite the great number of contributions in one manageable volume ; and to select properly was the chief difficulty in condensing. The main features, the great lines of a book or article had to be preserved ; subsidiary detail, however interesting in itself, had often to be sacrificed.

Translating, even where it was not a literal rendering of the original text but a condensation, had to be as faithful to the intention of the author as possible, and at the same time to result in a readable English text. Here the difficulty lay often in reconciling the demand for good English with the wish to reproduce the characteristic style of an author. The reader will understand that perfection was even less attainable than in other human enterprises and that much criticism is still justified. I can assure him, however, that the author of this book spared no effort to do full justice to the work of which he has become the mediator. The difficulties which arose at different occasions might have caused a less patient worker, one less devoted to his task, either to abandon the work completely or to finish it quickly without bothering any more about the niceties of style and meaning. Dr. Ellis never lost patience or courage, and to the end was guided by loyalty to his authors and their work.

This is a source-book, and therefore it has to be historically reliable in the sense that the translator had to give what the author actually said, not what he might have said had he written at a later date.

Does my very personal interest in the book and the material it contains deprive me of the right to wish it all possible success in the sense that it fills satisfactorily a need felt by students of psychology ?

K. Koffka.

Northampton, Mass.
January, 1938.

A SOURCE BOOK OF GESTALT PSYCHOLOGY

I. GENERAL PROBLEMS

Selection 1

GESTALT THEORY

By Max Wertheimer

Über Gestalttheorie [an address before the Kant Society, Berlin, 17th December, 1924], Erlangen, 1925.

39 What is Gestalt theory and what does it intend? Gestalt theory was the outcome of concrete investigations in psychology, logic, and epistemology. The prevailing situation at the time of its origin may be briefly sketched as follows. We go from the world of everyday events to that of science, and not unnaturally assume that in making this transition we shall gain a deeper and more precise understanding of essentials. The transition *should* mark an advance. And yet, though one may have learned a great deal, one is poorer than before. It is the same in psychology. Here too we find science intent upon a systematic collection of data, yet often excluding through that very activity precisely *that* which is most vivid and real in the living phenomena it studies. Somehow the thing that matters has eluded us.

40 What happens when a problem is solved, when one suddenly "sees the point"? Common as this experience is, we seek in vain for it in the textbooks of psychology. Of things arid, poor, and inessential there is an abundance, but that which really matters is missing. Instead we are told of formation of concepts, of abstraction and generalization, of class concepts and judgments, perhaps of associations, creative phantasy, intuitions, talents—anything but an answer to our original problem. And what are these last words but *names* for the problem? Where are the penetrating answers? Psychology is replete with terms of great potentiality—personality, essence, intuition, and the rest. But when one seeks to grasp their concrete content, such terms fail.

This is the situation and it is characteristic of modern science that the same problem should appear everywhere. Several attempts have been made to remedy the matter. One was a frank defeatism preaching the severance of science and life: there are
41 regions which are inaccessible to science. Other theories established a sharp distinction between the natural and moral sciences: the

exactitude and precision of chemistry and physics are characteristic of natural science, but "scientific" accuracy has no place in a study of the mind and its ways. This must be renounced in favour of *other* categories.

Without pausing for further examples, let us consider rather a question naturally underlying the whole discussion: Is "*science*" really the kind of thing we have implied? The word science has often suggested a certain outlook, certain fundamental assumptions, certain procedures and attitudes—but do these imply that this is the only possibility of scientific method? Perhaps science already embodies methods leading in an entirely different direction, methods which have been continually stifled by the seemingly necessary, dominant ones. It is conceivable, for instance, that a host of facts and problems have been concealed rather than illuminated by the prevailing scientific tradition. Even though the traditional methods of science are undoubtedly adequate in
42 many cases, there may be others where they lead us astray. Perhaps something in the very nature of the traditional outlook may have led its exponents at times to ignore precisely that which is truly essential.

Gestalt theory will not be satisfied with sham solutions suggested by a simple dichotomy of science and life. Instead, Gestalt theory is resolved to penetrate the *problem* itself by examining the fundamental assumptions of science. It has long seemed obvious—and is, in fact, the characteristic tone of European science—that "science" means breaking up complexes into their component elements. Isolate the elements, discover their laws, then reassemble them, and the problem is solved. All wholes are reduced to pieces and piecewise relations between pieces.

43 The fundamental "formula" of Gestalt theory might be expressed in this way [1]: There are wholes, the behaviour of which is not determined by that of their individual elements, but where the part-processes are themselves determined by the intrinsic nature of the whole. It is the hope of Gestalt theory to determine the nature of such wholes.

With a formula such as this, one might close, for Gestalt theory is neither more nor less than this. It is not interested in puzzling out philosophic questions which such a formula might suggest.

[1] "Man könnte das Grundproblem der Gestalttheorie etwa so zu formulieren suchen: Es gibt Zusammenhänge, bei denen nicht, was im Ganzen geschieht, sich daraus herleitet, wie die einzelne Stücke sind und sich zusammensetzen, sondern umgekehrt, wo—im prägnanten Fall—sich *das, was an einem Teil dieses Ganzen geschieht, bestimmt von inneren Strukturgesetzen dieses seines Ganzen.*"

Gestalt theory has to do with concrete research; it is not only an *outcome* but a *device*: not only a theory *about* results but a means toward further discoveries. This is not merely the proposal of one or more problems but an attempt to *see* what is really taking place in science. This problem cannot be solved by listing possibilities for systematization, classification, and arrangement. If it is to be attacked at all, we must be guided by the spirit of the new method and by the concrete nature of the things themselves which we are studying, and set ourselves to penetrate to that which is really given by nature.

44 There is another difficulty that may be illustrated by the following example. Suppose a mathematician shows you a proposition and you begin to "classify" it. This proposition, you say, is of such and such type, belongs in this or that historical category, and so on. Is that how the mathematician works?

"Why, you haven't grasped the thing at all," the mathematician will exclaim. "See here, this formula is not an independent, closed fact that can be dealt with for itself alone. You must see its dynamic *functional* relationship to the whole from which it was lifted or you will never understand it."

What holds for the mathematical formula applies also to the "formula" of Gestalt theory. The attempt of Gestalt theory to disclose the functional meaning of its own formula is no less strict than is the mathematician's. The attempt to explain Gestalt theory in a short essay is the more difficult because of the terms which are used: part, whole, intrinsic determination. All of them have in the past been the topic of endless discussions where each disputant has understood them differently. And even worse has been the cataloguing attitude adopted toward them. What they *lacked* has been actual research. Like many another "philosophic" problem they have been withheld from contact with reality and scientific work.

45 About all I can hope for in so short a discussion is to suggest a few of the problems which at present occupy the attention of Gestalt theory and something of the way they are being attacked.

To repeat: the *problem* has not merely to do with scientific work—it is a fundamental problem of our times. Gestalt theory is not something suddenly and unexpectedly dropped upon us from above; it is, rather, a palpable convergence of problems ranging throughout the sciences and the various philosophic standpoints of modern times.

Let us take, for example, an event in the history of psychology.

One turned from a living experience to science and asked what it had to say about this experience, and one found an assortment of elements, sensations, images, feelings, acts of will and laws governing these elements—and was told, "Take your choice, reconstruct from them the experience you had." Such procedure led to difficulties in concrete psychological research and to the emergence of problems which defied solution by the traditional analytic methods. Historically the most important impulse came from v. Ehrenfels who raised the following problem. Psychology
46 had said that experience is a compound of elements: we hear a melody and then, upon hearing it again, memory enables us to recognize it. But what is it that enables us to recognize the melody when it is played in a new key? The sum of the elements is different, yet the melody is the same; indeed, one is often not even aware that a transposition has been made.

When in retrospect we consider the prevailing situation we are struck by two aspects of v. Ehrenfels's thesis; on the one hand one is surprised at the essentially summative character of his theory, on the other one admires his courage in propounding and defending his proposition. Strictly interpreted, v. Ehrenfels's position was this: I play a familiar melody of six tones and employ six *new* tones, yet you recognize the melody despite the change. There must be a something *more* than the sum of six tones, viz. a seventh something, which is the form-quality, the *Gestaltqualität*, of the original six. It is this *seventh* factor or element which enabled you to recognize the melody despite its transposition.

However strange this view may seem, it shares with many another subsequently abandoned hypothesis the honour of having clearly seen and emphasized a fundamental problem.

47 But other explanations were also proposed. One maintained that in addition to the six tones there were intervals—relations—and that *these* were what remained constant. In other words we are asked to assume not only elements but "relations-between-elements" as additional components of the total complex. But this view failed to account for the phenomenon because in some cases the relations *too* may be altered without destroying the original melody.

Another type of explanation, also designed to bolster the elementaristic hypothesis, was that *to* this total of six or more tones there come certain "higher processes" which operate upon the given material to "*produce*" unity.[1]

This was the situation until Gestalt theory raised the radical

[1] Compare *Selection 32*, below.

question: Is it really true that when I hear a melody I have a *sum* of individual tones (pieces) which constitute the primary foundation of my experience? Is not perhaps the reverse of this true? What I really have, what I hear of each individual note, what I experience at each place in the melody is a *part* which is itself determined by the character of the whole. What is given me by the melody does not arise (through the agency of any auxiliary factor) as a *secondary* process from the sum of the pieces as such. Instead, what takes place in each single part already depends upon what the whole is. The flesh and blood of a tone depends from the start upon its role in the melody: a *b* as leading tone to *c* is something radically different from the *b* as tonic. It belongs to the flesh and blood of the things given in experience [*Gegebenheiten*], how, in what role, in what function they are in their whole.

48 Let us leave the melody example and turn to another field. Take the case of threshold phenomena. It has long been held that a certain stimulus necessarily produces a certain sensation. Thus, when two stimuli are sufficiently different, the sensations also will be different. Psychology is filled with careful inquiries regarding threshold phenomena. To account for the difficulties constantly being encountered it was assumed that these phenomena must be influenced by higher mental functions, judgments, illusions, attention, etc. And this continued until the radical question was raised: Is it really true that a specific stimulus *always* gives rise to the same sensation? Perhaps the prevailing whole-conditions will themselves determine the effect of stimulation? This kind of formulation leads to experimentation, and experiments show, for example, that when I see two colours the sensations I have are determined by the whole-conditions of the entire stimulus situation. Thus, also, the same local *physical* stimulus pattern can give rise to either a unitary and homogeneous figure, or to an articulated figure with different parts, all depending upon the whole-conditions which may favour either unity or articulation. Obviously the task, then, is to investigate these "whole-conditions" and discover what influences they exert upon experience.

49 Advancing another step we come to the question whether perhaps any part depends upon the particular whole in which it occurs. Experiments, largely on vision, have answered this question in the affirmative. Among other things they demand that the traditional theory of visual contrast be replaced by a theory which takes account of whole-part conditions.[1]

[1] See, e.g., *Selection 8*.

50 Our next point is that my field comprises also my Ego. There is not from the beginning an Ego over-against others, but the genesis of an Ego offers one of the most fascinating problems, the solution of which seems to lie in Gestalt principles. However, once constituted, the Ego is a functional part of the total field. Proceeding as before we may therefore ask : What happens to the Ego as a part of the field ? Is the resulting behaviour the piecewise sort of thing associationism, experience theory, and the like, would have us believe ? Experimental results contradict this interpretation and again we often find that the laws of whole-processes operative in such a field tend toward a meaningful behaviour of its parts.

This field is not a summation of sense data and no description of it which considers such separate pieces to be *primary* will be correct. If it were, then for children, primitive peoples and animals experience would be nothing but piece-sensations. The next most developed creatures would have, in addition to independent sensations, something higher, and so on. But this whole picture is the opposite of what actual inquiry has disclosed. We have learned to recognize the " sensations " of our textbooks
51 as products of a late culture utterly different from the experiences of more primitive stages. Who experiences the sensation of a specific red in that sense ? What the man of the streets, children, or primitive men normally react to is something coloured but at the same time exciting, gay, strong, or affecting—*not* " sensations ".

The programme to treat the organism as a part in a larger field necessitates the reformulation of the problem as to the relation between organism and environment. The stimulus-sensation connection must be replaced by a connection between alteration in the field conditions, the vital situation, and the total reaction of the organism by a change in its attitude, striving, and feeling.

There is, however, another step to be considered. A man is not only a part of his field, he is also one among other men. When a group of people work together it rarely occurs, and then only under very special conditions, that they constitute a mere sum of independent Egos. Instead the common enterprise often becomes their mutual concern and each works *as* a meaningfully functioning part of the whole. Consider a group of South Sea Islanders
52 engaged in some community occupation, or a group of children playing together. Only under very special circumstances does an " I " stand out alone. Then the balance which obtained during harmonious and systematic occupation may be upset and give

way to a surrogate (under certain conditions, pathological) *new* balance.[1]

Further discussion of this point would carry us into the work of social and cultural science which cannot be followed here. Instead let us consider certain other illustrations. What was said above of stimulus and sensation is applicable to physiology and the biological sciences no less than to psychology. It has been tried, for example, by postulating sums of more and more special apparatus, to account for meaningful or, as it is often called,
53 purposive behaviour. Once more we find meaninglessly combined reflexes taken for granted although it is probable that even with minute organisms it is not true that a piece-stimulus automatically bring about its corresponding piece-effect.

Opposing this view is *vitalism* which, however, as it appears to Gestalt theory, also errs in its efforts to solve the problem, for it, too, begins with the assumption that natural occurrences are themselves essentially blind and haphazard—and *adds* a mystical something over and above them which imposes order. Vitalism fails to inquire of physical events whether a genuine order might not already prevail amongst them. And yet nature *does* exhibit numerous instances of physical wholes in which part events are determined by the inner structure of the whole.[2]

These brief references to biology will suffice to remind us that whole-phenomena are not " merely " psychological, but appear in other sciences as well. Obviously, therefore, the problem is not solved by separating off various provinces of science and classifying whole-phenomena as something peculiar to psychology.

54 The fundamental question can be very simply stated : Are the parts of a given whole determined by the inner structure of that whole, or are the events such that, as independent, piecemeal, fortuitous and blind the total activity is a sum of the part-activities ? Human beings can, of course, *devise* a kind of physics of their own—e.g. a sequence of machines—exemplifying the latter half of our question, but this does not signify that *all natural* phenomena are of this type. Here is a place where Gestalt theory is least easily understood and this because of the great number of prejudices about nature which have accumulated during the centuries. Nature is thought of as something essentially blind in its laws, where whatever takes place in the whole is purely a sum of individual

[1] [The suggestions given in this paragraph have been worked out in further detail by Schulte. *Selection 31*.]

[2] See *Selection 3*.

occurrences. This view was the natural result of the struggle which physics has always had to purge itself of teleology. To-day it can be seen that we are obliged to traverse other routes than those suggested by this kind of purposivism.

Let us proceed another step and ask: How does all this stand with regard to the problem of body and mind? What does my knowledge of another's mental experiences amount to and how do I obtain it? There are, of course, old and established dogmas on these points: The mental and physical are wholly heterogeneous: there obtains between them an absolute dichotomy. (From this point of departure philosophers have drawn an array of metaphysical deductions so as to attribute all the good qualities to mind while reserving for nature the odious.) As regards the
55 second question, my discerning mental phenomena in others is traditionally explained as inference by analogy. Strictly interpreted the principle here is that something mental is meaninglessly coupled with something physical. I observe the physical and infer the mental from it more or less according to the following scheme: I see someone press a button on the wall and infer that he wants the light to go on. There *may be* couplings of this sort. However, many scientists have been disturbed by this dualism and have tried to save themselves by recourse to very curious hypotheses. Indeed, the ordinary person would violently refuse to believe that when he sees his companion startled, frightened, or angry he is seeing only certain physical occurrences which themselves have nothing to do (in their inner nature) with the mental, being only superficially coupled with it: you have frequently seen this and this combined . . . etc. There have been many attempts to surmount this problem. One speaks, for example, of *intuition* and says there can be no other possibility, for I *see* my companion's fear. It is not true, argue the intuitionists, that I see only the bare bodily activities meaninglessly coupled with other and invisible activities. However inadmissible it may otherwise be, an intuition theory does have at least this in its favour, it shows a suspicion that the traditional procedure might be successfully reversed. But the word intuition is at best only a *naming* of that which we must strive to lay hold of.

This and other hypotheses, apprehended as they now are, will not advance scientific pursuit, for science demands fruitful penetration, not mere cataloguing and systematization. But the question is,
56 How does the matter really stand? Looking more closely we find a third assumption, namely that a process such as fear is a matter of

consciousness. Is this true? Suppose you see a person who is kindly or benevolent. Does anyone suppose that this person is feeling mawkish? No one could possibly believe that. The characteristic feature of such behaviour has very little to do with consciousness. It has been one of the easiest contrivances of philosophy to identify a man's real behaviour and the direction of his mind with his consciousness. Parenthetically, in the opinion of many people the distinction between idealism and materialism implies that between the noble and the ignoble. Yet does one really mean by this to contrast consciousness with the blithesome budding of trees? Indeed, what is there so repugnant about the materialistic and mechanical? What is so attractive about the idealistic? Does it come from the *material* qualities of the connected pieces? Broadly speaking most psychological theories and textbooks, despite their continued emphasis upon consciousness, are far more "materialistic", arid, and spiritless than a living tree—which probably has no consciousness at all. The point is not what the material pieces are, but what *kind* of whole it is. Proceeding in terms of specific problems one soon realizes how many bodily activities there are which give no hint of a separation between body and mind. Imagine a dance, a dance full of grace and joy. What is the situation in such a dance? Do we have a summation of *physical* limb movements and a *psychical* consciousness? No. Obviously this answer does not solve the problem; we have to start anew—and it seems to me that a proper and fruitful point of attack has been discovered.[1] One finds many processes which, in their dynamical form, are identical regardless of variations in
57 the material character of their elements. When a man is timid, afraid or energetic, happy or sad, it can often be shown that the course of his physical processes is Gestalt-identical with the course pursued by the mental processes.

Again I can only indicate the direction of thought. I have touched on the question of body and mind merely to show that the problem we are discussing also has its philosophic aspects. To strengthen the import of the foregoing suggestions let us consider the fields of epistemology and logic. For centuries the assumption has prevailed that our world is essentially a summation of elements. For Hume and largely also for Kant the world is like a bundle of fragments, and the dogma of meaningless summations continues to play its part. As for logic, it supplies: *concepts*, which when rigorously viewed are but sums of properties; *classes*,

[1] Compare *Selection 17*.

which upon closer inspection prove to be mere catchalls; *syllogisms*, devised by arbitrarily lumping together any two propositions having the character that . . . etc. When one considers what a concept *is* in living thought, what it really means to grasp a conclusion; when one considers what the crucial thing *is* about a mathematical proof and the concrete interrelationships it involves, one sees that the categories of traditional logic have accomplished nothing in this direction.[1]

58 It is our task to inquire whether a logic is possible which is *not* piecemeal. Indeed the same question arises in mathematics also. Is it *necessary* that all mathematics be established upon a piecewise basis? What sort of mathematical system would it be in which this were *not* the case? There have been attempts to answer the latter question but almost always they have fallen back in the end upon the old procedures. This fate has overtaken many, for the result of training in piecewise thinking is extraordinarily tenacious. It is not enough and certainly does not constitute a solution of the principal problem if one shows that the axioms of mathematics are both piecemeal and at the same time evince something of the opposite character. The problem has been scientifically grasped only when an attack specifically designed to yield positive results has been launched. Just how this attack is to be made seems to many mathematicians a colossal problem, but perhaps the quantum theory will force the mathematicians to attack it.

59 This brings us to the close of an attempt to present a view of the problem as illustrated by its specific appearances in various fields. In concluding I may suggest a certain unification of these illustrations somewhat as follows. I consider the situation from the point of view of a theory of aggregates and say: How should a world be where science, concepts, inquiry, investigation, and comprehension of inner unities were impossible? The answer is obvious. This world would be a manifold of disparate pieces. Secondly, what kind of world would there have to be in which a piecewise science would apply? The answer is again quite simple, for here one needs only a system of recurrent couplings that are blind and piecewise in character, whereupon everything is available for a pursuit of the traditional piecewise methods of logic, mathematics, and science generally in so far as these presuppose this kind of world. But there is a third kind of aggregate which has been but cursorily investigated. These are the aggregates

[1] Compare in this connection *Selection 23*.

in which a manifold is not compounded from adjacently situated pieces but rather such that a term at its place in that aggregate is determined by the whole-laws of the aggregate itself.

Pictorially: suppose the world were a vast plateau upon which were many musicians. I walk about listening and watching the players. First suppose that the world is a meaningless plurality. Everyone does as he will, each for himself. What happens together when I hear ten players might be the basis for my guessing as to what they all are doing, but this is merely a matter of chance and probability much as in the kinetics of gas molecules.—A second possibility would be that each time one musician played *c*, another played *f* so and so many seconds later. I work out a theory of blind couplings but the playing as a whole remains meaningless. This is what many people think physics does, but the real work of physics belies this.—The third possibility is, say, a Beethoven symphony where it would be possible for one to select one part of the whole and work from that towards an idea of the structural principle motivating and determining the whole. Here the fundamental laws are not those of fortuitous pieces, but concern the very character of the event.

Selection 2

THE GENERAL THEORETICAL SITUATION

By Max Wertheimer

Untersuchungen zur Lehre von der Gestalt, I, *Psychol. Forsch.*, 1922, 1, 47–58.

47 The fundamental attitude towards mind prevailing in most scientific psychology, when its real implications are appreciated, appears to the naïve man alien, wooden, monstrous. Yet its advantages in scientific precision over mere opinion have led to its acceptance as obvious—especially since an attitude of this sort seems essential for clean-cut scientific work. The hypothesis has appeared obviously sound that scientific comprehension of a mental phenomenon required the discovery of its "elements" and then, by laws applicable to those elements, a reconstruction of the phenomenon.

But it is good in science to subject our principles themselves to investigation, and not merely in some general, discursive fashion
48 but by a concrete and positive inquiry. Although the attitude and hypothesis we have mentioned were supported by certain findings, there were others where this point of view *should* have been submitted to suspicious scrutiny. Instead, they were either somehow forced into line or simply carried along. Let us formulate some of these underlying principles. In doing so we shall express the positions more bluntly than is customary in order to bring out the maximum force of their concrete meaning.

I. *The mosaic or " bundle " hypothesis.*—Every " complex "
49 consists of a sum of elementary contents or pieces (e.g. sensations). Example: If I have a_1 b_1 c_1 and b_2 c_2 are substituted for b_1 c_1, I then have a_1 b_2 c_2. We are dealing essentially with a summative multiplicity of variously constituted components (a " bundle ") and all else is erected somehow upon this and-summation. Thus to sensations are added " residues " of earlier perceptions, feelings, attention, comprehension, will. Also memory attaches itself to the sum of contents.

II. *The association hypothesis.*—If a certain content *A* has frequently occurred with *B* (" in spatio-temporal contiguity "), then there is a tendency for *A* to call up *B*. (*Typical* case : nonsense syllables.) This is the ground plan of associationism. The principle here is one of merely *existential connection*, a union only as regards the appearance of these or those contents, a concatenation essentially extrinsic in character.[1] The concatenated contents are arbitrary; the question of their intrinsic relations to one another is *on principle* never raised.

50 In both hypotheses we find the *identical principle*: and-summation, i.e. a construction from pieces—a first, a second, a third, and so on—which, as primarily given fundaments, underlie all else. Their contents are adventitious with respect to one another. Now from this assemblage of pieces there may emerge higher structures, unifications, complexes—erected, as secondary, upon the *and*-summation of pieces. It is on principle quite arbitrary *what* is coupled in simultaneity and succession. For the togetherness itself the "content" or the relation of contents is really irrelevant. No intrinsic moments determine the aggregation; there are instead such foreign, extrinsic factors as frequency or simultaneity of presentation (of the constituents), and so on.

51 The severity with which these hypotheses have been characterized may seem unwarranted, and the question can be anticipated. Yes, but who would to-day defend such a position? But we are not examining "general doctrines"; the aim is to inquire what actually is *done*, what the positive content underlying the terminology of experimental reports really *is*, how a concrete problem is attacked and how the stages in a piece of strict research really follow one another. We are dealing here not with opinions but with practical questions, and the aim is to sketch outlines as sharply as possible. In the exact sciences one naturally expects a serious treatment when questions of principle regarding progress and fruitful endeavour are at issue. Quite objectively considered there can be no doubt that these hypotheses do prevail in a great deal of concrete psychological work.

52 *In contrast to the foregoing hypotheses*: Only rarely, only under certain characteristic conditions, only within very narrow limits and perhaps never more than approximately do we find purely summative relationships. It is inappropriate to treat so special a case as typical of all mental events.

In saying "only rarely", the point is that only in exceptional cases is an "and-summation" in experience possible. These may arise under conditions of extreme fatigue; they may occur when

[1] [The word "extrinsic" is used for Wertheimer's "*sachfremd*". By this term Wertheimer means a relation which is determined not by the *nature* of the related terms, but by the mere external fact of their contiguity. Correspondingly the word "intrinsic" is often used for "*sachlich*".]

one encounters a kind of stone wall in thinking ; or, again, when a situation is artificially so arranged as to present a succession of irrelevant and unrelated objects ; or, when, as part of a certain experimental procedure, the instructions specifically require an attitude favouring " piecewise " reception of the presented material.

The expression " within very narrow limits " reminds us that the " span of consciousness " for unrelated elements is exceedingly small, varying directly with degrees of structuration ; the same may also be said of immediate and extended memory.

" Never more than approximately " is intended to suggest that closer scrutiny frequently discloses how an apparently unrelated aggregate of elements may really be a united, organized whole. Even the impression of a chaos is not a case of and-summation. Indeed the realization of an and-group is possible only in approximation and then at the risk of artificiality or of having altered, flattened, and emptied the pieces themselves.

The given is itself in varying degrees " structured " (" gestaltet "), *it consists of more or less definitely structured wholes and whole-processes with their whole-properties and laws, characteristic whole-tendencies and whole-determinations of parts. " Pieces " almost always appear " as parts " in whole processes.*

53 Empirical inquiry discloses not a construction of primary pieces, but gradations of givenness " in broad strokes " (relative to more inclusive whole-properties), and varying articulation. The upper limit is complete internal organization of the entire given ; the lower limit is that of additive adjacency between two or more relatively independent wholes. To sever a " part " from the organized whole in which it occurs—whether it itself be a subsidiary whole or an " element "—is a very real process usually involving alterations in that " part ". Modifications of a part frequently involve changes elsewhere in the whole itself. Nor is the nature of these alterations arbitrary, for they *too* are determined by whole-conditions and the events initiated by their occurrence run a course defined by the laws of functional dependence in wholes. The role played here by the parts is one *of* " parts " genuinely " participating "—not of extraneous, independent and-units.

Combination, integration, completion, far from being the adventitious results of blind extrinsic factors (such as mechanized habit) are determined by concrete Gestalt laws. " Elements " are therefore *not* to be placed together as fundaments in and-summation and under conditions involving extrinsic combinations.

Instead they are determined as parts by the intrinsic conditions of their wholes and are to be understood "as parts" relative to such wholes. Nor are "Gestalten" the sums of aggregated contents erected subjectively upon primarily given pieces: contingent, subjectively determined, adventitious structures. They are not simply blind, additional "*Qualitäten*", essentially as piece-like and intractable as "elements"; nor are they merely some-
54 thing added to already given material, merely "formal". Instead we are dealing here with wholes and whole-processes possessed of specific inner, intrinsic laws; we are considering structures with their concrete structural principles.

Expressed in terms of the foregoing hypothesis (marginal page 52) we may assert that the scientific study of perception will not be grounded in a "purely summative" point of view; a total array of stimulus points over against a total of sensations plus the secondary factors necessary to bind these into an additive total. Instead, perception must be treated from the point of view of stimulus-constellations on the one side and actually given mental Gestalt phenomena on the other. And this leads in physiological theory to the assumption of whole processes. The cells of an organism are *parts* of the whole and excitations occurring in them are thus to be viewed as part-processes functionally related to whole-processes of the
55 entire organism.[1] This does not mean, however, a rejection of the psychological approach—as if, in emphasizing physiology, the psychological treatment were being excluded. What *is* repudiated is the piecewise handling of psychological data. Indeed psychological penetration of this problem is not only *demanded* but really now for the first time *permitted* by an hypothesis such as ours.

But quite apart from the problems of stimulus configuration and physiology it is clear that in psychology itself the possibility of advance requires a procedure "from above", *not* "from below upward". Thus the comprehension of whole-properties and whole-conditions *must* precede consideration of the real significance of "parts". Observe, for instance, the different implications of the following: (1) I have *a* and *b* and *c* and . . . ; these are the self-subsistent constituents of a total reached by coupling together a series of "ands". (Each is, say, a sensation determined only by its own corresponding stimulus.) Or, conversely, (2) here is a whole, determined by concrete properties and laws, from which parts may be derived *not* by mere changes of attention, bare

[1] Compare *Selection 15*.

subtractive abstraction or the like, but by a genuine dismemberment. Such derivation yields a group of subsidiary wholes any alterations in which (as a consequence of dismemberment) may be clearly ascertained.

In " completion " phenomena[1] we may again see the operation of these principles. Thus the *completion* of an incomplete experience is effected not by the bare addition of just any, arbitrary datum, but through the operation of whole-factors and concrete Gestalt laws.

Memory, too, is concerned primarily with the whole-properties and structural unity of the thing remembered. Memory processes and " experience " do not consist in a bare sequence of events
56 each essentially alien to all the rest. Contextual indifference in association or habit (" mechanical " memory in general) is simply a limiting case. In this connection consider the nature of a genuine thought process: the solution of a problem, the act of comprehending and grasping what one hears or sees, the process of discovering what a problem is, in seeing the point, the act of passing in thought from *in*comprehension to comprehension of a given situation. Here is no " sequence of images ", nor could anyone confuse such mental activities with and-like additions and subtractions of knowledge. Instead the essential property of these processes is that they are Gestalt processes.[2] (Analogies may be seen also in the processes of perception, feeling, and will.)

The whole-conditions to which we have referred are proposed as objects of scientific investigation, not as topics for generalization and speculation. Of fundamental importance is the difference between processes whose factors are externality and adventitiousness *and* those exemplifying genuine meaningfulness. The
57 processes of whole-phenomena are not blind, arbitrary, and devoid of meaning—as this term is understood in everyday life. To comprehend an inner coherence is meaningful; it is meaningful to sense an inner necessity. A prediction may be meaningful in this sense as may also a completion of something incomplete; behaviour is meaningful or not, and so on. In all such cases meaningfulness obtains when the happening is determined not by blindly external factors but by concrete " inner stipulation ". Hence we may say in general that a whole is meaningful when concrete mutual dependency obtains among its parts. The mosaic or associationistic hypothesis is therefore on principle unable to supply *any* direct approach to the problem of meaning. Whether there is such a thing as meaningfulness or not is simply a question of fact.

[1] *Selection 29.*

[2] Cf. *Selections 22* and *23.*

Selection 3

PHYSICAL GESTALTEN

By Wolfgang Köhler

Die physischen Gestalten in Ruhe und im stationären Zustand, Eine naturphilosophische Untersuchung, Erlangen, 1920.

ix *Introduction for Philosophers and Biologists.*—When spatial, visual, auditory and intellectual processes are such as to display properties other than could be derived from the parts in summation, they may be regarded as unities illustrating what we mean by the word " Gestalten ".

x In order to orient itself in the company of natural sciences,
psychology must discover connections wherever it can between its
xi own phenomena and those of the older disciplines. If this search
fails, then psychology must recognize that its categories and those
of natural science are incommensurable. And indeed a first glance
does not give one much encouragement, for the *exactitude* of
science does at first seem incompatible with inquiry in a field
devoted to the study of compounds possessing their own " specific
unity ". When, further, it is said that these whole-phenomena
disclose properties and influences that are " more than the sum
of their parts ", the suspicion becomes even greater that a search
for them elsewhere than in psychology would somehow violate
the fundamentals of exact science.

xii Let us nevertheless see whether physics discloses whole-
phenomena of this type. At first we may despair of success, for
without some guiding hints the immense domain of physics seems
xiii to reveal but little of the sort of thing we are seeking. However,
we must not expect a ready-made answer to our problem right
at the start. The thought and language of physics were established
in accordance with other points of view than those with which our
search is concerned ; hence if these alone were consulted, they
would hinder more than they might help—despite their admirable
fitness for the purposes of the research physicist.

It seems wiser, therefore, to abandon the idea of reaching our goal immediately—i.e. by a systematic survey of the whole body of physics as ordinarily presented. Probably, if our search is to succeed at all, a more special point of departure and a less ambitious method will prove advantageous.

In biology the controversy has centred around the problem whether life processes can be explained physio-chemically or whether " vital " forces must be postulated. Indeed, the properties of life processes with which biology is concerned are not unlike
xiv the psychical phenomena responsible for the Gestalt problem in psychology. This does not mean, however, that the vitalists' doctrine in biology recommends itself as particularly fruitful, for *their* answer precludes the possibility of success in a search for physical Gestalten. The biologists have of course made some attempts at discovering analogies in physics, but thus far little more than vague comparisons with crystal formations have been achieved. The problem was formulated much too generally.

The closest approach between general biology and psychology occurs in the theory of nervous functions, particularly in the doctrine of the physical basis of consciousness. Here we have an immediate correspondence between mental and physical processes and the demand seems inescapable that at this point organic functions be thought of as participating in and exhibiting essentially Gestalt characteristics. The import and extraordinary significance of this was first recognized by Wertheimer who thereby attached to Gestalten a degree of reality far beyond any they had previously possessed. This implies, as Koffka emphasized, that central physiological processes cannot be regarded as sums of individual excitations, but as configured whole-processes.

xv *Now* we find ourselves in a very different position regarding physics, for the brief reference to biology has suggested the thing we lacked, viz. a special but far more concrete problem—and surely nothing is lost if one begins by attacking this problem alone. A successful solution here would supply not only the beginnings of a physiological Gestalt theory but also definite instances of physical (in this case neurological) Gestalten. If we were successful in a discovery of such Gestalten in physics we should be able to derive the principles necessary for a generally satisfactory outcome of our original search. If there are *some* cases of Gestalten in physics, even these few will suffice to guide subsequent inquiry. It follows that this special path—i.e. from individual instances of Gestalt processes in the nervous system to physics—may carry
xvi us into yet wider avenues eventually leading back into biology and thus permit a much more comprehensive physical treatment not only of nervous but of all organic Gestalt processes.

Introduction for Physicists.—Let us consider under what conditions a physical system attains a state which is independent of time (i.e. a state of equilibrium or a so-called stationary state). In general we can say that such a state is reached when a certain condition is satisfied for the system *as a whole*. The potential energy must have reached a minimum, the entropy a maximum, or the like. The solution of the problem demands not that forces or potentials assume particular values in individual regions, but that their total arrangement relative to one another in the whole system must be of a certain definite type. The state or process at any place therefore depends in principle on the conditions obtaining in all other parts of the system. If the laws of equilibrium or stationary state for the individual parts can be formulated separately, then these parts do not together constitute a *single* physical system, but each part is a system in itself.

Thus an electric circuit is a physical system precisely because
xvii the conditions prevailing at any given point are determined by those obtaining in all the other parts. Contrariwise, a group of electrical circuits completely insulated from each other constitutes a complex of independent, single systems. This complex is a " whole " *only* in the mind of one who chances to think of it as such ; from the physical standpoint it is a summation of independent entities.

Now, although these facts are obviously familiar to physicists, they are often neglected in the theoretical treatment of biological problems. An example from the psychophysiology of space perception will illustrate this : when a number of stimuli act on different points of the sense organ at the same time, it has been the custom to interpret the action of each stimulus separately, and the total process has been considered a summation of the elementary processes which
xviii each stimulus would have aroused. A visual perception was thus physiologically ascribed to a mosaic of local nervous excitations in the visual cortex, each excitation corresponding to a single stimulus point on the retina and a single point of the object in space. Even Helmholtz proceeded in sense physiology upon this presupposition, although it is clear that the nervous system would have to satisfy very special conditions to make such a view tenable—namely, the nervous system could not be *a single physical system*.

For a time this method of treatment seemed adequate but, with the progress of psychology, difficulties began to appear which could not be covered up by the introduction of " psychological " hypotheses. And it was essentially this which led v. Ehrenfels to raise the " *Gestalt* " problem.

If, in the case of vision, we assume that each physically isolable

stimulus produces an independent optical excitation, the *problem*, then, is to explain the unity of visual experience. As so-called optical illusions show, we do not see individual fractions of a thing; instead, the mode of appearance of each part depends not only upon the stimulation arising at *that* point but upon the conditions pre-
xix vailing at other points as well. Since this fact does not bear out the assumption of isolated excitations, its explanation has been sought in terms of "higher mental processes". And yet, had it not been for this assumption probably no one would have thought to maintain that visual "Gestalten" occur only as products of mental activity. The *real* assumption, of course, was that to be scientific one had to treat wholes as bare aggregates.[1]

The work of Wertheimer and Koffka has proceeded not on the basis just suggested but rather in conformity with our earlier remarks about physical systems. The facts of vision require that we treat them as properties of a *single* physical system in which the totality of stimulus conditions both individually and collectively is determined by the whole which they comprise. This mode of
xx attack denies the validity of the assumption mentioned above and denies also that that assumption was really scientific. It is the aim of this essay to support the Wertheimer hypothesis on physical grounds.

The Derivation of a First Physical Gestalt Factor

1 *The characteristic qualities of stationary somatic fields.*—We feel and see Gestalten in the ordinary sense of the word[2] when the spatial field of perception is *not* homogeneous. A tactual Gestalt is experienced only when a limited area of the skin is touched; colour differentiation is essential for the visual perception of Gestalten, etc. This leads us to inquire whether any significant changes occur in the nervous system when we turn from a homo-
2 geneous to an inhomogeneous field? If such changes *do* occur, does the nervous system itself possess Gestalt properties?

Let us assume that adjacent elements of a sensory surface correspond to adjacent elements in the neuro-somatic field and brain. And that every difference in position upon that sensory surface involves a corresponding change of place among the elements of the somatic field. This schematic view of nerve cell relations is to serve us merely as a preliminary sketch and lays claim to no more than that. Returning now to the question of homogeneity

[1] Compare *Selection 1*.
[2] [i.e. "forms", "patterns", or "configurations".]

we find that if all points of a sensory surface are identically stimulated, the corresponding brain excitation will be likewise undifferentiated. With this in mind let us now consider certain types of excitation.

3 G. E. Müller has proposed a chemical theory of visual excitation according to which the processes of the retina and optic nerves involve reversible chemical reactions. This means that complementary colours are believed to initiate mutually opposite chemical
4 processes in the optic system. We propose to generalize upon this view by assuming that all excitations in the somatic field are potentially reversible chemical reactions in a broad sense of the term.

In attacking the problem of variations of nervous activity let us consider once more the concept of stationary processes mentioned above, and notice, first, the several types of process of which this is one. These include (*a*) perfect equilibrium or rest, (*b*) stationary processes, (*c*) quasi-stationary processes, (*d*) periodic stationary processes, and (*e*) dynamic processes. A state of *equilibrium* is most simply illustrated by any physical body such as a book
5 resting upon the table—let the book fall, however, and a *dynamic* process will arise. *Periodic stationary processes* are illustrated by membranes resonating with a constant and continuous vibration. A system is said to be in the stationary (or steady) state when the *same process* is going on in it continually, without changing any of its systemic properties. A steady stream of water in a pipe is an example. Change the conditions of a stationary process, however, and you have a dynamic process with accompanying changes of
6 system-characteristics. A system is said to be in a quasi-stationary state when the process taking place in it changes very gradually with time—so gradually that the specifically *dynamic* factors are negligible. Gradual depletion in the electric current of a galvanic battery is an example.

In the nervous system the excitation produced by a continued stimulus does not, in general, remain constant with time; but the excitation of the sensory surface and the corresponding somatic field will, with sufficiently protracted stimulation, reach a stationary, or at least quasi-stationary, state.

[7-11 : omitted] There is to-day a general tendency to treat nerve activity as a case
12 of reactions in dilute solutions, and this point of view is adopted here
13 also. The most important solvent in nervous tissue is water, and since water enhances the ionization of molecules, it is likely that nervous substance (like all living matter) contains dissolved

material that is to a large extent electrolytically dissociated. This would seem to justify the assumption that ionization of this type plays an essential part in the chemical reactions of the somatic field. Thus with constant external conditions, excitations in the somatic field may be considered quasi-stationary chemical reactions in dilute solutions in which ions participate. Hence the state prevailing at any given moment during the excitation is completely determined by the concentrations of reacting molecules and ions obtaining at that moment.

15 *The electric behaviour of inhomogeneously stimulated fields.*—It was
proposed above that each adjacent element of a sensory surface
be thought of as represented by similarly adjacent elements of the
central nervous field. Let us now supplement this by the addition
of certain physical principles; viz. the nature of field-excitation
as illustrated by chemical reactions in dilute solutions. The manner
in which neighbouring solutions affect one another is through
diffusion or (what amounts to the same thing) equalization of osmotic
16 pressures. This interrelationship of parts constitutes a physical
system. We assume nervous elements to be so connected that
diffusion can take place.

When the sensory surface is *in*homogeneously stimulated,
reactions of the corresponding (stationary) nerve processes are
*dis*similar. If two sensory areas are thus dissimilarly stimulated,
then two different stationary processes of different concentration
occur in the corresponding nerve areas. Hence all along the
boundary between these there is a difference of osmotic pressure
(with ensuing diffusion and migration of ions) and, owing to the
19 difference in the velocity of the positive and negative ions, a consequent difference of electrostatic potential—and it follows that this
21 potential difference is a function of the excitation-conditions of
both somatic fields together.[1] The principle of diffusion and
consequent difference of electrical potential is applicable also to
the case in which one area is stimulated while the other is devoid of
22 stimulation. Indeed our theoretical considerations are verified by
the fact that electromotive forces are operative between excited and
unexcited regions not only in the nervous system but almost
24 everywhere in living substance. Yet although electromotive forces
in physiological processes have been widely studied (e.g. muscles,

[1] Example: two bordering dilute solutions of HCl, the one with a high and the other with a low osmotic pressure (i.e. high or low concentration). In this case ions from the solution of higher pressure will migrate to that of lower pressure, the H ions preceding, however slightly, the much slower Cl ones [p. 17].

retina, etc.), the changes occurring in the somatic field in cases of spatially inhomogeneous excitations have not been investigated. If there is really a quantitative or qualitative difference in the excitations of adjacent fields under these conditions, then the following conclusions may be drawn:

25 *A.* Nervous fields excited by pressure, pain, or temperature stimuli display electromotive forces when circumscribed parts of the sensory surface are stimulated or when the type of stimulation is different at different places on this surface.

B. If the nerve regions corresponding to the two ear labyrinths are unequally stimulated, an osmotic communication of this dissimilarity will result, and a difference of electrical potential will arise between the two.

C. Most important of all is the nervous field corresponding to the retinas, for these are not peripheral sense organs like the cochlea, but parts of the brain itself. Two colours simultaneously seen have each a particular excitation-equivalent in the nervous system, and the contour between them is the equivalent of an electromotive force in the nervous system between the two areas. The amount and direction of the potential difference are thus determined by the nature of the stimulating colours. If the two colours are gradually made to resemble one another, both the electromotive force and the contour diminish and disappear also. So long, however, as there is differentiation in the visual field—e.g. that of figure and ground—there will be a corresponding electromotive force in the nervous field. Figure perception is represented in the optic field by differences of potential along the entire outline or
27 border of the figure. Similarly, movements of the eyes are governed almost completely by the contours of the things seen, and every executed eye-movement is accompanied by a change in the locus of electromotive force. Likewise a visual object is a total form bounded by definite contours enclosing a surface and this whole is experienced as set off against the surroundings in which it occurs. The less this condition of " being set off against " becomes, the less we are likely to consider the object a " *thing* ". Along the boundaries of every perceived thing there arise electromotive forces in the optic sector of the nervous system.

According to these considerations one cannot treat the complex of physical processes which correspond to a given visual field as a mosaic of individual excitations in purely *geometrical* (as opposed to dynamic) interrelation. The process in the somatic field includes something *more* than this.

28 *The first physical Gestalt factor.*—The foregoing has brought to
light a factor which marks the distinction between homogeneously
and inhomogeneously stimulated fields. The importance for our
29 inquiry of the physical nature of this factor is that in apprehending
it we are apprehending a simple *Gestalt* property of the systems
we have studied. To elucidate this we now raise the question
whether the characteristic properties of such physical systems are
derivable from similar characteristics possessed by their *parts*?
30 In answering this question let us suppose first that the "similar
characteristic" of the parts is, say, the *weight* of each. In this
case it is true that the characteristic quality of the whole *is* a sum of
those of the parts and no more.[1] But this does not resemble the
cases of potential difference discussed above. In those cases the
"difference" arose only when the two fields were in *physical
communication*—it was not a mere difference between two previously existing potentials, but something that only came into
31 being with the interplay of the two. The potential difference,
then, is a primary characteristic of the *two* fields and impossible
without *both* of them. The absolute potentials of the solutions
taken alone would be another thing altogether, and it is in no
sense true that the potential difference of the pair is derived
additively from previously existing potentials. Indeed, the *reverse*
is the case, for the electrical properties of the two parts are
determined by those of the system as a whole. In instances of the
34 kind we have discussed (osmotic communications of two solutions)
the material nature (ionization, concentration) of the pair determines
a new systemic property for the whole system, with simultaneous
changes in the properties of the parts. In other words, when
brought together the solutions communicate in a way such that
a system of typical Gestalt attributes appears. A system of this
kind is an internal unity precisely because its *parts* are determined
by the material nature of the whole. From all of which it is self-
evident that physics does not arbitrarily consider one group of
parts a "whole" and another not, for the question is decided by
very real and actual properties of the phenomena themselves.

35 Two characteristics of mental phenomena were considered by
von Ehrenfels as criteria of Gestalten. First, when the separate
stimuli (tones) of a melody are presented, one each to a number
of persons, the totality of experiences is poorer than the total
experience of *one* person to whom all the tones are presented.

[1] e.g. we weigh each electrolyte, then, afterwards, weigh both together. The weight of the whole is the sum of the two weights.

36 This criterion seems rather definitely to take for granted that both the stimuli and their specific "sensations" are all the while identical in themselves whether they are presented together or separately—and that the distinguishing feature of the richer experience rests upon a "*Gestaltqualität*" added to the other elements. This, however, does not cover the facts. Actually von Ehrenfels's first criterion, though necessary, demands too little, for not only must the stimulations occur in a single phenomenal (or physiological) system, but they must also be able to influence each other reciprocally in the sense already suggested.

37 Von Ehrenfels's second criterion of phenomenal Gestalten is based on transposition, i.e. it is characteristic of phenomenal Gestalten that they may retain their specific properties even when the absolute constituents upon which they rest are varied in certain ways. While transposibility is undoubtedly a characteristic of many, it does not apply to all cases of Gestalten; thus this is a sufficient but not a necessary criterion and therefore it must be said that whereas the former criterion demanded too little, this one requires too much. The criterion is correct in this, however, that transposition demonstrates the independence of Gestalten of the specific parts contained in them.

[38–40: show that the electromotive force at the boundary of two differently excited areas satisfies both of v. Ehrenfels's criteria.]

Electrostatic Structures

41 "*And-Summations*" *and* "*Physical Systems*".—If the electromotive force in heterogeneous systems has not been recognized as a Gestalt property of such systems, perhaps these properties
42 have also been overlooked in still *other* physical phenomena. To repeat our former question: Are there physical whole-states or whole structures in which the parts are not mere and-summations (Wertheimer, Koffka) of elementary individual states and individual structures? The first step is to determine an accurate and precise definition of the word "summation". An aggregate of "parts" or "pieces" is a genuine "sum" only when its constituents may be added together one after another without thereby causing any alteration in any of them; and conversely, a summation is that kind of togetherness from which any one or more units may be removed without any effect either on the ones remaining or on the ones removed. This preliminary characterization is, however, not sufficient for the purposes of the

43 following inquiry. The grouping may under certain circumstances
be quite unimportant, or it may be the essential feature of a
" togetherness ". The latter is a case of " summative grouping "
when, although each piece occupies a definitely prescribed place,
no change in property of the parts themselves is thereby involved.
And again conversely: from a summative grouping, parts or
pieces may be removed without any change occurring either in
the distribution of the remaining ones or in those removed. If
there are six coins on the table it will not alter them to be laid
out as points of a six-sided figure, nor does any change of arrangement occur in the remaining ones when three are removed.

44 This specification of what summations are in physics is necessary
in order that there be no misunderstanding when we come to speak
of super-summative physical structures. Physical quantities are
usually divided into scalar and vector quantities, both of which a first
survey reveals to be summative. As regards the former: the *mass*
of a system may be increased or decreased by specific amounts;
45 the electrical *charge* of a system may be increased by partial charges
until a desired sum of such charges is reached, and vice versa, the
energy of a system may be removed in small quantities. Physics
accordingly speaks of conservation of mass, electricity, and energy.
46 With vectors the situation, while somewhat more complicated, is
similar in that the addition of two or more vectors (e.g. velocities,
forces) gives a vector that is the (vectorial) sum of those vectors.

47 We now turn to groupings and distributions. Three stones,
one in Australia, another in Africa, and a third in the United States,
might formally be said to constitute a group, but displacement of
one has no effect on the others, nor upon their mutual relation.
And this may be said also in general even when the stones are
48 but 1 metre apart. Since such examples abound in our everyday
49 experience, we are apt to acquire a deeply rooted prejudice about
the nature of *all* groupings.

In physics it is not customary to investigate purely additive
distributions because the investigation of a distribution consisting
50 of *n* independent objects divides itself into *n* separate and distinct
investigations. Contrariwise, when the independent displacement
of particles in a distribution brings about reciprocal influences, the
relations within such a distribution are no longer summative.
In this case one displacement can and will determine other displacements—and we now have a " physical system ". With increasing
mutual dependence among the parts we reach systems where no
displacement or change of state is without its influence throughout

the entire system. An example of this can be seen in an electric charge, for changes in charge at one point of an insulated conductor involve immediate corresponding changes in the whole system. Physical systems and their distributions behave throughout differently from summative groupings of " objects " ; the groupings of physical systems are of a non-additive nature and the distinctions between *distributions of physical objects*—where summation is possible—and distributions in *physical systems* must never be lost sight of.

51 The second law of thermodynamics deals specifically with physical systems and designates the *direction* taken by their processes. Consider an isolated system of constant mass, volume, and energy. What is meant when we say that each later state possesses a greater *entropy* or is " a more probable state " than the preceding one? Since the system at last reaches a maximum entropy, the " state of equilibrium " thus attained shows us, by comparison with earlier stages, in what manner the increase of entropy has occurred: according to the particular kind of system we find that temperature and pressure have become the same throughout and that there is now also a definite distribution of velocities in the entire system.
52 Thus the second law, in referring to distribution, refers to the system as a *whole*, and any attempt to apply it to *parts* of a system would lead to extremely bad errors. This is because satisfaction of the second law by the *entire* system requires that one or more parts (considered alone) shall proceed in the *opposite* direction from that of the larger system. Consequently an attempt to derive the validity of this law additively from parts of a system would necessarily fail. The law of the system prescribes what must take place in the parts, not the reverse.

54 *Electric charge structures.*—We have already mentioned the case of electrostatic distributions (p. 50) and our first example (p. 15 f.)
55 was also of electric phenomena. Taking up this matter again now we observe that, as a result of the conditions of equilibrium and the law of force between electric charges, the charge upon an insulated conductor is confined to its outer surface, and further that this surface is one of constant potential. The charge distributes itself in such a way that these two conditions are fulfilled. Since this distribution is, as we shall see, not a summative one, we shall, to avoid ambiguity, call it a *structure*.

Considering somewhat more closely the behaviour of a charge upon a conductor we find: (*a*) If the conductor is supplied at a given instant with an electric charge of any arbitrary distribution

and thereafter left alone, there results a spontaneous arrangement of equilibrium distribution so rapid as practically to preclude an
56 investigation of its course. If now the conductor remains undisturbed and ideally insulated, no change of this state takes place. Upon a conductor of definitely determined properties to which a certain charge is conveyed and whose state of charge is dependent only upon itself, one encounters either a definite, unchanging distribution of charge or an extremely brief dynamic displacement-process leading to a static distribution peculiar to this conductor. It is therefore correct to designate this distribution the "natural structure" of the charge upon the given conductor.[1] (The mathematical expression of a natural structure would thus be called its "natural function".)

(*b*) It is impossible to decrease, increase, or displace any part of this charge alone; for with any such change there occurs a reaction throughout the entire natural structure. This does not
[57–67: omitted] refer, of course, to *amount* of charge which can be summatively increased or decreased without reference to structure (p. 45).
68 In a word *the structures of static charges upon conductors of given shape are physical Gestalten.*

70 *Field Structures.*—We turn now to a consideration of the *fields*
71 surrounding these electric structures. Whatever the medium between bodies may be in itself, we find in practice that the vicinity of a charged surface is a static field whose properties may be
72 expressed in terms of the natural structure of the charge, hence also in terms of the conductor's shape. Just as equilibrium of an electric structure on a surface involves a constant potential throughout this surface, so also is the field in equilibrium characterized by its
74 potential which satisfies the Laplace equation. Thus a field in equilibrium is itself a "structure", as follows from the fact that any effective change in the electric structure causes changes both in
76 the structure of the charge and in the surrounding field. For simplicity's sake we spoke above of charge-structures alone, but this is really inadmissible, for a state of equilibrium in a charge is possible only when the structure is completed in its surrounding field. Finally also there is the question of electric (potential)

[1] ["*Eigenstruktur*", like "*Eigenschwingung*" (natural frequency) will here be expressed in English as "natural structure".] Text, p. 62: If one asked a physicist, "What is the difference between the natural structure of two charges upon similarly shaped conductors when the charges are different in amount?"—the answer would presumably be: "There is no difference between them; the larger charge assumes the same natural structure as the smaller one." [Mathematical justification for this answer is given in the text (p. 62 f.).]

energy which a charge possesses even when in a static state. Amount of energy depends not only upon the amount of charge but also upon the shape of conductor and hence upon the natural structure assumed by the charge. This dependence is due to the fact that when the structure is formed, as much energy will be transformed into heat as corresponds to the difference between the original energy and the remaining electrostatic energy. Hence we see that electrostatic energy is determined by the *entire* natural structure including, that is to say, the field also. Therefore the
78 *complete* electric structure consists of charge and field and electrostatic energy together.

[79-152: (79–84): the difficulties of experimental treatment of this problem are discussed. (85–113): give the mathematical treatment showing that piecemeal methods are necessarily inapplicable. (114–133): the mathematical treatment of *strong* and *weak* Gestalten is discussed. Natural structures are instances of the former. The following is an example of a weak Gestalt [taken from the text, p. 69]: a number of conductors, so isolated that there is but a negligible reciprocal influence between them, are connected by fine wires. When a charge is introduced into this system an electric current passes along the wires until there is a uniform potential throughout and hence a static state is reached. Nevertheless the structures assumed by the charge upon each conductor are (almost wholly) the *natural* structures of each. In other words (see p. 190), the structural moments of each conductor are in *principle* dependent upon the conditions of the whole system but in extreme cases their *specific* articulation is not noticeably influenced by *specific* events in remote parts of this system; the articulation of such limited regions depends instead upon the systemic conditions within each region itself.—Furthermore [p. 106 f.] we may expect the mathematical treatment of weak Gestalten to be somewhat simpler than that of strong Gestalten. (This follows from the general principle that the method of attacking a problem is more or less determined by the object of study itself.) This simplification is due to the fact that the determining parts of a weak Gestalt (e.g. the several strong Gestalten: cf. p. 127) are finite in number. A *weak* Gestalt is nevertheless a *Gestalt* as may be determined by reference to the v. Ehrenfels criteria: the *structure* is unchanged even when the capacities of the conductors are increased or decreased proportionally (i.e. the structure is transposible: second criterion). (134–152): it is shown that *steady electric currents* have Gestalt properties the same as those of static states, i.e. [p. 142] that there are also physical *processes* of a Gestalt character. This is also confirmed by reference to the v. Ehrenfels criteria (pp. 141 and 148).]

153 *Summary.—One* point of view would be that nature is composed of independent elements whose purely additive total constitutes reality. *Another* that there are no such elements in nature, that all states and processes are real in a vast universal whole, and hence that all " parts " are but products of abstraction. The first proposition is completely wrong; the second hinders comprehension
154 of the Gestalt principle more than it helps. Take for example the case of radioactive substances whose disintegrations occur according
155 to their own laws and regardless of their surroundings. An outstanding exception such as this justifies us in rejecting the second hypothesis; this does not mean, however, that all states and
156 processes are indifferent to other events around them. The *size* of an area beyond which interaction between a process and its surroundings may be ignored is a matter for specific determination: and the first step in all physical experimentation consists in making just this determination. The hypothesis of universal interaction, however, far from helping us in this, gives instead a picture of nature that is completely misleading.

157 If natural science has never been greatly concerned with the doctrine of universal interactionism, philosophy, unhampered by concrete examples of physical phenomena, has suffered all the more. The doctrine appears to be a complete acceptance of the Gestalt principle; in point of fact it only corrupts that principle. The trouble is, no one can take so general and indefinite an hypothesis seriously. "The whole world," which would really be involved in each investigation, cannot be manipulated in this way. The outcome, therefore, is either a romantic scepticism or a position such as this: to obtain a picture of nature we must, for better or worse, overlook universal interaction and deal only with the abstracted parts or pieces of nature. Hence we return in practice to the assumption of independent elements and their and-summations.

In psychology the situation is closely analogous. The worst enemy of a fruitful Gestalt theory—fruitful, i.e. because it is pledged to accept the concrete implications of its position—is the doctrine that only the total consciousness as such is directly given. But since nothing can be *done* with a reality of this sort, there remains on the one side a purely platonic agreement with the modern thesis, and on the other, a feeling that all abstractions are

equally founded (better: equally unfounded) anyhow; and consciousness is thereupon treated as piecemeal as it was, say,
158 by Hume. The outcome is a confused misdirection of emphasis leading eventually to a position diametrically opposite to Gestalt principles. The *important* point is missed: viz. the existence of self-enclosed, finitely extended Gestalten with their scientifically determinable, natural laws [*Eigengesetze*]. *In the physical world*, as has been shown in the foregoing pages, *it is precisely segregated physical systems to which the laws of nature apply.*[1]

159 Whereas the doctrine of universal interactionism results in no responsible scientific inquiry, but leads in practice to a purely additive point of view, consideration of finite structures deals
160 instead with definite, non-additive properties. The Gestalt principle, in harmony with its own empirical objects, involves a *finite* application and leads therefore to direct results. It would be indeed surprising if these results were not apparent in the treatment of biological and psychological problems.

161 The concepts of parts, of summations, etc., do not lose their important significance when we deal with Gestalt phenomena. One must be clear, however, about *what* it is to which the concepts are applied. (A distinction implicit in our previous treatment may make this clear.) In none of the Gestalt phenomena treated above have the physical components (electricity, electric current, migrating substance, etc.) been unconstrained (free) in their own structures; instead in each case there was a complex of *unchangeable conditions* spatially delimiting the structural material and at the same time specifically determining its *mode of extension*. The shape of a conductor was frequently mentioned in discussing strong Gestalten (p. 55 f.), but this form as well as other physical topography was not included in the Gestalten themselves, since *it* may exist whether the Gestalt phenomenon is present or not. The electric conductor was for our purposes the same whether charged or not. It follows that supra-summative Gestalt properties in no way imply supra-summative characteristics in their determining
162 topography. It is for a Gestalt in such cases immaterial whether its topography be additively constituted or not. Hence we may readily assume that such topographies are physically composite. Therefore the term "part" may be used here in its ordinary

[1] The example of an electric field and its theoretically infinite extent would seem to contradict the view just expressed. That this is not the case will be apparent, however, when we recall that the influence exerted upon this field by receding objects decreases steadily as the distance increases. The only difference is that the boundaries of such a Gestalt are not abrupt.

meaning: we saw, for example (p. 15 f.), how two dissociated solutions of unequal ionic concentration could be brought together or separated. Only the stationary process occurring when they are together has any bearing on the Gestalt question, not the conditions obtaining in the two solutions separately. In this respect the physical conditions for the occurrence (and the properties) of a potential difference are not essentially different from the properties of the topography in which a stationary electric current develops. The entire system or any of its parts may exist, and the question whether or not an additive complex be involved has nothing to do
163 with the question of the current-Gestalt. In general, distinguishing between Gestalten and their topographies at once frees one from conceptual difficulties, and apparent contradictions disappear. This clarification is especially helpful in the field of nerve physiology.[1]

[164–167: show in what sense Gestalten are additive.]

168 As against summations we have, in the case of Gestalten, finitely composed unities dependent upon a finite topography—and hence there are physical grounds why we are compelled to treat such organized wholes *as* unities. There is here nothing of a choice whereby, for example, we might at will think of one arrangement of parts rather than another. Instead the Gestalt laws observed by such phenomena and the specific structure spontaneously and objectively assumed *prescribe for us* what we are to recognize "as one thing". From which it follows that the moments of a structure,[2] unlike the items of a geometrical grouping, are *not logically prior* to the total structure itself. To treat the moments of a Gestalt as if they *were* independent elements would be intrinsically and objectively fallacious. It would be intrinsically and objectively self-contradictory to treat a *structure* as one would a *geometric grouping* in which every element and its locus may be considered

[1] It need not follow, of course, that the topography *must* be additive.

[2] [The term "moment of a structure" is defined earlier (pp. 58–60) in connection with some general questions of terminology, especially as regards the concept "part". The word "part" has assumed a concrete meaning in connection with "things": 6 is *part* of 25, a pencil is a *part* of the room's contents, and the electric charge at a certain place is *qua* amount a part of the entire amount of the charge. The surface density of the charge at one point is, however, certainly not in this sense a part of the extended natural structure. But since in theoretical considerations one often speaks with special reference to the *structure* of the density of a charge at a certain point on a surface, we must seek a simple term for this. The expression "moment of the structure at a certain place" is therefore proposed. This expression is colourless enough to have little prior meaning; yet it is not wholly new because it appears in philosophy where it designates "dependent [*unselbständige*] parts". The moment of a natural structure at a certain point (or limited area) of a conductor thus means: "carried by and carrying the remaining structure".]

as independently variable factors. *A physical structure upon a given topography is not logically secondary relative to its moments.*

169 In physics the mode of thinking suitable for Gestalt problems is induced by *experience* itself. It is different in sciences that keep themselves remote from experience (e.g. modern philosophy) or are able only with great difficulty to make decisive observations (e.g. psychology and biology). Here the pressure of undeniable facts and hence restrictions upon purely additive thinking is lacking. Until recently it has been impossible to give conclusive answers to the speculations of additive thinking; *now*, however, from physics comes evidence to *demonstrate* the errors of such thinking.

[170–172: omitted]

First Application to Psychophysiological Gestalten

173 "*Denn was innen, das ist aussen.*" [1]—From his observations of static and dynamic phenomena in vision, Wertheimer concluded that events in the somatic field could not be a series of separate excitations. He therefore proposed the hypothesis of transverse-
174 and totality-processes. In this he did not (as some of his critics believed) unjustifiably project upon physics certain phenomenal concepts; rather he specified fundamental properties of physical Gestalten, which may be accurately demonstrated in physics at
175 any time. Our own task will be to show how the general properties of phenomenal Gestalten and of physical structures are not only analogous but indeed "parallel".

176 With but few exceptions the dominant point of view prior to Wertheimer was, briefly, this: an extensive process in a neural area is a summation of single and separate local excitations (or stimulations). This means a sum of a large number of adjacently situated physical systems. Now this is perfectly possible; only, if *this* hypothesis is accepted, another possibility of equally strict physical application must be excluded: the hypothesis, namely, that the process or state of an extended area corresponds to its *whole requirements*, in other words, that the area is one physical system.

177 The choice between these alternatives was not made, however, after careful consideration of both. Almost nowhere in the psychophysiological literature are the physical concepts with

[1] [In his *Gestalt Psychology*, p. 174 n., Köhler says of this section, "Who reads the chapter will see at once that that title refers to the similarity between sensory experience and the physiological process accompanying it, not to the relationship between organic processes and the environment."]

which we have dealt in this paper mentioned—not even by those *physicists* who had much to do with the creation of psychology as a science. The history of the Gestalt concept in psychology proves sufficiently that the properties of true physical systems had no influence upon the *mode of thought* used in psychology: otherwise the ideas of v. Ehrenfels and Wertheimer would not have seemed such obscure innovations.

Gestalt theory is not in the unpleasant situation of proposing bold changes in a well established, clearly envisaged line of thought; it insists only that a conscious choice between alternatives should be made. It holds that no theory of psychophysiological events should simply ignore that kind of physical structure which is richest and most valuable of all in its properties and effects. We
178 have seen that the doctrine of mutually independent sensory processes was not arrived at from actual (psychological or physiological) observation, and it follows, therefore, that the hypothesis is merely an *inference*. If it could be shown that all elementary segments of a sensory surface and the corresponding central field were physically absolutely insulated, then we should be justified in concluding that there were as many physical systems and hence
179 local processes as there are individual pathways. But where is the evidence for such an assumption? Indeed we find abundant evidence for the opposite point of view, e.g. between two unequally stimulated parts of the retina there is an electromotive force, but this would be impossible without functional (osmotic) communication between the two regions (cf. p. 15 f.). Since there is a multiplicity of such transverse functional connections between successive niveaus of sensory sectors, the histological reasons given for studying chains of neurones as physically independent systems are without foundation.

As a matter of fact the theory of independent neurones seems not to have been inferred from the facts of anatomy; instead, it seems to have been developed in order to explain the specific
180 function of our organ of sight. With normal eyes and a healthy nervous system our visual experiences do not merge into one another but remain sharply and clearly distinct. Because the relation between stimulation (form, amount) and these visual images is often quite simple one's conviction is strengthened that the dynamics of the phenomena, and therewith of their psychophysiological correlates, are distinguished by precise order. It would, however, be a grave error to assume in biology that spatially ordered processes must either be explained in terms of

underlying mechanisms or else are physically incomprehensible. The hypothesis of rigorously separated neurones and their sensation processes has a decidedly mechanistic character. *We* create the intended spatial order in machines by prescribing for partial functions their place and for the group its organization. Hence in turning to organisms we inquire after the contrivances (" innate mechanisms ") responsible for ordered activity because from a system of unconstrained local processes we expect only disorder and confusion. Against this, consider the foregoing discussion of extended physical systems where, even with complete lack of such contrivances, rigorous spatial order was found—not so much despite but rather because of the functional unity obtaining within them.

181 When applied to space perception the word " order " has usually meant correspondence with the geometry of stimulus patterns. Hence it would seem to follow that the *parts* of a visually experienced grouping are as independent as *parts* in the things seen. And indeed to a certain extent this is true, for changes in one region of the visual field do not usually bring about changes in the entire
182 field. *But* this fact led to the assumption that the visual field could therefore be treated as a congeries of *points* individually corresponding to points in the stimulus field—and hence as mutually independent as these. If there *were* a relationship of this kind, we could conclude now that although spatial Gestalten are to be found in physics they will not occur in space perception and also not in the psychophysiological processes underlying space perception. This is a necessary consequence of the theory of local sensation processes.

The theory of visual Gestalten is based on a more intensive observation. In the *first* place, visual space possesses characteristic properties which do not occur in a geometry of stimulus elements; phenomenal space is therefore in these respects simply not comparable to the geometry of stimulus arrangements. Insofar, however, as a comparison is possible, we find, *secondly*, no law of rigid *point* relationships according to which each minute region of the phenomenal field shall be individually dependent solely upon a corresponding minute stimulus region.

183 A homogeneous field in visual space is practically uniform and, being without " points ", there are no " relations between points " within this field. When Gestalten appear we see firm, closed structures " standing out " in " lively " and " impressive " manner from the remaining field. It is for this reason that terms

such as "figure" and "ground" may be used in visual space with perfect assurance that they designate concrete and phenomenally real modes of being. In the accompanying diagram the narrower spaces are "strips" while the area between them is "mere ground". Objectively the drawing contains so and so many reflecting elements in every possible kind of spatial relationship. But none
184 of these relations is more important than any other; all points here are geometrically equivalent. Narrow intervals are not at all superior geometrically to wider intervals; the local kind of stimulation coming from between the more adjacent lines is the same as that from the other spaces. Naturally there is no difference in the objective figure that corresponds to the difference between the firm, lively areas and the mere ground.

[185–188: proceeding as in *Selection* 4 below, it is shown that psychophysiological processes in the optic system display the general properties of physical Gestalten.]

FIG. 1.

189 The claim that psychophysiological processes in the optic system are Gestalt processes signifies that:—

(1) Temporally independent (i.e. invariable) states arise and persist for the system as a whole. The processes of each limited region are influenced ("carried") by those in other parts of the system and vice versa. They occur not independently but only as moments in the total process.

(2) Every actual psychophysiological process is subject to a definite complex of conditions including: (*a*) the total stimulus configuration upon the retina in the given case; (*b*) relatively constant histological and material properties of the optic-somatic system; (*c*) relatively variable conditioning factors primarily of the remaining nervous system and, secondarily, of the vascular system. As with the Gestalten of physics, so also here: no psychophysiological state is in principle independent; its local moments must therefore conform to the *total* "topography".

190 (3) Assuming constant conditions and an invariable state, it follows from (1) that the process represents an objective unity which is not dependent upon intentional unification by an observer.

For nowhere in the entire area is any moment completely autonomous relative to the state of any other region. The spatial coherence of the psychophysiological process corresponding to a given visual field has, therefore, a supra-geometric, i.e. dynamically real, constitution.

(4) Physically real unity of structure does not signify here (any more than in physics) undifferentiated diffusion or disorder; it is, rather, fully compatible with rigorous articulation. The type of articulation depends upon the specific type of psychophysiological process and the systemic conditions at the time of its occurrence. The supra-geometric dynamic articulation of the process is, however, in every case (i.e. for each complex of conditions) precisely as much a physically real property of the larger region as are, e.g., psychophysiological colour reactions.

(5) As with inorganic physical Gestalten, so here we may distinguish *degrees* of inner coherence within the system. Thus, although the moments of each minute region are in principle dependent upon the conditions of the entire system, their dependence varies according to a distance function such that the determining influence exerted by topographical conditions in adjacent areas is greater than that of more distant ones. In extreme cases (here as with the Gestalten of physics) the *specific* articulation of limited regions is no longer noticeably dependent upon *specific* topographical features of other regions. In these cases although the " total moments " of such areas are mutually dependent, the specific articulations of limited regions develop relative only to the systemic conditions of each such region alone. (Compare the distinction between strong and weak Gestalten.) As regards spatial articulation or structure, such limited and internally coherent regions can thus be relatively independent—without impairing the Gestalt coherence of the entire system upon which the Gestalt moments still depend. These limited regions are thus
191 in a very real sense circumscribed unities within the unitary total process. Provided the general assumption is not lost sight of (viz. that the process of the whole system is of a Gestalt character), we may designate such circumscribed unities as themselves Gestalten. Wertheimer's physiological hypotheses refer directly to structures of just this type—viz. specific wholes within the larger precincts of optic-psychophysiological Gestalt events.

(6) No matter how the spatial articulation of psychophysiological Gestalten may be constituted, it denotes in any event a specific type of intensity distribution and therewith of energy density.

Under appropriate conditions the energy densities of individual regions in the system can be extremely different. Again, however, this is determined by conditions of the system *as a whole.*

These properties are arrived at on physical grounds on the mere recognition that the optical sector has to be treated as one physical system. When now we turn to the phenomenal field and find it possessed of corresponding properties, we know that this correspondence is not an artifact resulting from a method which constructs psychophysiological processes to fit phenomenal data. These properties of the phenomenal field are as follows :—

(i) Visual phenomenal fields make their appearance as self-contained unities, and always have supra-geometric properties. Phenomenal subsidiary regions are never present as wholly indifferent " parts " ; in this they correspond to the *moments* of a physical Gestalt.

(ii) Phenomenal unity involves order and structure, and the specific articulation of the visual field (correlate of the structured state in physical Gestalten) represents a *super*-summative property whose experiential reality is the same as, e.g., that of colours.

(iii) Within the field there appear—without at all impairing its unity as a whole—subsidiary phenomenal unities limited in area and relatively independent over against the remainder of that field.

192 (iv) In particular do lively, close-knit areas (" Gestalten " in the narrower sense) segregate themselves as a rule from the remaining " mere ground " of the visual field.

193 In the case of vision it is already apparent from the foregoing that our theory leads to a concrete resemblance between psychophysiological events on the one hand and Gestalt properties of the phenomenal field on the other. Nor is this merely a general similarity due to both involving Gestalt phenomena ; we refer rather to specific correspondence in individual cases. More radical than any traditional theories of psychophysical correspondence (e.g. Johannes Müller) we mean here that *actual consciousness resembles in each case the real structural properties of the corresponding psychophysiological process.*

195 *The physics of optical Gestalten.*—Three questions which arise regarding the *physics* of psychophysiological Gestalten are these : (1) Which of the possible kinds of constant states (with respect to time) is realized in the case of visual perception ? (2) Through what regions of the nervous system do the coherent Gestalten of the optic processes extend ? (3) What is the physico-chemical material of these Gestalten and what are the forces acting in them ?

It would be difficult to undertake an answer to one of these without simultaneously considering the other two. As regards the *first* question, the following points must be considered: Gestalten which are independent of time may be either in a state of no process (rest), they may be processes in the steady (stationary) state, or they may be periodic-stationary processes.

196 It is unlikely that psychophysiological Gestalten are in a state of rest, for both physiological and psychological evidence indicates a type of *process* as the correlate of optical Gestalten. We must therefore choose between stationary and periodic-stationary processes as well as combinations of these. So far as I know there is as yet no experimental evidence in nerve physiology (optic sector) to guide us in this choice.

The *second* question suggests that psychophysiological Gestalten have a much greater significance for the optic sector than we have
197 hitherto assumed. The retina being a part of the brain, the so-called optic nerve is really a brain commissure. Therefore there is no occasion to deny that peripheral parts of the optic system can have the same type of function that one ascribes to central fields.

We know, moreover, that the functioning retina develops electromotive forces, and we have seen that electromotive forces exhibit Gestalt characteristics. Hence we find that there really are Gestalt processes in the peripheral eye. It is thus impossible to claim that the realm of optic-somatic Gestalten is restricted solely to central nervous processes. Now let us consider two different possible conceptions of what occurs when the retina is stimulated.

(i) There are Gestalt processes upon the surface of the retina, then a point for point conduction process, and then a *second* Gestalt process in the brain based on the topography of single cell excitations thus conducted.

(ii) There is *one* Gestalt process in which the *whole* optic sector from retina to central field, is involved. What is ordinarily called the *conduction* of stimulation from retina to cortical field *is* simply a part of this total process. The same process where it embraces the level of the cortex to which consciousness is adjunct is the correlate of phenomenal Gestalten in the visual field.

198 Compared with the customary notion of the relation between a sensory surface and the brain the second of these viewpoints appears quite radical. This idea shares with (i) in starting with the retinal image and the corresponding complex of colour excitations in the retina; but from this point onward the process is to be envisaged according to physical and not geometric-mechanistic

principles. The retina is thought of as belonging to that *single* physical system in whose entirety the optical Gestalt-process takes place.

As regards the first hypothesis above we observe that it presupposes an absolutely isolated conduction on the part of each nerve fibre. The conduction in these elementary pathways simply establishes a complex of " physical conditions " for the process in the central field. Regarding these " conditions " two hypotheses are possible: (*a*) The conditions do not themselves belong to the central Gestalt but constitute rather the summatively grouped and invariable " topography " *for* the Gestalt process. They are themselves, however, local, psychophysiological states in the sense that consciousness corresponds to them individually. Being reciprocally independent, these local consciousness conditions constitute what we are accustomed to call " sensations " (cf. p. 176). Hence it follows that what we reach by this procedure is a kind of " physiological production theory " since the Gestalt process (and the Gestalt consciousness) is thought of as arising only *subsequent to* a purely summative array of prior sensation
199 processes. It is easy to see that this does not agree with phenomenal experience, for we do not have a double consciousness of this sort. It is not true that we experience first a purely summative manifold of sensations and *then* a Gestalt consciousness. The same arguments which attack the psychological-intellectualistic production theory may be used against its physiological form also.[1]

(*b*) The same general description given in (*a*) is maintained but no claim is made for a conscious equivalent of the several material conditions underlying the central Gestalt process. The local conduction processes establish the conditions for a central Gestalt process which is throughout the physical correlate of perception. There are no independent sensations, but all parts of the phenomenal field are experienced only as parts of a *structure*.

Both (i, *b*) and (ii) are agreed upon the important point that consciousness and the Gestalt process correspond directly. The choice between them must ultimately depend, therefore, upon which agrees most adequately with the facts of physiological and psychological observation. Despite its radical appearance the point of view set forth in (ii) will be maintained in the following discussion. One reason for this is that physiological experience demands recognition of Gestalt processes in the *retina*; there can be no doubt that there are electromotive forces between unequally

[1] See *Selection 32*.

200 stimulated retinal regions. It would be difficult from a physical standpoint to imagine conduction processes proceeding inward from these regions without being influenced by Gestalt factors. The conduction in *one* nerve tract is not insulated from that taking place in the *remaining* tracts. Hence there is a Gestalt relationship from retina on into the central fields. If there is, therefore, a Gestalt process in the conducting tracts, it follows that this *same* process (and its consequences) is, in the psychophysiological niveau, the correlate of the phenomenal field—and this is the position set forth in (ii).

The assumption, then, is this : *the region in which optical Gestalt processes occur is at least the entire optic sector.* The topography of
201 these processes is given by the retinal image resulting (as a more or less steady state) from the incoming rays of light. And in the first approximation we may overlook the retroactive influence exerted by the ensuing Gestalt upon this topography. The local retinal process depends, we may therefore say, *only* upon the incoming light.

202 Our *third* question asked: What is the material nature of the Gestalt processes which occur in the optic sector?

203 It is known that all nervous processes involve electrical forces. A consideration of electromotive forces alone, however, would not lead to an understanding of spatial structures in psychophysiological processes, for they do not depend upon the form or size but only upon differences on either side of the boundary joining the substances (p. 15 f.). The development of electromotive forces at this boundary does lead, however, at least at first, to displacements throughout the entire system: and these are electric currents. We have (since p. 15) seen that such electric currents are directly determined by the form and size of the conducting medium.

[204–205 : show that, the purely electrical hypothesis being too simple, transportation of substances must be assumed.]

206 Let us now see what follows if we apply the principle of the conservation of electricity here. Every displacement of electricity in a transverse section of the conducting system implies equivalent displacements in other transverse sections of the path. It follows that if the transverse section of the system is different at different places, the *density* of the current through these transverse sections will be unequal. Let us suppose that we have a small white figure (say a disk) on a homogeneous background of grey. The light in the retinal image of the disk will give rise to a chemical reaction

and the (grey) background will give rise to a different sort of reaction. Potential differences will appear, first at a and a^1 (Fig. 2), i.e. at the boundary between the unequally stimulated retinal regions and, second, between the stimulated regions and the optic tracts. Displacement of electricity in this simple system must follow the lines indicated by arrows in the diagram. (In this diagram the direction of current has been arbitrarily assumed; it is irrelevant for our argument anyway). The important point is this: the same total quantity of electricity must be displaced across the homogeneous background of the disk as is displaced
207 across the retinal field corresponding to the disk itself. Since the figure is so much smaller than its surroundings, the average current density in the disk-field must be much greater than in the ground-field. This relation between the current densities, and

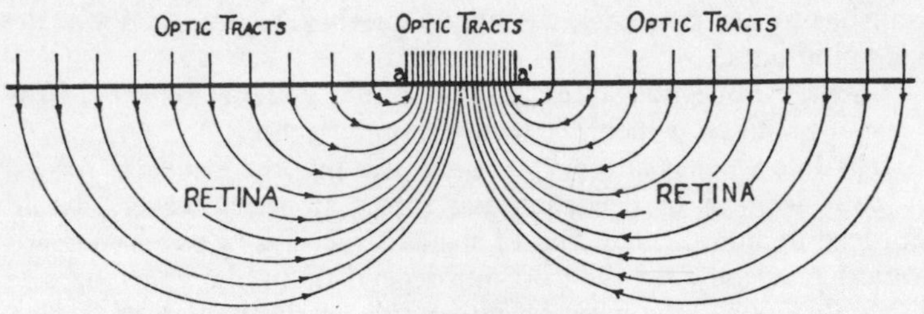

FIG. 2.

hence between the energy densities, must persist in the nervous pathways and on into the corresponding central fields. The disk ("figure") area corresponds in the Gestalt process (so far as this is of an electrostatic nature) to a much more lively state than that of the extended "ground". Throughout the system the directed energy of the electrical flow will be superposed on whatever other energy content the somatic fields possess. But "in the figure" or "Gestalt" in the narrower sense this energy is concentrated in a small space. In the "ground" the same total amount of energy is spread out to yield a lower density. It is not difficult to think of such a difference at the cortical level as giving rise to a decided difference in phenomenal appearance between figure and ground.

209 Electrolytic currents cause a displacement of *substance* in the region they traverse. Assuming that this is a stationary process (like

an ordinary electrolytic current), the concentration of the participating solutions will not vary at any point of the system which permits *free passage* of the current, for whatever amounts of the solution flow away from a given point will be replaced by an influx from other points in the system. Therefore the chemical state of the system will be disturbed only if some obstruction hinders this equal displacement of substance. At such places there would arise a damming up of the substance being moved by the current with the result that an increase in concentration would occur and hence that chemical reactions would be possible at these points. Now the psychophysiological correlate of the experience of *colour* is presumably a chemical reaction, and this we may suppose occurs at surfaces of discontinuity in the conducting system. According to this we may assert that a coloured
210 surface in vision corresponds to a cross-section of the current where the conditions for conduction undergo an abrupt change and the displacement of substance is hindered.

211 *Weber's Law*.—We have seen (p. 206 f.) that an average density in the disk-field greater than that in the ground-field produces the distinction in vision between "figure" and "ground". The specific densities of these regions, however, depend not only upon their *size* but also upon *the objective difference between the two colour reactions*. If the ground colour is made gradually to approach that of the figure so that the colour difference between them becomes eventually less than the so-called difference-threshold, the liveliness with which the figure is "lifted out from its ground" diminishes and eventually the "Gestalt" (narrow sense) disappears entirely.

Now the electric currents already discussed in this connection are dependent upon the electromotive forces in the somatic field. Hence when the field colours become more and more similar, the electromotive forces diminish, and the intensity of electric dis-
212 placements decreases also. But, in an electrolytic system such as the nervous system, the electromotive forces must attain a certain minimum value before a current is possible. An electric displacement whose occurrence (as a whole) is determined by electromotive forces between unequal colour reactions will therefore be impossible when the colour difference sinks below a certain threshold. At this threshold the electromotive forces have a definite value and it is this relationship with which we are here concerned.

In reactions of an unequal type there are molecular and

particularly ionic differences such that regions differ not only in concentration but also in the chemical nature and velocity of migration of their ions. Identical reaction types with difference only of reaction speed, on the other hand, differ from one another only in the concentration of whatever ions are involved. Now, since Nernst in the theory of galvanic chains employed just this case in his derivation of the potential difference between identical solutions of unequal ionic concentration, we select this simplest case for our hypothesis and can then take over his computations, as follows :—

Let us consider a surface-element q at the boundary between two regions of unequal ionic concentration ; let us call the direc-
213 tion toward the normal of this element n ; finally let us suppose that the concentration and osmotic pressure are continuously varying (i.e. without discontinuities) and quickly in the direction n. Let the velocity of the positive ions under the influence of a force 1 pro g.-ion (i.e. the " mobility ") be U, and that of the anions V. The osmotic partial pressure of each ion we shall call p (and this is therefore a magnitude varying rapidly along n). The electrostatic potential (referred to 1 g.-ion as unit of the quantity of electricity) we shall designate with ϕ.

The ions are acted upon by forces arising on the one hand from the spatial variations of p, and on the other from ϕ. Since, however, the movements involve enormous friction, the *velocities* are proportional to the effective forces. If c is the ionic concentration at the cross-section q, and if the force 1 pro g.-ion acts perpendicular to q for the brief time dt, there migrate through q in this interval of time and in the direction of the normal the quantities of substance :—

$$-Uqc.dt \text{ and } -Vqc.dt \text{ (of the cation and of the anion).}$$

In reality the osmotically derived force for a g.-ion is $\frac{1}{c} \cdot \frac{dp}{dn}$ and the electrostatic force $\pm \frac{d\Phi}{dn}$; hence the migrating amounts under the influences of both forces together are :—

$$-Uq\left(\frac{dp}{dn} + \frac{d\Phi}{dn} \cdot c\right)dt \quad \text{and} \quad -Vq\left(\frac{dp}{dn} - \frac{d\Phi}{dn} \cdot c\right)dt.$$

A separation of the two ions can occur only in imponderable quantities, for in the briefest interval a stationary state must ensue in which the generated electrostatic force (between the two) retards the ion which rushes ahead, and forces onward the lagging one. The result is that both assume the same speed and the two migrating quantities therefore represent the same amount. From this follows the equation:—

$$\frac{d\Phi}{dn} = - \frac{U - V}{U + V} \cdot \frac{1}{c} \frac{dp}{dn}.$$

In dilute solutions the equation of condition of ideal gases holds, viz.

$$p = cRT,$$

where R is the gas constant, T the absolute temperature, and p the osmotic (instead of the gas) pressure. If now, in accordance with this, c is introduced as an independent variable instead of p,
214 it follows for the potential difference between partial fields of the ionic concentrations c_1 and c_2 that

$$\Phi_1 - \Phi_2 = - \frac{U - V}{U + V} RT \int_{c_2}^{c_1} \frac{dc}{c} = \frac{U - V}{U + V} RTln \frac{c_2}{c_1}.$$

Here *ln* signifies the natural logarithm.

In the nervous system absolute temperature has a fixed value practically independent of local reactions; U and V are for a given temperature the characterizing properties of the particular *kind* of ion and therefore in the present case fixed numbers. Since we are concerned only with the dependence of the potential difference upon the variables, we may hence write

$$\Phi_1 - \Phi_2 = \text{const. } \log \frac{c_2}{c_1}$$

215 and will have the Weber-Fechner law in its customary form.

From this it is apparent that the amount of potential difference depends not upon the absolute concentrations, but upon the *ratio*: if both concentrations were tripled—a condition corresponding to complete change of reaction velocities and hence also of "absolute colours"—the potential difference would nevertheless remain the same. If the two regions are identically stimulated, then c_2 is equal to c_1; if c_1 is held constant and c_2 is gradually increased, we reach the threshold where

$$c_2 = c_1 + \Delta c_1, \text{ and } \frac{c_1 + \Delta c_1}{c_1} \left(\text{thus also } \frac{\Delta c_1}{c_1}\right)$$

is therefore the ratio at which the potential difference just causes a displacement. It is clear from this that if both initial concentrations are increased, say, 10 times, Δc will also be 10 times greater

and that the ratio $\frac{c + \Delta c}{c}$ $\left(\text{and thus also } \frac{\Delta c}{c}\right)$ will bring about the
216 same threshold value as in the first case above. This means that, in its required dependence upon the concentrations, the potential difference must satisfy Weber's law ; or, that the relative difference limen, determined by the electric displacement, has a constant value.

217 But only for achromatic colours, so far as we know, is the relative difference threshold always the same. And experience
218 shows that Weber's law does hold for achromatic colours within the range of light intensities in the ratio 1 : 50. That the law does not hold outside this range in no way minimizes its importance for the zone where it *does* apply. Indeed for practical purposes this zone is actually very large, since the brightness ratio between deep black paper and newly fallen snow is but 1 : 40.

Evidently therefore it is not a matter of chance that a physical theory of inhomogeneously stimulated fields should carry us to Weber's law precisely at the point where that law is in formal agreement with experimental findings regarding perception. The
219 identity between Weber's law as applicable, on the one hand, to the threshold of reaction differences, and, on the other, to psychological phenomena, is however established only if the ionic concentrations of the two fields (figure and ground) are proportional to the light intensities of the stimulation. If we call the light intensity upon a certain part of the retina R_1 and that of another part R_2 and if these radiations maintain stationary (retinal) reactions with the ionic concentrations

$$c_1 = \alpha R_1 \text{ and } c_2 = \alpha R_2$$

it follows that

$$c_1 : c_2 = R_1 : R_2,$$

since α signifies the constant of proportionality. The relative difference threshold then has a constant value not only in the form $\frac{\Delta c}{c}$, but also (as regards the *stimuli*) in the form $\frac{\Delta R}{R}$. Thus it
220 can be seen that the theory is capable of being carried out if we assume that the achromatic colours correspond to a series of identical reaction types.

[221–227 : estimation of the value of the difference limen in microvolt.]

228 *The conditions of psychophysiological space-structures.*—We return now to the simple case of a disk of homogeneous colour, let us say white, on a homogeneous grey background. Let us suppose that the disk is viewed with steady fixation, so that the retinal colour

reactions, and their boundary lines, have a constant locus. A definite process-structure will be established throughout the entire optic sector which at present we know only through its phenomenal correlate.

If we interchange the colours of the disk and its surroundings, the retinal reactions will also be interchanged. The electric vectors will be reversed, and there will no doubt also be change in the type of substance displacements which take place at various regions of the optic paths. But since the conducting system, and the determining *forms* are unchanged, the space-*structure* of the process will remain the same as before.

If we keep constant the retinal *locus*, the size and the *spatial form* of the reacting regions, and vary the colours of figure and ground—e.g. increase or decrease their qualitative resemblance—various qualitative and quantitative changes in the conduction process may occur, but within wide limits its *spatial form* will not change.

229 This corresponds to phenomenal experience, and in the older summative-geometrical theory was simply taken as a matter of course. But since *form* has supra-geometrical properties, the summative interpretation is inadequate; instead of solving the problem this interpretation overlooks it.

In discussions regarding the possibility of a physiological theory of *memory*, a difficulty has been seen in the fact that the reproductive effects of a figure of given *form* are relatively unaffected when the same figure is presented in different *colours*. We can now regard this difficulty as removed. For the essential outcome of our investigation is this, that the structure of the process [*Strömung*] is just as much a physically real datum as a colour process and that therefore a form process can as well (in reality better) arouse reproductive effects as can a colour process. If the same *structure* of the process has the same reproductive effects despite changes of colour, this is no more remarkable than that the same colour retains its reproductive effects when form is changed. An obstacle for the physiological interpretation of memory remains only so long as we regard the "figure" as corresponding not to something psychophysiologically real but to a mere geometry of sensation processes. (In saying this we have not, of course, answered the question how *in general* reproductive effects are produced in the nervous system. It is maintained only that the problem is in no way more puzzling in the case of space-structures than in that of colours.)

231 Let us now ask the following question: What must be the nature of the conducting system in order that retinal configurations should give rise to phenomenal structures having the properties we observe them to have? Let us consider the following:—

(*a*) Suppose, once more, that a homogeneous disk is seen upon a homogeneous ground. If the figure is moved about, the phenomenal field as a whole varies in character, but the seen figure,
232 varying only in position, remains unchanged *qua* figure. The same would hold for figures of any shape we might select.

(*b*) If the retinal image is enlarged or decreased but its proportions maintained, the spatial Gestalt as such is unaffected; only its phenomenal size and, in general, its liveliness will be changed.

(*c*) The simpler and more distinctive the figure is, the better the above conditions (independence of retinal location and of absolute size) will be fulfilled. The circle is of all figures the best in this case.

The conclusion in each of these three is the same. As regards (*c*): from the phenomenal symmetry of circles we may suppose that the psychophysiological processes in the "figure" region are also
233 symmetrical.[1] Conversely, geometrically irregular figures are not as a rule experienced as symmetrical. If we would avoid a theory of pre-established harmony between stimulus forms and perceptual properties, we must conclude that geometric symmetry in the stimulus *determines* the supra-geometric-physical symmetry of the dependent psychophysiological Gestalt process.

[234–236: physical instances of symmetry are discussed.]

237 Turning now to (*a*) and (*b*) let us consider the following physical example: if we move a charged conductor into the vicinity of other conductors, the electrostatic structure is changed. If, however, a *homogeneous* environment is provided, no disturbance occurs. Now the fact that retinal images do not materially change when moved about indicates that the optical system behaves *like* a *homogeneous environment* relative to the figure-process.

As regards increasing or decreasing the size of a conductor (the proportions being held constant), we again find that if no change in the physical Gestalt is to occur, homogeneity of the medium surrounding the conductor must be assured. Since the same result

[1] It should be noticed in this connection that symmetry of the psychophysiological process may exist even when the anatomical *space* is certainly *not* symmetrical. We are dealing here with a *functional* relationship which in itself need not at all coincide with geometrical relationships.

is found in the optical system we may again assert that this system is to be viewed as homogeneous.

238 In practice, however, such ideally simple conditions do not obtain, for the optical conduction system is not completely homogeneous. And as regards the visual field this is anything but
239 homogeneous : it possesses a fairly fixed " above " and " below ", a vertical, a horizontal, a right and a left. Nevertheless, the properties of the optical system remain clear and ordered because these (visual) inhomogeneities apply throughout the system. This is the reason why merely changing the retinal location of an image causes no considerable alteration in vision whereas *turning* the object *about* usually involves a considerable change in our perception of it. Hence when we speak of " homogeneity of the conducting system " we refer to uniformity of the conditions of conduction including the known deviations therefrom.

240 In science the term " homogeneous " has two meanings : in the one case it refers to similarity of the minute constituent elements of a medium ; in the other it designates uniformity of systemic regions relative to a process or state taken as a whole. With the possible exception of electromagnetic space or a vacuum there are probably no homogeneous media in the former of these senses. Far more important, therefore, is the second meaning, and it is this which we are here using when we say that the optical system
241 behaves as if it were homogeneous. The optical conduction system is a network of variously constituted tissue, but this tissue must by and large (and within the aforementioned limitations) provide uniform conditions for the optical process. Such " homogeneity in the large " does not apply to anatomical-geometric space as such ; it has to do only with " functional space ". Schematically we may illustrate thus : The transverse connection between points in two regions of the visual cortex (e.g. transverse commissures through the *corpus callosum*) is several centimetres long ; that between two other points (of a *single* region in the visual cortex) is but 1 millimetre long—yet *functionally* (e.g. change in potential) the two intervals may be the *same*.

The problem of the relation between retina and central field has customarily been approached from a starting point quite
242 different from our own. The attempt to make perception comprehensible from a purely geometric and summative point of view (i.e. without reference to physical Gestalten) inevitably means assigning to the visual cortex something like a geometrical copy of the retinal stimulus. For if this sort of relationship were not

assumed, how could the additive totality of "sensations" in the case of, say, a circle give rise to anything like a phenomenal circle and its symmetry? It is a necessary consequence of *this* formulation of the question that one should thereupon seek to answer the problem in terms of a projection, element for element, of the retina upon the cortex. It was in this manner that the conception of a one-to-one, anatomically fixed correspondence between retina and cortex developed. One may disapprove of such mechanistic theories as much as one likes; they can scarcely be avoided by summative thinking in physiology.

It is unnecessary to stress the incompatibility between the starting point of such a theory and that of a theory which regards the optic sector as a *single* physical system. It is more profitable to try, by developing the following consequence, to make the contradiction as concrete and vivid as possible.

Even those who, for good reasons, do not assume *geometrical similarity* between the retinal image and its cortical projection, usually hold nevertheless to the assumption that (1) the local central
243 processes are independent *parts* of the entire central process, and (2) that there is an anatomically fixed correspondence between *particular* retinal elements and *particular* cortical elements. Gestalt theory not only denies that local processes in the optical cortical elements are independent; it asserts also that its meaning is insufficiently represented by the notion that the entire central process is in principle dependent upon the whole retinal distribution, although this in itself would exclude a genuine "point-for-point correspondence" in the ordinary sense. In addition, according to the theory of physical Gestalten, a "line of flow" which begins at particular retinal elements does not necessarily and invariably go to one and the same place in the visual cortex. For Gestalt theory the lines of flow are free to follow different paths within the homogeneous conducting system, and the place where a given line of flow will end in the central field is determined in every case by the conditions in the system as a whole.

This is not a new assumption, but is a simple consequence of the physical conception with which we started; its acceptance or rejection hinges on the acceptance or rejection of our starting point. By contrast with the prevailing theory, this idea seems at first strange, but it is in no way contradicted by the facts of experience.

244 The general foundations of the theory, as we have taken them from physics, contain no assumptions which would apply exclusively to the *visual* system. If to the sensory surfaces of the tactual

sense there correspond central somatic fields, in the same way that the visual cortex corresponds to the retina, then in such regions there must arise currents of similar origin and of similar structural properties to those in the optic sector. The chemical reactions will of course be different, but this does not imply a difference in the *kind* of process involved. Hence in terms of type of process there is no physical reason why tactually perceived Gestalten should not be considered just as primary and genuine as are the visual. There is no need here for associationistic constructions for the purpose of deriving tactual from visual Gestalten. There is diversity of (specific) qualities, but agreement in general Gestalt properties: this does not mean, however, that we are
245 compelled to assume a super-sensory intellectual activity (" production ") capable of dealing in the same way with these unlike " sensations ".

247 Since experienced space does not consist of independent elementary experience, it is possible to conceive physically of " pure space Gestalten " devoid of specific qualitative contents. Example: on a billiard table one " sees " the path which the cue ball must take if it is to strike the other two. What is the colour of this path? Can it have a definite form without definite colour? " Imagined structures " are sometimes clearly experienced and
248 one's behaviour governed accordingly. " Pure space Gestalten " may occur also in other than the visual and tactual sector of the nervous system. A great deal of our *thinking* apparently takes place " as if in space " even when it involves neither visual perception nor the visual cortex.

249 *The tendency toward Prägnanz*.—Every state of rest or stationary equilibrium which occurs in nature is *a unique case* in contrast with an infinite manifold of other states. If, in a given physical system there is, at the beginning of our observations, a particular grouping of matter and a particular distribution of velocities, and if an *invariable* state is sooner or later reached, this end-state must be distinguished from the earlier states by some special property in virtue of which the change ceases when this stage is attained.

In theoretical physics it is shown that a unique condition holds for all invariable states: the energy of a Gestalt is a function of its spatial structure. A stationary state is reached when the energy of the structure as a whole has become as small as the given topography permits. Therefore, no matter what their dynamic route has been, all states which have occurred *prior* to that of the invariable structure possess a greater energy than the end-state. In other words: *In all processes ending in a state independent of time, development is in the direction of minimal energy in the ultimate structure.*

250 An example is furnished by a simple electric current which divides into two branches (*weak* Gestalt). We ask: For what distribution of current will the energy of the process be a minimum? Assuming there are no electromotive forces in the branches, the total quantity of Joulean heat generated in the wires gives a measure of the energy of the process. Let us call the main current I, the currents in the two branches I_1 and I_2, the resistance in the branches R_1 and R_2. We have to determine when the total heat generated

$$R_1 I_1^2 + R_2 I_2^2 \quad \text{or} \quad R_1 I_1^2 + R_2(I-I_1)^2$$

becomes a minimum, i.e. for what value of I_1 the expression

$$\frac{d}{dI_1}[R_1 I_1^2 + R_2(I-I_1)^2]$$

vanishes. This is the case when

$$\frac{I_1}{I-I_1} = \frac{I_1}{I_2} = \frac{R_2}{R_1}$$

251 that is, when the distribution of current follows Ohm's law for stationary currents. This distribution corresponds in fact to a minimum of Gestalt energy. (It corresponds to a *minimum*, not a maximum, for the second derivative of the energy expression given is always positive.)

The same holds for more complex current networks.

From an application of the foregoing (with appropriate modifications of mathematical procedure) to *strong* Gestalten we may deduce still more far-reaching consequences: a physical Gestalt is, among other things, a grouping of forces which operate upon the topography of its occurrence. These forces will change the
252 topography unless the latter is absolutely rigid. When the topography is not rigid the changes wrought in it involve changes in the Gestalt also, since the Gestalt is dependent upon its topography. In such cases, therefore, the Gestalt is supplying the energy needed for doing work (e.g. overcoming friction or elastic resistance). If the process begins with a stationary (or quasi-stationary) state of minimal energy content for the given topography, a displacement of this topography (and consequent self-reformation of the Gestalt) will be in the direction of still less energy in the ultimate Gestalt.

253 Applying this to the nervous system: Stationary psychophysiological Gestalten always assume that distribution which, under the given conditions (retinal and otherwise), yields the least possible energy in the Gestalt as a whole. Furthermore we may conclude that psychophysiological Gestalten, retroactively influencing their own topographical conditions,[1] produce these displacements not adventitiously but only in such a way as to bring about a further decrease of their own energy.

There is no way of telling from mere phenomenal observations whether a seen figure corresponds to an energy minimum or not. For the energy condition of a Gestalt does not refer to the distribution of the state or process *as such* but to a quantitative magnitude (energy) which varies with and is a function of this distribution. It is the *structure*, and not the corresponding energy, which is given to us phenomenally. Only if we knew some simple relation between quantity of energy and type of structure could we infer from the observed structure whether or not the principle of minimal
254 structural energy is fulfilled in the nervous system. However, no such simple relation seems to have been demonstrated even in the domain of inorganic Gestalten. What would be the "appearance" of a Gestalt which corresponded to a minimal value of energy?

255 Although we have no general solution of the problem of the relation between structure and quantity of energy, we know some special cases which give indications as to the general nature of the solution [cf. text, p. 254].

256 Consider a fine inelastic wire which carries electric current. We lay this wire on a flat, smooth surface, and bend it into any arbitrary, irregular form. If the current is strong enough, the wire will not remain at rest when current is passed through it, for the induction lines of the magnetic field pass through the surface enclosed by the wire. Every segment of the wire is acted on by a force so long as the number of enclosed lines of force can be increased by movement of the segment. Thus the wire changes its form until the whole contour encloses a maximum number of lines of force. Since for a contour of given circumference the shape enclosing the greatest surface is a *circle*, the *final* form will be circular, provided the current is strong enough, no matter what the *initial* form may have been.

257 A very different example shows that we are not dealing here with peculiarities of electromagnetic and electrodynamic processes,

[1] *Selection 4.*

but with general properties of nature. The illustration is taken from van der Mennsbugghe. A soap film is enclosed by a plane frame of wire and a small loop of very fine thread is placed in an irregular form upon it. If one pricks the film *inside* the loop, this part of the film vanishes, and the thread is exposed only to the surface tension of the outer film. These forces tend to give to the region enclosed by the thread the largest possible area, so that the remaining film has the smallest possible area. The thread thus immediately becomes a *circle*.

Where a physical form of homogeneous material properties can yield sufficiently to the systemic forces acting upon it, it seems to be a general rule that very *simple* and *regular* spatial arrangements are reached in the stationary state.

This behaviour of physical systems in their progress towards stationary states has been emphasized by the physicists P. Curie
258 and Mach. Curie writes that before natural processes can take place " it is necessary that certain elements of symmetry be absent. *Asymmetry* creates natural processes ".

259 The law exemplified in cases of this sort may be called the tendency towards simple Gestalten, or the law of *Prägnanz*—provided, of course, that we consciously leave the terms somewhat indefinite as a means of reminding ourselves that the theoretical physical problem itself is as yet unsolved.

This designation comes from Wertheimer, not as a description of inorganic physical behaviour, but of phenomenal and therefore also of physiological process-structures. Nevertheless it is possible to apply the terms to physical phenomena also, for the general tendency and line of development observed by Wertheimer in psychology and designated by him as the law of *Prägnanz* is obviously the same as we have here been discussing. We are not in a position to derive for individual cases their physiological and phenomenal characteristics, but the direction of process expressed therein shows clearly enough that Gestalten of the same fundamental character as those in physics must be involved.

SELECTION 4

SOME GESTALT PROBLEMS

By WOLFGANG KÖHLER

"Gestaltprobleme und Anfänge einer Gestalttheorie," *Jahresbericht ü. d. ges. Physiol.*, 1922, **3**, 512–539.

512 The name "Gestalt theory" denotes a way of thinking which seems to be of productive significance for the problems of various sciences. This paper will suggest the kind of answer to physiological questions which this mode of thinking engenders.

I. Every part of an organism is constantly being influenced both by the outside world and by all other parts within. Now since all these influences combine at any one time haphazardly, why are not the results themselves haphazard? Actually, of course, no such thing happens, for local processes are *not* arbitrary but evince, rather, a clearly defined organization relative to the needs and conditions of the organism as a whole. Indeed this co-operation resembles much more a state of "mutual agreement" than of mutual independence among the parts, and the result is not a jumble of independent processes but an ordered and meaningful activity of the whole organism. What are we to conclude from this?

513 This problem, well known as the starting point of vitalism, is an urgent problem of present day science. In insisting upon the urgency of the problem, Gestalt theory sides with vitalism—much as it rejects its solution. Nor will a solution be found for the problem of "causal harmony" merely by increasing our information about independent processes. The solution can be achieved only when an entirely different mode of attack is adopted.

Human beings construct machines and compel natural forces to operate in defined and controllable ways. A system of this sort is one of fixed "connections" in the sense of analytical mechanics. Thus by directing its forces and operations into fixed pathways from without we cause the activity at each mechanical point of the machine to conform with the total activity of every other point. Accordingly most biologists, physiologists, and psychologists think of organic harmony and co-ordination of processes

Grateful acknowledgment is hereby made to *Julius Springer*, *Verlagsbuchhandlung*, Berlin, for permission to reproduce the illustrations used in this SELECTION.

as achieved by the same mechanical principle of copious morphological connections. It seems that unwillingness to accept vitalism necessarily commits one to the mechanistic alternative. Only rarely is a point of view proposed which involves an essentially different, third mode of thinking.

Everyone knows how greatly the mechanistic point of view was stimulated by Darwinism. Eventually, however, it was realized that many organic phenomena do not conform with the mechanistic theory. Thus embryos and in varying degrees also adult organisms possess the ability, by changing the processes taking place within them, to compensate for irregularities of conditions which might otherwise have been injurious. Of course adjustments of this kind can sometimes, in cases of frequent, natural injuries, be explained as due to reparation mechanisms, but the multitude of regulations and regenerations which could not possibly have been bred into the species is so great that the mechanistic explanation breaks down.

514 II. In psychology the problem of sense perception raises questions closely resembling those of general biology. The visual field, for example, is an ordered manifold in which objects of the outer world are differentially represented. As a mechanical device the eye satisfies a primary requirement of such differentiation in the exact point for point reproduction of objects upon the receptive sensory surface. Again we encounter the mode of thinking already mentioned: unless some additional, mechanical device conducts the various excitations to their proper places and terminal processes corresponding directly to phenomenal vision, each excitation might spread in all possible directions and the result would be a completely haphazard disorder and confusion. Instead, of course, we find order and differentiation (book, pencil, inkstand); therefore it has been assumed fixed connections must force each excitation to remain in its appropriate pathway, and since this holds for each elementary process, there is order also in their totality. The *origin* of this delicate machinery, it has been supposed, could be accounted for on evolutionary grounds.

515 This hypothesis could be tested in the following manner. Suppose that visual perception depends upon the operation of a large but finite number of discrete local processes anatomically separated from one another and especially so in the sense that what takes place at one part of the visual field is independent of that taking place in its *other* parts. It should follow that the mechanically fixed elementary regions and functional boundaries by which

order is achieved would somehow be detected in phenomenal experience. If the minute size of these elementary regions rendered this impossible, then other tests designed to verify the hypothesis should have been *sought.* But almost nothing has been done along this line and certainly no one has ever seen the visual field break up into such elementary areas. On the contrary, everyone now recognizes that local areas in the visual field do not enjoy an isolated existence. But mechanism, rather than doubt the basic assumption of its theory, has introduced instead a series of supplementary hypotheses whereby, for the most part, "*mental*" factors are held accountable for contradictory findings. An instance of this procedure can be seen in Helmholtz's doctrine of unconscious inference. Another attempt to salvage mechanism (in this case *physiologically*) has been the assumption of secondary mechanisms by which the discrepancies might be accounted for. But complexity of the phenomena to be explained would soon require so complex a network of interconnections and interconnections between interconnections that the original theory would eventually become unrecognizable.

516 It is false to imply that vision consists in a mosaic of separate sensations, for the subdivisions that do appear in vision are simply those given by natural subdivisions in the visual field itself (book, pencil, inkstand). Any other implication is merely an artificial construct imposed *upon* the facts of vision. And it is this which Gestalt theory decries when it demands that we stay closer to observed facts and repudiate descriptions leading to artificialities. Certainly it is no moderation of scientific severity that a candid return to facts should be proposed. Indeed the rejected hypotheses not only misrepresent the facts but are utterly incapable of explaining even the most ordinary experience—such, for example, as why it is that the book is one visual thing, the pencil another, and so on. That we see separate, well defined things cannot be derived from the principles of mechanistic theory. In my own opinion one cannot grasp the position of Gestalt theory until one has learned to wonder about the fact of concrete articulations in the visual field.

517 Such visual articulation does not depend upon extrinsic, anatomical conditions, but rather upon the concrete properties of the spatial stimulus distributions. Realization of this fact leads one to the conclusion that visual articulation might be a spontaneous articulation of the physico-chemical properties of optical processes themselves. In this case the mechanistic theory of order would obviously be abandoned.

Take, for example, a number of pencils arranged in pairs of alternate red and green colour: place them parallel and at an equal distance from each other upon a grey background. In the first glance one sees a single "stripe" whose parts are made up of two colours. Here is a case where the spontaneous influence of colour upon visual articulation is especially significant because, despite the intervals between the pencils, they are nevertheless seen as a coherent whole.

518 It would be extremely unfortunate if the problem were thrust aside at this point as being after all only another case of the influence of past experience. No one doubts that past experience is an important factor in *some* cases, but the attempt to explain all perception in such terms is absolutely sure to fail, for it is easy to demonstrate instances where perception is not at all influenced by past experience. Fig. 1 is an example. We see a group of rectangles; but the figure may also be seen as two H's with certain intervening lines. Despite our extensive past experience with the letter H it is, nevertheless, the articulation of *the presented object* which determines what we shall see.

Fig. 1.

These segregated visual objects ("Gestalten" in the narrower sense)[1] have properties which are absolutely incomprehensible from a mechanistic point of view, with its assumption of anatomically independent elements. Such properties—e.g. "round", "sharp", "symmetrical", "simple"—are psychologically as
519 concrete as "red", "blue", and "green". No atomistic physiological theory can explain such properties; "straight," e.g., is not a property of any local element, but refers to a specific characteristic of an extended structure. Any attempt to discover the correspondence between phenomenal data and brain processes seems compelled to accept *real*, *physical events* and their *real properties*
521 as objective correlates of perceptual properties. The type of physiological process that will correspond to structured Gestalten in perception must itself have an equivalent physically real "structure". Consider the case of phenomenal transposition where changes in the size, place, and even sometimes the sense organ do not cause great if any changes in our experiencing of certain objects. "Round" and "straight", for example, are phenomenal Gestalt properties regardless of absolute size or position or sense organ. There must, therefore, be a physically

[1] Cf. *Selection 3*.

real side to such processes, some psychophysiological correlate which does *not* materially change with such alterations of the stimulating objects as we have suggested.

Now let us once more take up the biological problem mentioned above. In vision it is obvious that the specific function of individual parts is derived from their place in the objects we see. A black point, for example, will be a " corner " because of its location relative to the lines constituting a seen rectangle, and so on. The physical correlate of phenomenal Gestalten which we are seeking must therefore be a kind of process in which local events are determined by their position in a larger whole. And in this we find formal agreement with the biological problem of regulation in embryos, for now we can see how " part " and " whole " in a visual field may be compared with " part " and " whole " in the developing embryo. Indeed the biological side of this comparison exemplifies the reality of part and whole relationships with amazing fidelity.

That the properties of visual Gestalten (in the
522 narrower sense) are derived from their place in the whole may also be seen in geometrical illusions. Similarly the results of recent inquiries have demonstrated that colour contrast and also the local appearance of colours (threshold phenomena) are dependent upon Gestalt conditions of the field in which they are seen.[1]

FIG. 2.

Relatively segregated units which stand apart in the visual field have been called Gestalten. The characters of local events depend upon their place in the Gestalt in which they occur, but this is also true of the segregation of Gestalten themselves as regards the entire visual field. It is not enough that a certain region should be homogeneously coloured in order for it to constitute an independent Gestalt, but the environment also must be appropriately coloured. This is especially clear in the distinction between " figure " and
523 " ground ". When, in Fig. 2, the propeller blades are seen as figure, this region becomes compact and more substantial ; the " mere ground " is loose and empty by comparison despite the fact that both stimulations come from the same white page. This phenomenon, first emphasized by Rubin, served to show that the property of solidity or substantiality is also the character of every " thing " in optical space.

The propeller blades of Fig. 2 are reversible so that now the

[1] See *Selection 16*.

broader, now the thin are seen as figure. But the thin blades are more stable and the figure-character persists longer with them than with the others. Thus the organization of this pattern depends on the relation of the angles. Figs. 3 and 4 supply further illustrations of the influence exerted by broader or narrower areas, for the " figures " in Fig. 3 become the "ground " in Fig. 4, and even the contour functions of the boundary lines have been reversed. These examples show how large regions of the visual field (to some degree probably its whole extent) determine the segregation of parts within it. Physiologically expressed: the unknown type of function of a somatic field-area which makes of that area a Gestalt process is not determined by that region alone, but rather by the entire visual field. (The principles applied here to spatial structures hold also for temporal processes.)

525 Whatever the process is which physiologically underlies Gestalt

FIG. 3. FIG. 4.

perception, we know that it occurs pre-consciously since articulation of the visual field is given simultaneously with the contents of vision. That these phenomena cannot in principle depend upon higher mental abilities but are instead a result of the fundamental nature of the sensory process can be seen from cases such as the following. A chicken is taught to choose the darker of two greys. After this is learned the animal is given a pair composed of the former dark grey and another still darker one. The fact that it now selects the new (darker) grey shows that its choices had throughout been made relative to the *pair* of greys. This determination of a part (one grey) by its whole (the pair) is characteristic of the problem with which we are dealing, yet in the case of the chicken it is obviously impossible that higher mental powers should have been responsible for the observed behaviour.[1]

526 III. " Mechanistic " and " scientifically comprehensible " are

[1] See *Selection 18.*

not synonymous terms. In physics, for example, though far too little recognized in biology and psychology, one finds a kind of process which cannot be classified as mechanistic at all. A genuine machine is only one *specialized* kind of physical system the spatial order of whose activities is not determined by the forces at work in the machine but by a pre-designed arrangement of " connections " permitting and determining the ways in which those forces shall be exerted. The physics of Gestalt theory, on the contrary, refers to those spatial orders of processes which are *determined by the forces within the system itself.* Of course the inner states of any finite system develop relative to more or less fixed conditions along its boundaries and in its interior. But it makes a great deal of difference whether the inner distribution of substances, of vector and scalar magnitudes is throughout established by rigid connections *or* depends also upon the inner dynamics of the system. The more completely a system is governed by constraints, the more adequately does it exemplify a machine. The more freely the inner dynamics of a system are left to regulate themselves, the farther the system is from being a machine. Thus the fundamental operations of living organisms even if they be of the latter type remain thoroughly amenable to scientific treatment. Indeed, the range of possible activities in systems of *this* sort is much richer and more interesting than in those of the machine type. The question is : How are these processes related to the observable behaviour of living organisms ?

527 Every system to which the second law of thermodynamics can be applied sooner or later reaches an equilibrium either of rest or of a steady state under the given conditions.[1] The processes in the nervous system have repeatedly been treated from this point of view, but the necessary consequences of this have by no means been drawn. What properties must the final state display when individual regions of a system are not functionally isolated from one another but are, rather, to some degree in functional communication ? Physics can easily inform us about this. Since not only parts of a system which are exposed to the conditions prevailing at the boundaries must adjust themselves to these conditions, but since, also, every such produced change passes on its influence in turn, the system cannot reach an equilibrium merely by having each region alone become adjusted to the external conditions acting locally on it. *Instead* the final state is reached when, through continual displacements at each point, the resulting inner forces

[1] *Selection 3.*

and states eventually stand in such relation to each other throughout that they no longer bring about any change in the state or (now) stationary process of the system. There are systems in which this occurs very rapidly, others where it requires years to happen. In many systems the spatial side of the process is not particularly striking because, as with many solutions in test tubes, the end of a reaction is practically homogeneous. In other systems the spontaneously arising spatial distribution of equilibrium is without doubt the most interesting property. We are dealing here especially with cases of the *latter* type.

Theoretical physics treats such problems as " boundary problems ". It investigates what the spontaneous internal equilibrium distribution of a system of known material properties must be when definite conditions at its boundaries are prescribed. A well-known example of such a boundary problem is the following. Suppose that at the surface points of a body of known material and given form definite temperatures are externally maintained; the question then is to determine the internal temperature distribution and heat flow prevailing when the spontaneously arising steady state has been reached. The answer is obtained, as I need not describe here, by the solution of a differential equation or an integral equation for the given " boundary conditions ".

This simple principle of stationary distribution spontaneously arising from inner dynamics—in contradistinction to mechanical distribution governed by constraints—is characterized by just this, that the state of any region of the system is at any instant also determined by the state in every other region. This principle constitutes the fundamental thought underlying the theory of physical Gestalten.[1]

529 Another example. The distribution of an electric charge upon an isolated conductor constitutes a real structure. If another conductor of the same shape at a sufficient distance is similarly charged, we have the " same " distribution of equilibrium in both. And since these are physical realities, using the word " same " is justified because at the new place not merely the same geometry of parts but the identical dynamically balanced field and charge distribution exists. It is now easy to understand " transpositions " in psychology, for there too we have non-identity of constituent parts and still have identity of processes.

Now since a mere geometry of externally connected elementary excitations is unable to account for the facts of human perception,

[1] *Selection 3.*

and since the contradictory phenomena are remarkable in their conformity with the principles of physical spontaneous distributions, the following hypothesis naturally suggests itself: The somatic processes underlying static visual fields are stationary equilibrium distributions developed from the inner dynamics of the optical system itself; the spatial order and articulation of a visual field correspond to the physically real structure of this stationary process.

530 This hypothesis merely requires that we abandon the notion of insulated pathways leading from the retina to the region of psychophysiological processes. Since there are many cross-connections at various levels in the optic system between pathways extending inward from the retina, a spontaneous distribution for the entire system *must* result.

Gestalt theory favours this hypothesis rather than that proposed by mechanism for the following reasons :—

(1) Because only in this case does a physical reality in somatic events correspond to the spatial articulations, forms, and form-properties of visual fields;

(2) Because only in this case is it comprehensible that articulation and configuration in visual fields should harmonize with the *concrete* properties of the determining factors, notably stimulus-differences and -configurations;

(3) Because only on this assumption can (and must) parts and part-properties of visual fields and Gestalten [narrower sense] depend upon the total conditions (wholes) obtaining at the moment;

(4) Because in this case all types of " transposition " in the visual field follow directly from identical invariances of spontaneous stationary somatic distributions.

Naturally this means that spontaneous distribution in the somatic process can no longer be considered a more or less perfect representation of retinal stimulus-geometry. It is true, of course, that the picture upon each *retinal* area is practically independent of all the others, but the *field of vision* is spontaneously articulated into " seen things ", and in this it is far indeed from a mere geometry of stimuli. This fact is of the greatest importance for biology. Thus the distinction between " figure " and " ground " cannot be found in a geometry of stimuli to which in fact any real Gestalt properties are alien. Finally there is the proof supplied by illusory figures which show that our visual field is continually deviating from the relations obtaining in retinal geometry. Indeed there are probably endless unnoticed instances of the same thing in everyday life. But whatever the deviations between stimulus geometry and perception may be, they depend strongly upon the processes prevailing at the time in the optic sector of the nervous system.

Now these deviations between articulation of the field of vision and geometry of the retina disclose another striking resemblance to the spontaneously arising equilibrium structures of physics.
531 Such distributions in physics are distinguished by simplicity and regularity. Hence if optical structures follow this principle we should expect that they also would proceed in the direction of simplicity and regularity. And this tendency towards " *Prägnanz der Gestaltung* " was discovered in perceptual structures by Wertheimer. In optics the circle, a form unique in its properties, frequently tends to result even when the stimulus configuration deviates considerably from such extreme symmetry.

Although a completed theory of perceptual processes is as yet impossible, this much at least has been accomplished : we now see that the failure of mechanism does not signify the impossibility of treating perceptual problems scientifically. Furthermore it is now clear that even before specific knowledge of the forces and processes is available, psychological observations can also contribute to the study of physiological processes in the optic sector.

532 IV. Let us now apply the foregoing to problems of general biology. Mechanism is incapable of explaining either co-ordination or regulation in organic happenings. It is impossible that the host of fixed " connections " necessary for all cases of co-ordinated behaviour could lie ready in the organism. In applying the principle of dynamics to the entire organism (or large parts of it) two assumptions are made : first, that for a living system also inner forces are directed toward a state of equilibrium ; and, secondly, that this direction holds for the system and the grouping of forces as a *whole*, and that therefore the functions of its parts (organs) can only occasionally and with the greatest circumspection be looked upon as relatively self-sufficient. This second assumption contains nothing recondite but refers merely to a property of systemic regions which may or may not occur in nature—but which always *does* occur when the regions of a system are in functional communication. The degree of interdependence obtaining in a system depends upon the speed with which an alteration at one place is transmitted to every other place. The vascular and nervous systems of higher organisms mediate local alterations very rapidly, and even in the less differentiated protoplasm of embryos the speed must be great enough for the relatively slow processes of

morphogenesis. Therefore processes occurring independently in an organism may be admitted only as border-line cases.

When this is seen, however, the question of so-called "causal harmony" naturally takes on a very different aspect. Thus, when many *independent* processes arise and spread, any haphazard result may follow their coming together at any point. When, however, the processes of one region are dependent upon those of the remaining regions, and vice versa, then *arbitrary* effects can *not* result, either at points where the processes converge or in the relationship of processes in different parts of different organs. In the first case (independent forces) only a mechanistic theory of external connections can account for order; in the second it is obvious that a distinct direction of the whole happening is necessarily maintained, and this for the self-contained, functional system as a *whole*. This is true in so far as spatial, functional, and other displacements in the system mutually determine one another so that a steady state of the *whole* system, under the given conditions, is approached. Were a (macroscopic) process to arise at any place which opposed the direction taken by the system, this would call forth counter processes in the system that would at once nullify
533 this deviation. If such self-regulation seems surprising this is because we are unable to survey simultaneously so many mutually dependent processes. Yet all internally coherent systems in the inorganic world behave in this way; the arrangement of internal forces is always directed towards balance throughout. And so far as effects of inertia do not cause the system to overshoot a uniquely determined position, an equilibrium structure is reached and the displacements cease.

In the natural existence of an organism the steady state in the face of a given complex of actual conditions is often not reached because the conditions themselves change. This does not alter the fact, however, that the organism is constantly on the way towards a steady state under any given set of conditions.

In applying this mode of thinking to organisms it is not enough that we should take the organism alone into consideration since every organism through respiration, nutrition, etc., is in communication with an external source of energy. In many cases—such, for example, as that of embryonic development—the argument takes the following form: If, during an observed process, a system cut off from external energy-supply remains at constant temperature, it proceeds toward a steady end-state in which its energy capable of doing work decreases until a minimum value is reached. All distributions, displacements, etc., proceed in each place in such a manner that this direction will be that of the *whole*. If, however, the system is in communication with a reservoir of available energy of such character that the drain does not noticeably exhaust it, the theorem of constant loss of energy capacity must be applied to the larger whole—i.e. the system together with its energy reservoir. In *this* whole a minimum of available energy is attained if as much as possible of the reservoir's energy enters the transforming system. Here it is in part used up by the transformation processes, in part stored as working capacity. It follows that as a result of this connection with the reservoir, the system will increase its own available energy. For an embryo in the uterus the mother is an energy reservoir; its changes proceed in such a way that its own supply of available energy gradually increases, and changes at every place in the embryo are such that, as a whole, this direction is maintained.

The first consequence of our considerations is a resolution of the vitalistic paradox emphasized by Driesch. In an organism the end states are certain articulations and distributions *of the whole system* and therefore an event at a given place is determined by its location or situation in the whole. This is the only way that a continual approximation to the unique end-result can come about. If each partial region were functionally isolated, each would operate according to the second law of thermodynamics. When, however,
534 there is a functional *union* between them, then the second law can be satisfied for the whole only if each part functions according to its position in the given system.

Many embryos can be temporarily deformed (artificially) in ways utterly incongruous with their racial history and nevertheless regain by a wholly new route the same developmental stage reached by another, untouched embryo. Now a machine, says Driesch, cannot do this, and therefore regulations of this kind are outside the scope of scientific comprehension. But why should Driesch assume that the only alternative to a vitalistic organism is a machine? Such an assumption clearly betrays that nature is here being thought of as capable of ordered processes only when forced into them by external connections. Of course a machine will not regulate itself except as special regulatory mechanisms are provided for every case. A genuine machine has only one degree of freedom in the sense of analytical mechanics, i.e. its condition is expressed at any one time by one single variable. And this the engineer achieves from without by means of fixed

connections so arranged that, all others being eliminated, only the one desired kind of function remains possible. As a result the machine either operates along the line of this one degree of freedom, or not at all. Hence also the " lifelessness " and " monotony " of machines which is so repellent in the machine theory of organic events. But this dullness comes from the rigidity of the connections, the purely external direction of natural forces in the machine, *not* from the fact that machines belong to the inorganic world and are scientifically comprehensible. An inorganic system with several degrees of freedom would behave under other circumstances very differently from a machine, which can do one definite thing or nothing. In a system of this kind a change in external conditions, a disturbance of parts, etc., would bring about a reorganization of forces and processes relative to the new situation. And obviously each partial region would then change its state and process according to its place in the new whole. This is required by the tendency toward equilibrium in a system of communicating forces and processes. Hence instead of drawing a comparison between machines and self-regulating embryos one must extend the sphere of possibilities much farther into the inorganic world. Indeed machines can be omitted entirely from these possibilities as representing only a very special, and particularly unsuitable type of comparison. The systems that fulfil the conditions of comparison must possess freedom in their own forces, i.e. they must possess precisely that which (through the use of constraints) has been taken from machines in the interest of unalterable order. Many examples of systems with multiple degrees of freedom in their inner states disclose the formal properties of " regulation ". If, for example, I temporarily prevent an electric current in a conducting network from reaching its balance distribution, if I compel it through external means to quit the path it sought to follow, the first thing that happens when the " interruption " is removed is a change of course towards the end-state that
535 previously could not be achieved. In this change of course each part of the system behaves according to the state to which the whole was brought by the interruption, i.e. differently upon every occasion depending upon the nature of the interruption. This is the only way a change of course can always lead to the same end-state—and the same is true of the embryo.

If the development of an organism is viewed as a physical process, then temporary interruptions need not at all signify a lasting deformation. If the organism is a system of manifold degrees of freedom, the route its development takes is relatively immaterial. Since it is part of a new whole, each individual cell will, in a now more intelligible way, have a new function, will perform new processes, and thus all of them together will, so far as possible, perform a total process such that the end-state prevented by the interruption shall be achieved as soon as that disturbance is removed.

Is not the co-ordination of various organs, and hence the much discussed " purposiveness " of organic behaviour, simply an approach by the entire organism toward a steady state—and
536 therefore a causally necessary process? It seems to me probable that if there were a process which did *not* conform in this way, it would either fail to bring the system closer to its equilibrium or, by introducing " tensions ", it would obstruct the progress towards equilibrium. But such processes do not occur in macroscopic systems.

The enormous precision of co-ordination in eye-movements affords an illustration of what is meant here. The mechanistic theory explains this co-ordination in one or other of the following ways. Either it is due to an elaborate network of mechanisms inherited by the organism, or it is due to mechanisms supplied by the individual as a result of his own experience. But both views, unsatisfactory in themselves, fail when called upon to explain eye-movement in *new*, artificially designed situations.

A very different kind of possibility is the following. The eyes of a person in the dark assume a position in equilibrium with the bulbar musculature. If, then, a bright, moderately sized object is suddenly presented at one side and at a distance of, say, 5 m., the eyes are at first neither directed nor accommodated to this object. Excitations nevertheless traverse the optic nerve setting up processes in the somatic perceptual field depending upon the retinal pattern, which in its turn is determined by the position of the eyes relative to the object. If now the somatic perceptual field is so connected with the eye muscles that some available energy of the optic processes passes into the nerves innervating the eye muscles, the eyes will turn and thus alter the location of the image (and the lens adjustment), and finally there will result from these changes a displacement of process in the somatic perceptual field, involving a change of its inner dynamics. This constitutes a complete circle of processes ; each position of the eyes results from the perceptual field and in turn brings about an immediate reciprocal effect in the state of that field. Hence the question arises whether, in a reciprocal process of this sort, arbitrary or unordered events can possibly

537 occur. The eye muscles were formerly in equilibrium and would not have departed from that state had there not been other processes influencing and supplying them with available energy. This energy comes from the somatic perceptual field and since each small eye movement introduces new conditions into this field, innervation of the eye musculature *can* only occur in such a way that the process of the perceptual field shall attain a " better " equilibrium than before.

Convergence and fixation agree well with this theory, for the most general law of eye movements states that they are always in the direction of maximum simplification (maximum horopter) of the perceptual field. We have already seen (p. 531) that spatial distributions of a self-contained process assume simple forms as equilibrium is approached.

Let us proceed another step. The development of an organism sometimes includes self-imposed curtailment of its own inner dynamics and reduction in its degrees of freedom by constraints. The question is whether such connections are *arbitrarily* imposed. The problem applies not only to the early stages of morphogenesis but also to the completion of a relatively rigid skeleton, of the visual cortex, and so on. Indeed all normal differentiation of organs must
538 be understood as relatively fixed morphological products resulting from dynamic processes in the developing organism, originally in the fertilized cell. Now the question is whether *just anything* can result or whether the processes are directed towards the construction of " appropriate " mechanisms. This question may be answered as follows.

Any initial step towards a relatively fixed connection would be a " constraint " either *favouring* the function which it begins to constrain, and thereby favouring co-ordinated activity in the organism—or *opposing* such activity. This is essentially the same situation as the guidance of eye muscles by optic processes. Just as this guidance (because of reciprocal influence) occurs only towards optimal equilibrium of the optic whole-process, so also can the processes in an organism develop only *such* relatively rigid connections as—through retroactive influence upon the (now less free) dynamics of these processes—will permit the best equilibrium relative to normal conditions. Hence we can see that not only will general physical causes lead to " co-ordinated " behaviour in completed organisms but also that the same causes will bring about the development of relatively fixed morphological forms—always assuming that co-ordination will result when there is constant pressure toward compensating, unique states and processes relative to the given conditions. Thus " purposiveness " and " goal activity " of organic differentiation and growth appear to be causally determined happenings in communicating systems, the inner dynamics of which are impelled toward equilibrium. Causality in such systems is, in virtue of their coherence throughout, free from " arbitrary coincidence ", yet (without any assumption of entelechies) at the same time constantly " directed " by the total pressure of the system.

With radical changes of condition there may thus be at one time a strict maintenance of function—when the organic structures are absolutely rigid—and at another, appropriate modifications of the organic forms. A surprising number of " mechanisms " of the latter type can be observed even in adults. The study of hemianopic patients, for example, has recently shown that the fovea which, in a normal individual, is morphologically differentiated as the place of greatest visual acuity, is, when necessary, movable so as to conform with new conditions brought about by injury.[1]

From these considerations it would appear that a " chance "
origin of organic forms may be referred to only with the greatest
caution. Instead of externally determined selection (Darwin) we
539 must consider *directly selective* factors which, operating in the
whole and relative to the given environmental conditions, will
not permit a haphazard origin of forms.

[1] See *Selection 30*.

II. SPECIAL PROBLEMS

First Group: Perception

A. PERCEPTION AND ORGANIZATION

Selection 5

LAWS OF ORGANIZATION IN PERCEPTUAL FORMS

By Max Wertheimer

"Untersuchungen zur Lehre von der Gestalt," II, *Psychol. Forsch.*, 1923, **4**, 301–350.

301 I stand at the window and see a house, trees, sky.

Theoretically I might say there were 327 brightnesses and nuances of colour. Do I *have* "327"? No. I have sky, house, and trees. It is impossible to achieve "327" as such. And yet even though such droll calculation were possible—and implied, say, for the house 120, the trees 90, the sky 117—I should at least have *this* arrangement and division of the total, and not, say, 127 and 100 and 100; or 150 and 177.

The concrete division which I *see* is not determined by some arbitrary mode of organization lying solely within my own pleasure; instead I see the arrangement and division which is given there before me. And what a remarkable process it is when some other mode of apprehension *does* succeed! I gaze for a long time from my window, adopt after some effort the most unreal attitude possible. And I *discover* that part of a window sash and part of a bare branch together compose an *N*.

Or, I look at a picture. Two faces cheek to cheek. I see one (with its, if you will, "57" brightnesses) and the other ("49" brightnesses). I do not see an arrangement of 66 plus 40 nor of 6 plus 100. There *have* been theories which would require that I see "106". In reality I see two faces!

Or, I hear a melody (17 tones) with its accompaniment (32 tones). I hear the melody and accompaniment, not simply "49"—and certainly not 20 plus 29. And the same is true even in cases where there is no stimulus continuum. I hear the melody and its accompaniment even when they are played by an old-fashioned
302 clock where each tone is separate from the others. Or, one sees
a series of discontinuous dots upon a homogeneous ground not

Grateful acknowledgment is hereby made to *Julius Springer*, *Verlagsbuchhandlung*, Berlin, for permission to reproduce the illustrations used in this Selection.

as a sum of dots, but as figures. Even though there may here be a greater latitude of possible arrangements, the dots usually combine in some "spontaneous", "natural" articulation—and any other arrangement, even if it can be achieved, is artificial and difficult to maintain.

When we are presented with a number of stimuli we do not as a rule experience "a number" of individual things, this one and that and that. Instead larger wholes separated from and related to one another are given in experience; their arrangement and division are concrete and definite.

Do such arrangements and divisions follow definite principles? When the stimuli *abcde* appear together what are the principles according to which *abc/de* and not *ab/cde* is experienced? It is the purpose of this paper to examine this problem, and we shall therefore begin with cases of discontinuous stimulus constellations.

304 *I.* A row of dots is presented upon a homogeneous ground. The alternate intervals are 3 mm. and 12 mm.

• •   • •   • •   • •   • •   • •   • • (i)

Normally this row will be seen as *ab/cd*, not as *a/bc/de*. As a matter of fact it is for most people impossible to see the whole series simultaneously in the latter grouping.

We are interested here in what is actually *seen*. The following will make this clear. One sees a row of groups obliquely tilted from lower left to upper right (*ab/cd/ef*). The arrangement *a/bc/de*
305 is extremely difficult to achieve. Even when it can be seen, such an arrangement is far less certain than the other and is quite likely to be upset by eye-movements or variations of attention.

(ii)

This is even more clear in (iii).

(iii)

I.e. :— *c* *f* *i* *l* *o*
b *e* *h* *k* *n* etc.
a *d* *g* *j* *m*

Quite obviously the arrangement *abc/def/ghi* is greatly superior to *ceg/fhj/ikm*.

Another, still clearer example of spontaneous arrangement is that given in (iv). The natural grouping is, of course, *a/bcd/efghi*, etc.

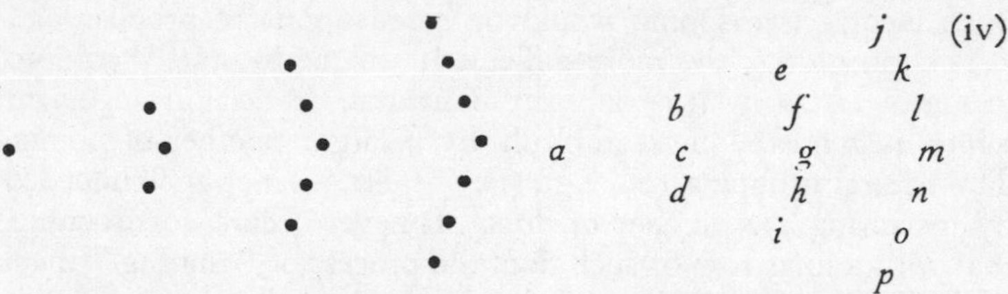

Resembling (i) but still more compelling is the row of three-dot groupings given in (v). One sees *abc/def*, and not some other (theoretically possible) arrangement.

(v)

306 Another example of seeing what the objective arrangement dictates is contained in (vi) for vertical, and in (vii) for horizontal groupings.

(vii)

(viii)

(ix)

(x)

In all the foregoing cases we have used a relatively large number of dots for each figure. Using fewer we find that the arrangement is not so imperatively dictated as before, and reversing the more obvious grouping is comparatively easy. Examples: (viii)–(x).

307 It would be false to assume that (viii)–(x) lend themselves more readily to reversal because fewer stimulus points (dots) are involved. Such incorrect reasoning would be based upon the proposition: "The more dots, the more difficult it will be to unite them into groups." Actually it is only the unnatural, artificial arrangement which is rendered more difficult by a larger number of points. The natural grouping (cf., e.g., (i), (ii), etc.) is not at all impeded by increasing the number of dots. It never occurs, for example, that with a long row of such dots the process of "uniting" them into pairs is abandoned and individual points seen instead. It is not true that fewer stimulus points "obviously" yield simpler, surer, more elementary results.

308 In each of the above cases that form of grouping is most natural which involves the smallest interval. They all show, that is to say, the predominant influence of what we may call *The Factor of Proximity*. Here is the first of the principles which we undertook to discover. That the principle holds also for auditory organization can readily be seen by substituting tap-tap, pause, tap-tap, pause, etc. for (i), and so on for the others.

II. Proximity is not, however, the only factor involved in natural groupings. This is apparent from the following examples. We shall maintain an identical proximity throughout but vary the colour of the dots themselves :—

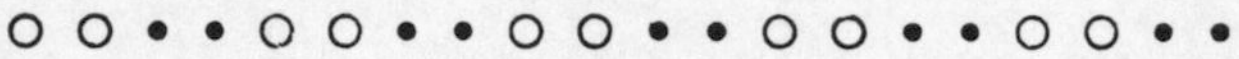

○ ○ • • ○ ○ • • ○ ○ • • ○ ○ • • ○ ○ • • (xi)

309 Or, again :—

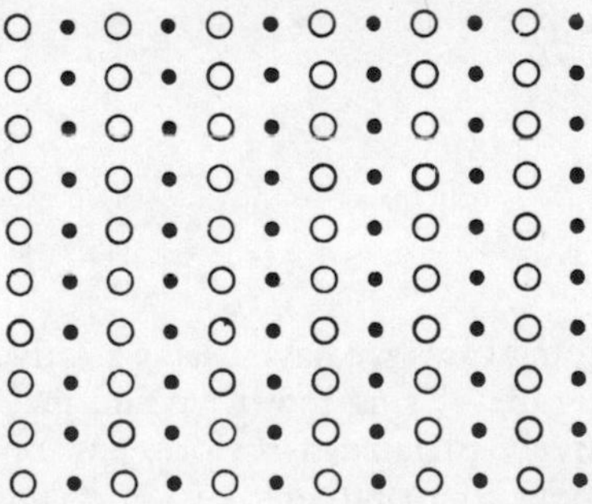

○ • ○ • ○ • ○ • ○ • ○ •
○ • ○ • ○ • ○ • ○ • ○ •
○ • ○ • ○ • ○ • ○ • ○ •
○ • ○ • ○ • ○ • ○ • ○ •
○ • ○ • ○ • ○ • ○ • ○ • (xii)
○ • ○ • ○ • ○ • ○ • ○ •
○ • ○ • ○ • ○ • ○ • ○ •
○ • ○ • ○ • ○ • ○ • ○ •
○ • ○ • ○ • ○ • ○ • ○ •
○ • ○ • ○ • ○ • ○ • ○ •

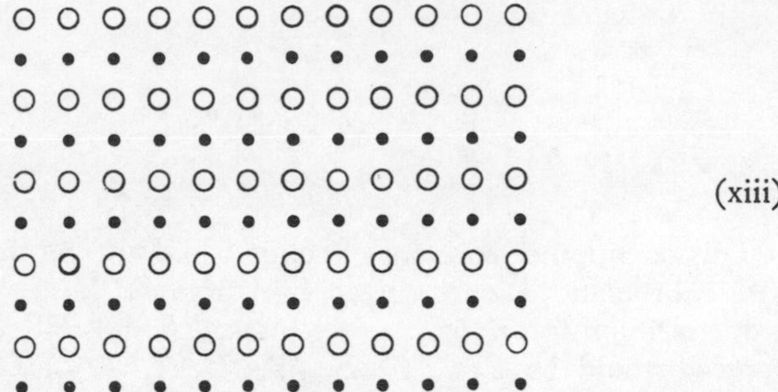

(xiii)

Or, to repeat (v) but with uniform proximity :—

○ ○ ○ • • • ○ ○ ○ • • • ○ ○ ○ • • • ○ ○ ○ • • • (xiv)

Thus we are led to the discovery of a second principle—viz. the tendency of like parts to band together—which we may call *The Factor of Similarity*. And again it should be remarked that this principle applies also to auditory experience. Maintaining a constant interval, the beats may be soft and loud (analogous to (xi)) thus: . . ! ! . . ! ! etc. Even when the attempt to hear some other arrangement succeeds, this cannot be maintained for long. The natural grouping soon returns as an overpowering " upset " of the artificial arrangement.

310 In (xi)–(xiv) there is, however, the possibility of another arrangement which should not be overlooked. We have treated these sequences in terms of a *constant* direction from left to right. But it is also true that a continual *change* of direction is taking place between the groups themselves: viz. the transition from group one to group two (soft-to-loud), the transition from group two to group three (loud-to-soft), and so on. This naturally involves a special factor. To retain a constant direction it would be necessary to make each succeeding pair louder than the last. Schematically this can be represented as :—

                • •
            • •
        • •   (xv)
    • •
• •

Or, in the same way:—

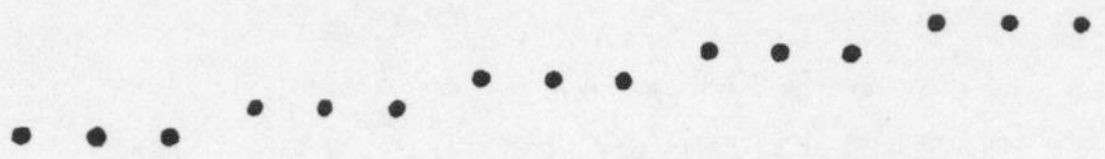

(xvi)

This retention of constant direction could also be demonstrated with achromatic colours (green background) thus: white, light
311 grey, medium grey, dark grey, black. A musical reproduction of (xv) would be *C*, *C*, *E*, *E*, *F*♯, *F*♯, *A*, *A*, *C*, *C*, . . .; and similarly for (xvi): *C*, *C*, *C*, *E*, *E*, *E*, *F*♯, *F*♯, *F*♯, *A*, *A*, *A*, *C*, *C*, *C*, . . .

Thus far we have dealt merely with a special case of the general law. Not only similarity and dissimilarity, but *more and less dissimilarity* operate to determine experienced arrangement. With tones, for example, *C*, *C*♯, *E*, *F*, *G*♯, *A*, *C*, *C*♯ . . . will be heard in the grouping *ab*/*cd* . . . and *C*, *C*♯, *D*, *E*, *F*, *F*♯, *G*♯, *A*, *A*♯, *C*, *C*♯, *D* . . . in the grouping *abc*/*def* . . . Or, again using achromatic colours, we might present these same relationships in the manner suggested (schematically) by (xvii) and (xviii).

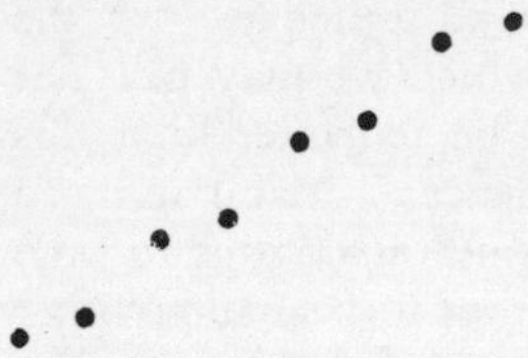

(xvii)

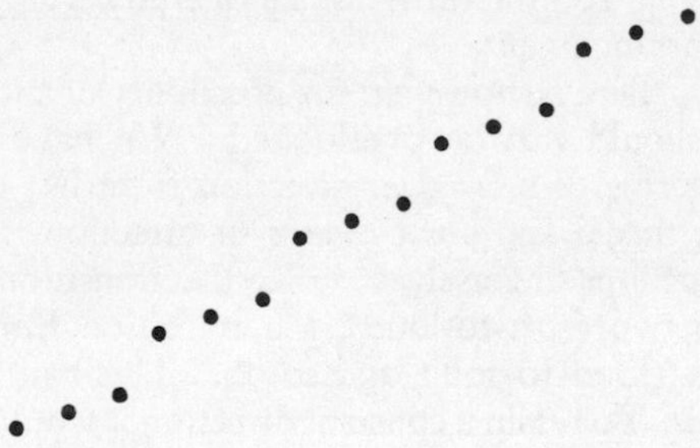

(xviii)

(It is apparent from the foregoing that quantitative comparisons can be made regarding the application of the same laws in regions—form, colour, sound—heretofore treated as psychologically separate and heterogeneous.)

III. What will happen when *two* such factors appear in the same constellation? They may be made to co-operate; or, they can

be set in opposition—as, for example, when *one* operates to favour *ab/cd* while the *other* favours */bc/de*. By appropriate variations,
312 either factor may be weakened or strengthened. As an example, consider this arrangement :—

(xix)

where both similarity and proximity are employed. An illustration
313 of opposition in which similarity is victorious despite the preferential status given to proximity is this :—

(xx)

A less decided victory by similarity :—

(xxi)

Functioning together towards the same end, similarity and proximity greatly strengthen the prominence here of verticality :—

(xxii)

Where, in cases such as these, *proximity* is the predominant factor, a gradual increase of interval will eventually introduce a point at which *similarity* is predominant. In this way it is possible to test the strength of these Factors.

315 *IV*. A row of dots is presented :—

and then, without the subject's expecting it, but before his eyes, a sudden, slight shift upward is given, say, to *d*, *e*, *f* or to *d*, *e*, *f* and *j*, *k*, *l* together. *This* shift is " pro-structural ", since it involves an entire group of naturally related dots. A shift upward of, say, *c*, *d*, *e* or of *c*, *d*, *e* and *i*, *j*, *k* would be " contra-structural " because the common fate (i.e. the shift) to which these dots are subjected does *not* conform with their natural groupings.

316 Shifts of the latter kind are far less " smooth " than those of the former type. The former often call forth from the subject no more than bare recognition that a change has occurred; not so with the latter type. Here it is as if some particular " opposition " to the change had been encountered. The result is confusing and discomforting. Sometimes a revolt against the originally dominant Factor of Proximity will occur and the shifted dots themselves thereupon constitute a new grouping whose common fate it has been to be shifted above the original row. The principle involved here may be designated *The Factor of Uniform Destiny* (or of " *Common Fate* ").

V. Imagine a sequence of rows of which this would be the first :—

Row A.	••	••	••	••	••
	a b	*c d*	*e f*	*g h*	*i j*

The intervals between *a-b*, *c-d*, etc. (designated hereafter as S_1) are in this row 2 mm. ; those between *b-c*, *d-e*, etc. (S_2) are 20 mm. We shall hold *a*, *c*, *e*, *g*, and *i* constant while varying the horizontal position of *b*, *d*, *f*, *h*, and *j* thus :—

$$S_1 + S_2 = 22$$

317

Row A	S_1 = 2 mm.	S_2 = 20 mm.
B	5	17
C	8	14
D	11	11
E	14	8
F	17	5
G	20	2

Experimentally we now present these rows *separately*.[1] It will be found that there are three major constellations : The dominant impression in Row A is *ab/cd*, and in Row G it is */bc/de*. But in the middle row (represented in our schema by D) the predominant impression is that of uniformity. These three constellations thus constitute " unique regions " and it will be found that intervening

[1] The above classification of but 7 rows is intended merely as a schema. In actual experimentation many more than 7 (with correspondingly more minute variations of intervals) are needed.

rows are more indefinite in character and their arrangement less striking; indeed they are often most easily seen in the sense of the nearest major constellation. Example: intermediate rows in the vicinity of D will be seen *as* " not quite equally spaced " (even when the difference between intervals S_1 and S_2 is clearly supraliminal).

318 Or to take another example. Suppose one side of an angle is held horizontal and the other passes through an arc from 30° to 150°. No more here than in the preceding case is *each* degree of equal value psychologically. Instead there are three principal stages: acute, right, and obtuse. The " right angle ", for example, has a certain region such that an angle of 93° appears *as* a (more or less inadequate) right angle. Stages intermediate between the major ones have the character of indefiniteness about them and are readily seen in the sense of one *or* the other adjacent *Prägnanzstufen.*[1] This can be very clearly demonstrated by tachistoscopic presentations, for in this case the observer frequently *sees* a right angle even when objectively a more acute or more obtuse angle is being presented. Although the observer may report that it was " not quite correct ", " somehow wrong ", etc., he is usually unable to say in which direction the " error " lies.

319 In general we may say, as in the case above where the location of *b* between *a* and *c* was varied, that our impressions are not psychologically equivalent for all positions of *b*. Instead there are certain *Prägnanzstufen* with their appropriate realms or regions, and intermediate stages typically appear " in the sense of " one of these characteristic regions.

VI. Suppose now that the variations from A to G are carried out before the observer's eyes. This procedure leads to a discovery of *The Factor of Objective Set* [*Einstellung*]. As one proceeds from A towards G or from G towards A the *original* grouping in each case (i.e. *ab/cd* in the former, */bc/de* in the latter) tends to maintain itself even beyond the middle row. Then there occurs an upset and the opposite grouping becomes dominant. The constellation of Row C, for example, will be different when preceded by A and B from what it would be when preceded by G, F, E. This means that the row is *a part in a sequence* and the law of its arrangement is such that the constellation resulting from *one* form of sequence will be different from that given by some

[1] [" *Stufen* " = steps or stages; the term " *Prägnanz* " cannot be translated. In the present usage " *Prägnanzstufen* " means *regions* of figural stability in a sense which should be clear from the text.]

other sequence. Or, again, a certain (objectively) ambiguous
320 arrangement will be perfectly definite and unequivocal when given as a part in a sequence. (In view of its great strength this Factor must in all cases be considered with much care.)

Parenthetically: it is customary to attribute influences such as these to purely subjective (meaning by this "purely arbitrary") conditions. But our examples refer only to *objective* factors: the presence or absence of a certain row of dots in a sequence is determined solely by objective conditions. It is objectively quite different whether a Row M is presented after Row L or after Row N; or, whether the presentations follow one another

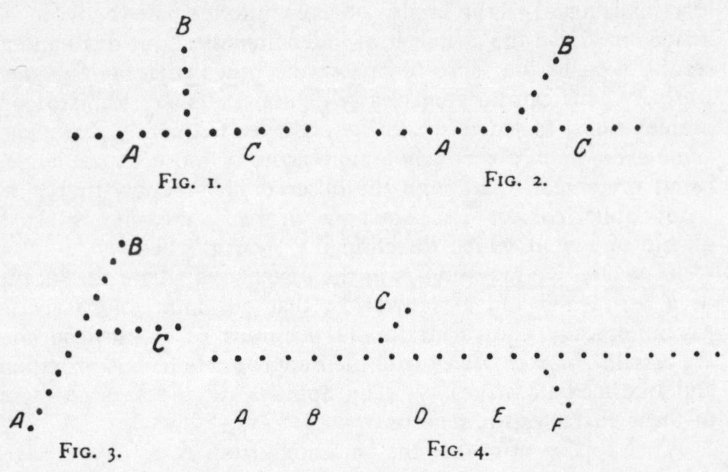

FIG. 1. FIG. 2.

FIG. 3. FIG. 4.

immediately or occur on different days. When several rows are simultaneously presented it is of course possible to select one row or another quite according to one's (subjective) fancy; or any certain row may be compared with another just above or below it. But this special case is not what we are here concerned with. Such subjectively determined arrangements are possible *only* if the rows of dots permit of two or more modes of apprehension. Curiously enough, however, it has been just this special case (where objective conditions do not themselves compel us to see one arrangement rather than another) which has usually been thought of as *the* fundamental relationship. As a matter of fact we shall see below how even purely subjective factors are by no means as arbitrary in their operations as one might suppose.

VII. That spatial proximity will not alone account for organiza-
321 tion can be shown by an example such as Fig. 1. Taken individually the points in *B* are in closer proximity to the individual points of *A*

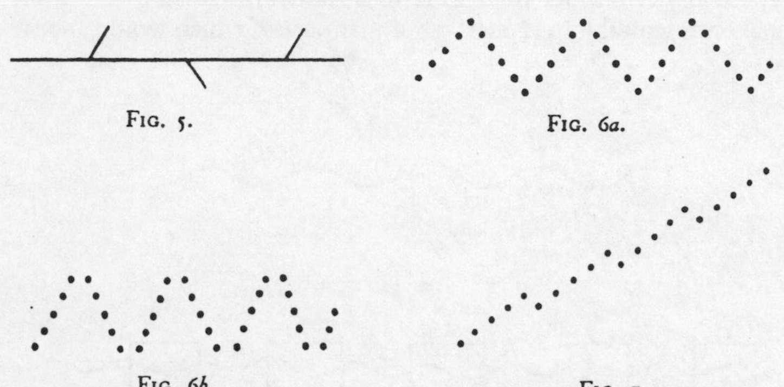

FIG. 5.

FIG. 6*a*.

FIG. 6*b*.

FIG. 7.

(or *C*) than the points of *A* and *C* are to each other. Nevertheless the perceived grouping is not *AB/C* or *BC/A*, but, quite clearly " a horizontal line and a vertical line "—i.e. *AC/B*. In Fig. 2 the spatial proximity of *B* and *C* is even greater, yet the result is still *AC/B*—i.e. horizontal-oblique. The same is true of the relationship
322 *AB/C* in Fig. 3. As Figs. 4–7 also show we are dealing now with a new principle which we may call *The Factor of Direction*. That direction may still be unequivocally given even when curved lines are used is of course obvious (cf. Figs. 8–12).
323 The dominance of this Factor in certain cases will be especially clear

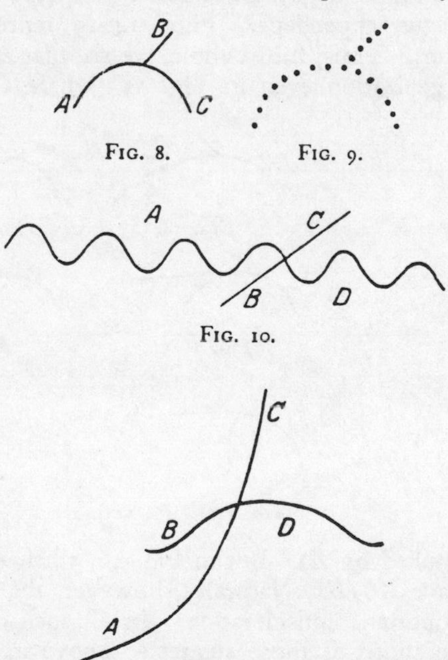

FIG. 8.

FIG. 9.

FIG. 10.

FIG. 11.

if one attempts to see Fig. 13 as (*abefil* . . .) (*cdghkm* . . .) instead of (*acegik* . . .) (*bdfhlm* . . .).

Suppose in Fig. 8 we had only the part designated as *A*, and suppose any two other lines were to be added. Which of the additional ones would join *A* as its continuation and which would appear

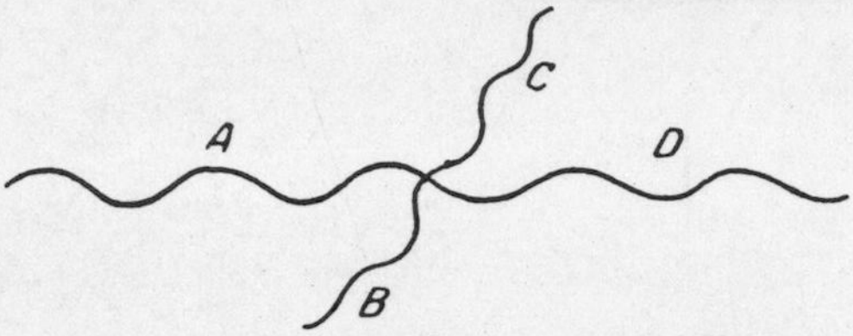

FIG. 12.

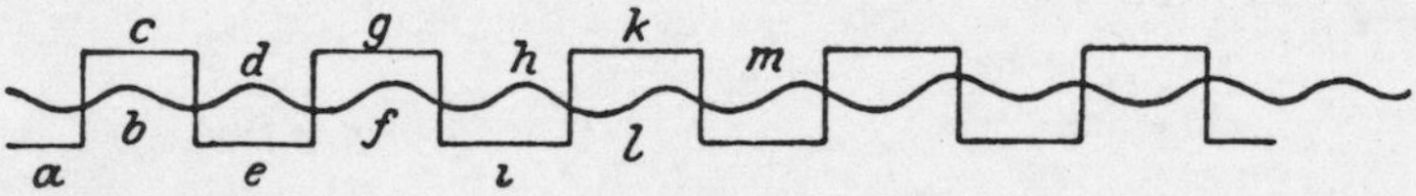

FIG. 13.

as an appendage? As it is now drawn *AC* constitutes the continuity, *B* the appendage. Figs. 14–19 represent a few such variations. Thus, for example, we see that *AC*/*B* is still the dominant organization even in Fig. 15 (where *C* is tangent to the circle

324

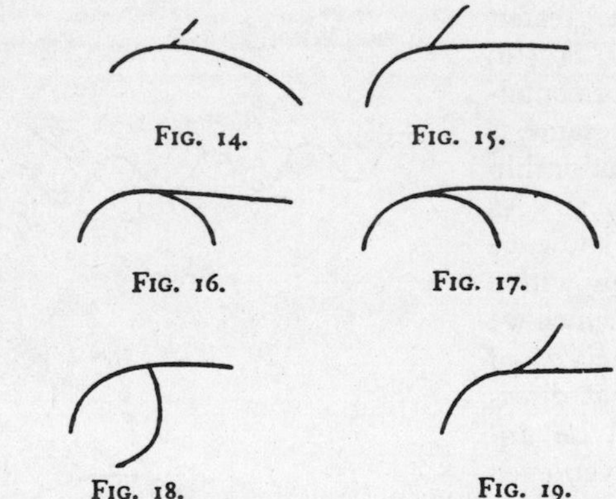

FIG. 14. FIG. 15.

FIG. 16. FIG. 17.

FIG. 18. FIG. 19.

implied by *A*). But in Fig. 16, when *B* is tangent to *A*, we still have *AC*/*B*. Naturally, however, the length of *B* and *C* is an important consideration. In all such cases there arise the same questions as those suggested above in our discussion of *Prägnanzstufen*. Certain arrangements are stronger than others, and seem to "triumph"; intermediate arrangements are less distinctive, more equivocal.

On the whole the reader should find no difficulty in *seeing* what is meant here. In designing a pattern, for example, one has a feeling how successive parts should follow one another; one knows what a "good" continuation is, how "inner coherence" is to be achieved, etc.; one recognizes a resultant "good Gestalt" simply by its own "inner necessity". A more detailed study at this juncture would require consideration of the following: Additions
325 to an incomplete object (e.g. the segment of a curve) may proceed in a direction opposed to that of the original, or they may *carry on*

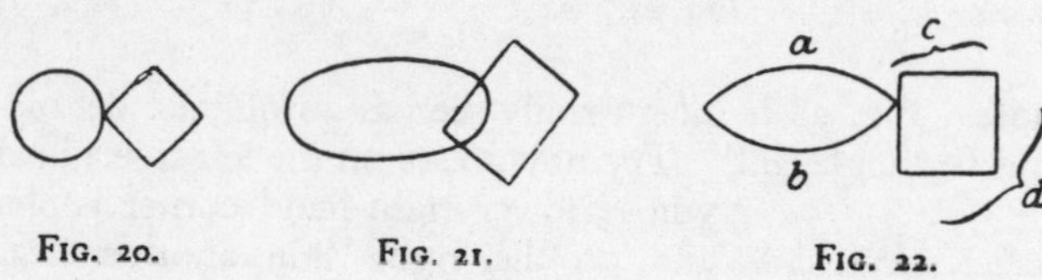

FIG. 20. FIG. 21. FIG. 22.

the principle "logically demanded" by the original. It is in the latter case that "unity" will result. This does not mean, however, that "simplicity" will result from an addition which is (piecewise considered) "simple". Indeed even a very "complicated" addition may promote unity of the resultant whole. "Simplicity" does not refer to the properties of individual parts; simplicity is a property of wholes. Finally, the addition must be viewed also in terms of such characteristic "whole properties" as closure, equilibrium, and symmetry.[1]

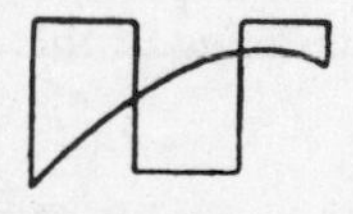

FIG. 23.

From an inspection of Figs. 20–22 we are led to the discovery of still another principle: *The Factor of Closure.* If *A*, *B*, *C*, *D* are given and *AB*/*CD* constitute two self-enclosed units, then *this*
326 arrangement rather than *AC*/*BD* will be apprehended. It is not true, however, that closure is necessarily the dominant Factor in all cases which satisfy these conditions. In Fig. 23, for example, it is not three self-enclosed areas but rather *The Factor of the "Good Curve"* which predominates.

It is instructive in this connection to determine the conditions under which two figures will appear as *two* independent figures, and

[1] Symmetry signifies far more than mere similarity of parts; it refers rather to the logical correctness of a part considered relative to the whole in which that part occurs.

those under which they will combine to yield an entirely different
327 (single) figure. (Examples: Figs. 24–27.) And this applies also to surfaces.[1] The reader may test the influence of surface wholeness by attempting to see Fig. 24 as three separate, closed figures. With coloured areas the unity of naturally coherent parts may be enhanced

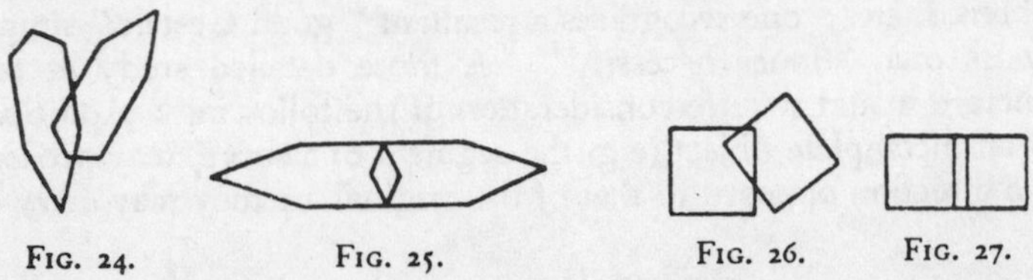

FIG. 24. FIG. 25. FIG. 26. FIG. 27.

328 still more. Fig. 28 is most readily seen as an oblique deltoid (*bc*) within a rectangle (*ad*). Try now to see on the left side a hexagon whose lower right-hand corner is shaded, and on the right side another hexagon whose upper left-hand corner is shaded [viz. Figs. 28*a* and 28*b*].

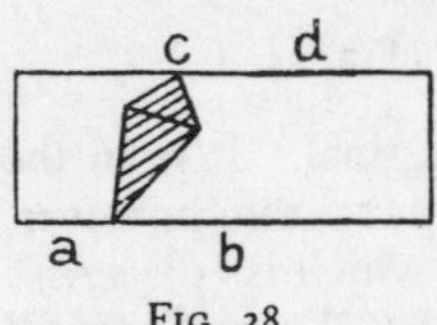

FIG. 28.

Once more we observe (as with the curves of Figs. 9–12) the influence of a tendency towards the "good" Gestalt, and in the present case it is probably easier than before to grasp the meaning of this expression. Here it is clearly evident that a unitary

FIG. 28*a*.

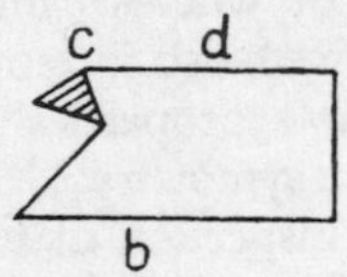

FIG. 28*b*.

colour tends to bring about uniformity of colouring within the given surface.[2]

Taking any figure (e.g. Fig. 29) it is instructive to raise such questions as the following: By means of what additions can one so alter the figure that a spontaneous apprehension of the original
329 would be impossible? (Figs. 30–32 are examples.) An excellent

[1] Compare in *Selection 6* the application which Fuchs makes of this.

[2] The Factor of similarity can thus be seen as a special instance of *The Factor of the Good Gestalt*.

method of achieving this result is to complete certain "good subsidiaries" in a manner which is "contra-structural" relative to the original. (But notice that not all additions to the original

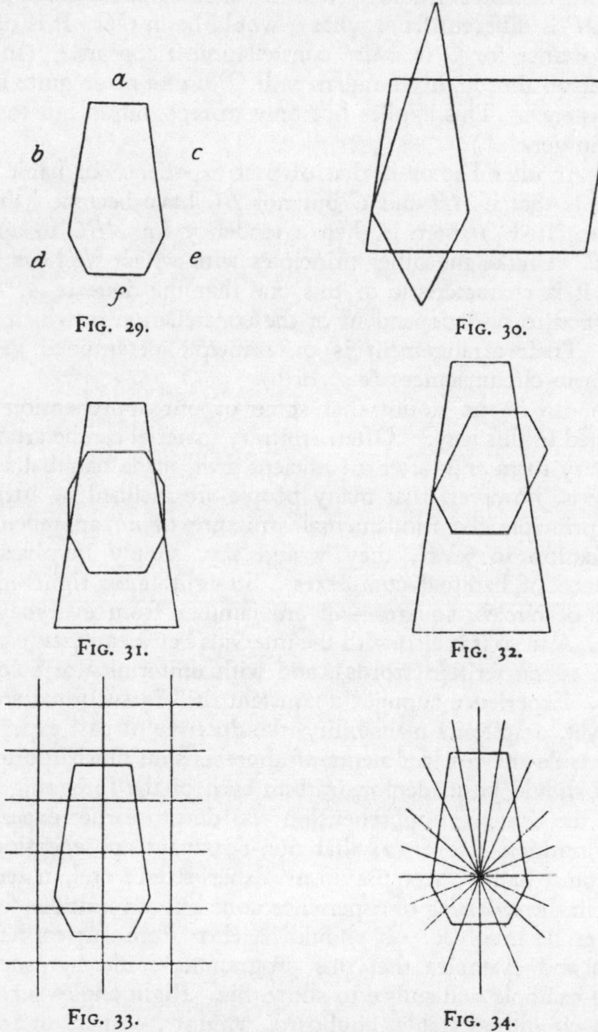

FIG. 29. FIG. 30.

FIG. 31. FIG. 32.

FIG. 33. FIG. 34.

will have this effect. Figs. 33–34, for example, represent additions which we may call "indifferent" since they are neither "pro-structural" nor "contra-structural".)

Let us call the original (Fig. 29) *O* and any contra-structural addition *C*, while any pro-structural addition we shall call *P*. For our purposes, then, *O* is to be thought of as a subsidiary of some more inclusive whole. Now *O* whether taken alone or as part of *OP* is different from what it would be in *OC*. It is of the first importance for *O* in *which* constellation it appears.[1] (In this way a person thoroughly familiar with *O* can be made quite blind to its existence. This applies not only to recognition but to perception in general.)

331 *VIII*. Another Factor is that of past experience or habit. Its principle is that if *AB* and *C* but not *BC* have become habitual (or "associated") there is then a tendency for *ABC* to appear as *AB/C*. Unlike the other principles with which we have been dealing, it is characteristic of this one that the *contents A*, *B*, *C* are assumed to be independent of the constellation in which they appear. Their arrangement is on principle determined merely by extrinsic circumstances (e.g. drill).

332 There can be no doubt that some of our apprehensions are determined in this way.[2] Often arbitrary material can be arranged in arbitrary form and, after a sufficient drill, made habitual. The difficulty is, however, that many people are inclined to attribute to this principle the fundamental structure of *all* apprehension. The situation in § VII, they would say, simply involves the prominence of habitual complexes. Straight lines, right angles, the arcs of circles, squares—all are familiar from everyday experience. And so it is also with the intervals between parts (e.g. the spaces between written words), and with uniformity of coloured surfaces. Experience supplies a constant drill in such matters.

And yet, despite its plausibility, the doctrine of past experience brushes aside the real problems of apprehension much too easily. Its duty should be to demonstrate in each of the foregoing cases (1) that the dominant apprehension was due to earlier experience (and to nothing else); (2) that non-dominant apprehensions in
333 each instance had *not* been previously experienced; and, in general, (3) that in the *amassing* of experience none but adventitious factors need ever be involved. It should be clear from our earlier discussions and examples that this programme could not succeed. A single example will suffice to show this. Right angles surround us from childhood (table, cupboard, window, corners of rooms,

[1] Compare *Selections 9a* and *9b*.

[2] Example: 314 cm. is apprehended as *abc/de*, not as *ab/cde*—i.e. as 314 cm., not 31/4 cm. nor as 314c/m.

houses). At first this seems quite self-evident. But does the child's environment consist of nothing but man-made objects? Are there not in nature (e.g. the branches of trees) fully as many obtuse and acute angles? But far more important than these is the following consideration. Is it *true* that cupboards, tables, etc., actually present right angles to the child's eye? If we consider the literal reception of stimuli upon the retina, how often are *right angles* as such involved? Certainly less often than the *perception* of right angles. As a matter of fact the conditions necessary for a literal "right angle" stimulation are realized but rarely in everyday life (viz. *only* when the table or other object appears in a frontal parallel plane). Hence the argument from experience is referring not to repetition of literal stimulus conditions, but to repetition of phenomenal experience—and the problem therefore simply repeats itself.

Regardless of whether or not one believes that the relationships discussed in § VII depend upon past experience, the question remains in either case: Do these relationships exhibit the operations of intrinsic laws or not, and if so, which laws? Such a question requires experimental inquiry and cannot be answered by the mere expression "past experience". Let us take two arrangements which have been habitually experienced in the forms *abc* and *def* many thousands of times. I place them together and
334 present *abcdef*. Is the result sure to be *abc/def*? Fig. 35, which is merely the combination of a W and an M, may be taken as an example. One ordinarily sees not the familiar letters W and M, but a sinuation between two symmetrically curved uprights. If we designate parts of the W from left to right as *abc* and those of the M as *def*, the figure may be described as *ad/be/cf* (or as */be/* between */ad/* and */cf/*); *not*, however, as *abc/def*.

Fig. 35. Fig. 36.

335 But the objection might be raised that while we are familiar enough with W and M, we are not accustomed to seeing them in *this* way (one above the other) and that this is why the other arrangement is dominant. It would certainly be false, however, to consider this an "explanation". At best this mode of approach could show only why the arrangement W-M is *not* seen; the positive side would still be untouched. But apart from this, the objection is rendered impotent when we arrange *abc* and *def* one above the other (Fig. 36) in a fashion quite as unusual as that

given in Fig. 35. Nor is the argument admissible that the arrangements /*ad*/ and /*be*/ and /*cf*/ in Fig. 35 are themselves familiar from past experience. It simply is not true that as much experience has been had with /*be*/ as with the *b* in *abc* and the *e* in *def*.

[330–347: omitted]

348 *IX*. When an object appears upon a homogeneous field there must be stimulus differentiation (inhomogeneity) in order that the object may be perceived. A perfectly homogeneous field appears as a total field [*Ganzfeld*] opposing subdivision, disintegration, etc. To effect a segregation within this field requires relatively strong differentiation between the object and its background. And this holds not only for ideally homogeneous fields but also for fields in which, e.g., a symmetrical brightness distribution obtains, or in which the " homogeneity " consists in a uniform dappled effect. The best case for the resulting of a figure in such a field is when in the total field a closed surface of simple form is different in colour from the remaining field. Such a surface figure is not one member of a duo (of which the total field or " ground " would be the other member) ; its contours serve as boundary lines only for *this* figure. The background is not limited by the figure, but usually seems to continue unbroken beneath that figure.

349 *Within* this figure there may be then further subdivision resulting in subsidiary wholes. The procedure here as before is in the direction " from above downward " and it will be found that the Factors discussed in § VII are crucial for these subdivisions.[1] As regards attention, fixation, etc., it follows that they are *secondarily* determined relative to the natural relations already given by whole-constellations as such. Consider, e.g., the difference between some artificially determined concentration of attention and that spontaneously resulting from the pro-structural emphasis given by a figure itself. For an approach " from above downward ", i.e. from whole-properties downward towards subsidiary wholes and parts, individual parts (" elements ") are not primary, not pieces to be combined in and-summations, but are *parts of wholes*.

[1] Epistemologically this distinction between " above " and " below " is of great importance. The mind and the psychophysiological reception of stimuli do *not* respond after the manner of a mirror or photographic apparatus receiving individual " stimuli " *qua* individual units and working them up " from below " into the objects of experience. Instead response is made to articulation as a whole—and this after the manner suggested by the Factors of § VII. It follows that the apparatus of reception cannot be described as a piecewise sort of mechanism. It must be of such a nature as to be able *to grasp the inner necessity* of articulated wholes. When we consider the problem in this light it becomes apparent that pieces are not even experienced as such but that apprehension itself is characteristically " from above ".

SELECTION 6

ON TRANSPARENCY

By WILHELM FUCHS

"Experimentelle Untersuchungen über das simultane Hintereinandersehen auf derselben Sehrichtung" ("Untersuchung über die psychologischen Grundprobleme der Tiefenwahrnehmung, iii." Herausgegeben von F. Schumann), *Zeitschr. f. Psychol.*, 1923, **91**, 145–235.

146 This paper deals with problems suggested by the following
questions. Can there be in visual space a simultaneous perception
of two objects one behind the other? When I look through a
transparent object do I really see a complete, unbroken surface
147 in front and absolutely at the same time another, more distant
surface? Or is this the case: I see only parts of the nearer object,
and, through gaps in its surface, parts of the other object and
from these fractional sections I mentally construct the two surfaces?
Further: are we able to see two complementary colours as one
behind the other even though both are stimulating the same retinal
149 area? [1] It is easy from common experience with transparent glass
or gelatine, to confuse the issue here. We are not referring to the
"real space" in which, of course, one object is closer to the
observer than the other. Our problem deals rather with phenomenal,
visual space.[2]

150 *First series of experiments.*—I. When a vertical black rod is seen
binocularly and monocularly at a slight distance in front of an
ordinary white projection screen, the following modes of apprehending these objects may be discriminated: (1) If the difference
in depth between the two objects is clearly apprehended, the surface
of the screen does not appear broken; it is apprehended as a
whole-surface, part of which is merely "hidden" by the rod.
151 (2) Depth being overlooked, the rod may have the appearance of

[1] Hering denied the possibility of simultaneous perception of two colours, one behind the other in the same visual direction ("*Sehrichtung*"); Helmholtz held that it was possible even with complementary colours.

[2] (p. 149) Terminology: colours will be referred to in the manner suggested by D. Katz. [I.e. terminology here will be the same as that in *Selection 16*.] (p. 150): "Transparency" and "simultaneous perception of two colours one behind the other", being equivalent terms phenomenally, will be used interchangeably.

Grateful acknowledgment is hereby made to *Johann Ambrosius Barth, Verlagsbuchhandlungen*, Leipzig, for permission to reproduce the illustrations used in this SELECTION.

a black strip or charcoal mark across a white area. But the white is nevertheless seen as an unbroken colour; it is, of course, not actually seen at the place where the strip falls, but one has the impression that white is present beneath the strip as well as elsewhere on the screen. (3) Unity of surface and even of colour are lacking now although the screen's general shape and form are still perceived. The strip has become a stripe woven into the white surface, and as such it is now an integral part of the screen. This appearance gives way quite readily, however, to still another impression (4) in which the screen appears divided into three independent objects: in the centre a long, narrow rectangle of
152 black and on either side a white surface. Finally, (5) the screen appears cut in two by a crevice into whose black depth one's gaze seems to penetrate.

II. A useful device for seeing one object through another is pictured in Fig. 1. The tilted pane of glass reflects an image of
153 one colour while permitting direct vision of the other.[1] Care must be taken to secure equal brightnesses and it is therefore usually necessary to illuminate the mirrored object more than the one seen directly. In our present experiment the objects were rectangles of variously coloured paper cut in the various sizes. In what follows we shall take blue and yellow as our examples.

Two cases of *non*-transparency may be mentioned first. When
154 the rectangles are arranged as shown in Fig. 2 there is no transparency if the smaller figure is seen (whether directly or by
156 mirroring) to lie *in front of* (i.e. above) the larger one. Transparency is also lacking when rectangles of equal size are used and so mirrored as to coincide exactly. In this case one sees only one surface whose colour is a mixture of the two colours.

Transparency does occur with the arrangement of Fig. 2 when the smaller rectangle appears *behind* (i.e. below) the larger one. Now one has a clear impression of, say, a yellow (smaller) rectangle seen *through* blue. This impression is stronger the more one looks
157 upon the two surfaces as separate wholes. It disappears entirely, however, if one isolates a point and concentrates upon this alone: at this place *one* small area appears in the mixed colour.

158 As already stated, the smaller rectangle is not transparent if seen above and within the larger one. Transparency of the smaller figure can be achieved, however, even for a position above the

[1] [With different inclinations of the glass it is possible to cause the mirrored image to appear either *behind* (i.e. below) or *in front of* (i.e. above) the object which is seen directly.]

larger one if it is moved so as to fall partly upon and partly outside the larger rectangle (Fig. 3).

160 Thus conditions have been established under which naïve subjects will experience the transparency phenomenon, i.e. perceive one plane behind another in the same visual direction. This holds true for complementary colours as well as for others. It should be repeated, however, that transparency is *not* possible if a point common to the two surfaces is fixated. When this is done one sees only *one* colour. *The simultaneous perception on two surfaces of*

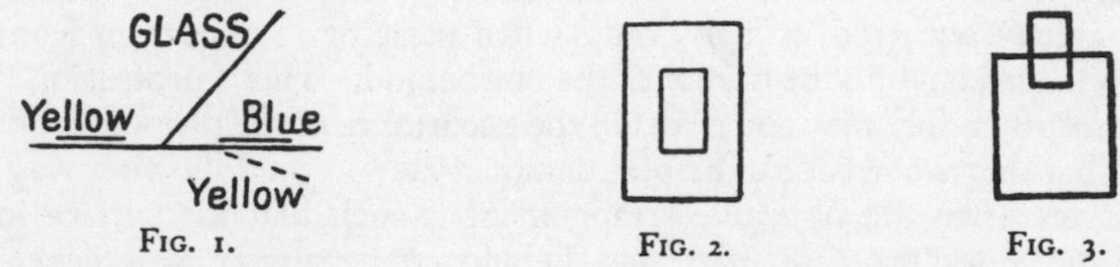

FIG. 1. FIG. 2. FIG. 3.

161 *two points qua points in the same visual direction is impossible.* And this holds also for individual contours of the lower surface (i.e. when yellow is beneath blue [cf. p. 156]): one sees neither blue nor even a glassy surface above (i.e. "in front of") the yellow contour. It is only when the two surfaces are simultaneously apprehended as whole-surfaces that an unbroken blue can be seen in front of (i.e. above) the points and contours of yellow.

FIG. 4.

FIG. 5.

[162–169: protocols of the subjects' reports are given; it is also pointed out that transparency is much better with binocular than with monocular vision. (165–168): various modes of appearance of the two colours (glassy, "colourless," bulky) are discussed.]

170 When the smaller surface is enclosed by straight lines which more or less resemble those enclosing the larger surface (Fig. 4) it is easy and rather obvious to see the area surrounding this smaller figure as itself a unified, closed figure ("border"). When,

on the other hand, the smaller surface is of an irregular shape (Fig. 5) it is often easier and more obvious to apprehend the parts
171 *a*, *b*, *c*, *d* as independent figures than to grasp this surrounding area as *one* unified border whose outer contours are straight lines and
173 inner contours curved lines. In general, transparency depends upon a perception of the yellow contours as boundary lines solely
[174–175: omitted] for yellow without any boundary function relative to blue; and vice versa for the blue contour lines.

176 Comparing the conditions under which transparency did and did not occur we are led to recognize still another factor. Transparency occurred, namely, only when parts of the figure in front extended beyond the border of the one behind. This " protrusion " must therefore play some part in the occurrence of the phenomenon. That this is correct can be best demonstrated in the following way. Even when the objective arrangement is such that the surface in front does protrude past that behind, transparency will nevertheless disappear at once (or will never have occurred) if the observer's mode of apprehension—e.g. concentration upon the region " common " to both figures, or upon some point or contour,
[177–178: omitted] or apprehension of the protruding parts as independent figures—is such as to disrupt figural cohesion between the protruding
179 parts and that " common " to both figures. And in this connection it should be noted that transparency will in fact disappear whenever one adopts a " critical " attitude and concentrates upon individual points or contours to the exclusion of whole-surfaces.

[180–210: the experiments which led Hering to deny the possibility of simultaneous perception of two objects one behind the other are repeated. Since positive results were obtained it would seem likely that Hering had ignored the need for apprehending both surfaces as unified wholes. (191–210): omitted.]

211 *Second series of experiments*.—I. It is possible, though difficult, to " invert " a yellow disk upon a blue surface—i.e. to see the yellow disk lying below blue. The glassy, sometimes bluish surface which then lies in front of the yellow is the result of psychical totalization of the blue surface. The inversion can be effected more easily, however, if an arrangement such as the following is used.

As shown in Fig. 6 a strip of blue paper is placed upon a black background and some distance above there is (at right angles) a yellow strip. When looked at from above these appear in the shape of a cross (Fig. 7).

When the subject (observing monocularly) visually " inverts "

the cross of Fig. 7 and sees blue as the upper colour, yellow as the
212 lower one, he experiences a glassy area at the intersection. This
critical region seems as a rule to be quite colourless, in some cases
[213–214: omitted] slightly bluish. The impression disappears, however, if one
allows the yellow or the intersection to stand out alone.

215 II. Very often in our preceding experiments the subjects referred to "shadows" and "shadow-like effects" in connection with transparency phenomena. We therefore turn now to a more specific study of two shadow effects.

Fig. 6. Fig. 7.

216 (1) The shadow is not transparent; it lies on or in front of the
surface. The surface itself constitutes a figural whole to which the
shadow does not belong. That part of the surface "hidden"
by the shadow is invisible. This mode of appearance is enhanced
(*a*) if there is adequate figural appearance of the
surface; (*b*) if contours of the shadow are diffuse
217 (penumbra) and, further, if the shadow itself is
somewhat diffuse in form.

Fig. 8.

(2) The shadow is transparent; then one sees
both it and, through it, a portion of the surface as
well. This situation is most easily obtained when
both the shadow and the shadowed object constitute very clear-cut figures whose relation to one another is
such that they do not easily merge. Fig. 8 is an example which
meets these requirements. The E is composed of yellow paper
and from a distance some centimetres above it there falls a not too
intense blue shadow. (This is achieved by holding a strip of blue
[218–219: omitted] gelatine in the beam of light falling upon E.) It is possible under
these circumstances to see an unbroken, uniformly coloured E
despite simultaneous perception of the blue shadow.

220 III. In all our experiments it was found that moving the head or one or both of the objects enhanced the transparency phenomenon. The colour of the more distant object was stronger in these cases than otherwise. To study this more systematically we used the following apparatus. Strips of variously coloured paper were

222 pasted upon a white kymograph drum upon which there fell a beam of coloured light. When the drum was at rest a separation between the colours of the light and the strips was impossible with many colours; when the drum slowly revolved this separation was at once experienced. Thus, for example, one saw quite clearly that a green strip passed behind a red rectangle. The movement prevented the two figures from merging and one therefore saw two different colours one of which moved behind the other.
[223–235 : omitted] These effects were, if anything, even stronger when both colours were in motion. This again shows that transparency is a function of the figural adequacy of the two objects.

Selection 7

THE INFLUENCE OF FORM ON THE ASSIMILATION OF COLOURS

By Wilhelm Fuchs

"Experimentelle Untersuchungen über die Aenderung von Farben unter dem Einfluss von Gestalten" ("Angleichungserscheinungen"), *Zeitschr. f. Psychol.*, 1923, **92**, 249–325.

250 In the preceding *Selection* it was shown that a simultaneous perception of two colours in the same visual direction is possible
251 when both objects are seen as independent figural wholes. The necessary separability of these objects cannot be achieved when they coincide perfectly, however; it is imperative that some part of one object shall extend beyond the corresponding boundary of the other. But this protruding part not only serves to bring about a separation between the two objects; it also acts to influence the colour of the overlapping (i.e. the "critical") area. Suppose, for example, that one sees a cross made of a transparent blue strip upon a yellow strip. If, looking through the aperture of a hole-screen, only the intersection is visible, this area will be seen to have a whitish grey colour. But this changes immediately when one lays aside the screen and sees the entire blue, or yellow strip, or both together. The critical area now assimilates the colour of the figure to which it is seen as belonging.

It is to a systematic investigation of this phenomenon that we now turn. We shall be interested primarily in answering the
252 following questions: Is there any uniformity in the influence exerted upon the critical area by the overlapping one (or vice versa)? Do these phenomena also make their appearance in the case of contrasting colours and of after-images?

253 *Experiments with the episcotister.*—Upon a black cardboard a yellow or orange E (8 × 1 cm.) was pasted. At a distance of 1·2 m. sat the observer, while approximately half-way between him and the cardboard an episcotister (radius 12 cm., opening 30°, blades dark blue) was placed. Illumination came from an open window 1·5 m. away.

254 When completely covered by the episcotister a yellow E will appear grey. When but half of the figure is covered one usually

Grateful acknowledgment is hereby made to *Johann Ambrosius Barth, Verlagsbuchhandlungen*, Leipzig, for permission to reproduce the illustrations used in this Selection.

sees the one part grey and the other yellow. If, however, one
apprehends the figure as an entire E, then its colour is yellow
throughout with the covered portion having the appearance of
shadowed yellow. If only the lower horizontal is covered, a
comparatively stable division may occur whereby this covered
part will be grey while the protruding part is seen as a yellow F.
If much the larger portion is covered, the entire E will then be
255 greyish in colour.

From these results it would appear that except where a stable
division is possible, the colour of the largest part tends to determine
the colour of the entire figure. Might one assume, then, that
256 only the *smaller* portion undergoes any change—i.e. that no
reciprocal modification takes place in the larger portion? That
such is not the case may be seen from the following. When the
figure, seen as a partly covered yellow E, is slowly moved out from
behind the episcotister the *entire* E—i.e. including even those parts
which from the beginning were outside the episcotister—will be
seen to grow yellower. This shows that the colour of this protruding, larger part had to a certain extent been under the influence
of the smaller, covered part.

257 Another demonstration of this effect is the following. At a
short distance from the E and outside of the blue field one places
a small piece of paper of any desired shape and of the same colour
as the E. If now the covered and uncovered parts of E are seen
as two things, the uncovered area will be seen to have the same
colour as the extra piece of orange paper. When, however, the
E is apprehended as an undivided (orange) whole, a clear distinction can be experienced between the colour of the extra piece and
that of the protruding part of the E. This is true even when the
episcotister does not cover the larger part of the E. In other words,
that the portion covered by blue has brought about a change in the
uncovered portion is evident because this uncovered part is not
identical with the adjacent piece. Analogous (reverse) results can
be obtained by placing the extra piece within the blue field.

259 Much depends upon *which* part of the E is covered and which
uncovered. The centre of gravity [*Schwerpunkt*] of an E-figure
lies not in one or other of the horizontal arms, but in the upright
line. We found, therefore, that even though the three arms and
part of the upright piece (i.e. geometrically the largest amount of
the figure) protruded beyond the episcotister, the E in this case
260 nevertheless assumed as a whole the colour of its smaller but more
"important" part.

261 As regards the blue surface of the episcotister it need only be remarked that the more this surface was apprehended as an entirety, the bluer and more compact appeared that part which covered the E, i.e. the more this part resembled the remaining portion of the episcotister surface.

264 We asked above (p. 252) whether or not a mutual influence is exerted by the covered and uncovered parts of the E-figure upon one another. The experiments have shown that there is such an effect. The uncovered portion influences the critical part making it more yellow than it would otherwise have been; and, conversely, this critical area causes the uncovered part to approximate somewhat to its colour. This is an example of mutual assimilation
265 [*Angleichung*], and it was found to be more pronounced, the more adequately one succeeded in apprehending the E as an unbroken figure. The opposite of assimilation occurred when the covered and uncovered parts were apprehended as independent of one another. We conclude then that colour assimilation is one result of whole-figure apprehension [*Gestaltauffassung*].

Experiments with discontinuous figures.—I. In the foregoing experiments the mutually assimilating colours were contiguous, and the question might therefore be raised whether the observed phenomena were not perhaps due to mutual influences (e.g. a "diffusion" effect) between the correspondingly contiguous retinal areas. That colour assimilation does not depend upon such peripheral factors will, however, be apparent from the following experiments.—We shall here employ the mirroring device described in *Selection* 6, Fig. 1.

266 When a small yellow disk (diameter 2 cm.) was reflected deeply into a blue rectangle (length 6 cm.) it appeared white. When another yellow disk was added which lay outside the blue, the disk in blue now appeared a yellowish-white and somewhat darker than before. If, outside the blue, three disks in line with the critical one are used, the disk in blue becomes a much stronger yellow than
267 before. This effect is still further strengthened when five such disks (at intervals of 3 cm.) are used: in this case two disks are placed on each side of the blue rectangle and one, the critical disk, appears in the centre. If all five are seen as a single row, they will all have the same yellow colour.[1] When the disks 1, 2, 4, and 5 are

[1] This colour is slightly inferior to the yellow of the outside disks when seen alone, for, as shown above, there is a *mutual* assimilation involved here and those outside the rectangle therefore suffer a slight greying effect from the disk within the blue.

attended as one group, No. 3 (the critical disk) is no longer yellow but pinkish white, and it seems also to have risen above the plane occupied by the remaining disks (although of course still below the surface of the blue rectangle). The critical disk often appears in this case to be smaller than the others and also not in line with them. Similar appearances of the critical disk were also observed when 1 and 2 or 4 and 5 were attended alone.

268 A modification of the foregoing procedure may be carried out
in the following way. Disks 1 and 5 are covered by a shield and
the remaining three are seen as a single row. These three will
assume the same colour. When 1 and 5 are uncovered all three
of the other disks thereupon become yellower than formerly.
If No. 3 alone is seen, then 2-3-4, and then 1-2-3-4-5, three distinct
[269–272: omitted] stages of yellow can be clearly observed. In other words, the
more yellow disks there were added to No. 3 the yellower it became.

273 The experiments were repeated with a blue shadow so cast that
it fell upon disk No. 3. No mirror or blue rectangle was involved
in this set-up. The results were throughout as above described for
the mirror and rectangle apparatus.

275 II. Since it has been shown that one of the two coloured objects
may consist of physically discontinuous parts without greatly
impairing the assimilation phenomenon, we shall from now on
employ arrangements of the two colours in which the blue as well
as the yellow will be divided up into separate areas in order to
eliminate contrast effects as far as possible. As shown in Fig. 1
this was accomplished by mirroring four yellow disks (1 cm.
diameter) in such a way that one of them coincided with one of
276 the blue disks. In this case the yellow was reflected so as to fall
on the same plane as the blue. In order to secure exact coincidence
of the critical disk all observations were made monocularly. Great
care was also taken to regulate the illumination so as to insure
277 a perfect grey in the critical disk. Fixation was upon the overlapping
disk.

The results may be summarized as follows. If one sees the four
yellow disks as a square, the critical disk becomes the same yellow
as the other corners of this square. If one sees the four blue disks
as a square, the critical disk becomes blue. When all else is ignored
and only the critical disk attended, its colour is white or grey.
[278–280: omitted] This was true also when the six outside dots were seen as corners
of a hexagon.

281 Another step suggested by the preceding experiment is to use
actual grey disks for the overlapping position. To investigate this

we prepared a cross with a grey centre and blue and yellow
283 arms. When one attends only the yellow arms, the central disk seems to become yellow; with an apprehension of the blue arms the grey disk becomes blue.[1]

284 We propose now to examine the possibility that these results might be due not to figural factors but to the influence of attention:

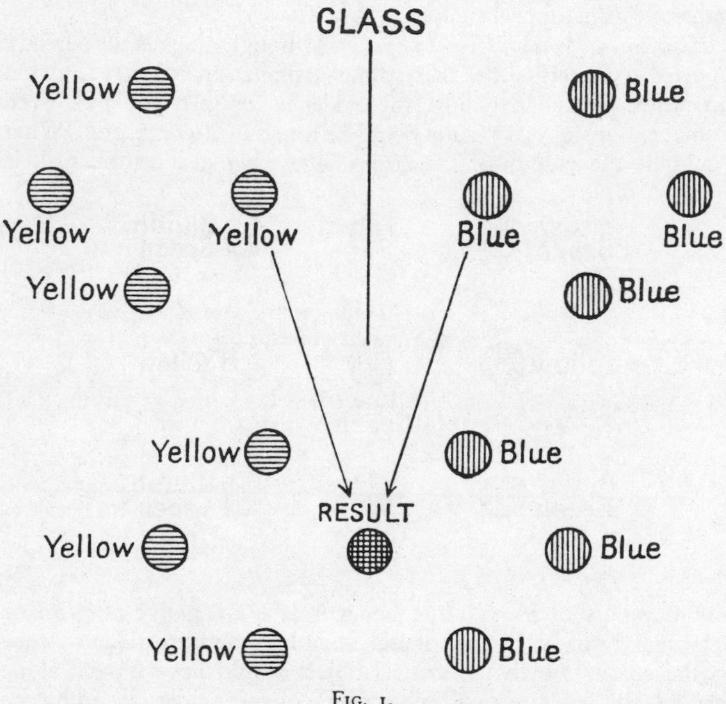

Fig. 1.

i.e. attention in the sense that concentrating one's attention upon the yellow disks makes the central grey disk assume a yellow colour, and vice versa for blue. This explanation could not be applied, however, if the same results were obtainable even when yellow and blue *both* occupied the centre of attention at the same time. Fig. 2 shows an arrangement of disks which satisfied this require-
285 ment. With this figure it is possible to see, at the same time, a

[1] The results in both cases were not sudden and it sometimes required several seconds before the grey had completely adopted the appropriate colour.

bluish-green square and a yellow cross. In this case the central disk is yellow. Or, one can, again simultaneously, see a bluish green multiplication mark and a yellow diamond. Now the central disk is bluish-green. Since in both instances attention has been concentrated upon yellow and bluish-green
[286–290: simultaneously, the effect must be due not to attention but to the
omitted] factor of figural apprehension.

291 *Experiments with After-Images.*—Although the results already reported definitely show that colour assimilation is not peripheral but rather central in nature, the evidence for this would be even stronger if analogous results could be found in after-images. What would be the colour of the after-image when the central disk is

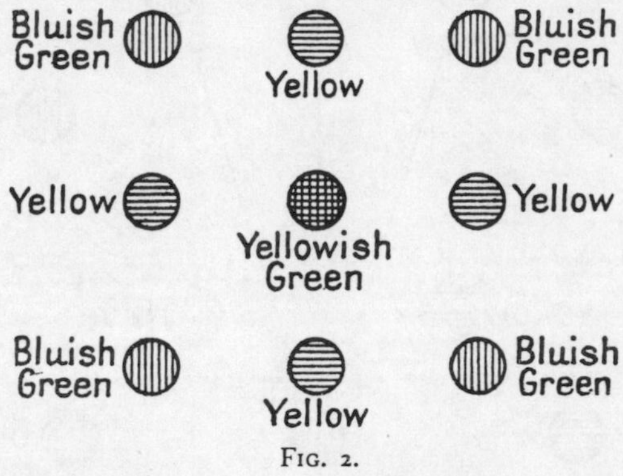

FIG. 2.

seen as yellow or blue? In other words, is a negative after-image determined solely by peripheral stimulus conditions (and hence by the colour which the critical object would have if seen alone through the aperture of a hole-screen), or is it under the influence of central factors? That is to say, does the colour of an after-image depend upon the colour of the original stimulus object?

Using a cross one of whose arms was bluish-green, the other yellow, and whose centre was yellowish-green, our subjects secured after-images of this cross first apprehending the *yellow* as a complete cross-piece, then the *bluish-green.* The images were projected upon a medium grey field. The results were as follows.
292 When the yellow cross-piece predominated in the original, the after-image—*including the critical disk*—was a uniform row of blue disks. Corresponding results were obtained when the blue

cross-piece constituted the original. But more than this. When neither blue nor yellow was allowed to predominate in the original perception and the figural prominence of one colour or the other was brought about only *after* the after-image had appeared, it was nevertheless possible to see the critical disk as blue *or* as yellow according to which row it joined. Indeed it was even possible to see a yellow (or blue) row originally, and then *reverse* the figural membership of the critical disk when the after-image appeared.

Thus we see that the after-image assimilates itself to the figure to which at any given time it is *seen* as belonging, and this even when doing so involves reversing the conditions of the original apprehension.—The experiment was repeated with variously coloured crosses as well as with the arrangement shown in Fig. 2. It was also carried out with disks of grey paper at the critical position. In all cases the same results as those already reported were obtained.

[293–296: that these results do not depend on attention is shown by a detailed study of after-image phenomena in connection with Fig. 2.]

297 *Assimilation and Contrast.*—In agreement with the foregoing it was found that as regards contrasting colours there are assimilation processes operative in two directions: (1) between the contrasting colours themselves, and (2) between each colour and its own background.

If two crosses are cut from the same grey paper and placed upon white and black backgrounds respectively, a marked brightness difference between them can be noted. When, however, the crosses are connected by a strip of the same grey, they will become
298 identical in brightness. Wundt, who was the first to make this experiment, attributed the result to a process of "mutual associative influence", but in the light of our own findings it is evident that such assimilation effects result from the altered figural apprehension brought about by the connecting strip.

The same type of explanation applies also to the sudden disappearance of simultaneous contrast in the Hering squares shown in Fig. 3. Upon fixating the middle point of this figure one observes that the indirectly seen intersections are greyish. This
299 effect disappears at once, however, when one sees the white lines as wholes, forming, e.g., a kind of network. It can furthermore be observed that either from an active apprehension to that effect or of its own accord the grey of any particular intersection will disappear while other intersections are still grey. Introspection

shows that these changes invariably accompany an attainment of figural prominence by the particular white lines in question.

[300–316: (300–303): omitted. (304–316): instances of colour assimilation may be found in various experiences of everyday life. Examples: (1) perception of slightly inhomogeneous coloured surfaces as really homogeneous; (2) failure to see objects actually present in one's visual field; (3) apprehension of the wall of a room as uniformly coloured even though its parts are at various

FIG. 3.

distances from the window; (4) perception of peripherally seen colour as approximately the same as that seen at the fovea.]

317 (*Appendix*). *Size and localization assimilation.*—In the experiment with three disks (one mirrored within and two flanking a blue rectangle, cf. p. 265 f.) it happened that in one case the middle disk was slightly larger than the other two. (Diameters 2, 2·6, and 2 cm.) Nevertheless, if the three disks were seen as a unified row, they appeared equal not only in *colour* but also in *size*. If, however, the two outside disks were attended to the exclusion of the middle one, or if this latter alone were attended, then a distinct difference in size (and colour) would be observed.

319 Another instance of the assimilation phenomenon is the following. In Fig. 4 the lowest line, although objectively equal in length

to the one above it, is ordinarily seen as longer than this one. It is possible, however, to see these lines as equal if one apprehends the four upper lines as an independent, separate whole,[1] or if,
320 ignoring these upper lines, one sees the two lower lines as sides of a rectangle.

323 As regards assimilation phenomena in connection with localization the case mentioned on p. 267 may be recalled. A row of five yellow disks was mirrored so that No. 3 fell within a blue rectangle while 1–2 and 4–5 appeared on either side. It will be recalled that when not apprehended as part of the yellow row No. 3 seemed above and out of line with the other four disks. In an apprehension of 1-2-3-4-5 as a single row not only was there uniformity of colour throughout but there were also no irregularities of location either. This does not mean to imply, however, that colour and localization assimilation are necessarily parallel phenomena. Instead it was found that the displacement undergone by No. 3 supplied still further evidence for the significance of figural apprehension—and this in the following sense. If the five disks were seen not as a straight line but as an angle, a curve, or a triangle, there would be *colour* assimilation but no alteration of *place* by the critical member. In this case No. 3 continued to appear above the plane of the other four disks.

FIG. 4.

[1] In this case the space between the lines will appear somewhat greyish (assimilation effect from the black lines), and there seem also to be diagonal "lines" marking off the left and right boundaries of this greyish area.

SELECTION 8

THE INFLUENCE OF FORM ON BRIGHTNESS CONTRAST

By WILHELM BENARY

"Beobachtungen zu einem Experiment über Helligkeitskontrast," *Psychol. Forsch.*, 1924, 5, 131–142.

131 Upon a white surface there is a black cross *beside* and *within* which two objectively equal grey triangles are placed in the manner shown by Fig. 1.[1] Let us call the upper (embedded) triangle g_1, and the lower one g_2. It can be shown that g_2 has in its vicinity more black and less white than has g_1. According to a summative theory of colour contrast, g_2 should therefore be brighter than g_1, but this is not the case; g_1 is clearly brighter than g_2. (Until

FIG. 1.

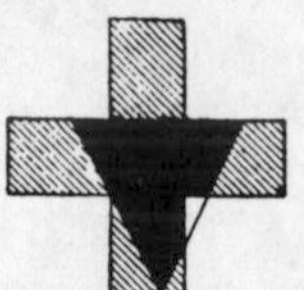

FIG. 2.

actual geometric measurements are shown them, even experienced observers will often declare that, embedded as it is within the cross, the upper grey really *does* have more black in its vicinity than does the lower one.)

Another example will show this relationship more forcibly. Take the black cross of Fig. 1 and place a small grey triangle in one corner, then cut away, as indicated by the hatched portion of Fig. 2, all of the black with the exception of a large triangle. In this way *white* is added and *black* taken away from the total picture—i.e. there is now more white background than before. Within the triangle nestles the former g_2 (which we shall, in Fig. 3, call g_t—i.e. "grey in triangle"). If now we compare the brightness of these greys in Fig. 3, we observe that g_t is clearly *brighter* than g_2.

[1] This experiment was suggested by M. Wertheimer.

Grateful acknowledgment is hereby made to *Julius Springer*, *Verlagsbuchhandlung*, Berlin, for permission to reproduce the illustrations used in this SELECTION.

132 In this latter case it is quite apparent that essential for the contrast effect is the question of *appurtenance* of the critical field—i.e. the question in which figural whole the grey triangle appears as part. In these examples brightness differences are the *reverse* of what a summative theory would have demanded.

Proceeding now to investigate this phenomenon somewhat more closely we may inquire first whether it will also appear when other types of figures are used. This question was affirmed by the analogous results obtained with Fig. 4. As regards observation

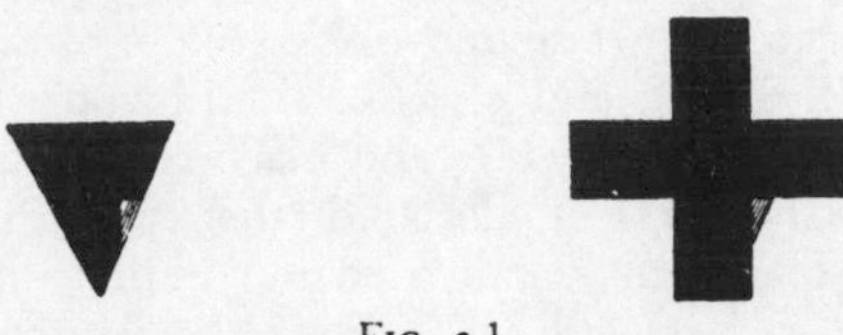

Fig. 3.[1]

distance the optimum was found to lie between 4 and 8 m., but, provided the two critical areas were distinctly visible and the figural relationships clear, the brightness difference could still be noticed anywhere between ½ and 14 m. When, for Fig. 3, a white cross and white triangle were used upon black backgrounds the

Fig. 4.

brightness difference was reversed: g_t was under these circumstances clearly darker than g_2. Nor did the use of various identical greys (light, medium, dark) alter the fact of brightness difference.

133 The effect could also be demonstrated with successive presentations as follows. Upon the cross (and small triangle) of Fig. 3 was placed a white shield out of which a large triangular opening had been cut so that only that part of the black cross (and small triangle) remained visible which can be seen in Fig. 2 as a large black triangle. In other words the object seen was the large triangle of Fig. 3. When the shield was removed (exposing the

[1] Size of these figures as used in the experiments reported below was *triangle*: 6·8 × 7·9 × 7·7 cm.; *cross*: width of arms 3 cm., length of protrusion 4 cm.; *small triangles* both 0·8 × 2 cm.

remainder of the cross) the small grey triangle thereafter looked darker than before.

134 Since it was possible to compensate for the described effect by variations in the *objective* brightness of the two grey triangles, we were able to measure the amount of phenomenal difference in the following manner. The small triangles (Fig. 3) were cut out and a colour wheel placed directly behind each opening. The duration of observation was, for each comparison, 20 sec. or less. The method of limits was used and each subject made two comparisons for each value: g_2 remained throughout a constant medium grey (i.e. the white and black sectors of the rotator were each 180° at all times), and g_t was varied in objective brightness (by changing the size of white and black sectors upon its colour wheel) until the subject declared the two greys to appear equal. The experiment was carried out both with black figures upon a white background and with white figures upon a black background.

135 The results (8 subjects) with black figures were as follows: to compensate for the original brightness difference required that 41·25° more *white* be present in the rotator of g_t than was present in that of g_2. With white figure g_t required 48·75° more *black* than was present in g_2. Although there was no appreciable change in results where figures twice the original size were used, changes were noted when the positions of triangle and cross (triangle left,
136 cross right: see Fig. 3) were reversed, for in this case the amount of brightness difference between the critical greys was lessened. This was true also when the figures were partially rotated to new positions. Using larger "grey openings" (i.e. increased size of the small triangles) did not materially alter the results. The
137 difference in brightness between the grey rectangles in Fig. 4 (I–H: deep black figures on white) was found to be 40° and more for various subjects. With *grey* I–H figures this difference between the small rectangles was less, and with *light grey* I–H figures upon a white ground the brightness difference between their small rectangles was only 10°.[1] These latter results show a clear uniformity in the dependence effect of contrast upon the amount of brightness difference between figure and ground. When this difference was greatest (black or white figure upon a

[1] Whenever grey figures were used the critical greys were always half-way between the brightnesses of figure and background just as they were when black/white figures on white/black grounds were being studied. In this latter case the critical greys resulted from 180° black and white sectors on the colour wheel.

white or black ground) the difference between critical greys was also greatest.

The preceding measurements were secured by varying the brightness of the critical greys while the brightness relation between
138 figure and ground remained constant. We shall now employ another method: the critical greys will be held constant while changes in brightness of the figure or ground will be made. Procedure was as follows. A cross and a triangle were cut out of a large sheet of cardboard, then two small grey triangles were pasted into place (cf. Fig. 3). Behind each opening a colour wheel was placed.

Unlike former cases, *extreme* brightness differences between the two figures were necessary in this instance. So long as the critical areas were lighter than the figures, compensation was as a rule impossible; indeed even when the small triangles were *very* light grey—thus permitting wide brightness differences to be made between the two figures—compensation could not be achieved for all subjects. Typical values were: large triangle 240° White, and cross 30° White.

To study the effect of changes in brightness of the background a black cross and large triangle (both with their respective grey triangles) were cut out and suspended in front of two colour wheels whose surfaces thus served as backgrounds for the two figures. Here compensation was more easily achieved, for the small triangles (medium grey) were made to look alike when the rotator behind the large triangle was set at 360° White and that behind the cross at 260° White.

Fig. 5.

Another mode of compensating for brightness differences between the small triangles of Fig. 3 was to reduce the size of the larger triangle by means of a white shield such as that shown in Fig. 5. This shield was slowly moved to the right and downward
139 so that, while reducing the figure in size, it did not alter its triangular shape. It was found, however, that even with a considerable coverage by the shield, g_t nevertheless remained for some time brighter than g_2. Indeed it was not until practically all of the black triangle had been obscured by the shield that g_t became noticeably darker. But accompanying this there were strong figural changes also. One no longer saw a black figure which contained a grey one [1] but rather a duo of two adjacent *equivalent* small triangles —one black and the other grey.

[1] Cf. *Selection 12*, p. 246, and the footnote summary of p. 247.

With the I-figure (Fig. 4) appurtenance [*Zugehörigkeit*] of the grey to the I exhibited especially interesting changes as a shield was drawn across the figure: large excursions of the shield caused no brightness changes until a figurally "critical" region was affected, then even very small movements of the shield brought about immediate darkening of the grey rectangle. And similarly with the triangle and cross it was found that large parts of the (originally white) background could be covered by a black shield without causing noticeable changes of brightness in the small grey triangle; but if the shield were brought quite close to the grey (say 0·7 cm.), then changes of figural relationship and simultaneously of brightness in the grey would be observed.

140 In all these experiments g_1 (in Fig. 3 g_t) belonged to the *figure* while g_2 did not. Is union with the figure as against that with the ground an essential condition for the occurrence of the described effect? An answer to this question is given by the following experiment. In Fig. 6 the grey triangle in black corresponds to the g_t of Fig. 3, that in white corresponds to g_2. One normally sees this grey-in-black as brighter than the grey-in-white. With a little effort it is possible to see Fig. 6 as two simultaneous, *equivalent figures*. Since, however, this does not alter the brightness relation between our greys (i.e. the grey-in-black is still brighter than the grey-in-white), we conclude that the observed brightness difference (here as in Fig. 3) depends not upon figure and ground but upon surface appurtenance.

Fig. 6.

141 Our experiments have shown that the influence of contrast upon a figural part [*Feldteil*] is not determined simply by the kind, amount, and proximity of the other parts; rather, the effect depends upon figural relations between the critical part and its whole. In the foregoing instances the greatest contrast effect was that deriving from surface appurtenance, despite the fact that the amount and proximity of contrasting brightnesses favoured effects just the opposite of those which we have demonstrated.

Selection 9a

GESTALT FACTORS AND REPETITION

By Kurt Gottschaldt

"Über den Einfluss der Erfahrung auf die Wahrnehmung von Figuren, I."; "Über den Einfluss gehäufter Einprägung von Figuren auf ihre Sichtbarkeit in umfassenden Konfigurationen," *Psychol. Forsch.*, 1926, **8**, 261–317.

261 It is the purpose of this and the following paper [1] to study the influence of past experience upon the perception of visual forms.

Although many theories of perception ascribe great significance to the part played by experience [*Erfahrung*] [2] it is difficult to find
262 any avowed specification of what the concept really means. In usage, however, "experience" as a psychical factor usually has the following meaning. Former experiences [*Erlebnisse*] with arrangement *A* of a certain stimulus complex, *S*, leave behind a disposition favouring the apprehension of *A* upon a repetition of *S*. Thus if *abc* has been previously experienced, the presentation of *abcde* will tend on a later occasion to be experienced as *abc/de*.

We agree with other investigators in distinguishing between the origin of a datum of experience (learning, habituation) and the *influence* exerted by that earlier upon a subsequent experience. In seeking to determine what this influence is in the case of visually perceived forms we shall study the significance for a later experience of (1) the *number*, and (2) the *type* of antecedent experiences as well as (3) the *time* elapsing between original presentation and subsequent test. And, congruent with this, we shall also examine the role played by the figural properties of the presented objects and by the experimental procedure itself.

The implication of any appeal in psychology to "past experience" [*Erfahrung*] as an explanatory concept is that such experience constitutes an independent force capable of modifying subsequent perception in a specific manner. According to this, experience would be an executive factor causing a segregation of
263 the familiar unity *abc* from *abcde* even when *abcde* would *not*

[1] *Selection 9b.*

[2] [We have in English but one word, "experience", for the German terms *Erfahrung* (datum of past experience) and *Erlebnis* (current happening).]

Grateful acknowledgment is hereby made to *Julius Springer*, *Verlagsbuchhandlung*, Berlin, for permission to reproduce the illustrations used in this Selection.

otherwise have been apprehended in this way. Some of the questions to which this gives rise are: What effect does past experience as a dynamic factor have upon the perception of figures? Is past experience able to exert modifying effects upon any and all figures, or are there some whose "internal unity" or cohesion is such that past experience is powerless to affect them?

Statement of specific problem.—If "experience" theories are correct, then the more *often* a certain figure (e.g. "*abc*" in the preceding example) has been presented, the easier it should be to apprehend *this* figure when it appears in a larger one (e.g. in "*abcde*"). If memorizing the original figure (hereinafter designated as the "*a*"-figure) has been accomplished with sufficient frequency and recency, then when presented as a geometrical part

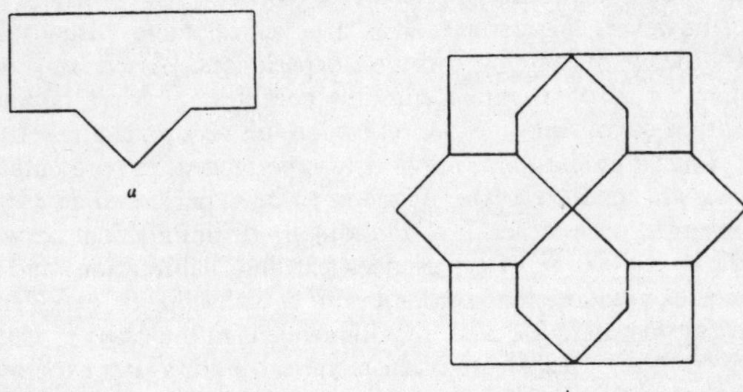

FIG. 1.

of the larger ("*b*"-)figure, the memorized one should "stand out" so clearly that all other *b*-parts would appear as mere subsidiaries. Furthermore, the more *often* the "*a*"-figure (composed of the parts *a*, *b*, *c*) has been presented and memorized as a unified
264 complex before the "*b*"-figure is seen, the more readily may we anticipate that with presentation of the "*b*"-figure (consisting of *a*, *b*, *c*, *d*, *e*) the unified complex *abc* will stand out or be recognized.

Our primary interest lay in discovering how variations in the memorial prominence of *a* would influence the manner of *b*'s appearance. Examples of the *a*- and *b*-figures used are given in Figs. 1–2. The *b*-figure consisted in each case of a black line-
[265–266: omitted] drawing upon a white background: the *a*-figure was a geometrical part of *b*.

267 *Experimental technique.*—Five *a*-figures [1] were presented (individually) to two groups of subjects by means of an episcope projection lantern. The presentations lasted 1 sec. and there were 3 sec. intervals between them. In order to test the influence of experience, the number of presentations was very different for the two groups. Group I saw each *a*-figure 3 times; Group II received 520 presentations of the same figures. To insure ignorance by the subjects of the real purpose of the experiment, instructions were to memorize the *a*-figures in order that they could later be drawn. The *b*-figures were (individually) shown for 2 sec. to each group after the memorizing series (3 or 520) had been completed.[2]

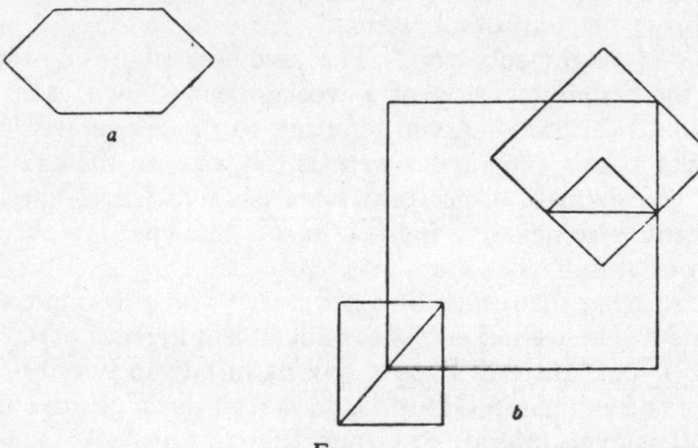

FIG. 2.

268 The subjects were told that the memorizing series would be resumed later; they were asked to describe these (*b*-)figures and were told that if their attention were attracted by anything in particular they should describe this in detail. Stenographic records were taken of the reports.

269 *Results.*—In accordance with the subjects' reports the following classification of results was compiled:—

(1) The *a*-figure instantly stood out from *b* without any assistance from the subject.

(2) The *a*-figure was "discovered" in *b* after the description of *b* as such had already been given.[3]

[1] Cf. Figs. 3–18 below.

[2] It will be observed in Figs. 3–18 that an *a*-figure may be part of several different *b*-figures. Thirty-one *b*-figures (six each for the five *a*-figures except one for which there were seven) were used in the present experiment.

[3] Included here also are all those cases where, following the 2sec. exposure of the *b*-figure, the memory image of *b* underwent a change such that it "fell apart" into *a* and something else.

(3) There was a suspicion that *a* might be present in *b* but it was never actually seen.

(4) An incorrect *a*-figure was suspected.

(5) No trace of *a* was perceived or suspected—the *b*-figure was described *as such* without reference to *a*.

Group I (three subjects): 92 reports on the 31 *b*-figures were obtained. Only *one* report was of an immediate perception of the *a*-figure (i.e. Type 1 above). There were five reports of the 2nd Type; no report of Type 3 was given; two cases of Type 4 were reported; 84 of the reports were of Type 5. Summarizing: positive reports, i.e. Types 1–3, six (i.e. 6·6 per cent); negative reports, i.e. Types 4–5, eighty-six (i.e. 93·4 per cent). Type 5 alone: 91·3 per cent of all reports.

271 *Group II* (eight subjects): The members of this group had, during the training period of 2 weeks, been shown each of the 5 *a*-figures 520 times. Again referring to the above classification the results of this experiment were as follows: of the 242 reports on the 31 *b*-figures, 5 per cent were positive (i.e. Types 1–3); 95 per cent were negative (i.e. Types 4–5). Type 5 alone: 93·8 per cent of all reports.

273 In comparing the results obtained after 3 and after 520 presentations one might well expect a considerable difference in reports of the first Type. Instead Type 1 appears in Group II only 0·6 per cent more often than in Group I, and as regards *all* positive reports, Group II is even inferior to Group I.[1]

Influence of instructions to search for "a".—In this experiment the subjects were told to look for the *a*-figure when *b* was exposed.
274 The instructions were as follows: "I shall now show you the figures you were last shown yesterday and you are to search for the 5 memorized figures in these. There is never more than one *a*-figure in any *b*-figure, but there are some *b*-figures which contain no "*a*"-part at all. I shall not tell you beforehand which will be exposed. If an *a*-figure *is* present in a *b*-figure, it will always be the same size and in the same spatial position as when you saw it alone for the purpose of memorizing it."

On the day following their first test, the three subjects of Group I were shown the 5 *a*-figures twice more. Ninety-three descriptions

[1] [In a later experiment (reported in text p. 310 f.) the objection is examined whether such excessive repetition might not perhaps have introduced extraneous (e.g. affective) factors making any comparison between our present Groups inadmissible. As check also on another possible objection, only one *a*-figure was used. There were 12, 24, 50, 100, or 200 presentations of the *a*-figure. Results: increasing the number of presentations does *not* increase the number of positive reports.]

were secured. Their results in this case were: Types 1–3, 31·2 per cent; Types 4–5, 68·8 per cent. Type 1 was not aided particularly, however, by instructions to seek *a*, for whereas its value in the original case had been 1·1 per cent, in the present instance it constituted but 2·2 per cent of all reports.

275 With Group II (8 subjects) 540 presentations of *a*-figures were made (i.e. the original 520 + 20) and instructions to look for *a* in *b* were given. There were 248 descriptions. Reports of the Types 1–3 totalled 28·3 per cent in this case; those of Types 4–5 totalled 71·7 per cent. Again Type 1 showed no marked improvement as a result of instructions to search for *a*: originally (p. 271 above) it had represented 1·7 per cent, now it constituted but 2·0 per cent of all reports.

277 Summarizing, we find that although mere difference in frequency of past experience failed to elicit any marked differences between the two Groups, *changing the instructions* resulted, in both Groups, in an increase of approximately 24 per cent in the number of positive reports (Types 2–3). We conclude, then, that in cases such as ours, whereas frequency of earlier presentation is practically without influence upon subsequent experience, modification of experimental procedure (i.e. passive *versus* active attitude of the subject) is of much greater significance.[1]

Discussion.—Our results have shown that the bare frequency with which an object appears in the subject's presence [i.e. its mere "*Oft-Dagewesensein*"] affords no reliable index as to its possible influence upon a later experience. Since our findings indicate that there are at all events *some* cases where "past experience" (in the sense of bare repetition) is practically without effect, it follows that important changes must be made in "experience theory" itself. Any appeal to "past experience" as an explanatory concept must limit itself in one or other of the following ways. The theory may renounce all claim to universal validity and indicate instead its own range of application, in which case a reformulation of the entire concept seems inevitable. Or, if the claim to universality is maintained, the admission must be made that the degree of such influence is in many cases well-nigh negligible in comparison with that of other factors. And it would then be these *other* factors (apart from the influence of instructions and other subjectively induced factors) which would play the principal

[1] As we shall presently consider still other factors it would be incorrect to assume here that the only, or even the essential, condition is that of passivity *vs.* activity of the subject.

roles. The influence of such forces is not dependent upon "past experience" with the object in question, but depends rather upon organizational conditions of the perceptual field itself; these
279 forces are determined by the *intrinsic* properties of the stimulus object, not by such contingent conditions as those postulated by "experience theory".

When approached from the point of view of Gestalt theory the results of our experiments are perfectly clear. A consideration of the figural properties of our *b*-figures discloses that the *a*-figures were psychologically not present in them at all. Though reappearing in *b* as a mere geometrical constituent, the *a*-figure is almost completely altered when presented in *b*, and it is only by a thoroughgoing disintegration (and consequent modification) of *b* that *a*-in-*b* can be seen. The ways in which a constellation (e.g. "*b*") appears, its subdivisions, the appearance of any certain portion of it, etc., are matters which depend primarily upon autochthonous Gestalt factors. In our experiments even the greatest multiplication of "past experience" with the *a*-figure was incapable of offsetting
281 these latter forces.—We propose now to examine certain *b*- and *a*-figures with special reference to internal unity. We shall designate various degrees of such unity or cohesion and then compare these with the results of our earlier experiments.

Internal unity of the b-figures.—It is important for a proper evaluation of our results to know the degree of figural cohesion
282 of our *a*-figures in their respective *b*-complexes. One way of determining this is to record the average time required by a large number of subjects before *a* is located in *b* when the two are presented simultaneously. Procedure was as follows: each of 112 subjects was given a slip of paper upon which an *a*- and *b*-figure had been printed. The instructions were to search for *a* in *b*, but only visually (i.e. tracing, etc., was prohibited).

For all 31 figures the average of the medians was 10·8 sec. The maximum time permitted was 3 min. The average numbers of
283 subjects who were able to find *a* in *b* within the 3 minute limit was, for all cases, 108, while in no case did the number of those succeeding fall below 94 of the total 112 subjects. From these results it is evident that the figures used in our experiment had not been unreasonably difficult.

284–286: reports procedure of weighting results to equalize practice effects; attention is called to the fact that whereas bare repetition of an *a*-figure yielded practically no after-effect, the 112 subjects engaged in this latter task improved greatly in their ability as a result of this kind of repetition.]

287 In this way 5 degrees or "grades" of figural unity or cohesion in our 31 *b*-figures could be discriminated. The degree of difficulty with which *a* could be discovered in *b*, together with the time required in each case may be tabulated as follows:—

1. Very easy.	Average time required to find *a* . . .	9·5 sec.
2. Easy . .	,, ,, ,, . . .	13·3 ,,
3. Medium . .	,, ,, ,, . . .	18·0 ,,
4. Difficult .	,, ,, ,, . . .	26·9 ,,
5. Very difficult .	,, ,, ,, . . .	36·1 ,,

(The average of 10·8 sec. given above for all figures is lower than an average of those in this table because it was obtained without computing the influence of practice which latter has been taken into consideration in the present table.)

288 Comparing this classification with the 675 reports obtained in our earlier experiments, we find that *b*-figures with a high degree of figural cohesion (viz. Class 5 in the above table) are precisely those in which the *a*-figure least often influenced the perception when *b* was shown. (This applies to both Groups of subjects under both types of instruction.) On the other hand the comparison also shows that cases where *a* " stood out " are those in which the *b*-figures of lesser figural cohesion (e.g. Class 1 in the above table) were used. Summarizing this comparison we have:—

Kind of b-*figure.*	*Average number of positive reports.*
Very difficult (there were 5 such) . .	1·2
Difficult (there were 6) . . .	2·0
Medium (7 figures)	3·3
Easy (10 figures)	5·7
Very easy (3 figures)	6·3

290 *Phenomenal characteristics of internal unity.*—In view of the theoretical and practical significance of "internal unity" or cohesion as already defined, let us now study the figural factors involved when an *a*-figure is presented in *b*. The protocols of our earlier experiments were useful in this connection, but reports from a new group of trained subjects will also be considered. Each subject was shown 6 or 8 *a*-figures together with one *b*-figure which might or might not contain one of the *a*-figures. They were asked to see if they could discover an *a*-figure in *b*, and to describe how they went about this.

The descriptions dealt on the one hand with the appearance of *a* itself, and on the other with its appearance in *b*; they also referred to the procedure whereby *a* was " lifted out " of *b*. Except for the

291 cube shown in Figs. 3, 9, and 10, all *a*-figures were seen as plane surfaces whose contour lines served as *boundaries*. The importance of this for our present consideration lies in the fact that changing

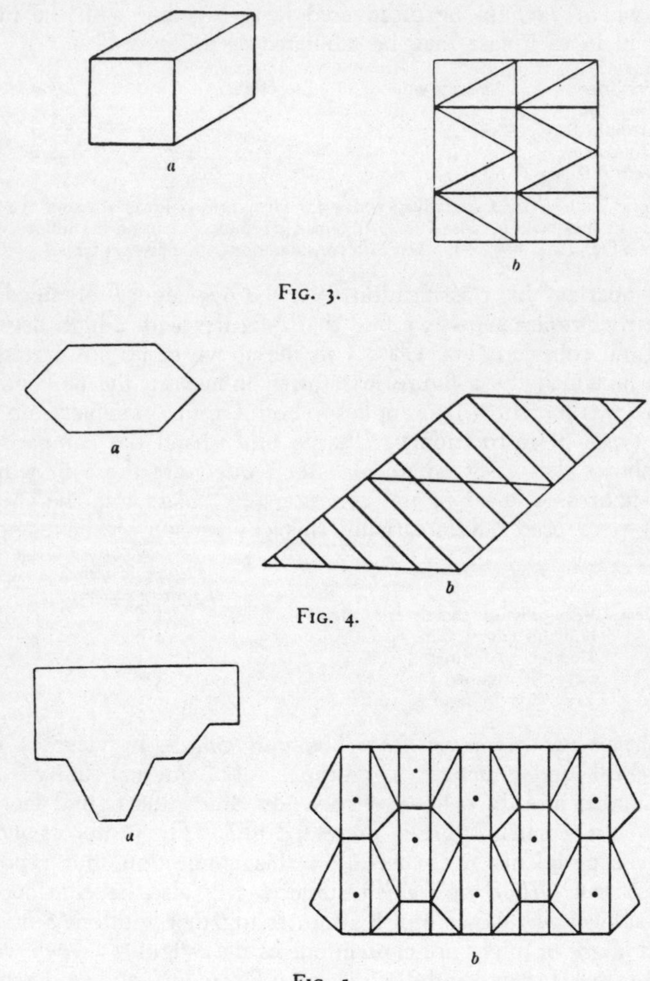

Fig. 3.

Fig. 4.

Fig. 5.

the *boundary function* of a contour line is almost certain to bring about a dissolution of the figure in question when seen in *b*. No change need be made in the actual contour line itself in order

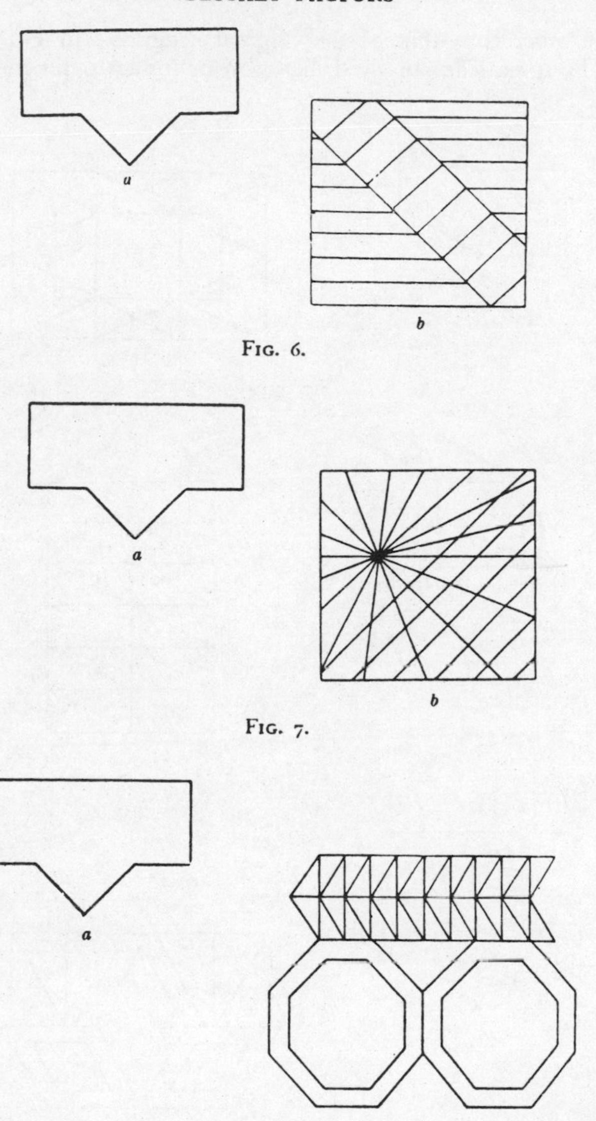

Fig. 6.

Fig. 7.

Fig. 8.

for there to be a change in the boundary-function of that line. It is enough if the line serves in the *b*-figure as contour line for a surface other than that of the original *a*-figure. In Fig. 4, for example, three sides of the *a*-hexagon continue to function in *b*

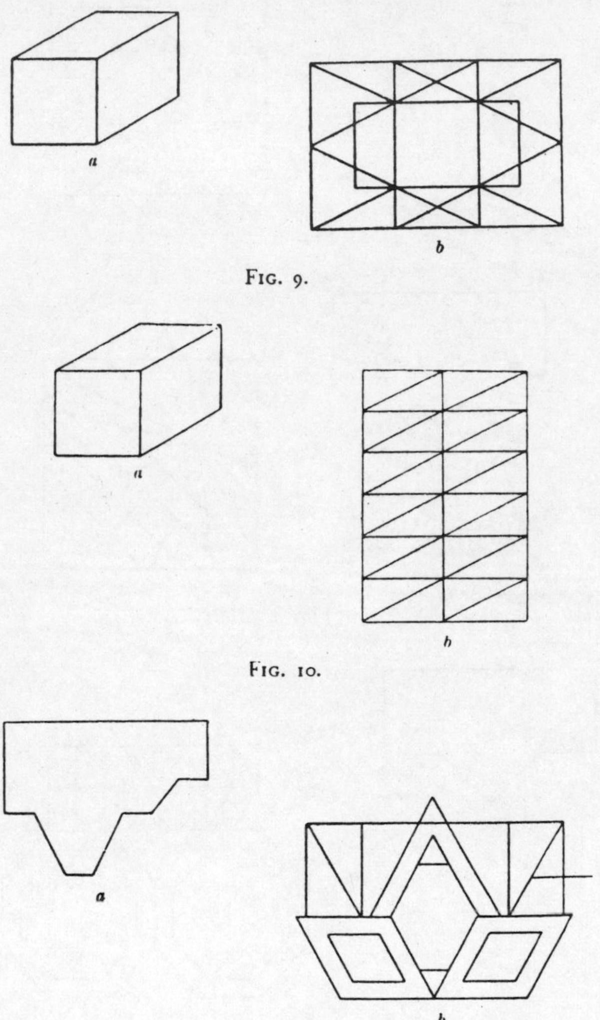

FIG. 9.

FIG. 10.

FIG. 11.

as contour lines—but now they merely assist in enclosing the large oblique figure, and in so doing, have lost the limiting character which they possessed in the hexagon. Notice also how, in Fig. 5, the lower, stair-step *boundary* of *a* has become in *b* an *interior* line.

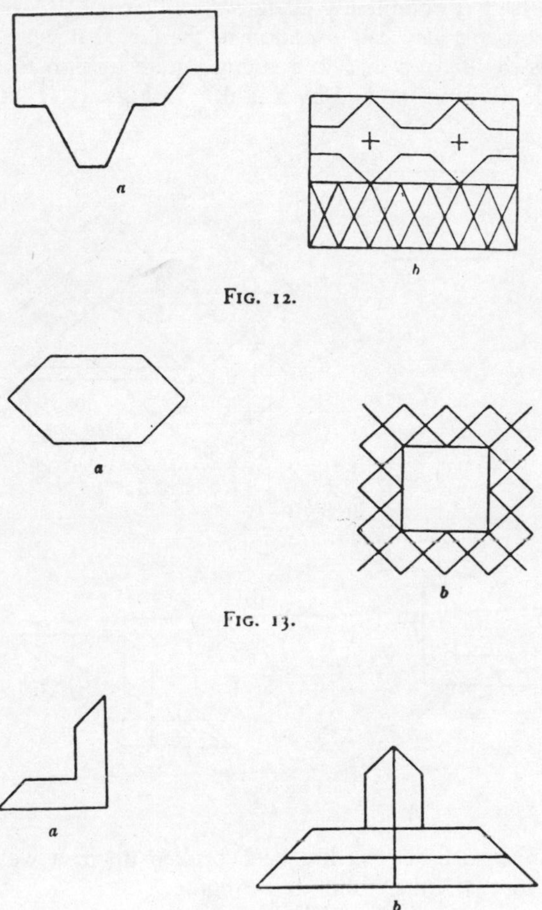

FIG. 12.

FIG. 13.

FIG. 14.

In Fig. 6 the boundary-function of the lower *a*-contour has disappeared entirely in *b*.

A second principle also noted in this connection was that of
292 changes in the surface-character of *a*. It not infrequently occurred
that an *a figure* would, in *b*, appear as *background* for some other

part of *b*: Figs. 7 and 8 are examples. Another type of change in the surface-character of *a* can be seen in Figs. 3, 9, and 10 where, with the disappearance of its depth-surfaces in the various *b*-figures, the cube itself is completely changed (i.e. " lost ").

The protocols also call attention to the fact that very often the *a*-figure is divided up in *b* in a manner quite foreign to the mode of possible division implied by *a* itself. In Figs. 5, 11, and 12, for

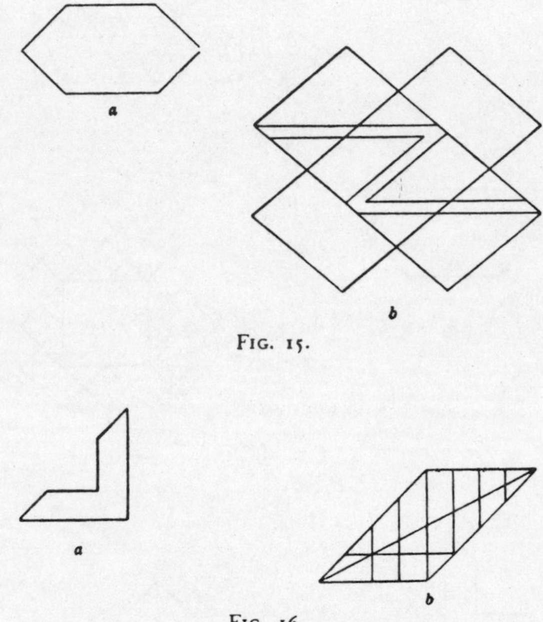

FIG. 15.

FIG. 16.

example, the surface of *a* has been broken up in a way directly opposite to that inherent in the *a*-figure.

Dissolution of *a* is especially easy when asymmetrical portions of it are enlarged into symmetrical parts of *b*. This can be seen in Figs. 10, 12, 13, and 14. The same holds also for cases (e.g. Figs. 10, 15, and 16) where the *direction* given by *b* is other than
293 that manifested by *a*. And the result is similar also when *b*'s centre of gravity does not conform with that of *a*. (Examples: Figs. 4 and 13.)

294 Since not all the lines which make up the *a*-figure are equally

important in supplying the character of that figure, some of our observers called attention to "figurally emphasized" and "figurally unemphasized" *a*-lines. The wedge-point of Fig. 1 was thus spoken of as "figurally emphasized" (in *a*). When the appearance of *a*-in-*b* is such that a formerly emphasized part is now unemphasized, the result is usually a dissolution of *a* in the manner

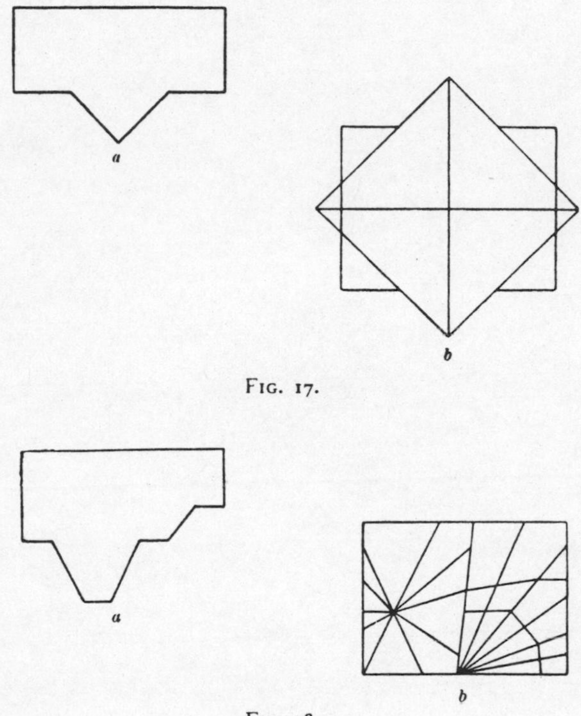

Fig. 17.

Fig. 18.

295 already discussed and illustrated. This may be seen in Figs. 4 and 17, where the decisive or emphasized characteristic of the *a*-figure appears, in *b*, to have suffered demotion to the rank of one-among-many. That the converse also holds (i.e. promotion of an unemphasized portion of *a* to the focal point in *b*) can be seen in Figs. 7 and 18.

[296–306: drawings and further descriptions of the individual *a*- and *b*-figures.]

307 The foregoing account of the phenomenal characteristics of " internal unity " has designated a number of principles in terms of which the perception of *a*-in-*b* can be understood. And it should also be clear how and why a search for *a* frequently gave false results.

[308–317: see above, footnote to p. 273; (313–317): omitted.]

(Continued in *Selection 9b.*)

SELECTION 9b

GESTALT FACTORS AND REPETITION (*continued*)

By KURT GOTTSCHALDT

" Über den Einfluss der Erfahrung auf die Wahrnehmung von Figuren, II." " Vergleichende Untersuchung über die Wirkung figuraler Einprägung und den Einfluss spezifischer Geschehensverläufe auf die Auffassung optischer Komplexe," *Psychol. Forsch.*, 1929, **12**, 1–87.

2 In the preceding *Selection* we studied the effect of frequent presentations of " *a*-figures " upon the perceptibility of these figures when presented as geometrical parts of various " *b*-figures ". The results showed that under the conditions of that earlier study, and with the degree of figural cohesion there employed, the after-effect of experience was so small as to be virtually non-existent. In the present paper we shall use figures whose internal cohesion is much less opposed to the perception of *a*-in-*b* than formerly ; and we

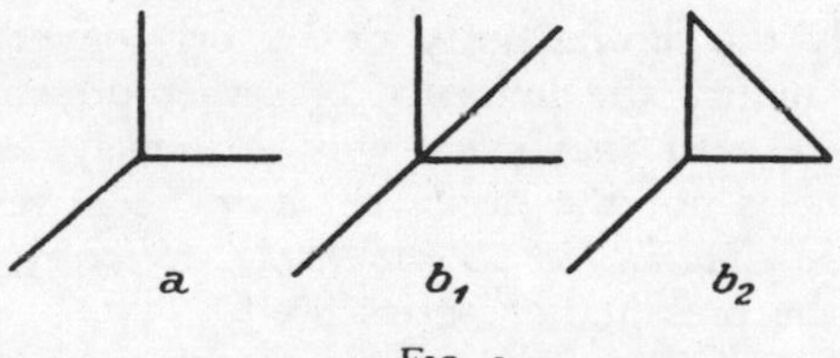

FIG. 1.

shall also study the influences exerted by the character of the situation prevailing for the subject at the time when *b* is presented.

Structural properties of the memorizing series.—What effect will frequent presentation of *a* have upon the perception of *b* when *very easy b*-figures are used ? Fig. 1 shows the *a*- and *b*-figures with which we began our attempt to find an answer to this question. The experiment itself was conducted as follows. The 15 subjects were divided into two groups with identical instructions regarding the *a*-figure but (as stated below) with a difference in the time
3 at which mention of the *b*-figure was made. The *a*-figure was shown and after an interval of 2–20 sec. it was again exposed. The subjects did not know, however, that the *same* figure appeared

Grateful acknowledgment is hereby made to *Julius Springer*, *Verlagsbuchhandlung*, Berlin, for permission to reproduce the illustrations used in this SELECTION.

in both exposures; indeed they were permitted to believe that there must be a difference because instructions were given to compare the two as regards their size.[1] After 20 such comparisons (i.e. 40 presentations of the *a*-figure) the *b*-figure was interposed between the 41st and 42nd presentations of *a*: that is to say, the order upon this occasion was *a–b–a*. Descriptions of *b* were then secured. The results were as follows:—

4 *Group I.*—The 7 subjects of this Group were told *before the experiment began* that at some time during the comparison series an extraneous (or "interrupting") figure would be shown. In the 14 tests (i.e. 7 subjects, 2 *b*-figures) there were 12 positive descriptions: *a* was at once seen in *b*.

5 *Group II.*—The 8 subjects of this Group were told nothing of a coming extraneous figure until *after the 20th comparison pair*, i.e. not until immediately before the triple exposition. In this case every one of the 16 reports was negative: not once was the *a*-figure seen in *b*.

These results clearly reveal the important part played by the *character* of the memorizing series itself, for by changing the time at which *b* is mentioned it is possible, as with Group I, to overcome almost entirely the figural unity of *b*; or, conversely, as with Group II, to nullify the influence of earlier presentations of *a*. Thus it can be seen that even with extremely easy *b*-figures repetition alone is not the decisive factor. The result depends rather upon *the situation set up within the subject* by the character (for him) of the presentation series itself.

The subjects of Group I, having been told at the start to expect
an interrupting figure, were at first constantly awaiting this inter-
6 loper. As one after another of the comparison pairs failed to bring
anything new, tension gradually relaxed and when *b did* appear,
they were so confidently expecting an *a*-figure that they *saw b* as *a*.
Very often the subjects were emotionally aroused by this unexpected interruption, some cried out and all reported having
found this appearance of *b* unpleasant.

With Group II the situation was quite different. Having just been told that an interrupting figure would occur between the next two presentations of *a* (i.e. within the 21st comparison pair) they thought of the new figure as a kind of parenthesized incident, having little if any connection with the comparison series. With the subjects in this frame of mind, and with no expectation of an *a*-figure anyway, their attitude was simply one of preparation to

[1] Most of the reports were of a difference in size between the "two" figures.

" leap across " to the second member of the interrupted comparison pair. In general, therefore, we conclude that whenever *a* is spontaneously seen in *b*, the decisive factor, without which preliminary repetitions of *a* are of no avail, is the subject's own *expectation* of *a*.

[7–12 : repeating the foregoing experiment it was found that with more difficult *b*-figures the internal unity of *b* proved to be a stronger factor than was the character of the memorizing series. That is to say, in these cases even Group I gave negative results.]

13 *Threshold experiments with " emerging " figures.*—It might be that the negative results of Group II above were due to the *manner* in which the *b*-figure was shown. That is to say, it may have been that the influence of past experience was " estopped " by the force exerted by *b* at the time of the test. The argument would thus contend that at the instant of testing *b* there is, in full swing, a " *b*-process " against which the influence of *a* is powerless.

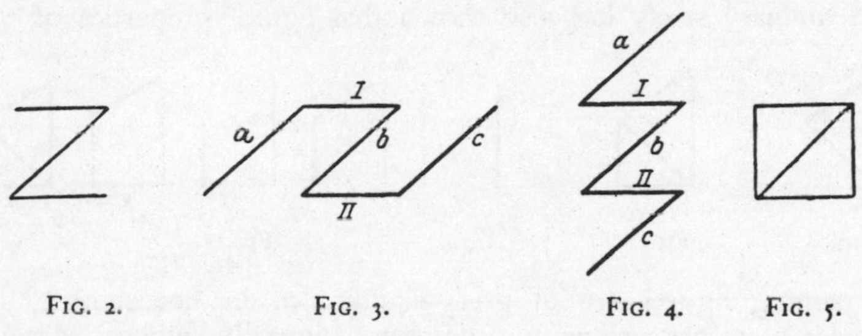

FIG. 2. FIG. 3. FIG. 4. FIG. 5.

Possibly an after-effect of *a* might be expected when the *b*-figure *gradually* comes into view (" emerges "), for in this case the *b*-figure might not at first be so closely knit as in the former mode of presentation. In the following experiments, therefore, the *b*-figure became visible upon the projection screen very slowly in order that if the threshold for its *a*-content were lower than
14 for any other part, this should be given the opportunity to appear *first* as the projected figure gradually became more distinct.

It is essential for an experiment of this kind that each figure used should be uniform in its mode of emergence. Preliminary experiments were therefore conducted to assure compliance with this requirement. A Z-shaped figure (Fig. 2), for example, will " emerge " in the following manner : first there appears one or other of the parallel lines, immediately thereafter (though sometimes simultaneously) the other one becomes visible, and only after some little time (during which the entire illumination has

been steadily increasing) does the oblique line come into view. The oblique line may be given an advantage over the horizontal ones, however, if the *Z* is enlarged as in Figs. 3 and 4. Now it is the three parallel oblique lines which appear first. On the other hand if the *Z* is submerged in a square such as that shown in Fig. 5, then all other contour lines will appear *before* the oblique line can be seen. That not all figures are uniform in their mode of emergence was clear from experiments using arrangements such as that given in Fig. 6. Here there was no regularity of appearance and on any given occasion this line or that might be the first to come
15 into view. But, when Fig. 6 was closed by the addition of two parallel lines (Fig. 7), regularity of emergence was restored. The stages of appearance in this case are given in Fig. 8.

On the whole these preliminary experiments show that with suitable figures we may feel confident of the constancy of emergence itself in the experiments to which we shall presently turn. The preliminary study has also shown that figural properties of the

Fig. 6. Fig. 7. Fig. 8.

emerging figures are of great significance in determining the order of emergence among the parts: figurally emphasized parts (in Figs. 2–8, parallel lines) are the first to appear.

16 *Procedure.*—Seated at a table 4 m. from a projection screen the subject had before him a sheet of paper arranged so that he could make drawings of the emerging figures without looking away from the screen. Nothing whatever was said by the experimenter about a *b*-figure.

In addition to the apparatus used for projecting the *b*-figure there was an extra lamp which maintained a constant, faint illumination upon the screen. In front of the projection lens an episcotister was placed whose opening could be gradually (and automatically) increased during rotation. It required approximately 40–60 sec. for the *b*-figure to become fully visible. A " ready " signal was given by the experimenter as the projection lantern was brought into action. As soon as any inhomogeneity in the projection field
17 could be observed, the subject signalled " one ". With each emerging addition he called out " two ", " three ", etc. When he

TABLE I

		a-figure	Stages of emergence of the *b*-figure as given by subjects' drawings					*b*-figure
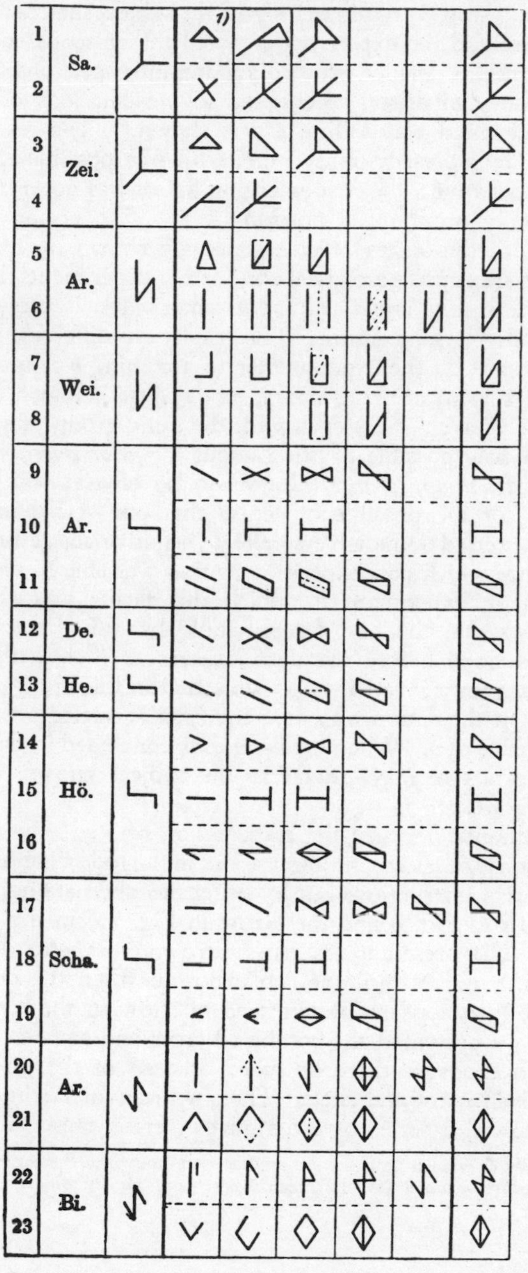 1	Sa.		[1]					
2								
3	Zei.							
4								
5	Ar.							
6								
7	Wei.							
8								
9	Ar.							
10								
11								
12	De.							
13	He.							
14	Hö.							
15								
16								
17	Scha.							
18								
19								
20	Ar.							
21								
22	Bi.							
23								

was confident that no additional lines would come into view he signalled " stop ". After each signal the subject sketched what he had just seen and the experimenter noted the episcotister opening at that instant. A detailed protocol of later introspections was kept.

Using the comparison technique, 40 presentations of *a* were made in the usual way before *b* was shown.[1] The results with 9 subjects (23 *b*-presentations) were, with one possible exception,
18 uniformly negative: the first emerging figure was not *a* but rather some figurally pronounced portion of *b*. The *a*- and *b*-figures together with the stages of emergence are shown in Table I.

[19–25: additional examples are given and further experiments described. (22 f.): the results are no different when *a* too is presented (50 times) as an emerging figure. The results *are* different, however, when reference by the experimenter to a coming *b*-figure is made (1) before the memorizing series, or (2) just before *b* is shown (cf. pp. 4 f. above). (24) even with the same group of subjects it was in this way possible to bring about the *prior emergence* (Condition I) or *non-appearance* (Condition II) of *a* at will.]

26 In view of the possible objection that our verbal instruction may have exerted some adverse effect (negative suggestion) upon the influence which past experience with *a* was able to display, we performed an experiment in which this factor was eliminated. Announcing that the next figure would be different from those which had gone before manifestly serves to " close the case ", so to speak, for *a*; and it is possible that in this break between *a* and *b* may lie the reason why no *a*-influence is carried over to affect the emergence of *b*. When the *a*-series is concluded in this manner the next exposure may, so far as the subject knows, show *any* possible figure.

27 Discontinuity between the presentation of *b* and the preceding presentations (of *a*) was brought about in the following experiment not by verbal instructions but by using *two* alternate figures (such as the cross in Fig. 9 and the arrow in Fig. 10) in the following manner. The presentations cross, arrow, cross, etc., occurred 6 times (i.e. 3 each) until the 7th exposure when the cross alone was " due " to appear. But instead of showing the cross at this exposure we presented the combined cross and square. Similarly in the 8th exposure there appeared, instead of the arrow alone, the combined arrow and circle. Then, without further interruption, there followed a series of cross, arrow, cross presentations until

[1] Naturally only such figures were used as were known to " emerge " in a consistently uniform manner (cf. the preceding account of preliminary experiments).

each had been seen 12 times. At this point, when the *cross* was due to appear next, we exposed instead the *arrow and circle*, and, following this, there appeared the *cross and square* instead of the *arrow*.[1]

29 In this way two tests with each *b*-figure were obtained: Test I was that occurring at the 7th or 8th exposure, and in this case the logically correct ("pro-structural") *b*-figure was shown. In Test II, on the other hand, the *b*-figure was presented "out of turn", so to speak (i.e. "contra-structurally"), for the arrow and circle was shown at an exposure when not the *arrow* but the *cross* was due to appear (and vice versa).

The results from 24 *b*-presentations with 6 subjects: Test I,
30 all reports are positive. That is to say, in every case *a* was the first figure to emerge. The 12 reports of Test II, on the contrary, contain only 2 positive cases despite the fact that by this time the number of previous experiences with both *a*-figures was much greater than when Test I had been made.

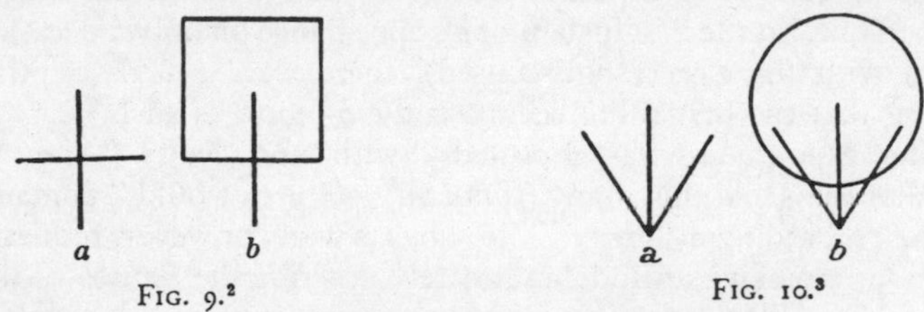

FIG. 9.[2] FIG. 10.[3]

[31–42: numerous other experiments along this line are reported. (37): the results show conclusively that even with easy *b*-figures direct perception of *a*-in-*b* is possible only when vectorial factors of the presentation situation themselves function to bring about *this* perception rather than that of *b* itself.]

43 *The factor of recency.*—It is ordinarily assumed that the effect of past experience is greater the less time there is intervening between that experience and a subsequent test. Although in the experiments reported above the *b*-figure usually appeared within 1–2 sec. after *a* had been extinguished, we now propose to investigate the influence of past experience when even shorter

[1] With some of the subjects this was reversed: i.e. cross and square first, arrow and circle second, but again, of course, with this *b*-figure appearing at a "wrong" place in the series.

[2] In preliminary experiments with this *b*-figure the square was found to emerge much sooner than the 5th line by which the cross is made [p. 25].

[3] Here the *b*-figure regularly emerges as a circle to which is then added the arrow-head with parts of the latter appearing either simultaneously or in succession.

44 intervals between *a* and *b* are used. We shall, moreover, take care to project the *a*-in-*b* image upon the identical retinal area just previously stimulated by *a* alone.

Twenty-five easy, medium, and relatively difficult *a*- and *b*-figures were used in this experiment.[1] These were photographed a_1–b_1, a_2–b_2, etc. upon successive frames of moving picture film and then projected upon a frosted glass plate in such a way that the *a* part in *b* occupied in each case the same position as when just
[45–47: presented alone. The images were 20 × 15 cm. in size; observa-
omitted] tion distance was approximately 2 m.

48 The 8 trained subjects were without knowledge of the *a* and *b*
relationships. An *a*-figure was exposed and a short description
of it requested, then, following an "attention" signal, the corresponding *b*-figure was shown and a description requested. The
49 results of 120 *b*-descriptions were as follows: whereas the *a*-figure
"stood out" at the first instant of *b*'s appearance on only 2 occasions
(both with the easiest figure used), there were 118 descriptions
stating that the first thing seen was the *b*-figure as such.[2]

50 The experiment was repeated "with knowledge"—i.e. the subjects were told that many (if not all) *b*-figures would "contain" the just preceding *a*-figure. The subjects were, however, requested to adopt a passive attitude and merely describe the figures as they saw them. This was necessary because an active search would in almost every case have brought *a* to light.

51 There were 210 descriptions (10 subjects): 11 of these descriptions mentioned immediate perception of *a*-in-*b*; 8 commented upon *b* as somehow under the influence of the just preceding *a*-figure; 191 failed to report *a*-in-*b*.

53 But the results were quite different when the vector of the *b*-situation was directed towards *a*. This was accomplished by a sudden and unexpected presentation of *b* at the instant when the subject was most intent upon his description of *a*. At such a moment the subject's own "inner situation" is often so directed upon the apprehension of *a* that (especially the first time this is done) the *a*-figure is much more likely to be seen in *b* than ordinarily even when strong figural cohesion opposes this.

54 But the factor of surprise is quickly compensated for by subjects in an experiment such as this, and in order to secure measurable

[1] All were easier than the *b*-figures shown in *Selection 9a*.

[2] The experiment was repeated with 5 new subjects and several additional figures, thus bringing the total number of descriptions to 245. Of the 125 descriptions obtained in this latter experiment only 1 was of an immediate perception of *a*-in-*b*.

results we therefore adopted a different technique. (We shall henceforth abandon the immediate presentation of *b* after *a*, but this is no great sacrifice since absolute recency apparently played little or no part in increasing positive results anyhow.) We now substituted a *rhythmic* presentation of the *a*-figure and then (without warning) showed the *b*-figure at an exposure when *a* was " due " to appear. The apparatus was so designed that every 2 seconds the *a*-figure appeared for $\frac{1}{2}$ sec. The subjects were told that several series of figures would be shown and that they were to notice
55 particularly the *transition* from one series to the next.[1] It was further understood that immediately following the first member of a new series there would be a pause during which they were to make their reports. The 4 subjects thus saw 15 *a*- and *b*-figures. With 2 of these subjects the easiest *b*-figures were used first, the medium and difficult ones coming later. This order was reversed with the other 2 subjects.

The great increase in positive reports under these circumstances can be seen from the fact that 25 of the 60 descriptions mention immediate perception of *a*-in-*b*.[2]

[56–63 : acoustic beats were used to strengthen the rhythm effect but the number of positive reports was not greatly increased (now 46 per cent). (58–61) : omitted. (62–63) : a new type of experiment is reported. The *b*-figure consisted in this case of a large number of small figures, among them *a* itself. The *a*-figure alone was presented 10 times (at different places on the exposure screen) to 3 naïve subjects, and then *b* was shown. The results of six tests were all negative, for in no case was *a* seen to stand out from the *b*-chaos. Repeating the experiment with *a* always appearing (when alone) at the same place on the screen which it was to occupy in the *b*-chaos, 4 out of 6 reports were positive.]

64 *Explanation of Rubin's figural after-effect.*—In his *Visuell wahrgenommene Figuren* (p. 6 f.) Rubin reports an experiment whose results are at variance with the general implications of the present inquiry. Repeating Rubin's work we proceeded as
65 follows : 36 black-white designs were prepared and submitted to three subjects for judgment regarding figure-ground relationships. The reports agreed that in 8 of our designs the spontaneous

[1] [The influence of such rhythmic series reaches its maximum strength in the vicinity of 9–15 repetitions of *a*. Fewer positive results were obtained when 3, 25, or 40 repetitions of *a* were made. (This latter fact shows once more that bare repetition cannot be the decisive factor influencing the apprehension of *b*.) (p. 60).]

[2] [In the experiment reported above (p. 49) only 1·2 per cent of the entire 245 reports were positive ; here 41·7 per cent were positive.]

figure was *black*, in 15 it was *white*; the remaining 13 designs were *ambiguous* since either black or white might equally well be seen as figure.

Still following Rubin's method we selected three mixed series of 12 designs each and showed our subjects the first series four times through (duration of each exposure for each design: 5 sec.) under instructions to apprehend *black* as the figure. Series II was then shown with instructions to apprehend *white* as the figure. After a pause of forty-five minutes filled with casual conversation, the entire 36 designs were presented singly and a judgment regarding the figure-ground relationships of each one was required. The subjects were also asked to state in each case whether or not the design was familiar. There were no other instructions for this latter half of the experiment except that the subjects were asked to remain passive and exercise no prior preference for black or white as the figure in any design.

Our results confirmed Rubin's findings, for there was an undeniable effect exerted by the earlier presentations of Series I
66 and II. We found, however (also in conformity with Rubin), that the subjects almost always identified familiar designs as familiar *before* apprehending them as black or white. This *urge* to identify the designs as familiar or unfamiliar was the more remarkable since our instructions had been to comment upon familiarity only *after* reporting upon the black or white of a design.

Must we accept Rubin's results and our own confirmation of them as evidence of an automatic experience effect? Viewing the experiment as a whole one finds that this conclusion would be
67 incorrect. The instructions and general procedure may have exercised a determining influence upon our results. The subjects' spontaneous comments revealed that they were *expecting* a "test" to follow the initial presentations of the designs. Such comments show that our instructions and procedure had set up a state of tension which could be resolved only by a "test" of what had been "memorized" before. The situation prevailing during the latter half of our experiment contained two main components: the figural character of the designs, and the "urge to identify familiar designs". The latter of these had remained in latent form from the attitude adopted (under instructions) towards the designs when first presented. To discover whether or not this interpretation was correct we repeated the experiment with the following changes.

In order to neutralize the residual " urge towards a test situation " it was necessary to conduct a kind of " test " before the
second half of our experiment began. This time the subject was
68 given a task to perform during the forty-five minute pause. Paper
and scissors were provided and he was asked to prepare designs of
the kind he had just been shown. The second half of our experiment
contained in irregular order both his own and the (36) other
designs. Once more the instructions were to report whether a
black or white figure was seen first. The subject was not asked
to report on the familiarity of designs. This time there was as
good as *no* evidence of former experience with the designs of
69 Series I and II. The experiment was repeated with three additional
subjects to whom only the decidedly black—or white—figure
designs were given in the initial presentations. The instructions
in this case were to apprehend the naturally black-figure designs
as white figures, and vice versa. The results were again practically
70 zero as regards figural after-effect. It thus seems clear that Rubin's
results must be ascribed to the experimental procedure which he
used and not to an automatic after-effect of earlier experience.

Concluding discussion.—In this study we have inquired into the validity of the theory which holds that the more often a part [*Teilfigur*] has been presented and apprehended, the more readily will the perception of a larger whole which includes this part be affected in a specific manner. The theory also maintains that the expected effect will be greater the less time there is intervening between the two presentations. Repetition of the initial figure is thus believed to set up a disposition which, when activated by a later appearance of the original stimulus, operates to influence in a definite way the subsequent mode of apprehension. This process is, to be thought of as self-operative or automatic. If there are other tendencies also favouring the expected effect, these will be strengthened by repeated presentations of the original figure. Conversely, opposing tendencies will to greater or less degree be compensated for by such repetitions.

Consulting the results of our experiments it is evident that within the range of our tests and under the conditions set forth, such automatic after-effects of earlier experience do not exist. Neither extreme increase in the number of presentations nor immediate sequence of *a-b* exposures was successful in demonstrating this automatic influence. The results were also no different whether the *b*-figures had a high or low degree of cohesion, nor did the *a*-figure " emerge " first in our threshold experiments.

72 It was also found that increasing the number of presentations did not improve the subjects' ability to find the initially presented figure, for with instructions to search for *a* the subjects with over 500 previous experiences did no better than those who had seen *a* but 5 times before this test was made.

As soon, however, as the b-*figure was exposed in a situation which directed the subject toward the perception of* a, *there resulted* (*quite apart from the number of earlier presentations*) *a tendency to see the* b-*complex in the manner given by this vector.*

With a very difficult *b*-figure the situational force was, of course, frequently incapable of splitting it up and there occurred instead (when *b* was encountered) a sudden disruption of the earlier experienced sequence. Conversely, with relatively easier *b*-figures a sufficiently strong situational force brought about a disruption of *b* such that the primary apprehension now was of *a*. Thus we see that the dissolution of *b* into *a*, and (with difficult *b*-figures) the disruption of a specifically constituted course of events [*Geschehensverlauf*] are phenomena depending respectively upon the strength of the situational force and the degree of figural unity exhibited by *b*.

Nor was the strength of situational forces increased by multiplying the number of *a*-presentations. This was shown by the fact that the results became *worse* when a certain optimal number of presentations [e.g. 9–15] was exceeded.

[73–80: discussion defending these conclusions against probable objections. (77–80): bare repetition does not guarantee which apprehension will occur at a later presentation even of the same object. Equally balanced black and white figure-ground drawings were presented every 5 sec. for 30 min. At each of the first 30 presentations black was seen as figure and white as ground. This repeated experience did not, however, prevent a reversal at the 31st presentation when, quite spontaneously, the white became figure and the black ground.]

81 In conclusion, then, there remains the question: How did the positive cases in our experiments come about, and what had
82 repetitions of *a* to do with this? We have already seen that everything depends upon the character of the situation obtaining for the subject when *b* is first seen. Consider once more the cross and square shown in Fig. 9 above. During the 4 or 5 *a*-presentations (i.e. of the cross alone) there is created a procession or stream which causes the subject to see a succeeding *b*-figure (cross and square) in the same manner as the *a*-presentations had been seen.

In thus establishing the character of the presentation situation the constitution of the *a*-series is of the greatest importance. But not in the sense that mere multiplicity of *a*-presentations will automatically serve to bring about self-reproduction. Instead the case here resembles that in music where the preceding tones of a melody create the need for a specific resolving tone.[1] The important consideration, then, has to do not with repetitions as such but with a specifically constituted process-Gestalt [*Geschehensgestalt*] within which the perceptions (of *a*) occur. Hence, if for any reason the presentation situation lacks at the critical moment the requisite character, mere repetitions of *a* are powerless to bring about a disruption of the *b*-figure.

From this point of view it is clear why repeated presentations of *a* had so little effect upon our results. Mere repetition of *a*-presentations will not cause the perception of *a*-in-*b*; instead the presence of *a* is necessary only as a means of directing the course [*Geschehensverlauf*] which the situation is to take. For this purpose there [83–87: omitted] is usually no more need of " repetitions " here than in the parallel melody example.

[1] In all of this discussion it will be apparent that the larger question is really that of temporal Gestalten [p. 83].

SELECTION 10

TENDENCIES IN FIGURAL VARIATION

By FRIEDRICH WULF

"Über die Veränderung von Vorstellungen (Gedächtnis und Gestalt)," *Psychol. Forsch.*, 1922, **1**, 333–373.

333 *Statement of the problem.*—The discussion of the laws which govern the sequence of ideas, resulting from the publications of Külpe's school, has forced the adherents of associationistic psychology, no less than members of Külpe's group, to make their concepts more precise and concrete. Thus G. E. Müller in defending associationism has re-introduced and more carefully defined the concept of the *directional image* [*Richtungsvorstellung*] in an attempt to explain an ordered sequence of ideas. But the success of such an explanation requires that the concept of directional imagery shall itself be adequately established. Our problem is to carry out a critical examination of this concept. Müller believes that directional imagery is possible because all memorial contents [*Vorstellungen*] gradually deteriorate in definiteness and come more and more to resemble one another.

334 This can be examined experimentally. We may ask: Do memorial contents suffer, with the passage of time, those and *only* those changes necessary for Müller's theory of the directional image? According to Müller, a "*convergence principle*" operates to minimize not only all qualitative but also certain quantitative differences by which an object was initially characterized. The
335 extreme toward which this converging process leads would thus be for any given image a state of maximum vagueness. In addition to the principle of convergence Müller has also proposed a theory of *affective transformation* to account for the special memorial advantage sometimes enjoyed by certain properties or aspects of an experience. The term "affective transformation" is used because memorial prominence of this kind is due, Müller holds, to the special attention with which the favoured portion has been regarded.

It is the convergence principle—of such crucial importance for Müller's entire theory—which we plan to investigate. Our

Grateful acknowledgment is hereby made to *Julius Springer*, *Verlagsbuchhandlung*, Berlin, for permission to reproduce the illustrations used in this SELECTION.

336 procedure was as follows. The subject was shown a simple drawing; after an interval he was asked to reproduce it from memory. These reproductions were then compared with the original to ascertain whether certain special characteristics had been retained, weakened, or strengthened. We shall speak of the changes respectively as *conservation*, *levelling*, and *sharpening*.

Preliminary experiments.—Since they were intended only for orientation, the initial experiments were all conducted with one subject. The instructions were to look at the drawing with the intention of reproducing it later as accurately as possible. The drawing was exposed for 5 sec.; observation distance 30–40 cm. A reproduction was requested in all cases approximately half an
337 hour later and for many of the drawings another recall after a 24-hour interval was also asked for. In all, 16 drawings (of which the two shown in Fig. 1 are typical) were used in the preliminary experiments.

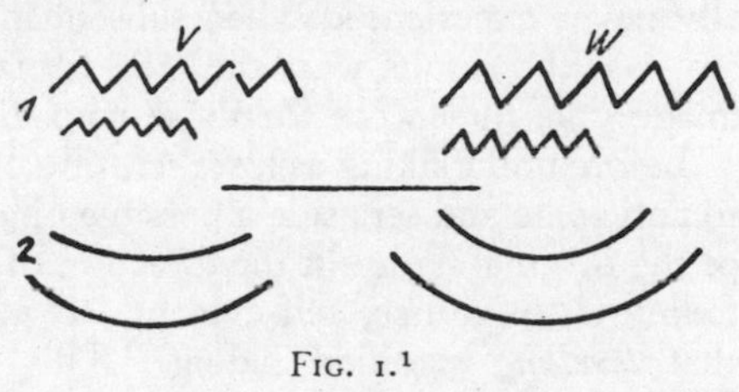

Fig. 1.[1]

It can be seen in Fig. 1 (1) that both zigzag lines have become sharper in the reproduction; the angles are somewhat smaller and the individual lines are larger; also the difference in length between the two has become more pronounced. This is throughout a case of *sharpening*. In Fig. 1 (2) the reproduction shows a *levelling* effect.

338 *The main experiment.*—The 26 figures used in this experiment were drawn with India ink upon pieces of white cardboard 8 × 10 cm. in size. Instructions were the same as above. There were six subjects. In order to detect any peculiarities of figural *apprehension* during actual exposition we called for the first reproduction just 30 sec. after the card had been removed from view. The subjects were asked not to think of the figure during the interval between presentation and recall. Upon making their drawings they were told to visualize the original as clearly as possible.
339 A second recall was requested after 24 hours, another after one week, and in a few cases again some two months later. Upon beginning the experiment a subject would be given only 2 figures

[1] The original drawing is indicated by the letter *V*, while *W* designates the reproduction.

in an experimental sitting; later this was increased to 4 figures per sitting.

For the recall made one week later we prepared cards showing a fractional part of the original. The subject was not told that this part really was accurate but was left to decide this for himself. His task was to complete the original design using this part if he acknowledged it as correct. When a subject had finished the entire series his memory for all the presented figures was tested.

340 *Results.*—It may be stated at the start that with but 8 exceptions (6 of which were invalid in any case) all reproductions which we obtained displayed clear deviations toward *sharpening* or *levelling*. Moreover, modifications manifested by the initial reproduction of a figure followed the same course in later reproductions of that figure.

[341–344: discusses the role of visual images (*Vorstellungsbilder*) in reproductions of this sort. Not every subject experienced visual images of the original figure even at the first recall, and they were practically never experienced when subsequent recalls occurred. But in any case the results were the *same* for subjects who used no visual imagery as they were for those who did.]

345 Before undertaking a closer scrutiny of these results it is necessary to anticipate and set aside a possible objection. That modifications of the original figure in the direction of *sharpening* are not cases of fading is, of course, self-evident. It might be thought, however, that *levelling* signified fading. This would be quite incorrect. In the protocols assembled during our experiment one finds
346 references to reduced distinctness of the memorial contents fully as often when the sharpening process was involved as when levelling was the case. This shows that the levelling process was in no sense a sign of forgetting. Further evidence of this was also given in cases where the subject voluntarily offered to attempt another recall after a lapse of several weeks' time. If the levelling phenomenon was really, in contrast to sharpening, an instance of fading, then the figures recalled after a longer interval should have been primarily those which had changed in the direction of sharpening. That this was not the case, however, may be seen from the fact that of 48 such reproductions 27 were of figures which had been undergoing a levelling process while but 21 were of the other type.

347 As can be seen in the figures given below, the designs used in this experiment were extremely simple. And yet they were not wholly unequivocal in determining the different subjects' apprehensions of them. The same design (e.g. solid line drawing in

Fig. 10) would be called, for example, "zigzag" by one subject
348 and "three points or 'peaks'" by another. Similarly, whereas for one subject the design shown in Fig. 2 (solid lines) was "two horizontal lines, parallel; the oblique ones not", two other subjects spoke of it as a "stairstep". The former saw the drawing as a *drawing*; the latter looked upon it as a picture of something.
349 In both cases the design was given a name, but the classes of objects designated were quite different. The former mentioned concrete things (lines) from the sphere to which the drawing as a drawing belonged; the latter specified an object from another sphere (stairstep) as characterization of the design. This is nearer to life; here the figure loses its dead half-reality and enters into relation with living things; in the other case it stands apart from such relationships. The two modes of apprehension ("lines" and "stairsteps")

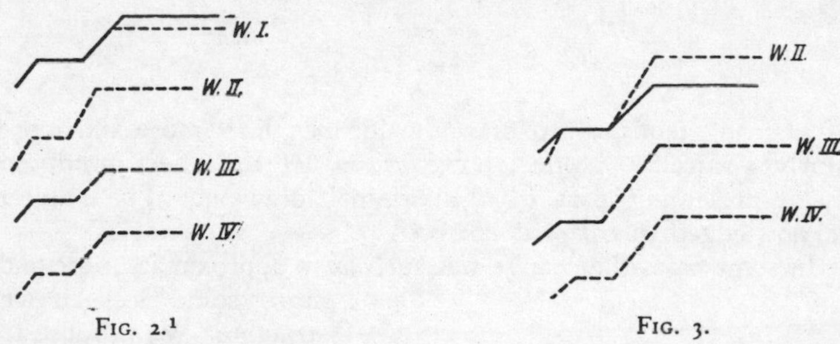

FIG. 2.[1] FIG. 3.

we shall call, respectively, the *isolative* and the *comprehensive*. The specific results of our experiment will be presented under these headings.

350 *Comprehensive apprehension.*—Fig. 2 (solid lines) was called by one subject "stairsteps with a platform above". The dotted lines (I, i.e. first recall) indicate a tendency to "level off" or reduce the difference between the stairsteps and platform by lowering the latter. In II (second recall) the structure has been still more levelled and the oblique lines are steeper. He again referred to the figure as a "staircase". In III the part given as solid lines was re-presented for judgment. He found the oblique line somewhat too short and not steep enough. This *levelling* tendency is still apparent in the reproduction (IV) made eight weeks after the original presentation. As may be seen, the original apprehension of this figure as a staircase

[1] The figures given here and in all subsequent cases are one-half the original size (p. 338).

has been borne out more and more in each later recall although, of course, no genuine staircase figure is ever attained.

With another subject (whose results are given by the dotted lines of Fig. 3) the figure was also seen as a staircase but here memorial changes took the form of a *sharpening* as well as a levelling. Levelling occurred only in the tread parts ; differences in length between the vertical and horizontal lines which compose a staircase became smaller. In connection with this, one may observe the operation

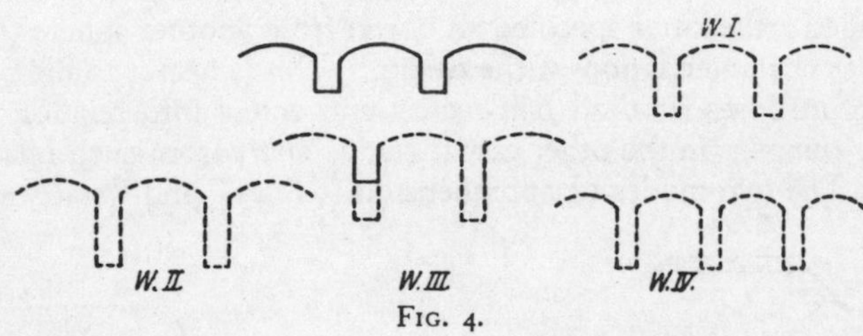

FIG. 4.

of a strong tendency to draw the inclined lines more and more nearly vertical. (Notice, however, in III the effect produced by re-presenting part of the original drawing. The subject acknowledged this part as correct.)

351 In some cases the change was such as to approximate more and more some well-known structure. We propose to designate changes of this sort by the term " normalizing ". A better example of this than the foregoing may be seen in Fig. 4. The object pictured here by solid lines was spoken of by four subjects as a " bridge " while another called it an " arch ". In all cases the " supports " were progressively lengthened. Three of the subjects were unwilling to acknowledge the part shown them in III and insisted upon lengthening it. Another example : with the object shown in Fig. 5 the impression of a " W " had been so strong for one subject that he was quite unable to recognize a part of the original which was represented at the third recall. He finally remembered a W, turned the re-presented part around (as shown here in III) and drew the lines necessary to complete a kind of W-figure.

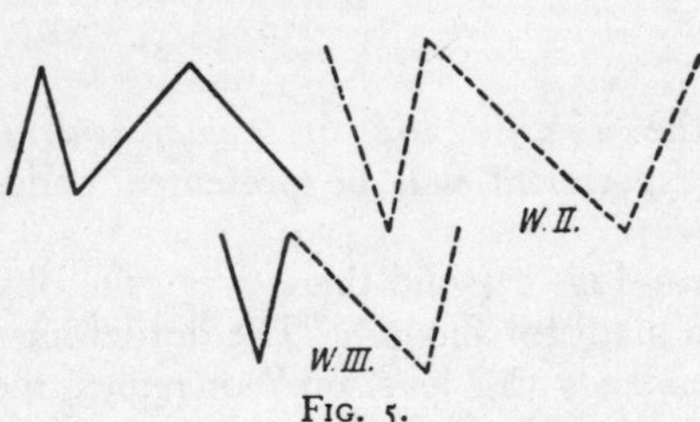

FIG. 5.

However, not every apprehension after the manner of well-known objects need proceed solely in the normalizing direction. The subject who saw Fig. 6 as " a descending arrow " exhibited more and more clearly with each reproduction a strong tendency to draw the object in a vertical position. Here the tilt given by the original was apparently insufficient and in subsequent drawings the subject emphasized or " pointed " this property more and
352 more. We shall therefore classify cases of this kind as " pointing " or emphasizing.

We turn now to a third kind of modification. Unlike " pointing ", it sometimes happened that without particular consideration for the properties given by the original figure, a comprehensive apprehension would proceed along a line directly opposed to normalizing. Thus, for example, had Fig. 7 been subjected to a normalizing process (" flask ") there would have been a sharpening of differences in size between the two rounded

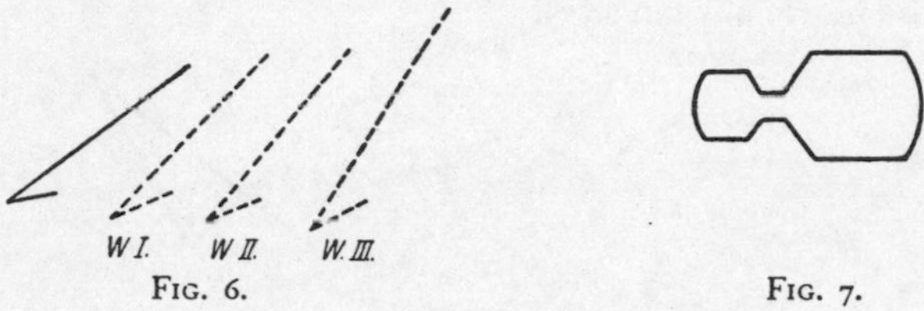

Fig. 6. Fig. 7.

areas. Instead with one subject a levelling process occurred whereby these areas tended to become more nearly alike. Changes of this kind reveal the operation of factors peculiar to the design itself, and we shall therefore speak of them as " autonomous changes ".

353 These are, of course, but a few examples chosen to illustrate the many phenomenal contents which influence the drawing made after a comprehensive apprehension of the presented figure. In addition to (or even instead of) purely visual data there were also general types or schema in terms of which the subject constructed his responses. The subject in such a case knows what he must draw; his reproduction is not " the copy of a picture " but the carrying out of an assigned task. The schema itself becomes with time ever more dominant; visual imagery of the original disappears, the number of details contained in the original is forgotten and incorrectly reproduced, yet even the last reproduction will usually show a steady progress towards representation of the type or schema originally conceived.

It is not that a presented figure is " associated " with some familiar idea gotten from earlier experience, but rather the law of the design is itself given by the comprehensive apprehension. It is *this* and not the recall of some specific object which remains in the subject's memory, and it is this structure which undergoes with time the changes appearing in the reproductions. Indeed, the
354 same general structure may be used with reference to very different original figures. One subject, for example, designated both Fig. 8 and Fig. 9 " an envelope ". The result was that in correspondence with the respective figures one (Fig. 8) underwent in memory a process of sharpening while the other (Fig. 9) shows the effect of levelling (i.e., in the latter case, the two triangles became more and more nearly alike in size).

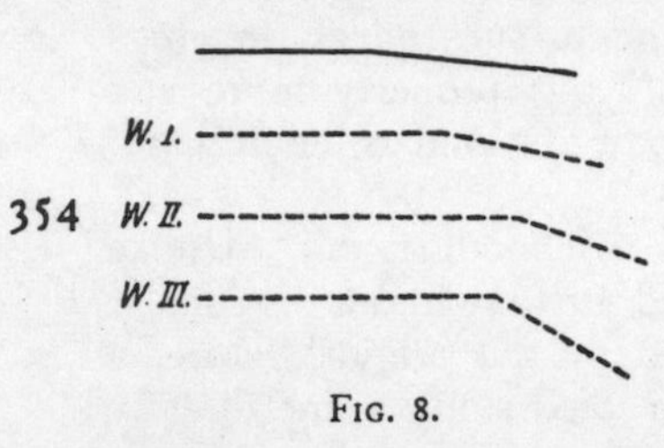

Fig. 8.

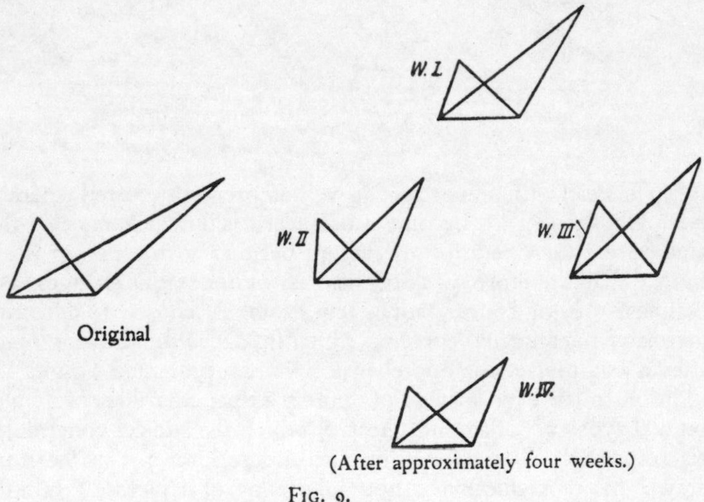

Fig. 9.

355 *Isolative apprehension.*—The principles involved here are essentially the same as those already discussed. A subject who, for example, designated Fig. 10 as " three equilateral triangles " gave as his subsequent reproductions the sharpened peaks shown by the dotted lines. Another subject spoke of " three peaks " [*Spitzen*],

and it may be seen from Fig. 11 how his reproductions emphasized this apprehension.[1]

356 The reproductions made by another subject when shown the object given in Fig. 12*a* changed in two directions. First the horizontal line was lengthened (Fig. 12*b*), and, secondly, the scallops became ever more alike—i.e. the figure tended steadily towards greater symmetry.

358 As regards the role played by phenomenal contents our findings

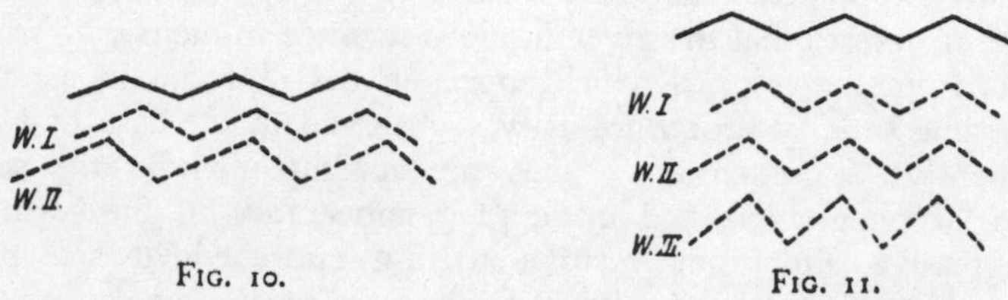

FIG. 10. FIG. 11.

here were essentially the same as in the case of comprehensive apprehensions (cf. p. 353): in many cases the subject " knew " what he should reproduce without there being any imagery of the originally presented figure. Thus the object shown in Fig. 9 was apprehended by one subject as " a figure with two triangles "

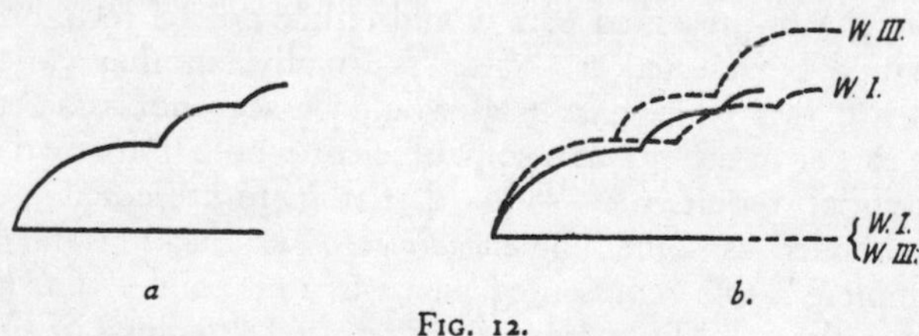

FIG. 12.

and his drawings represent fulfilment of the task of indicating two triangles upon the same base. He " knew " that certain relationships were involved. This does not mean, however, that recourse was had to this procedure as one method (among several others) of assisting memory for the original. Perception of relationships is, instead, a kind of " active detection " (Köhler); it is not something new over and above figural perception but rather a particular modification thereof. One is conscious of a figure between whose

[1] Another subject declared with reference to this figure that it was a " zigzag ", and he repeatedly emphasized its " flatness ". And yet, even in this case, the reproductions were successively sharper. Evidently to become more pointed must be a natural property of the object shown in Figs. 10–11 [p. 357].

structural parts there is " tension ". It is the relationship between these parts which very often supplies a stable frame-work in memory for the figure itself. The number of specific details which one can recall is often quite meagre ; yet the direction of change may nevertheless remain, for this is given by certain properties
359 of the original which had given to the initial apprehension its essential character.

Summarizing : Familiar structures also appear in the case of isolative apprehensions. It is relative to the special properties of these structures that the given figure is retained in memory. Variations from the original which appear in the reproductions reveal the same orderly procedure as was observed in the case of comprehensive apprehensions ; they are accompanied by the same kind of phenomena and make their appearance in the form of progressive alterations relative to the apprehended structure.
[360–362 : when parts of the original figure were re-presented one week later, one or other of the following reactions could be observed : (1) The part would be recognized immediately and the subject would be unaware that any changes of this part had occurred in his drawings. (2) The part would be acknowledged but would be used in the wrong place or even in some other figure. (3) Memorial changes of the original figure having gone so far in some other direction, the re-presented part would either not be recognized at all or would be rejected as " false ". Finally, another variety of reaction was this. The part itself would be seen not as a " part " of some earlier figure but as a self-sufficient whole in its own right. The essential requirement—viz. that the re-presented portion be apprehended as something *incomplete*—was lacking and hence to " complete " this represented part was impossible. Cf. in this connection the solid lines given in the dotted drawings of Figs. 2, 3, 4.]

363 *Our results and the principle of convergence.*—The actual *drawing* at any given reproduction is always definite and distinct ; the
364 *idea* underlying this drawing is rarely very distinct. In cases where the subject has a specific visual image of the object he intends to draw, we may assume that characteristics appearing in the reproduction were also present in the visual image. In all other cases we may conclude, from inspecting the reproductions given, that the characteristics thus appearing were also present in the subject's memory at the time of the recall. There were no cases of vacillation between *levelling* and *sharpening* as regards the modifications displayed by successive reproductions.

That is to say, in all cases the ideational content undergoes the same persistent changes as may be observed in the reproductions themselves. This means that hand in hand with increasing vagueness of the phenomenal contents, intensification of certain aspects of the object can take place either in the direction of levelling or of sharpening. It follows from this that the *kind of change* designated by the terms levelling and sharpening is not a form of increasing vagueness [*Undeutlichwerden*]. This was also shown by the fact that the direction of change—levelling or sharpening—had no influence upon any subject's assurance regarding whether a given reproduction was or was not a true representation of the originally exposed figure. Moreover, as mentioned above (p. 345 f.), if levelling were the same as vagueness, reproductions in which the levelling process was exhibited should involve less subjective assurance than those exhibiting a sharpening effect. This was not, however, the case.

Müller describes loss of clarity as an effacement of differences.
365 If levelling were this, then " levelling " would mean that each part of a figure becomes more and more like every other part as their differences disappear. Such a view assumes that each part is an independent entity whose loss of clarity causes differences to vanish. That this point of view is incorrect has, however, already been shown by the present discussion. The parts of our figures are parts of wholes and changes occurring within them are determined by changes of those wholes themselves. It is not true that fading and loss of clarity necessarily imply an increasing resemblance between parts. It is important in this connection to remember that the most significant properties and major outlines of a figure are not lost. Retained are the gross principles of the structure (which are, in fact, emphasized by the levelling or sharpening process) ; it is only subordinate details which fall prey to forgetting.

366 Indefiniteness is not due simply to increasing resemblance between parts (i.e. approximation to an average). Indefiniteness means : subordinate parts and minor characteristics disappear or lose specificity. This does not prevent other subordinate parts and whole-properties from attaining an enhanced significance.

Explanations of results : 1. *By assimilation and attention.*—The foregoing has shown that changes occurring in the reproductions are due to something other than inadequacy of perception or forgetting. In seeking the cause of these changes one may consider first the explanations offered by the theory of association and attention. Such an explanation would proceed as follows :—

367 The original apprehension of the presented figure is determined not only by the exposed object but also by memory residua from earlier experiences. The result of this mixture is a single perceptual image. But when a later reproduction is called for, the *older* residua will—by Jost's second law [1]—make themselves more strongly felt than those of more recent acquisition. In consequence changes in the reproduction will, as time goes on, be determined more and more unequivocally by the older residua.

The reader will at once recall in this connection the cases already cited as examples of normalizing. Without pausing here to determine whether normalizing can really be explained in this way two relevant considerations may nevertheless be mentioned: (1) Normalizing did not necessarily affect all parts of the figures in which its operation occurred; certain parts might proceed in this direction while others did not. (2) In no case was there a segregation of a figure into mere bits such as the theory of associative mixture-effects would require.

As regards the "pointing" of certain properties in the original,
368 Müller holds that such emphasis is due to *attention.* Having enjoyed a special place in the subject's attention at the time of exposition, such properties become overemphasized in the reproduction. But, concretely, just how is this accomplished? How can *attention* cause changes in memorial contents? Attention is said to cause an intensification of sensitivity (e.g. ability to hear a very soft tone), but where is the bridge between this case and progressive modifications in the whole-properties of figures such as those used in our experiments? And furthermore: the modifications apparent in these reproductions are not mere intensifications of attended parts; they are instead the characteristic changes manifested by a redistribution of equilibrium in whole-phenomena. As in so many other psychological problems, so here an appeal to "attention" cannot serve as an explanation; the concept of attention merely conceals the real problems which observed events set for us.

370 2. *By Gestalt principles.*—Rejecting the hypotheses of associationism, we are now in a position to propose our own theory. We shall first investigate the problem of autonomous changes, for it is this which a theory of associations is most patently incapable of explaining.

The laws of Gestalten (phenomenal as well as physical) cannot

[1] A. Jost, Die Assoziationsfestigkeit in ihrer Abhängigkeit von der Verteilung der Wiederholungen, *Zeitschr. f. Psychol.*, 1897, **14**, p. 472.

be derived from the phenomena of association and attention; yet memory is governed by Gestalt laws. Just as it is true that not every figure may be perceived in any arbitrary way one pleases, so also, not everything that is perceived will be retained in memory. That which remains in memory—the physiological "engram"—cannot therefore be thought of as an unalterable impression—a drawing scratched in stone—whose only modification with the passage of time is to fade and blur. Instead, the engram undergoes changes in accordance with Gestalt laws. In place of the originally perceived figure there occur, with time, deviations from this original and these changes are modifications of the figure as a whole.

We have seen that there are two mutually opposed lines of
371 directional change: levelling and sharpening. Both, however, have to do with changes toward "the good Gestalt".[1] Distinctness and inner articulation may, with time, diminish as they will; this does not affect directional modification toward the "good" Gestalt.

But, it is objected, though levelling may lead (by minimizing asymmetries, etc.) to a better figure, how can the *opposite* process—sharpening—achieve this *same* end? An example will make this clear. Suppose three strokes of a hammer, *a*, *b*, *c*, are to be reproduced. The interval between *a* and *b* is 10 units, that between *b* and *c*, 10·5 units. Now there are two possibilities. Either the two intervals may become equal, or the second may be increased relative to the first so that a group such as • •   • will result. True enough, this example does not refer to phenomena resolving from one stage into another over a period of time; it refers rather to variations of an experience-structure from a stimulus-constellation. Such variations may proceed in one direction or the other, but in either case the end approached is that of a pronounced Gestalt. And in general the same may be said of every limen: either a similarity-structure or a difference-structure stands in opposition to the stimuli which have been presented for comparison.

That changes of the same objective design may be very different in accordance with varying apprehensions may readily be expected in the light of our theory. The various phenomenal Gestalten, although all derived from the same design, will each in its own way be "incomplete" or "bad" and hence each must change in its particular direction so as to overcome this defect. These changes do not, however, lie within the subject's pleasure [*Willkür*] to determine. Indeed, the experimenter can even predict the changes

[1] Cf. *Selection 5*.

a certain figure will undergo: consider, for example, how in Figs. 10–12 the same changes occurred despite differences of apprehension by the subjects.[1]

And similarly as regards "pointing". With some subjects certain aspects of a given figure were outstanding, while with others
372 other aspects of that figure were the more prominent. In one case, then, the phenomenal or perceptual figure was so constituted that its point of equilibrium lay in one aspect of the whole; in another case the distribution of equilibrium would not depend upon this aspect. In consequence the same objective aspects of a figure will not in the two instances remain identical since the properties of every part are derived from the whole of which it is a member. The two figures will therefore develop in different directions. One may progress towards greater symmetry; the other may attain organizational "goodness" through special emphasis of specific aspects.

The most general law underlying all change is The Law of *Prägnanz* according to which every Gestalt becomes as "good" as possible. In perception the "possible" is strongly determined by the stimulus complex. When freed from this influence the "engram" is able to change in ways prescribed by the law of *Prägnanz*. It is for this reason that memorial Gestalten tend
373 towards unique forms. From this it is also possible now to understand the normalizing effect. Well known forms (structures) are themselves already stable. If the structure given in perception is such as to initiate processes proceeding along the same lines as those of already stable forms, they will eventuate in the same forms as their predecessors. The significant factor is not how frequently a form has been experienced, but whether its structure is stabilized in accordance with Gestalt laws.

[1] Cf. also the footnote given in connection with Fig. 11.

B. PERCEPTION AND MOVEMENT

SELECTION 11

THE PROBLEM OF PHENOMENAL IDENTITY

By JOSEF TERNUS

"Experimentelle Untersuchung über phänomenale Identität," *Psychol. Forsch.*, 1926, 7, 81–136.

81 The aim of this study is to investigate the category of identity with special reference to its functional role in actual experience.

Experience consists far less in haphazard multiplicity than in the
82 temporal sequence of self-identical objects. We see a moving object, and we say that "*this* object moves" even though our retinal images are changing at each instant of time and for each place which it occupies in space. *Phenomenally* the object retains its identity. And with resting objects the same situation prevails. My present desk is not merely equal to the desk of a moment ago; *the same desk* persists. Nor is change excluded by this, for an object may certainly change without losing its identity: the sun grows red; my friend's face pales, etc.

83 We are interested here in discovering the crucial conditions of such phenomenal identity. The first one can say in this connection is that neither temporal nor spatial continuity of stimulus conditions is necessary for the fact of phenomenal identity. This has been demonstrated by experiments with stroboscopic movement. A point *a* is projected upon a screen, then (after a brief interval of time and at another place upon the screen) *b* is shown. One sees "a moving point" traversing the distance from *a* to *b*. Or if *b* is shown at the same place as *a*, it is possible to arouse the impression of an identical, unmoving point.

84 From this we might formulate the following hypotheses. Phenomenal identity will result (1) when a light point is exposed continuously or with but minimal time intervals; (2) when the point moves—and this whether real or stroboscopic movement is involved. (3) Using several points at once and presenting some of them in Exposition I and (after a brief interval) some in Exposition II it would seem to follow from (1) that those points will be

Grateful acknowledgment is hereby made to *Julius Springer*, *Verlagsbuchhandlung*, Berlin, for permission to reproduce the illustrations used in this SELECTION.

seen as phenomenally self-identical and *at rest* which are *re*-exposed in Exposition II; and, from (2) it would have to follow that the remaining points would be seen as phenomenally self-identical and *moving*. In other words the perceived occurrence in each individual point would depend solely upon the conditions obtaining for that point alone. Our problem is to determine whether or not these hypotheses are correct.

86 *Standard experiment.*—The hypotheses just proposed may be tested in the following manner.[1] Three light points, *a*, *b*, *c*, are projected upon a screen and these are then supplanted by the points *d*, *e*, *f*, which overlap the first group in such a way that *d* is physically identical with *b*, and *e* is physically identical with *c* (Fig. 1).[2] Under optimal conditions one sees the original group, Exposition I, move, with Exposition II, from left to right. The points *b-d* and *c-e* do not seem to appear

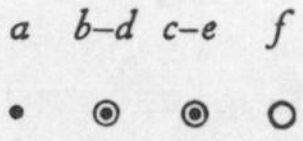

a *b–d* *c–e* *f*

• ◉ ◉ ○

FIG. 1.

87 twice; instead there is a movement from *a* to *d*, from *b* to *e*, and from *c* to *f*. It is apparent from this experiment that the kind of approach represented by the foregoing hypotheses is essentially unnatural and foreign to actual experience.

Further experiments: 1. *Exchange of identity.*—Restating our problem in the light of the standard experiment, the question is: What effect upon the phenomenon of identity will result when, using several points, some (the *i*-points) are re-exposed while others appear only in Exposition I or Exposition II?[3]

In the standard experiment the result, as we have seen, was an "exchange" of identity by the *i*-points: i.e. the *i*-points did not maintain their own self-identity in the two expositions. Other examples of the exchange phenomenon will now be given.

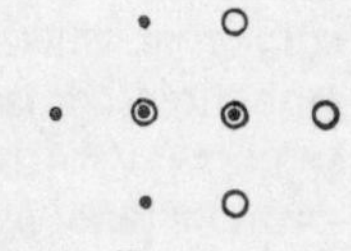

FIG. 2.

88 Exposition I in Fig. 2 is the cross at the left; Exposition II is the same cross appearing now at the right. Two of the points, it will be observed, are *i*-points. What one sees, however, is a *cross* that moves and the result is that the *i*-points undergo here the same kind of identity exchange as those in the standard experiment. The point in Exposition I which appears as the "middle" or centre appears in Exposition II as the left-hand extremity;

[1] Experiments of the type reported here were first made by J. Pikler (1917).

[2] Exposition I is indicated in this and all later figures by dots, Exposition II by circles. The overlapping or physically identical points (hereafter designated "*i*-points") are indicated by both dot and circle.

[3] The number of points remains the same in both expositions.

the right-hand side of Exposition I becomes in II the centre. Most observers are not even aware that there are *i*-points in the two expositions. In no case were these points spontaneously seen as
89 self-identical. The *i*-points of Figs. 3–6 were so far from obviously self-identical that most observers even had difficulty in " finding " them.

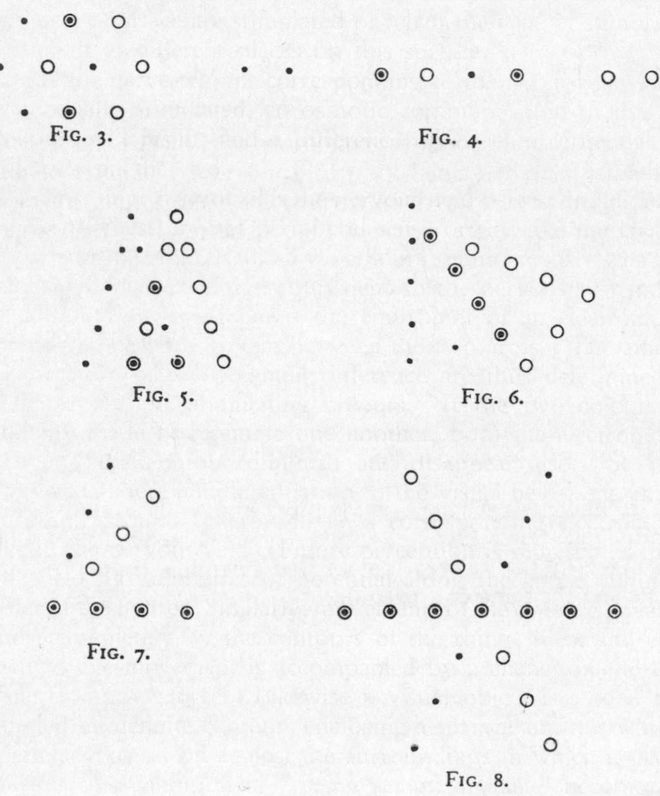

Fig. 3. Fig. 4. Fig. 5. Fig. 6. Fig. 7. Fig. 8.

91 2. *Retention of identity.*—As against cases of identity exchange, there are others where, just as forcibly and spontaneously, the phenomenon of identity *retention* (by the *i*-points) may be observed. An example of this can be seen in Fig. 7. The upper line moves to diminish the angle, but the *lower line* remains unchanged. Similarly in Fig. 8: the horizontal line neither moves nor do the *i*-points
92 of which it consists exhibit any exchange of identity. The results

with Fig. 9 were of the same character. A vertical middle line (" fence " or " barrier ") was seen as resting; the diamond-shaped figure moved from left to right—gliding with an uncanny sort of penetrability through the *i*-group.

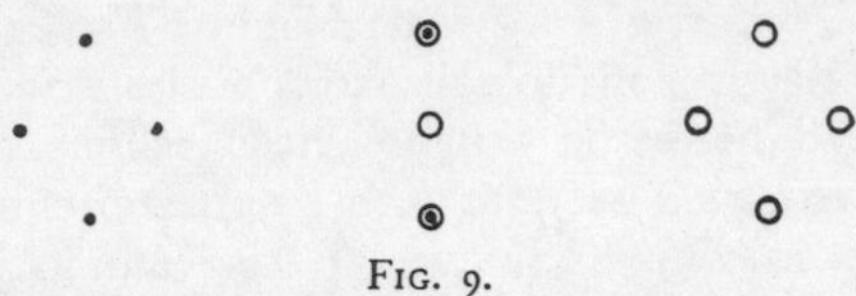

FIG. 9.

93 A comparison between the conditions of exchange and retention of identity may be gained from Figs. 10–11. The latter of these, it will be observed, has been derived from the former by raising the *i*-points above the common line. The result is that whereas

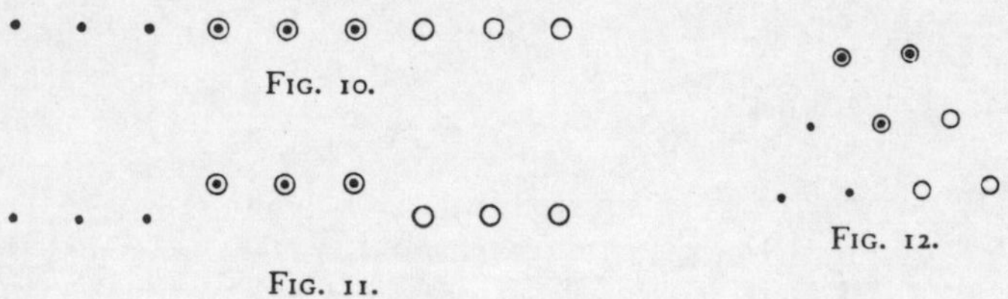

FIG. 10.

FIG. 11.

FIG. 12.

Fig. 10 exhibits exchange of identity, Fig. 11 is a clear case of
94 identity retention. Or, still another type: Fig. 12 involves both exchange (in the lower *i*-point) *and* retention (upper *i*-points) in one and the same constellation.

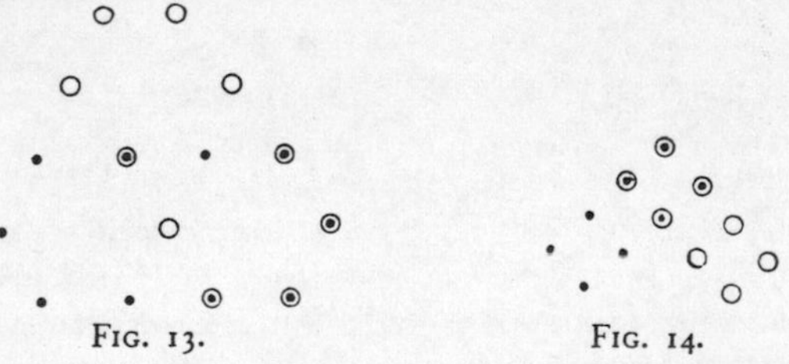

FIG. 13. FIG. 14.

3. *Ambiguous figures.*—In addition to cases of unequivocal exchange or retention of identity in the *i*-points, there are others of a more ambiguous nature. With Fig. 13, for example, the horizontal figure is seen to pivot upward—and yet one is not always sure whether the overlapping points (lower right) have retained or exchanged

their identity. Fig. 14 is also ambiguous in that one may experience either retention of identity (a constant diamond-shaped figure above) or exchange of identity (an oblique column pointing first to the left and then to the right). It is possible, by exerting oneself, to cause either of these to predominate. This is also true of Fig. 15
95 where artificial retention of identity can be achieved (despite the slight advantage enjoyed by exchange) if one makes the necessary effort.

97 *Another hypothesis.*—Let us call those points which are physically different in the two exposures "*d*-points". In describing cases of identity *retention*, then, we may say that the observer sees a moving *d*-figure and a resting *i*-figure. One experiences, that is to say, a "duo" or duality of figures one of which is in motion and the other not. With *exchange* of identity, on the other hand, the figure is experienced as a unitary whole or "unum" which moves *as* a

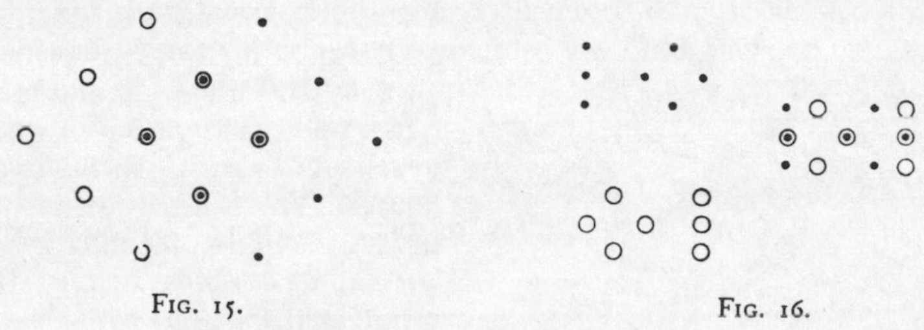

FIG. 15. FIG. 16.

whole. Nothing in this latter case is experienced which would give one the feeling of duality in the figure; phenomenally there are no *d- and i*-points.

98 To repeat: retention of identity is typical of duo-figures, whereas exchange of identity is characteristic of unum-figures. It does not follow from this, however, that no duo could ever exhibit exchange in an *i*-part. The important factor is *what* division occurs within the duo. Retention will result when the division into two figures is such that the *d*-part appears as moving, the *i*-part as at rest—i.e. such that the division corresponds to a separation into movement and rest. But the exchange phenomenon can nevertheless result in certain cases even when an obvious initial separation within the duo is given. Fig. 16, for example, appears as a duo (vertical line and diamond), but the *d-i* division does not correspond with the duo-cleavage of the figure itself (i.e. the two expositions
99 do not divide the figure into a moving part and a resting part

corresponding to the initially given line and diamond division), and the result is therefore exchange of identity by the *i*-points. Another example is that given in Fig. 17: the pair of circles moves to the right with consequent exchange of identity by the *i*-circle.

The results of our experiment show that one can see figures moving as wholes, either *one* or *two* in definite separation; but
100 the results reveal more than this. The point-constituents of our figures appear, in a most decided manner, *as parts of the whole in which they occur.* Consider once more the case of Fig. 2. One sees a moving " cross ". In describing the left-hand *i*-point one would say of Exposition I, " it is the centre or mid-point of the cross "; but, with Exposition II, this mid-point moves to the right. *Now*, in Exposition II, a description of the left-hand *i*-point states that it is the left arm of the cross. In other words the *i*-points of unum figures change their role from one exposition to the next. Phenomenal identity cannot be understood in terms of piecewise self-identity; it depends rather upon the *meaning* or role which the *i*-part has in the two figures. Phenomenal self-identity by the mid-point and by the left arm of our cross is certainly maintained, but not with reference to the same *i*-points in both cases: phenomenally the mid-point, for example, does not change even though it is represented in one exposition by one *i*-point and in the other exposition by the other *i*-point.

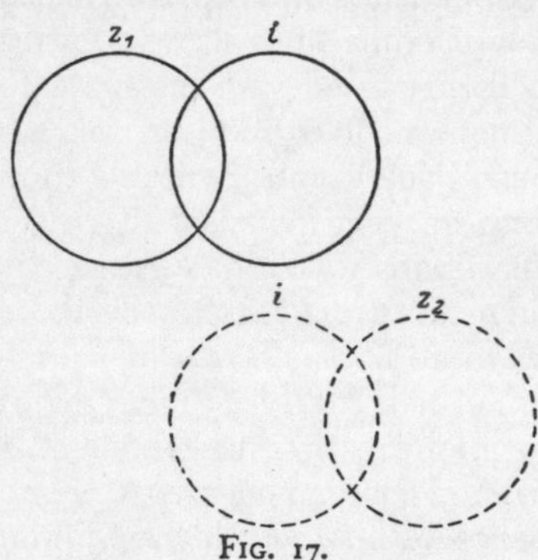

Fig. 17.

In Fig. 7, on the other hand, the *i*-points do not change their
101 role in the two expositions. They remain " Gestalt homologous " in the two exposures. And so, on the basis of these considerations, another hypothesis must be formulated: *Phenomenal identity depends upon Gestalt identity; homologous parts in two Gestalten will exhibit phenomenal identity; phenomenal identity is a characteristic not of piecewise relationships but of whole-phenomena.*

For the earlier hypothesis *exchange* of identity would have to be an " exception to the rule " whose explanation would require additional, supplementary hypotheses. Our own hypothesis, on the contrary, considers *retention* of identity to be a special case under a more general law. Retention of identity occurs, that is to say, only when there is Gestalt homology between the two exposed constellations.

102 *Special questions:* 1. *Fixation.*—If Fig. 1 (p. 86 above) is shown and the subject questioned regarding eye-movement, the customary answer is that his glance had fallen upon the middle dot and had moved from left to right with this dot when Exposition II occurred. The spontaneous fixation point in Fig. 3 is the empty middle area, and the eyes move with this area to a corresponding position for Exposition II. And this type of reply was given for all the figures. There is in each case a preferred point or area upon which the eye spontaneously fixes. Very often, however, the subject will report eye-movements when in reality there have been none at all. In order to determine whether eye-movement *necessarily* accompanies all cases of identity exchange we used the method of after-image fixation. The after-image of a small cross was projected (during successive expositions of the figures) upon a certain point on the screen. In most cases despite complete immobility of
103 the after-image (i.e. unwavering fixation), the subject nevertheless experienced exchange of identity of the kind already described.

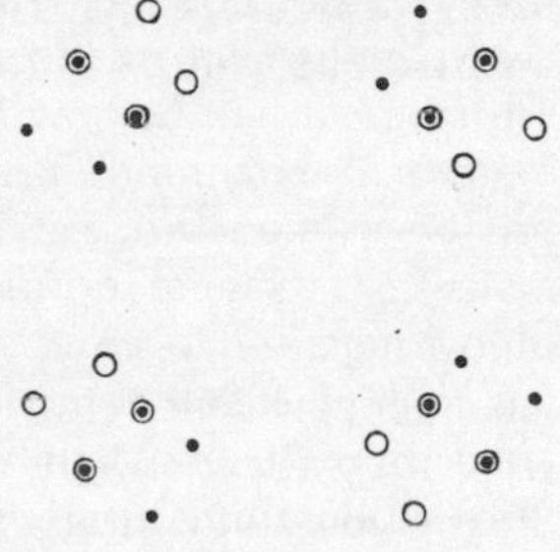

Fig. 18.

Using Fig. 1 the subjects were next given the difficult task of fixating the place at which one of the *d*-points appeared. No interruption in the usual exchange of identity occurred. With fixation upon the empty space between the two *i*-points, the end-point was seen to move " through " these from left to right and the *i*-points in this case retained their identity. This was true also when either of the
105 *i*-points itself was fixated. In general it was found that with
[106–107: omitted] successful fixation of an *i*-point, that point could usually (if not always) be made to *retain* its self-identity.

108 Two examples may be cited in this connection. When a single *i*-point in Fig. 18 was rigidly fixated, it was possible to achieve retention of identity in that point and its neighbour, but the circle itself nevertheless moved and all other *i*-points presented clear cases of identity exchange. Indeed, with successive presentations of Expositions I and II the entire figure was seen to rotate with, however, a " disturbance " at the fixated *i*-point. When Fig. 19 was used no fixation of any *i*-" point " could succeed in establishing

[109–111: omitted] retention of identity anywhere along the strip. Even the most rigid fixation was of no avail in this type of figure.

112 With fixation outside the figure (i.e. peripheral vision) *retentio* of identity was practically abolished for all cases—occasionally even for those which with direct vision would normally have exhibited retention.

113 2. *Attention.*—Our findings regarding attention are not essentially different from those already reported for fixation. Attention embraces the entire figure unless instructions to the contrary are given, and the centre of attention typically coincides with the figural centre of the presented object. Moreover, with successive expositions this centre also moves with that of the figure.

114 The most difficult task our observers were called upon to perform was to *attend* one part of the figure while *fixating* some other part. Using a figure which clearly exhibited exchange of identity, the instructions were to fixate some point other than the *i*-points while concentrating the attention upon the *i*-group. The only cases in which any measure of success was achieved were those in which the *i*-group could be apprehended as
115 an "independent figure". More often, however, even with unwavering attention, the following would occur [cf. Fig. 2]. In Exposition I attention was upon "the right side of the figure"; in Exposition II the centre of attention was "the left half of the figure". Considered from a piecewise point of view one would have to say that the centre of attention was upon the *same* place, the *same* points throughout. When viewed in terms of figural relations, however, it is apparent that this "same" place had, in the two expositions, the meaning of two different places.

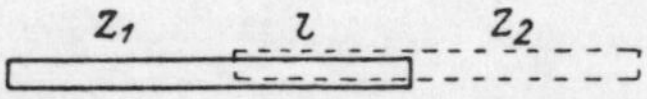

z_1 i z_2

FIG. 19.

3. *Distance and Size.*—Observation distance, objective size of the presented figures, and conditions of "surveyability" are factors of great importance. Figures in which exchange of identity in the *i*-points was not pronounced at close range usually exhibited excellent exchange phenomena when seen from a distance. And conversely, even the strongest cases of identity exchange could be made to exhibit retention of identity when the observer drew quite close to the projection screen. In this way we were able to determine approximate thresholds of exchange and retention: the observer would slowly approach the screen and report at which point the mode of appearance changed.

116 Similar tests were also made of the influence exerted by changing the size of dots and intervals. Thus reducing the figure was found to improve the chances of identity exchange while increasing its size functioned to favour retention of identity. It will be apparent from these results that any diminution of "surveyability" (close range observation, increased size) tended to obstruct exchange of identity by the *i*-points. Reducing surveyability diminished *figural* apprehension of the presented object and one then saw a number of individual points (those in direct vision being clear and sharp, those to one side being vague and hazy). With very close observation, however, it often occurred that whereas *i*-points directly in front of the observer would retain their identity those in peripheral vision would exhibit exchange. Summarizing, then: close range observation acted to favour identity retention *when* and *in so far as* it brought about a weakening of phenomenal unity within the perceived figures.

[117–121: 4. *Subjective factors*.—Illustrations are given of subjectively induced variations in typical point-figures. Example: four dots, arranged in the form of a square, *can*, with some effort, be seen as an arithmetical "times" mark, as a diamond lying on its side, etc. It is noteworthy that subjective variations of this kind are rare except when specifically requested by the experimenter. (P. 117): no subject described what he had seen in Fig. 3 as two points above, two in the middle, and two below (which would have been a correct specification of the stimulus points), but spoke instead of *the* hexagon, *the* figure. "There was a hexagon on the left, then on the right. . . ." No one thought to inquire which points were identical in the two expositions because *the hexagon itself* was identical and was seen as a moving self-identical object. (P. 118): with Fig. 15 the subjects sometimes exclaimed, "There! I suddenly saw a smaller, diamond-shaped figure in the centre." (Pp. 119–121): that subjectively induced changes of unitary constellations usually involve new identity relations is shown by various figures given in the text.]

122 5. *Subliminal influences*.—In all the foregoing presentations the shutters used in our projection lantern were so constructed that all points of Exposition I disappeared just before those of Exposition II
123 appeared. Now, however, a shutter was used which permitted the *i*-points to *remain* during both expositions. Two sets of shutters (Shutter I, the old type, and Shutter II, the new or continuous-*i*-point type) were prepared and each presented the points of Fig. 20 as here shown. The interval between exposures with Shutter II

was so small (subliminal) that no observer was aware that the *i*-points were continuous. And yet our results with the two shutters were quite different. With Shutter I there occurred a clear exchange of identity in which the oblique lines moved from lower left to upper right. With Shutter II, on the other hand, there was complete retention of identity by the middle band of points. The lower points moved through this band to their new position above. And the same was true of other point-constellations, but especially in cases where the figural conditions were not too strongly in favour of identity exchange. In cases where they were (e.g. Fig. 2), this type of "disturbance" (even when not subliminal) was incapable of preventing exchange of identity by the *i*-points.

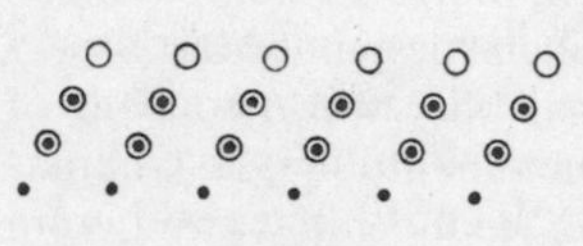

Fig. 20.

124 *Figural conditions and Transposition.*—In many of the foregoing cases the movement with which we were concerned was merely a shift of an entire figure from right to left, i.e. changes of location but not of shape. We propose now, however, to see what happens when something more than a mere shift of position is required of the figure. An example of this was given above in Fig. 13 where the movement was rotation upon an axis.

125 One consideration arising here is whether or not the required movement is in a direction already implied by the original figure of Exposition I. We saw in connection with Fig. 13, for example, that identity exchange by the *i*-points was not altogether compelling. When, however, we begin with the same original figure and introduce a movement such as that shown in Fig. 21, the exchange of identity is much clearer than in the earlier case.

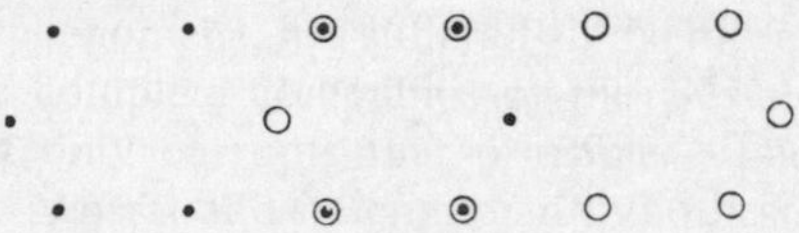

Fig. 21.

127 When figural conditions are such that the figure itself permits a relatively easy division into subsidiary *i*- and *d*-parts, identity *retention* is the most probable outcome. Fig. 22, for example, readily divides into a horizontal bar and an oblique appendage, and there is retention of identity by the *i*-parts. With Fig. 23, on the other hand, figural unity in the semicircle results in exchange of identity by the *i*-points.

But it should not be thought from our preceding examples that the exchange phenomenon is possible only when Exposition II is

(except for its position on the screen) the *same* as Exposition I. Exchange of identity can also be shown when the two expositions differ considerably in either colour, size, or other figural character-
128 istic. As an example of such figural dissimilarity let us consider Fig. 24 where Exposition II is *larger* than Exposition I. Here,

Fig. 22. Fig. 23.

as before, the entire figure shifts to the right, but in addition there is also *an expansion in size*. This shows that exchange of identity does not depend merely upon a literal reproduction in Exposition II of the figure given by Exposition I, but is possible also in the sense of a *transposition*. The left-most line of Exposition II in Fig. 24 is exactly the same line as the one next-
129 to-left in Exposition I, and yet a clear *exchange* of identity nevertheless occurs in it. Figs. 25–26 provide still other examples of this phenomenon: viz. identity exchange *and* change within the figure
130 itself (i.e. a shift to the right and an expansion in size). In all of these cases there is a change by the entire figure as a whole; it is not a piecewise process with expansion occurring at one place and some portion of the
[131–132: omitted]- original (i.e. of Exposition I) breaking off at another place. Instead the *figure* itself changes its place in one unbroken movement.

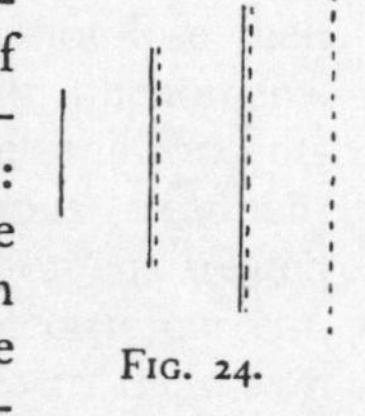

Fig. 24.

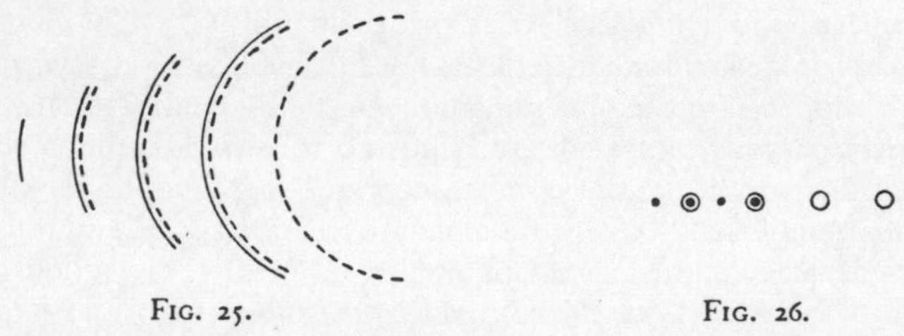

Fig. 25. Fig. 26.

133 We turn now, and in conclusion, to the results obtained with alternate colours. When, for example, the arm of a cross was red in Exposition I and blue in Exposition II, the observer nevertheless saw the *same* arm now one colour and now another. In another
134 experiment along this line the arrangement given in Fig. 1 was

used, thus: Exposition I consisted of white, light grey, and middle grey points; Exposition II was then light grey, middle grey, and dark grey. When Exposition II was shown there was a decided exchange of identity in the sense of a transposition from left to right; the *line* of points both shifted to the right *and* grew darker.

Selection 12

INDUCED MOTION

By Karl Duncker

"Über induzierte Bewegung (Ein Beitrag zur Theorie optisch wahrgenommener Bewegung),' *Psychol. Forsch.*, 1929, **12**, 180–259.

181 In normal vision objective motion can be experienced both when
a moving stimulus traverses the resting retina and when the eye
182 itself follows the stimulus. There is, however, a type of perceived
[183–185: motion quite different from all others, and this is the so-called
omitted] " induced motion ". When, for example, one is sitting in a railway
186 coach and a nearby train moves, it seems for a time as if one's own
train were moving in the opposite direction. This is a case of
187 induced motion.

The standard experiment.—A beam of sunlight reflected by a
small stationary mirror (2 cm. in diameter) was thrown upon a
piece of cardboard (66 × 48 cm.). Observation distance 1 m.
When the cardboard was moved back and forth, the fixated spot
188 of light appeared to move also but in the opposite direction.
If the light point itself is occasionally set in motion also (either
with or against that of the cardboard), it is impossible to tell at
any given moment whether the point *is* objectively moving or not.
It is only when two light points are used—one objectively moving
and the other at rest—that the difference can be detected.

The principle of phenomenal frame of reference.—These results
cannot be reversed, for moving the light point alone does not pro-
189 duce an induced motion in the cardboard. The reason is, of course,
that whereas in the standard experiment there was a small object
embedded in a larger, wholly moving surface, in this case the same
small object would have to induce its entire environment to move.
The *point* exists in both cases wholly with reference to its
surrounding framework (the cardboard), and is both spontaneously
and primarily " located " or oriented relative thereto. The cardboard is the natural *place* and primary frame of reference for the
point—not the reverse. Moreover, the unmoving room in which
the experiment takes place has a very different meaning for the

Grateful acknowledgment is hereby made to *Julius Springer*, *Verlagsbuchhandlung*, Berlin, for permission to reproduce the illustrations used in this Selection.

point from what it has for the cardboard. The point has only an indirect or mediated relation with the room-environment, for between them stands the cardboard. The cardboard itself, on the other hand, has an immediate connection with the remaining environmental features of the room, and *it* is "located" relative to the room just as the point is relative to the cardboard. To bring
[190–191: omitted] about an induced motion in the cardboard one would have to move its environmental background (the room).

192 If the cardboard is moved back and forth rapidly and in quick succession, the point itself will often come to a standstill. This is because the point loses, so to speak, its phenomenal relation to the cardboard as its sole background. The point is no longer able to maintain its "foothold" within the cardboard-environment and suddenly the observer sees that the point, ceasing its motion, has become a resting, "anchored" object in the unmoving environment of the room—an environment which formerly existed for the point only secondarily. In a word, when the immediate frame of reference fails, there occurs a spontaneous shift bringing the point into direct contact with the room environment where it becomes anchored.

193 *Pendulum experiment.*—A cardboard (66 × 48 cm.) with a 3 cm. black border was suspended by two strings 70 cm. long in front of a fairly homogeneous wall of the room. In the centre and directly in front of the cardboard hung a small round plummet. Observation distance 2·5–3 m.

When the cardboard was swung to and fro and the plummet (or, better, the point from which it was suspended) was fixated, an induced motion of the plumb-bob was seen. The induced pendular motion of the bob was, however, somewhat paradoxical, for it was the reverse of ordinary pendular motion (in which, of course, the bob *descends* from the sides towards the middle). The result
194 was that the string of our pendulum seemed to be alternately expanding and contracting as the bob appeared to move this way and that. If the two were moved objectively in the same direction although at a somewhat different frequency, it was possible to achieve a relationship of these motions such that the objective and induced motions of the plummet would cancel each other, so to speak, and it would then be seen for a moment as practically
195 at rest. When objective motion of the bob was given an amplitude (8 cm.) much smaller than that of the cardboard and both were moved in the same direction, objective motion in the pendulum was over-compensated for and the observed motion of the bob was

reversed. This finding is especially important because it shows that induced motion is commensurable with objective motion.

196 In these experiments no noticeable influence was exerted by the induced motion of the plummet upon the experienced motion of the cardboard. Objectively the lateral relative displacement between the cardboard and plummet is merely the length of swing made by the former. Phenomenally, however, it is considerably greater (nearly double), for *it* consists in the combined motions of the two (cardboard to the right, plumb-bob to the left, etc.). This apparent discrepancy between phenomenal and objective displacement may at first seem paradoxical. The " paradox " disappears, however, with more careful consideration of the situation.

The lateral displacements right and left between cardboard and plummet are not the only relevant displacements in this experimental set-up. There is also a relationship of displacement between the cardboard and the room-environment, and another between the cardboard and the person of the observer. The plummet secures its phenomenal motion only from the cardboard; the phenomenal
197 motion of the latter, on the contrary, depends upon its relation to the room-environment and to the egocentric system of the observer. In other words the cardboard obtains its phenomenal motion precisely because of those systems of relationships which would destroy motion in the plummet (cf. above *Frame of reference*).

Briefly: cardboard and plummet are moving in two different systems (there prevails, that is to say, a " separation of systems ") and hence to this extent there is, theoretically, no paradox. Why should the sum of *two* phenomenal motions (resulting from change of position in different systems) be the same as the phenomenal motion in *one* of these systems? The former resulted from changes taking place in two separate systems, i.e. in two sets of distance relationships; the latter is due to but one such set of distance relationships. The visual space in which these separate systems are seen is itself not divided into two because the plummet shares directly the fate of the cardboard. That is to say, its place within the cardboard changes with each change of place by the cardboard.

But the situation is less complex if we eliminate the influence exerted by the room-environment and by the ego-system of the observer. The following section reports experiments in which these were both ruled out.

198 *Dark room experiments; slow motion.*—By conducting the experiment in darkness we are able to eliminate the influence of

room-environment just discussed. The subjective or egocentric system can be eliminated if the objective motion is so slow as to be subliminal. In this case any phenomenal motion appearing in the objectively unmoved (i.e. " induced ") object must result entirely from their mutual relationship.

199 The set-up was as follows. In a dark room two projection lanterns cast spots of light upon mirrors which in turn reflected the light from behind upon a screen. On the other side of this screen and at a distance of 2 m. sat the observer. The light points were 2·4 cm. in diameter and their distance was at no time less than 5 cm. One was held steady and the other moved horizontally at the rate of 3·8 cm. per second.[1] The duration of each observation period was 8 sec. and the distance traversed by the moving light was therefore approximately 30 cm.

200 It was found (1) that in this case the total phenomenal motion of both objects equalled their phenomenal displacement; (2) that four of the six observers saw the *fixated* point as moving regardless of whether this point was the objectively moving one or not.[2] (For the other two observers the motion of both points was more
201 symmetrical.) (3) That when no fixation instructions were given, the experienced motion was usually symmetrical.

When light squares of different sizes (dimensions 20 cm. sq. and 2·2 cm. sq.) were used the results were not essentially different from those obtained before: the fixated light, whether it was the larger or the smaller, moved more than the other regardless of which was in objective motion. Applying this result to the discussion of
202 irreversibility in the standard case (p. 189) we can see that mere difference in size cannot have been responsible for the phenomena observed there. To test our earlier hypothesis regarding the role of " localization " the following experiment was carried out.

One of the objects was a point (diameter 1 cm. in Series I, 2 cm. in Series II) and the other a contour rectangle (18 × 14·5 cm. in Series I, 36 × 39 cm. in Series II). The point was inside the rectangle. The speed of objective motion (whether of the point or of the rectangle) was always the same. In all cases the unmoving object was the one fixated. There were ten observers.

In *all* cases of both Series the strongest movement was that observed in the point, *not* in the rectangle. Ordinarily (e.g. with two points) it is the *fixated* object which is seen to move; here

[1] In this case a just liminal motion was used. Naturally, however, the subjects were not informed whether the left or right hand light was in motion objectively.

[2] Eye-movements were reported even when the stationary point had been fixated.

the fixated rectangle never moved. It is clear that the influence exerted by fixation in our earlier cases is not sufficient to overcome
203 the figural factor of enclosure. The issue now is, not which object is *fixated*, but which one is *enclosed* by the other. Thus we have encountered two determinants of perceived motion: (1) Other
204 things being equal, there is a greater tendency for motion to appear in the *fixated* object than in the non-fixated one; (2) the same as regards the enclosed rather than the enclosing object. Stated in general terms we may say that when an object shifts relative to its frame of reference, phenomenal motion of that object occurs.

206 Now arises the question of relationship between the observer and these moving objects. Are the motions of the observed objects independent of the observer's status as phenomenally at rest or in motion? To answer this question we performed the following experiment.

The former observation distance of 2 m. was shortened to from 100–30 cm. and the exposed objects were those of Series II above. Here the point or dot was always at rest, objectively, while the rectangle was given objective motion. When the subject now fixated the point he experienced the feeling of being moved with it to and fro. In some cases this was so strong as to cause dizziness.
207 The subject had himself become a part of the induced motion system and was (phenomenally) "carried along with it". When, however, something of the room-environment was visible, the subject usually did not have this experience, for now his own phenomenal status of rest was too stable, and in this case only the rectangle was seen to move.

208 *Normal illumination; rotating fields.*—We turn now to a study of induced motion in daylight but with the inducing motion occurring in one direction only. Two concentric disks were attached to a common axle in such a way that the one in front could be revolved *upon* the axle while that in back was attached to and revolved *with* the axle. By using two motors it was thus possible to revolve the disks independently of one another. The disks were grey with 32 black (equidistant) radii; only the outer rim of the rear disk was visible. The forward or smaller disk we shall designate as the "inner" or "enclosed" field, the larger, rear one as the "outer" or "enclosing" field. One metre behind these disks was a homogeneously greyish wall. Observation distance 30 cm.

209 In the first experiment disks of 16 cm. radius (rear) and 2 cm. radius (forward) were used. The outer disk was revolved in a

clockwise direction (4° per sec.), the inner field (i.e. the forward or smaller disk) was held stationary.[1] Fixation was upon the inner field; the exposition lasted 3 sec.[2]

211 Phenomenally both disks were seen to move (in opposite directions).[3] In order to measure the amount of induced motion the inner disk was revolved (also clockwise) at different rates until the point was found for each of six observers at which this disk was no longer seen to move. (Dimensions in this case: inner disk 10 cm. radius, outer disk 16 cm. radius.) This was observed monocularly through a circular hole in a screen and with tachistoscopic presentations ($\frac{2}{3}$ sec.) of the revolving disks. Results: with a speed of 8° 44′ per sec. in the larger disk the average speed required in the smaller one in order to compensate for its induced motion was 5° 36′ per sec.

[212–215: see footnotes to p. 209.]

216 The phenomenon of induced motion in the smaller disk was diminished or cancelled (1) by moving this disk objectively in the same direction as the other; (2) by increasing the speed of the larger disk; (3) by increasing the exposure time. These effects may all be explained in the same way. All are due to an increased conflict with the observer's own phenomenal status of motion or rest. If, with a constant exposure time, one increases the speed of the inducing motion, then there arises a steadily increasing discrepancy between the objective and experienced location of the radii of the small disk. Since this is seen in induced motion, the positions of its radii change continuously in experience while objectively they remain unaltered. One can express this somewhat picturesquely by saying: the inner disk incurs a steadily increasing "debt of location or direction". The same argument applies to the other changes mentioned.

The radial markings upon the disks constitute the only points of contact between them. If any change of condition is introduced

[1] [212–214]: At speeds above 5° per sec. the induced motion, although greater, became less intense. At a speed of 15° and more the induced motion seems no longer able "to keep up with itself".

[2] [214–215]: With increased observation time (e.g. 4 or 5 sec.) induced motion in the inner field is considerably lessened.

[3] [209–210]: That the phenomenon of induced motion is not due to eye-movement may be seen in the following way. (1) With very small inner fields (1½ cm. radius) the *entire* disk can be seen all at once. This means that its upper portion is seen as moving to the left, its lower portion as moving towards the right, its left-hand side as moving downward, and its right-hand side as moving upward. Since the four opposed motions are simultaneous it is difficult to believe that they are due to separate eye-movements. (2) Intentional, wandering movements of the eyes do not disturb the perceived induced motion.

which reduces the clarity of this contact, the induced motion is jeopardized accordingly. With a speed of 20° per sec., for example, the larger disk begins to fuse into a relatively homogeneous background and its former relationship to the inner field (as
217 frame of reference for this latter) is changed. This was found to apply also as regards fixation. If the eyes are permitted to move freely in such a way that the two disks are seen peripherally and unclearly, the distance relationship between them is less clear and the induced motion consequently diminished.

[218–223: omitted. Pp. 218–219 report a study of figure-ground and of inner-outer (i.e. enclosed-enclosing) relationships. The following arrangements were used: figure enclosed, ground enclosing; ground enclosed, figure enclosing. It was found that the *figure* exhibited better induced motion than the ground and that the best motion of all was that occurring when the *figure* was *enclosed*.]

224 *Dark room experiments; stroboscopic motion.*—In this experiment the *inducing* motion arises from alternate presentations of an outline or contour rectangle similar to the cardboard used in the standard experiment. In a darkened room two dimly lighted rectangular figures were alternately exposed upon a screen by two projection lanterns. Each exposure thus constituted a complete picture consisting of an inducing part (the rectangle) and an induced part (the dot) as will be seen in
225 Fig. 1. Each rectangle was 100 × 86 cm. with contour lines 3·5 cm. wide; the dots (4 × 6 cm.) were at a position 16 cm. inward from the right end of one rectangle and the same distance inward from the left end of the other rectangle. The projection frames were so arranged that the *dots* appeared at the same spot on the screen with each exposure.[1] The dot was fixated.

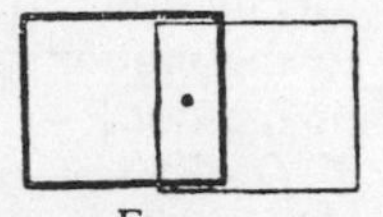

FIG. 1.

With alternate exposures of the two pictures the rectangle was seen to move (stroboscopically) back and forth, but in addition
[226–227: omitted] to this the dot also moved: forth and back. The result was thus essentially the same as that of the standard experiment.

228 In order to test the effect of giving the dot also a certain (opposed) stroboscopic component we shifted the projection frames so that the dots no longer overlapped objectively. The problem in this case was to see if the induced motion of the dot could be so compensated for that it would be *seen* as stationary. This condition was found almost impossible to produce. With a distance of

[1] Optimal exposition time approximately $\frac{1}{2}$ sec. duration for each picture. Observation was from a position about 4 m. in front and 1 m. to the left of the screen.

4 or 8 cm. between the screen-points upon which the dot(s) appeared, no interruption whatever of its induced motion (in the opposite direction) could be detected.[1] In general an increased interval between the screen-points was not accompanied by a decrease in the induced motion; instead there occurred a break or "separation of systems" in the following sense. The dot moved first in the opposite (induced) direction, and *then* in the same direction as the rectangle(s)—i.e. in the latter case in accordance with the requirements of its alternate positions (upon the screen) relative to the observer himself.

[229–238: further variations of the rectangle and results for the induced motion are reported (e.g. removal of all or part of the side farthest from the dot, use of lines drawn from the dot to the four corners of the rectangle); variations of exposure time and of observation distance are also reported (e.g. induced motion in the dot disappeared at 1·5–1 m. observation distance). A slight objective motion of the dot in the induced direction greatly strengthened this motion; the addition of a vertical (stroboscopic) component to the motion of the rectangle also strengthened induced motion in the dot.]

239 *Dark room experiments; translatory rotation.*—When we see a rolling wheel we usually see not only the motion of its peripheral points around the hub but also the forward motion of the wheel itself. We do not see cycloids such as result physically from this combination of rotary and translatory motions; instead the cycloidal motion is resolved phenomenally into rotary and trans-
240 latory motions. This is another instance of separation between two systems such as we have already mentioned: the periphery constitutes one system with its point of reference (the hub); the hub and wheel as a whole constitute another system whose frame of reference is the surrounding terrain and the observer. We propose here to study this phenomenon.

Upon a wheel of 10 cm. radius (which could be made to roll along a track), two dim lamps were attached—one at the hub and the other 5 cm. from this centre. The path of these lights is indicated in Fig. 2. When seen, the peripheral light (solid line) rushes *ahead* of the hub light from *a* to *b* and lags *behind* from *b* to *c*. The track was long enough to permit five revolutions of the wheel in each direction. Observation distance was 3 m.

[1] It is in general astonishing with what tenacity a good mode of apprehension will persist despite increasing obstacles. Induced motion was usually seen in the dot even when the initial interval between screen-points was 40 cm.

241 The observers were ignorant of the nature of the set-up. Fixation was upon the peripheral point.

With a speed whereby the hub moved 4·5 cm. per sec., and with only the peripheral light illuminated, some observers saw no motion at all, some saw a wave-motion similar to that indicated by the solid line in Fig. 2. When the hub light was added all that approximately half the observers saw was the peripheral light describing a circle around the hub light; the *other* half saw the same circular motion of the peripheral point around the hub light
242 combined with a translatory motion of both points.[1] When the motions are seen as an ordinary *wheel* this means that an induced motion is involved in the following manner. With a translatory motion towards the right the hub point (which—Fig. 2 *b-c*—is rushing ahead of the peripheral point) *induces* an opposite motion (*towards the left*) in the peripheral point. This brings about the phenomenally experienced circular motion of the peripheral point.

Fig. 2.

With a speed of 20 cm. per sec. all observers saw the peripheral point (when alone) describing "bridge spans" very like the physical, objective path. When, however, the hub light was added[2] there occurred (as previously, p. 241) a splitting up of the motion, and this was found to assume various forms: (1) the peripheral light circled around the hub light; (2) it described loops;
243 (3) both lights appeared to revolve around an imaginary point midway between the two. Common to all these modes of appearance, however, was the periodic induced backward motion of the kind already discussed.

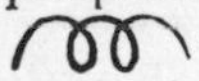

When the *hub* point was fixated the induced backward motion of this point was much more striking than before. With no par-
244 ticular fixation (e.g. roving eye-movements) neither light seemed to be the point of reference for the other; instead their motion was more like that of a tumbling stick with lights at each end.

245 *Theoretical considerations.*—Let us suppose that one or both of two visible objects, *a* and *b*, move objectively along a straight line in the frontal parallel plane in such a way that the distance between them changes. This would be the case if *a* remained fixed and *b*

[1] This shows that the separation of a translatory component from the rotary one is possible even when no more than one peripheral point and the central point (i.e. two points in all) are given.

[2] Fixation point is still the peripheral light.

alone moved, or vice versa; or if *a* and *b* moved apart by similar or different amounts; or, finally, if *a* and *b* moved in the same direction but at different velocities. In all such cases the interval between them will be altered by their movement. Suppose further that nothing but these two objects is seen and that neither object has any appreciable motion relative to the observer himself (i.e. the motion of either alone would be subliminal).

246 Under these circumstances the phenomenal motion of *a* and *b* will be such that

$$A \text{ (phen.)} + B \text{ (phen.)} = \Delta R_{ab} \text{ (phen.)}$$

That is to say, the sum of the phenomenal distances through which *a* and *b* are seen to move is equal to their phenomenal displacement. Hence the *total* phenomenal distance traversed by *a* and *b* is unequivocally co-ordinated with their objective displacement. The *individual* phenomenal motions, on the other hand, are not unequivocally co-ordinated with the objective motions of the individual objects *a* and *b*. In other words although ΔR_{ab} (phen.) conforms with ΔR_{ab} (obj.), this is not true of A (phen.) and A (obj.), nor of B (phen.) and B (obj.), and the ratio A (phen.) : B (phen.) is independent of the ratio A (obj.) : B (obj.). From these considerations and in the light of our foregoing findings the following " Law of Motion Distribution " may be formulated :—

The phenomenal motions of separating objects is determined by the kind and degree of mutual " localization " of these objects, and this whether one of them is localized relative to the other or both are localized with regard to each other respectively.[1] In other words: phenomenal motion is displacement in a natural frame of reference.

249 Still retaining the condition that in the presented objects (*a* and *b*) there shall be no appreciable motion relative to the observer, let us now inquire what takes place when a third object, *c*, is introduced. Here phenomenal motion in *a* and *b* is no longer determined

[1] Localization here means something quite different from the ordinary theory according to which each stimulating point (in space, upon the retina) has its own place-value. We are referring instead to the concrete figural properties of perceived constellations in the sense that *localization* depends upon such properties. It is these properties which determine whether (and how) one object (or part) is localized relative to another. A waiting room is localized relative to the railway station, a button relative to its coat, a blot relative to its piece of paper—not the reverse. These examples signify that localization is not directed by purely spatial conditions; rather it appears as a special case of the more general one: one datum finding its place under the influence of another datum [p. 247].

merely by the relations of *a* and *b* alone but usually by the relations obtaining between *a*, *b*, and *c*. Three possibilities should be considered :—

(1) *c* has no influence upon the phenomenal motions of *a* and *b*. This would be true, for example, if *c* were so remote from or for any other reason so completely out of touch with *a* or *b* as to play no phenomenal part in the *a-b* relationship. It would also be true if the interval between *a* and *c* or between *b* and *c* were constant so that either *a* or *b* might readily compose with *c* a single unit (*ac*) or (*bc*). The entire relationship would thus be either [(*ac*) and *b*] or [*a* and (*bc*)].

250 (2) *c* may be so closely related to *a* and *b* respectively that the previous phenomenal relationship between *a* and *b* disappears. This would be the case, for example, if *c* enclosed *a* and *b* in such a way that each was primarily "*c*-related".

251 (3) *c* influences the phenomenal motion of *b* but that of *a*
is determined by *b* as before. This is the case in a hierarchy where,
for example, *a* is enclosed by *b* and *b* is enclosed by *c*.[1] It is in such
instances as this that there can occur the separation of systems about
which we have already spoken. The *ab* system, which is for *a*
the system of first or *primary* reference, separates itself from
253 the *bc* system to which *a* enjoys but *secondary* reference. The prerequisite of such separation is that the two systems shall be as
strongly differentiated as possible, i.e. that the *ab* system shall be
maximally self-enclosed relative to *bc*.

We have up until now considered only those cases where there
was no appreciable motion of the objects *a* and *b* relative to the
observer. In practice, however, such cases are comparatively
rare. Actually the observer plays the part of an additional object
254 such as the object *c*. Thus, for example, where it was said that
c had no influence upon the phenomenal motions of *a* and *b*, we
could now say that *o* (the observer) will also have no influence
upon *a* and *b* when the objective motions are subliminal, or when
o concentrates his fixation so steadily upon the induced motion
of *a* that he is "carried along" by *a*. Or, the analogy may be drawn
for the case where *o* does influence the phenomenal motions of
a and *b*. This occurs, for example, when the observation distance
255 is too short. Finally, the influence exerted by *o* may bear chiefly

[1] This was illustrated above in the case where an object, *a*, was presented upon a cardboard background, *b*, in a room, *c*. The sum of the opposite distances traversed by *a* and *b* is greater than the separation between *a* and *b*. That is to say, *A* (phen.) + *B* (phen.) is not equal to *R* (phen.), and this is the source of the "paradox" discussed above (p. 196 f.).

on *b* while *a* continues, as before, to be determined by *b* alone. Here the situation is the same as that discussed above, pp. 251 f. (viz. case 3). In the hierarchy *a-b-o*, the *ab* system is subordinate to the *bo* system. In order for *a* to be free from the influence of *o* it is necessary that egocentric (i.e. " *o* ") *localization* of *a* shall be [256–257: omitted] prevented. This can be achieved, for example, by indirect vision, eye-movements, etc.

258 It would, of course, carry us too far afield to examine all the problems of perceived motion in terms of the foregoing experiments, but the treatment of one of these on the basis of our results may be suggested. Resting objects are usually seen at rest even when our eyes are moving and the images of the objects therefore move across the retina. The explanation of this can be derived from our findings in the following way. The point of regard moves among the objects of vision and is thus surrounded by them: it is itself a system embedded in a larger, enclosing system; its localization is acquired from these objects which thus act as its frame of reference. It is for this reason that the objects do not appear to move to the left when one's glance (moving towards the right) passes across them. The " things " upon which one's regard is directed supply for visual space the determinative system of reference into which the moving glance enters.

SELECTION 13

GAMMA MOVEMENT

By E. LINDEMANN

"Experimentelle Untersuchungen über das Entstehen und Vergehen von Gestalten," *Psychol. Forsch.*, 1922, **2**, 5–60.

6 It was not by chance that Gestalt theory had its origin in a study
of movement phenomena. As an example of the numerous problems
in this field we shall report an investigation (carried out as a continuation of the studies by Koffka and Kenkel) of how Gestalten
arise and disappear and in what manner these phenomena are
related to those of perceived movement. More specifically we
shall study the occurrence of movement when but a single object is
exposed for a brief interval of time. Kenkel has called this γ-
movement. The present author was at the start ignorant of what
7 his inquiry might produce and could not himself have predicted
the theoretical relationships he might later discover among his
results. The findings may at first, therefore, appear to the reader
[8–10: omitted] quite unrelated until he has reached the theoretical discussion with
which the report closes.

11 *Apparatus and procedure.*—The stimulus objects used in this experiment were figures cut in sheets of black cardboard with tissue paper covering the opening and illuminated from behind. Both surface and outline figures were used; the contour lines in the latter case were ½ mm. wide. Figures of the following sizes were used: circle 2½ cm. radius, ellipse 6 and 3 cm. axes, equilateral triangle 4 cm. sides. The cards were placed 60 cm. from the opening of a telescope (magnification 3 diameters) whose reception of light from the figure could be interrupted by the opaque rim of a Schumann tachistoscope. An opening or slit in this rim exposed the figure for an interval of time whose duration depended upon the speed of the wheel and the size of the slit. At no time was this opening less than 5° so that the entire figure could always be seen during the exposition period.

12 The figure could be presented as a single exposure or in a succession of exposures according to experimental procedure.

Grateful acknowledgment is hereby made to *Julius Springer*, *Verlagsbuchhandlung*, Berlin, for permission to reproduce the illustrations used in this SELECTION.

Only one of our five subjects reported any experience of movement in the figures when intervals of 30 secs. elapsed between presentations; all reported movement when but 1 sec. intervals were introduced. With the longer pause the subject's first experience was usually of a figure "bursting" upon him and then "vanishing". When the 1 sec. pause was used the subject reported that after 10–15 appearances of the figure (e.g. a circle: radius 2 cm.) it could be seen to expand and contract; fleeting shadows across the circle were also experienced.

13 *Objective determinants.*—The γ-phenomenon will make its appearance at exposure durations as long as 220 and 111σ according to intensity differences in the illumination, but it is more pronounced and its amplitude is greater when exposures of 70 and 35σ are used. With durations of 30–20σ it usually disappears entirely. The phenomenon is quite different when contour and surface figures are used. Let us first consider the former of these.

With contour designs (circle) the outline rapidly expands and
14 contracts; even with a long exposure time the first impetus towards expansion can be seen. The excursions are increased as the exposure is shortened: several subjects compared them to the movements of a rubber band. If a very short exposure is given, the expanding-contracting motion diminishes and a rapid rotation of the outline can be observed. Turning now to surface figures we find movement not only in the outer boundary but inside the circle as well. Sometimes one or other of these will predominate; again they will be co-ordinated as a unified γ-phenomenon of
15 the entire figure. At other times the internal motion would take the form of a shadow. At exposures of 130–60σ this shadow appeared as a faint elliptical movement in the horizontal direction.[1] Its form did not depend at this exposure time upon the shape of the stimulus object. With shorter exposures, however, the shadow accommodated itself more and more to the circular contour.

16 As regards the influence of light intensity it was found that an increase in this had to be offset by a reduction of the exposure time if optimal γ-movement was to be retained; and in general it can be said of the figures which we used (circle, triangle, ellipse)
[17–18: omitted] that the tendency to movement at every exposure time could be strengthened by lowering the intensity at which the figure was
19 illuminated. This rule does not hold, however, for every shape

[1] Varying the angle at which the tachistoscope slit exposed the figure did n alter this horizontal effect.

of figure. The circle, triangle, and ellipse are quite different geometrically, but psychologically they are all alike in being simple, closed figures of considerable coherence. With irregularly shaped figures (such, for example, as the outline of an inkblot), we found the γ-movement to be stronger and more extensive when greater rather than less intensity of illumination was used. These results
20 show that intensity plays a crucial role in the Gestalt process itself and hence that its influence depends upon the kind of shape under investigation.

[21–25: the amount of expansion and contraction in a circle of 2 cm. radius (outline figure) was found to be approximately 2·5 mm. in the vertical and somewhat more than 3 mm. in the horizontal direction. The contour movements of a surface figure this size did not exceed 1·5 mm. (P. 23): if γ-movement is present, a figure looks smaller when it first appears than the same figure does when seen at rest. During the expansion stage it attains or even exceeds its resting size. In the contraction phase it once more becomes noticeably smaller. (P. 25): objectively small figures exhibited less γ-movement than larger ones and this improvement continued with increase of size as long as a survey of the whole figure was possible. If this extreme was exceeded, the movement was no longer unified; it became an unsystematic aggregate of movements by various relatively independent parts.]

26 *Distribution of movement.*—Not every part of a figure exhibits an equal amount of γ-movement, for horizontal movement is considerably greater than that in the vertical direction. This was true of the circle and was especially marked in ellipses turned so that the long axis was horizontal. An equilateral triangle, if presented with the base line horizontal, was seen to expand upward and outward and then return; if presented obliquely, all three sides moved away from and towards the centre. A square, if resting on one side, exhibited strong horizontal movement in the upright sides, some in the upper part
27 and almost none in the base line. When a cube drawn in perspective was seen as a three dimensional figure, movement of the various surfaces was observed to proceed from a central point in all three directions; if seen as an irregular hexagon, the movement (stronger than before) was restricted to a single plane and was uniform in all directions. A solitary line exhibited but little movement unless the subject saw it as a long, narrow rectangle, in which case the movement was considerably strengthened. An irregular group of dots displayed very little movement, but if certain of

them together were seen to form, say, a square or triangle, there was a movement of this figure in which the dots tended to pull away from and strive towards each other.

With designs such as those shown in Figs. 1–2, the point *A*
28 remained almost at rest while the base line made wide excursions; in Fig. 2 the base angles spread and narrowed very strongly. The normal movement of a vertical ellipse is indicated by the arrows in Fig. 3.

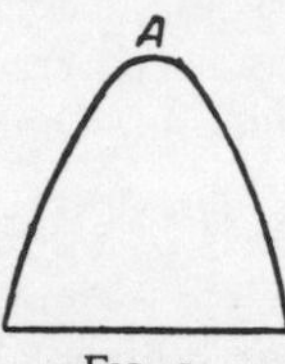

FIG. 1.

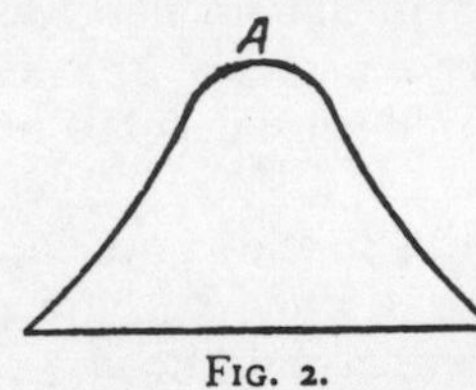

FIG. 2.

The strongest movement here was in the horizontal direction. If a small piece is removed from the centre of both sides, a strong movement towards re-closing the figure will result. If a much larger section is taken out (Fig. 4), the two parts act independently and in the direction of flying still farther apart. Similar results can also be observed with triangles. The movement in Fig. 5 is toward closure whereas that in Fig. 6 proceeds from a quite different centre of gravity and has the effect of further disrupting "triangularity". If but a small piece is missing from each side of a triangle, most subjects do not notice these gaps at all.

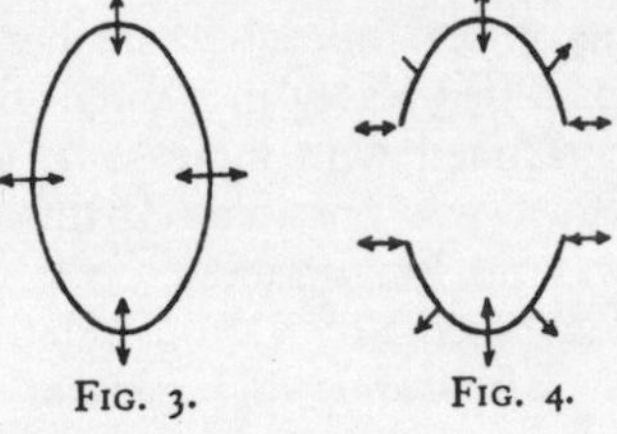

FIG. 3. FIG. 4.

Subjective factors.—The γ-phenomenon disappeared entirely or became very weak if a real object
29 (e.g. a lemon) was exposed in the
30 place of our geometric figures. It returned if the subject succeeded in seeing the object as a mere two-dimensional shape. Con-
31 versely, if (as was the case with two visiting subjects) the drawings already studied were seen as "thing-like" in character, they too would fail to exhibit γ-movement. "Things" are rigid and unmoving by nature. The two subjects who failed where all the others succeeded in seeing this movement were doubtlessly apprehending the drawings as "things". They were "set" by a very natural predisposition to

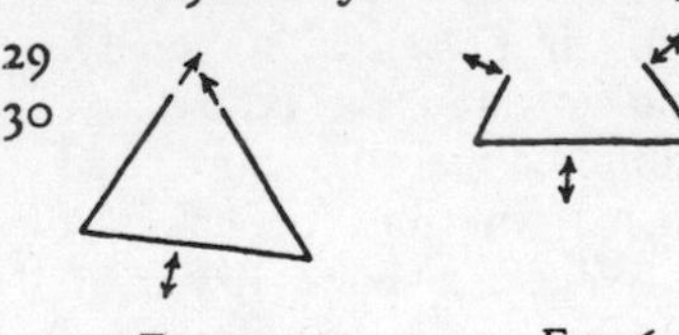

FIG. 5. FIG. 6.

see rigid objects. This accounts also for the fact that the objects of everyday experience do not exhibit γ-movement. It would be much more difficult to live in a world where each rapid movement
33 of the eyes brought about a γ-movement in the objects seen. That the phenomenon is not, however, a purely laboratory artifact can be gathered from the common experience of expanding movement which comes when a room in which we stand is suddenly illuminated. Both the light itself and other objects exhibit a strong tendency to expand. Another factor which tended to reduce the phenomenon, even with practiced subjects and favourable conditions, was fatigue.

34 The general instructions in all the foregoing observations were to fixate the centre of the figure and attend all of it. If, however, the subject is asked to pay particular attention to some part of the figure, at once the movement in this part is improved. Thus even

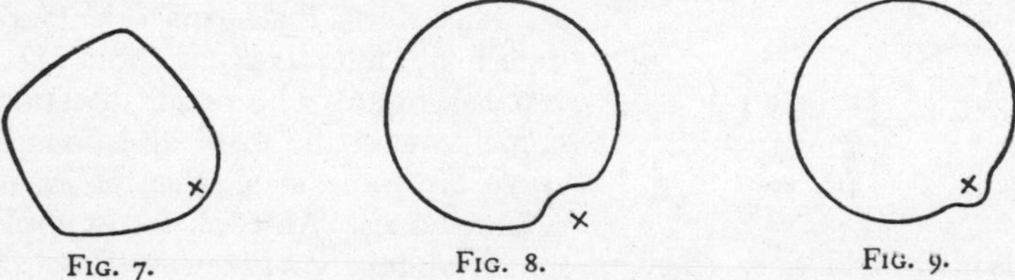

Fig. 7. Fig. 8. Fig. 9.

the horizontal base-line of a triangle would exhibit movement if attention was directed towards it. A very different result came,
35 however, with changes of fixation. If a fixation point was marked in the figure, movement in the vicinity of this point was weaker than it would normally have been, while that in other parts of the figure became stronger. Fig. 7 illustrates the kind of deformations which this method sometimes brought about. That part of the periphery adjacent to the fixation point seems in this case to remain fixed; in Fig. 8 the effect of locating the point outside the circle is shown.

36 If the small cross was alternately presented alone and with the circle, its position relative to the latter varied considerably even though objectively it lay just inside the circle. When seen alone it appeared to occupy a place definitely outside the circle; when the circle was presented also, there was a disproportionately wide excursion of the contour at this point—" as if it wanted to ensnare the cross " (cf. Fig. 9). One is reminded of the remark by Fuchs [1]

[1] Compare, e.g., p. 116 of *Selection 28*.

that "Errors of localization are in the direction of the area upon which maximum attention is focused. Normally this means towards the point of fixation because the centre of attention is usually at this point." When the small cross alone was seen, it naturally was the centre of the perceptual field. When both are seen, the *circle* is, relative to the centre as given by the cross, *off-centre*. The fixation point shifts towards the circle because it is now this figure which occupies the centre of attention.

38 *Gestalt factors.*—In studying the dependence of the γ-phenomenon upon exposure time we found that γ-movement influenced the manner in which our figures were perceived. A simple figure was not disrupted even when the shortest possible exposures were made. If a special exposure technique was used and different parts of a figure (e.g. the two halves of a circle) were presented for slightly different lengths of time, the figures would either break apart or transmogrify into some other figure. It was also discovered that spatial orientation determines figural organization. That is to say, figures whose main directions coincide with the main directions of space are more stable than obliquely oriented ones. An oval, for example,
39 is deformed only when presented obliquely. Likewise if a circle contains a horizontal diameter it is much more stable than if this line is in an oblique position. Good figures, when presented under unfavourable circumstances, displayed disruption far more often than they did deformation.[1] If the two halves of a circle were slightly different, either uniform movement would be seen, or (if the difference was too great) a disruption into two independent halves would occur.

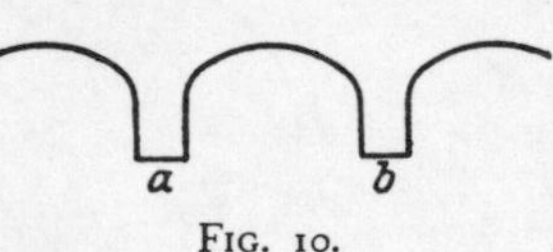

Fig. 10.

Much more important, however, than these influences of movement upon the perception of forms are the numerous cases where the distribution of movement is influenced by the form or structure of the exposed figure. Thus, as we have seen, a triangle resting upon one side displays an upward movement, whereas if it rests on one corner the movement is in all directions. Another example
40 may be seen in Fig. 10 (taken from Wulf: *Selection 10*). When this design was presented (as here) with arches uppermost, no movement occurred in *a* and *b*; when turned about so that *a* and *b* were uppermost, the arches exhibited a strong movement while the

[1] I.e. the better the figure the more likely was disruption and the less likely deformation.

bowed lines showed little or none. With ambiguous figures such
41 as the Rubin vase and faces (Fig. 11) it was found that whereas the *vase* disclosed a decided expansion and contraction, the faces "were unable to draw nearer together", and movement was greatly inhibited. Likewise the movement exhibited by a contour cube varied with the way in which the drawing was apprehended. When seen as a plane irregular hexagon the figure exhibited much stronger movement than when seen as three dimensional. In the latter case if the cube was seen "from above", its lower surface acted as the base and the other surfaces, in moving, seemed to spread apart from one another. The base, however, maintained its position in space and merely expanded. If the cube was seen obliquely "from below", it was then the rear surface which

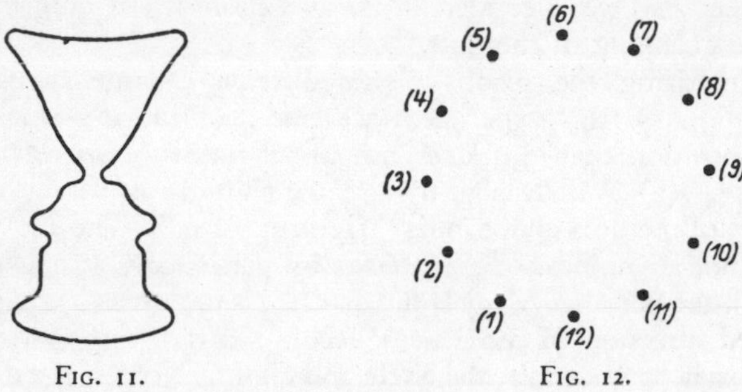

FIG. 11. FIG. 12.

42 remained in a fixed position. Thus we can see that changes in the figural apprehension of a drawing will cause changes in its γ-movement even though the stimulus conditions remain constant.

Pursuing still further the influence of Gestalt factors we next constructed the circle shown in Fig. 12. This circle was 18 mm. in diameter and the diameter of each dot was 1 mm. The figure was presented tachistoscopically as already described. One of the dots could be moved without the subject's prior knowledge. The subject was requested to report what kind of figure he saw, whether any dot had particularly attracted his attention, and what movements he had experienced. An example of the results may be
43 seen from the following table. The exposition time was approximately 36σ.

44–45 : tabular reports are given of the effects caused by shifting dots 8, 6, 3, and 2. Rarely were open, incomplete figures seen; instead the figures in nearly every case were finished, closed forms and the

TABLE 1

Position of dots	Observed phenomenon
1. As in Fig. 12.	1. The circle exhibits a good γ-movement in a directions.
2. Dot 12 shifted inward 3 mm.; it now lies on the line connecting 1 and 11.	2. There is a circle with a chord; it rests upon the chord as its base line. The chord stretches back and forth; it maintains its height-position. The circle's movements upward and sideward are good.
3. Dot 12 shifted 9 mm. inward.	3. Circle and chord; upon the chord a triangle whose base line (the chord) is at rest. The apex moves violently up and down.
4. Dot 12 shifted outward 6 mm.	4. A pear. The lowest dot jabs downward, the neighbouring ones make feeble movements inward.

movement also was strongest in the direction of attaining the best possible grouping of the dots.]

46 Summarizing the results obtained from a large number of observations in this experiment we find: (1) a very small shift in the position of a dot does not at all influence an established structure. (2) With a slightly greater shift the observer notices that one of the dots is not in its " rightful place ". The movement of this dot is emphasized; it strives by particularly strong thrusts to rejoin the periphery. (3) If the distance is too great, a completely
47 reversed direction of movement occurs; a new figural terminus is approached: example, the circle and chord. Now, if the distance from the periphery is too great, the dot moves towards this chord. (4) As the dot is shifted nearer the centre of the circle, its movement towards that middle point becomes very pronounced.

48 *Theoretical considerations.*—Bethe, Fuchs, and Wittmann have
49 all proposed explanations of the phenomena described in this paper,[1] but none succeeds in accounting for all of the facts. A
50 more satisfactory explanation can probably be found if we begin
51 with the hypothesis that γ-movement is a phenomenal expression of the arousal and disappearance [*das Entstehen und Vergehen*] of visual forms. The initial phase of this γ-movement we shall designate as *A*. As our foregoing report has shown, there are cases where quiescence in the stimulus object does not necessarily imply that the perceived form will be experienced as quiescent. The movement experienced in such cases may be thought of as the initial stage in a process whose terminus is a quiescent form.

53 Physiologically this means that quiescence in the somatic field

[1] [A brief critical examination of these theories is given in the text.]

will come about only after a brief but rapid physiological process.
54 This process must also be assumed to occur even with prolonged
exposures of the stimulus object. That ordinarily we do not
experience it, may have the following reasons: (1) Its effect may be
disturbed by other factors: example, the influence of real objects
(lemon, p. 29 f.) upon γ-movement. (2) The energy involved in
the process may be greatly exceeded by that of the stationary end-
process of the form in question. Generally speaking we may say
that the physiological γ-process will always occur, but that it will
not always be experienced.[1]

What has been said of the *A* phase of γ-movement holds *mutatis mutandis* for the last or *Z* phase also. No excitation ceases immediately when the stimulus is removed. The *Z* phase of γ-movement shows that the physiological process does not come to an abrupt halt but disappears rather by means of orderly displacement processes. Many of our subjects remarked that " even after the figure had vanished I still had the visual experience of something converging or drawing together ".

55 As Köhler has shown, every interruption of a physical steady
state produces a rapid process of displacement which can then
result in a new steady state. As regards vision this means that
stimulation of the retina produces throughout the optic sector[2]
a specific process (already designated in this paper as the γ-process)
which results in a quiescent final form. This terminal form is
governed by the law of *Prägnanz*: it must assume the best possible
56 shape. Of course where the stimulation lasts for any considerable
length of time, rigid conditions or " boundary values " are imposed
by the stimulus object itself and the γ-process is unable to bring
about a change of organization in the presented figure. If, however,
an appropriately short exposure permits it to do so, the perceived
form will tend to become as good as possible and the displacement
[57–60: omitted] processes which occur will proceed in the direction of this best
possible end.

[1] Evidence for this is apparent in the fact that with practice one can observe far more instances of γ-movement in everyday life than before.

[2] Cf. *Selection 3*, p. 197.

Selection 14

FURTHER STUDIES OF GAMMA MOVEMENT

By L. Hartmann

"Neue Verschmelzungsprobleme," *Psychol. Forsch.*, 1923, **3**, 319–396.

319 Although the phenomena of visual fusion have been extensively
320 studied before, the present inquiry will approach the subject from a new point of view. As a result of Koffka's studies of movement and in view of his conclusions regarding the close relation between movement- and fusion-phenomena, fusion itself now appears in a new light. The task now is to determine the laws holding for both movement and fusion. Our present study will deal with a limiting case following upon the results obtained by Koffka in experiments with moving stimulus objects seen by intermittent illumination. We shall expose a stimulus object twice with a pause between the two exposures. A second point of departure for the present study is the investigation of γ-movement by Lindemann (*Selection 13*). But whereas Lindemann used only a single exposure, we shall have two, separated by an interval of approximately the
321 same order of magnitude as the exposures themselves. Our experiments can also be considered as a limiting case for Wertheimer's movement phenomena, for whereas his two stimulus objects were separated both in space and in time, ours are identical in space and separate only in time.

Finally this study seeks to determine the influence of exposition time, light intensity, size of figure, and also that of fixation, fatigue, etc., upon the point (i.e. threshold) at which the fusion of two objects occurs.

322 *Apparatus.*—A Schumann tachistoscope in a dark room was used to interrupt the subject's perception (through a black metal tube) of illuminated geometrical figures 35 cm. the other side of the tachistoscope wheel. The duration of exposition was governed by the velocity of the wheel and the size of slits in it. The figures (e.g. circle, ellipse, triangle) were cut out of black cardboard and filled (by pasting from behind) with white tissue paper. They were lighted from behind but could also be illuminated by an electric

Grateful acknowledgment is hereby made to *Julius Springer*, *Verlagsbuchhandlung*, Berlin, for permission to reproduce the illustrations used in this Selection.

lamp in front and to one side. The lights could be moved along
323 calibrated measuring sticks and the amount of illumination thus varied in known quantities. These lights were turned on only while the wheel made a single revolution, at other times the subject looked at an illuminated white screen in order to maintain accom-
325 modation. Fusion was achieved by increasing the velocity of the wheel, not by merely shortening the interval between presentations of the stimulus object. If t is the total duration of an exposition-pause-exposition period ($t = e_1 + p + e_2$), any other method of securing fusion (e.g. reducing the duration of p) would mean a change of ratio within the series $e_1 + p + e_2$. The method used here maintains this ratio and hence leaves the total stimulus-configuration unchanged even though t itself is varied.

The following is an example taken from the reports of one subject.[1] The stimulus object was a single line (1 by 30 mm.) placed 10 cm. in front of an electric lamp. The slits were $e_1 = 8{\cdot}5°$, $e_2 = 8{\cdot}5°$ and the pause was 20°. A report was taken after each revolution (r) of the wheel:—

[326] TABLE I

r in secs.	Double presentation : $e_1 + p + e_2$
3·1	*Two* fairly isolated "individual impulses" each of which displayed a strong expansion and contraction movement.
1·73	A strong double-quiver, sometimes two individual parts with a length- and cross-wise expansion of each.
1·25	Double-quiver with a decided internal movement of the individual components. Also γ-movement.
1·06	Double-quiver, already more unified, with strong tremors within the figure. Flicker and a marked trembling in the individual components. Very little γ-movement.
0·9	A fairly strong flutter or fine flickering movement within; no longer a decided double-quiver.
0·8	A uniform movement, but some trembling within. The whole line expands a little in length and breadth.
0·69	No more vibration or disquiet within; fully unitary. The whole line now exhibits a more decided expanding movement than formerly.

From this report one can observe the qualitative changes which took place as the r-values were varied. The phenomenon seems, with

[1] [Quantitative data are given throughout this article but have been omitted from the present abstract.]

the increasing speed, to change in a *continuous* manner until fusion occurs. Nevertheless different stages may be discriminated:
326 $r = 3 \cdot 1$ sec. in this case is one of succession; from here to, say, $r = 1 \cdot 5$ sec. one finds duality (the two lines are "coupled" in such a way that the observer no longer has the impression of a temporal sequence); in the next stage the figure flickers, is unquiet,
327 and there is still some doubleness about it; then flicker gives way to oscillation or fluttering; and finally fusion (i.e. the stage of simultaneity).

[328–348: variations of p and of light intensity (i) show that the influence of i upon the fusion point is less than that of p. An account of the influence exerted upon fusion by variations of the figure is given below (p. 349 f.). As regards the relation of i and r it was found that to attain fusion an increase in i had to be offset by a decrease in r (i.e. faster revolutions of the tachistoscope wheel). (P. 341): the threshold for fusion was found to change with initial increases of e_2, but after a certain point this lengthening of the second stimulus no longer affected the fusion threshold. The fusion point was also much affected when a third exposition ($p_2 + e_3$) was added. The effects brought about by changing the shape of the slits were also observed. If part of the slit was covered so that only the upper half of the line was clearly visible, the upper portion would attain fusion while the lower half was still at the duality stage. Sometimes, however, the "quieter" upper half would be invaded by flicker from below. (P. 348): changing the *length* of the exposed line affected the fusion threshold much less than did changing its *breadth*. This was true even when the absolute increases of area were the same in both cases.]

FIG. 1.

349 *Objective figural influences.*—If the fusion point for a single line varies with the length and breadth of that line, what influence will be exerted upon this threshold by changing the *kind of figure* used? Before turning to the question of fusion, we may report that the points of the triangle shown in Fig. 1 (area 312 sq. mm.) exhibited extremely vigorous γ-movements whereas a circle (also 312 sq. mm. in area) displayed very little movement of this kind. This difference between the two types of figures made itself
350 apparent also in the next stage of our investigation. If the fusion point for the circle had been found and the triangle was then suddenly introduced (i and r being held constant), the triangle exhibited not fusion but vibration (or "twinkle"). The objection

might be raised that this was due to the considerable difference in radius (9·5 and 18 mm. respectively: cf. Fig. 1) of the two figures. To test this the experiment was repeated using a circle whose radius was 18 mm. But since approximately the same results as before were obtained, the objection must therefore be ruled out. Since, moreover, the outcome of this test is in conformity with our earlier findings [1] we may draw the conclusion that differences in figural character exercise a real influence upon the fusion threshold. We therefore proceeded as follows to classify a number of figures. The fusion point of a circle having been found, we substituted another figure for it and increased the velocity of the tachistoscope wheel until fusion of this figure
351 occurred. The order of fusions with the *r*-value at which they occurred was as follows: circle ($r = 1·22$ sec.), hexagon ($r = 1·18$ sec.), square ($r = 1·12$ sec.), triangle ($r = 1·12$ sec.), and, finally, the "concave" triangle shown in Fig. 1 ($r = 1·10$ sec.). As can be seen from this list the threshold, *r*, varied directly with the obtuseness of angles used. There was a considerable leap between the hexagon and square which showed that a figure (pentagon) between them was missing. Between the hexagon and circle, on the other hand, there was so little difference that the
352 subjects at first failed to realize that a new figure had been substituted. When the influence of figural character was compared with that of illumination intensity it was found that the latter is but secondary in importance. A further discussion of this difference will be given below.

[353–356: a study of certain subjective factors (fixation, practice, and fatigue).]

357 *Subjective figural influences.*—The preceding paragraph has shown that the fusion point for the figures mentioned there was determined by the super-summative characters of those figures. Lindemann's results (*Selection* 13, p. 19) corroborate this finding. But in our present inquiry the results reported on pp. 349 f. might seem to have depended primarily upon *brightness* intensity in the following sense. If one compares the concave triangle of Fig. 1 with a circle, one observes that its tapering, narrow points were surrounded (in our expositions) by darkness and were, therefore, by contrast effect, brighter than the circle. The more complicated field would thus be the brighter field, and this would hold for all of our figures.

[1] That sheer size differences were relatively unimportant with regard to the fusion threshold [p. 348].

In order to study this problem more closely we employed am-
358 biguous designs (Figs. 2 and 3). The reader will observe, for example, that Fig. 2 may be seen as a square with curved sides, or as a kite whose axis is the diagonal extending from the lower left to the upper right-hand corner. Fig. 3 is both a pair of right triangles, and a square with a broad diagonal cut away. One can more or less easily shift these apprehensions at will without really knowing how this is done. One sees the figure so, tries (sometimes without success) to shift; then suddenly it changes and one has a new apprehension of it without having known before what this would be. This subjective factor in figural apprehension supplies us with an excellent means for demonstrating the influence of figural character upon fusion. Since with such figures the objective stimulus is the same in both cases there can then be no question but that any threshold differences will be due to figural factors alone.

Two groups of subjects were used. The first was shown an ambiguous figure and allowed to practice reversing it until proficient. The second group was kept in ignorance of the kind of figure to be used. First Group: with the subject set for Apprehension I, we proceeded, as reported in the preceding sections, to determine the fusion threshold. Then Apprehension II would be requested and the threshold again determined. Second Group: nothing being said about the kind of figure, we merely exposed it as described above and determined its fusion point. Then the subject was asked to describe the figure. Which-
359 ever Apprehension was mentioned, the subject was told of the other and asked to see the figure in that way. If fluttering was now reported, the fusion point for this new Apprehension would be determined.

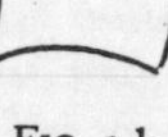

FIG. 2.[1]

FIG. 3.[2]

We may summarize the results thus: Fig. 2 as a "kite" (*k*) displayed greater disquiet and its γ-movement was stronger at the duality and flicker stages than when it was seen as a "square" (*s*). Correspondingly the fusion point for *s* occurred sooner than did that for *k*; moreover, even after *s* had attained fusion, *k* still continued to vibrate. If *s* was apprehended and its fusion had been accomplished, a shift of Apprehension (to *k*) brought about
360 vibration; if *k* was apprehended, the reverse shift (to *s*) abolished

[1] From K. Bühler.

[2] The diagonal, like the remaining background of this figure, was black.

vibration from the figure. Fig. 3 could be seen as a square with a broad diagonal cut out (Apprehension I) or as two right triangles (Apprehension II). It was found that fusion came about sooner with I than with II.

[361–374: additional figures were studied. With the Rubin cross it was found that the same objective area attains fusion sooner when it is apprehended as *ground* than when seen as the *figure*. (P. 364): the flickering and other movements within various figures (ellipse, circle, concave triangle, etc.), were more pronounced in the horizontal than in the vertical direction; they varied in character both with the type of figure and with intensity of illumination. (P. 367): with a ring (instead of a circle) the flicker stage was almost entirely eliminated; a square grating (such as would be obtained by adding screen wire to the tissue paper at the back of the figure) gave but very little flicker or vibration and progressed almost directly from duality to fusion.]

375 *Alternate (different) figures.*—If the same figure is presented in two positions,[1] vibration is not confined to the overlapping portion but pertains, in reduced amount, to the whole figure which shifts at the same time from Positon I to Position II

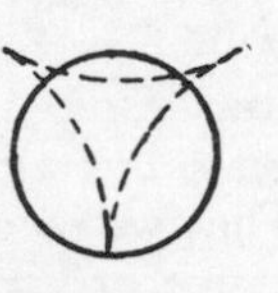

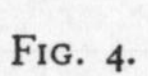

Fig. 4.

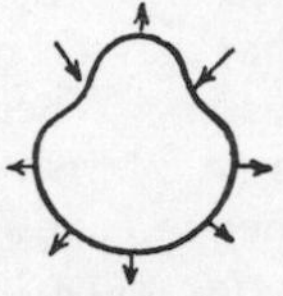

Fig. 5.[2]

(β-movement). Now we propose to use two different but overlapping figures, such, for example, as those shown in Fig. 4.[3] Each of
376 these was exposed by an opening in the tachistoscope wheel of 8·5°; the interval between exposures was 20°. The fluttering stage mentioned in connection with our earlier studies did not occur in the present experiment. The most interesting result obtained from these expositions is that depicted in Fig. 5—viz. deformation of the circle when the triangle was exposed first and the circle afterwards. Here the subjects saw a triangle, then a blank, and then a pear-shaped figure; they never saw the circle at all. The indentations of this "pear" are at precisely those points where, but an instant before, the upper points of the triangle had been. The experiment was repeated with a line first and a circle afterward. The "circle" appeared extended at its equator and flattened at its poles.

[1] Example: a square with horizontal base and the same square slightly tilted.

[2] The arrows indicate the direction of the γ-movement.

[3] There were two series: in one the triangle appeared first and the circle afterward; in the other a reversed order was used.

[377–387: (377 f.): omitted. (380 f.): results obtained here are compared with those of Korte, Koffka, Cermack, et al., with special reference to the laws of motion formulated by these authors.]

388 *Summary and theory.*—We have seen in this study that there is
a parallelism between γ-movement and fusion. Our experiments
have shown the same influence of figural character upon fusion
as is known to hold for γ-movement, for, as we have seen, the
fusion threshold depends upon the *kind* of figure used. With
389 ambiguous figures and with the Rubin cross we found that despite
objective invariance of the exposed figure, fusion occurred at
different thresholds for different apprehensions. And we discovered that the same objective area had a lower fusion point when seen as "ground" than when appearing as "figure". We learned also that when the figures exposed in e_1 and e_2 were different but overlapped, flicker and fluttering were reduced or eliminated entirely. Each of these figures possesses so definite a structure that they do not readily combine to produce flicker, fluttering, and fusion. When the same figure is exposed twice in succession there is an internal flickering, but with two different figures this phenomenon is absent. Thus we see that for fusion to occur the second figure must be the same or very nearly the same as the first, and that both must occupy the same spatial position. This resistance to fusion by two different figures serves to substantiate the law of Gestalt constancy. For the individual figures, entering into the larger union would mean an annulment of their status as individuals, and this they can sometimes prevent.

390 When a slight discrepancy of position was introduced for the
two exposures, or when two different figures were used (cf. p. 375),
flickering disappeared and β-movement was seen. In seeking an
explanation for this we may be guided by Wertheimer's conviction
that the perception of movement is not due to a *sum* of excitations
in individual brain cells. Instead one must assume a unified whole-
process, for whole-states and whole-processes play a crucial part
391 in the nervous system. Moreover, in view of Köhler's demonstra-
tions,[1] we may also assert that the physical Gestalten of the nervous system possess characteristics which "parallel" those of their phenomenal correlates. Like Lindemann we shall attempt here to extend Köhler's theory of stationary whole-processes to cover dynamic processes also.

The same rapid displacement-process which Lindemann speaks

[1] *Selection 3.*

of as the γ-process occurred in the present experiment twice in succession. Our task is to discover the relationship between (*a*) the occurrence of β-movement, and (*b*) fusion. To do this we must consider the following. When a region of the retina is stimulated by some object a displacement-process occurs at its boundaries along which a potential difference [*Potentialsprung*] arises in the somatic field. This displacement-process in the peripheral sense organ is, however, only one side of a much more extensive dynamic process involving the whole optic sector. The entire event may be compared to an electric circuit. At the moment of stimulation a retinal "topography" is established. This serves as a surface of transformation of light energy into electric energy, and at the same time as surface source or electrode and transition surface of an electrolytic circuit towards central parts of the somatic field and back to the periphery. The development of the dynamic circuit corresponds to the rapid displacement process due to the initial increase in energy density. Because of this rise of the energy density to a final value (stationary state) the numerically rapidly increasing flow lines (Köhler) passing through the retinal topography will at first mutually tend to repel each other and expand the contour (γ-process); but finally these dynamic changes will reach a final steady state in which during a unit of time the same amount of energy enters into as passes out of any closed surface
392 in the circuit. When stimulation ceases, energy density within the stimulated area is diminished and the result is a contraction phase of the γ-process.

What, now, is the physiological process corresponding to the phenomenal experience of β-movement? If a retinal area is stimulated by incoming light, the energy density of this region increases until a certain constant value is reached; the dynamic current becomes a stationary Gestalt. When the source of light is withdrawn, the energy density decreases—but more slowly than it arose.[1] If, now, another area is at this moment increasing in energy density, an exchange of energy between the two will take place and the latter will thus be influenced by the former. Designating the first as I and the second as II we may describe the result by saying that the distance between I and II will decrease—i.e. the current *passes* from I to II. The phenomenal correlate of this is an experience of β-movement.

393 An analogous phenomenon in hydrodynamics will illustrate this passing of a current (see Fig. 6). In the bottom of a large water

[1] This is the *Z*-phase of γ-movement according to Lindemann.

container there are two round holes. The water is shallow. At first both holes are closed. When one of them is opened the place where the water is sucked down can be readily identified by a little whirlpool upon the water's surface. If both holes are closed and one is opened for a brief time, closed, and the other opened after a short but definite interval, the transition from one whirlpool to the other can be easily observed. The current passes from I to II. In the case of a β-process the current passes from brain area I across an unstimulated region to brain area II.

Korte found that

$$\phi = f\left(\frac{s}{ip}\right)$$

where ϕ designates the phenomenal experience (of movement), s the spatial interval between the stimulus objects, i the light intensity, and p the pause or temporal interval. If s is increased, the new current arising at II will develop fully before any influences from I can reach II. The result is two independent processes or *simultaneity*. If, however, p is increased, the approximately circular boundaries of process I will have reached the vicinity of II by the time that II occurs and there will be an exchange of energy between I and II. If p is still further increased, ϕ must become smaller and the result is *succession*. This can be understood because if optimal movement had prevailed before p
394 was increased, Process I would now disappear before the arousal of Process II which would therefore have to build up anew; consequently no exchange of energy between the two places would be possible. Phenomenally this is experienced as two temporally separate impressions. An increase of i would, according to this theory, accelerate Process I so that it would be over before Process II arose: result, again, succession.

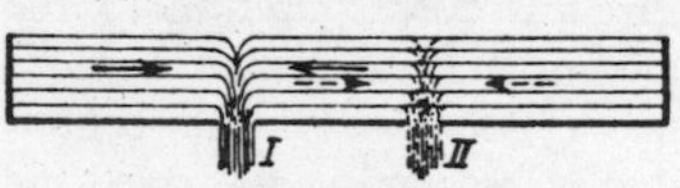

Fig. 6.

The phenomena of fusion can likewise be explained by our theory in the following way. Since both stimulations occur at the same place, if fusion has been established and i is increased, there is a proportional increase in the concentration, c, of ions; but the electromotive force of the stimulated area increases proportionally with log c. The rate of change of the dynamic current-Gestalt increases proportionally with the electromotive force, and hence, if fusion had been present before, now the first process is over too soon and the second one must build up anew. The result is *duality*.

[An analogous explanation is also given for the shadow effect or fluttering movement which appeared inside the figure. *Fusion* occurs when p is short enough so that there is no gap before the second process begins.]

C. PERCEPTION AND RELATED PHENOMENA

SELECTION 15

VARIATIONS IN TACTUAL IMPRESSIONS

By M. von Frey

"Über Wandlungen der Empfindungen bei formal verschiedener Reizung einer Art von Sinnesnerven," *Psychol. Forsch.*, 1923, **5**, 209–218.

[209–213: brief introduction; then examples which show that with the assumption of definite kinds of sensory nerves the quality of sensations is in no wise unequivocally given.]

214 Our sensations of pressure vary not only with the intensity and duration of stimulation but are also in their very nature different even though they all come from the same peripheral receptors. The same may be said also of superficial pain and sound sensations.
215 Of course to this it might be objected that sensations such as these are not simple, but constitute complexes and that it is, therefore, not surprising when the complex itself changes with alterations in the form of stimulation. This objection would have some weight if the experiences could be recognized *as* compound and not merely inferred to be such from the nature of experimental conditions. Indeed as regards such inferences there is as yet *no* evidence for the claim that a presumptive sensation-complex consists of subsidiary components—and the reason for this may be found in the fact that peripheral excitation processes are not conducted unchanged to the region of psychophysiological activity but undergo (and themselves initiate) changes along the way. Such reciprocal activity is especially operative in the grey matter of spinal cord and brain. Perhaps the most important of such modifications of excitation is the irradiation or induction especially characteristic of tactual experiences.

Thus I have found that even with the stimulation of but one pressure point, central representation is not restricted to this point only. Instead the representational correlates of adjacent nerve-endings are also involved. This is apparent from the fact that formerly subliminal stimulation of these adjacent nerve-endings is now sensed. Another such disturbance of the conduction process can be seen in the case of simultaneous pressure of two or more points on the skin. The degree of distinctness with which each is

experienced is diminished and the impression one has of their location is likewise altered under these circumstances. The two points seem closer when simultaneously than when successively
216 stimulated. It is even possible to cause a fusion of two stimuli such that the subject will report stimulation of but one point. This is especially true when the stimuli are unequal in strength: the stronger seems to suck in and absorb the weaker.

It is apparent from conduction disturbances such as these that a mosaic description of sensation would be impossible. Experimental evidence shows that sensation upon extended stimulation does not consist in a plurality of isolated excitations but is rather a closed whole whose locus is determined by the region of strongest stimulation. And the same is true of temporal phenomena in perception, for here too we find unified experience-wholes such, e.g., as the rapid diminution of contact sensations in contradistinction to the rather considerable duration of pressure sensations; or, as in hearing, the influence of temporal interval in determining whether we shall hear a tone, noise, or tremolo.

We are here considering structures which are *more* than a mere summation of peripheral excitations. Indeed the structure is such that the peripheral excitations cannot be discerned within it. How could one describe the psychic element supposedly common to, say, a tickle, a buzzing in the ears, and a sense of pressure? No such analytic element can be found because it is impossible to penetrate below the threshold of conscious experience.

217 Although these findings regarding sensation would seem to agree with v. Ehrenfels's doctrine of *Gestaltqualitäten*, they conform still more closely with Köhler's view of Gestalten as states and processes whose characteristic properties are not derived from their so-called parts. The advance which recent study of this question has achieved lies, however, not so much in an improved terminology as in the conviction that the somatic processes correlated with psychological Gestalt phenomena themselves possess a similar (Gestalt) structure. Thus Köhler, agreeing with Wertheimer and Koffka, assumes that organic processes correspond directly to higher mental happenings in that both are to be viewed not as sums of individual excitations but as structured whole-processes.

No field is better suited for experimental tests of this view than that of tactual experience: *first* because nerve-endings in the skin are genuinely discrete and can thus be independently excited, and *secondly* because the modification of excitation processes occurs

in part in the spinal cord and is therefore far less difficult to study than pure brain processes. Let us consider an experiment designed to investigate the nature of disturbances (raising of spatial threshold,
218 fusion) appearing when two or more pressure spots on the skin are stimulated :—

It can be shown that these disturbances cannot be adequately explained by irradiation of excitations in the grey matter. An explanation, however, *is* possible if one considers the discriminability of simultaneous excitations as a function of the slope of the excitation gradient between their terminal points. This meets the demands of Gestalt theory inasmuch as, on the one hand, irradiation makes it possible to connect the single excitations; while, on the other hand, the projection system of the second order based upon this appears as a selective device which creates new relations.

The foregoing has shown that Gestalt phenomena are not limited to the realm of higher mental processes, but can be demonstrated even in the processes underlying simple perceptions. And the discussion shows further that the search for "simple sensations" must halt precisely at the boundary of such Gestalt phenomena.

Selection 16

COLOUR CONSTANCY

By Adhémar Gelb

"Die 'Farbenkonstanz' der Sehdinge," *Handbuch der normalen und pathologischen Physiologie*, 1929, **12**, 594–678. [With the exception of the last experiment (pp. 674 f.) this paper is *itself* a summary of a large number of books and articles. As a further condensation of this text the English abstract does not adequately reveal the thoroughly systematic character of the author's inquiry.]

595 *Statement of the problem.*—We shall be concerned in this study
596 primarily with the relation between "illumination" and "colour".[1] White paper is recognized as "white" whether seen in daylight or in moonlight; the same holds for the "black" of black velvet. The paper will also be "white" when seen in the greenish shadows of an arbour or under an ordinary electric light. With coloured objects (blue, red, etc.) analogous although less extensive observations may be made; a blue paper is seen as practically "blue" even under the reddish-yellow light of a gas lamp.

These discrepancies between experience and physical light conditions give rise to the problem with which we are here concerned. If, for example, degree of whiteness were a simple function of the intensity of light reflected from the surface, then white paper in a reduced light *should* look blacker than intensely illuminated
597 black velvet. The fact that this does not ordinarily occur has been designated by Hering as "the approximate constancy of the colour of visual objects", or, as we shall hereafter call it, "colour constancy."

598 One of Hering's early observations was this: I stand with my back to the window and hold before me a piece of unglazed, dark-grey paper. From this position I look alternately at the grey and at a white wall on the other side of the room. Now in this case the grey, because of its better illumination, reflects much more light than the wall. Nevertheless it is seen as grey while the wall is seen as white. The grey paper is, of course, seen as more "insistent", "lively", and even, in this sense, "brighter"[2] than

[1] [The term "colour" as used throughout this paper refers to achromatic or neutral as well as to chromatic colours.]

[2] [Unless otherwise noted (e.g. by quotation marks) the terms *bright* and *dark* refer in this essay to perceived illumination. (This usage does not, of course, affect the meaning of standard terms such as "dark-grey paper".) The physical intensity of illumination will be indicated by the qualifying adjectives *strong* or *weak*.]

the wall which appears as "dull" or even "darker" than the grey. Nevertheless one does not lose the impression that the essential quality of the paper is "dark-grey" and of the wall "white".

In another experiment two identical white papers were used. Here although the one nearest the window is seen as "lighter" (i.e. more luminous) than the other, we nevertheless ascribe this difference not to the surface of our papers but to the illumination. We say that both are "white" but that one is more brightly illuminated than the other.

599 *Reduction screen.*—A "reduction" or "hole" screen is a fairly large piece of cardboard with two small, clean-edged holes cut in the centre. If the holes are appropriately spaced and the screen held at a comfortable distance from the eyes, one sees two objects behind the screen, e.g. the dark-grey paper and white wall, in accordance with their objective light intensities. The position of the screen should be such that the rays from one object reach the eye through one opening, those from the other through the other opening. The screen naturally does not alter the physical rays, yet the "hole colours" of our reducing screen have an entirely different appearance from the surfaces of the two objects seen directly. More intense physical rays cause brighter, whiter hole colours. If the dark-grey paper is reflecting the same amount and quality of light from its position (near the window) that the wall is from its position, the two hole colours will be identical. As soon, however, as one removes the screen, the paper will again be seen as dark-grey, the wall as white.

It must be emphasized, however, that under certain circumstances we can, *even without using a reduction screen*, see the dark-grey paper and the white wall in accordance with their objective light intensities. To accomplish this one must assume a special, "critical" attitude. (Artists, for example, are usually able to perform this feat with relative ease.) But neither the very naïve
600 perception nor that achieved by using a reduction screen or by adopting a "critical" attitude is alone characteristic of most visual experience. Instead there is a wide range between these extremes. An interesting and theoretically important illustration of variations which may occur in visual experience despite constancy of objective illumination was reported by Hering. This was as follows: Hang a small bit of paper by a thin silk thread in front of a lamp so that its shadow falls upon a piece of white writing paper. The shadowed area is merely an incidental darkness upon the white. Now, however, if a heavy black line (broad enough to

cover the penumbra) is drawn around the core of the shadow, it thereafter looks as if the white paper were coloured with grey paint. If one moves the thread or paper, the shadow reappears *as* a shadow upon a white.

[601–609: historical résumé of the problem as it developed under the hands of Helmholtz, v. Kries, and Hering. (For the best history of this subject in English see R. B. MacLeod, "An Experimental Investigation of Brightness Constancy," *Archives of Psychol.*, 1932, No. 135, pp. 19–57, also pp. 100–102 for references.)]

610 *Experimental: Katz.*—David Katz was the first to recognize that the problem of colour constancy must be studied not as an abstract and isolated phenomenon of light- and colour-sensation, but in terms of its relation to the structure of our spatially articulated
611 world of coloured objects. It was from this type of approach that he came to distinguish between the various modes of appearance of colours [*Erscheinungsweisen der Farben*], and hence also to make his distinction between "object colour" and "illumination". Let us notice some of the experiments which he reports.

612 In Katz's experiment on "light-perspective" an observer sits in a dark room under a high power lamp; in front of him and at a distance of 1 m. is a series of 18 achromatic colours progressing evenly from white to deep black. Behind this, and approximately 5 m. from the observer, various greys, white, black, etc., are displayed individually and in haphazard order. The subject's task is to identify these in terms of the scale of 18. Results: when a white was shown which was physically identical with *white* on the scale, the observers declared it to be the same as the second
613 or third of the nearer colours—i.e. they saw it the same as a white which under the conditions of the experiment reflected approximately twenty times as much light as itself. Nevertheless the identity was not complete in every respect and indeed the distant white could not be *identified* with any of the scale colours. The better illuminated white and greys seemed "lighter", "livelier", more "insistent", and more "intense" than the distant white. Some observers referred to the nearer white as "brighter" and the other as "darker" or "veiled in darkness"; others characterized the nearer one as more "pronounced" or "genuine". Katz himself also describes the difference as one of "*pronouncedness*" [*Ausgeprägtheit*]. With black, however, a new situation was encountered, for the nearer black was undoubtedly the more "insistent" but the remote one in this case was superior in pronouncedness or genuineness—i.e. it was a "better" black. It

appeared, then, that *the best illuminated of two colours is always the most insistent, but not always the most pronounced.*[1]

On the basis of his findings Katz concluded that, in the case of object colours, it would be incorrect to speak of *a* series from black to white. Instead we must consider this series to be *bi-dimensional*: that is to say, one can proceed from one quality to
[614–616 : omitted] another among the white, greys, and black, *or*, within the same quality, to varying degrees of pronouncedness.

617 *Experiments with oblique orientation of surfaces.*—Even more important in everyday colour perception than distance from the source of illumination is the matter of orientation relative to the source of light. All things are equally distant from the sun but not equally orientated towards it. Hering suggested the following observation. Stand at the window with a piece of white paper in one hand, grey in the other. If the grey is inclined towards the window and the white away from it, the stimulation intensity of grey becomes greater than that of the white. Nevertheless, even though a brightness difference can be noticed, the grey and white remain visually what they were before. (With a reduction screen, of course, it is easy to see the grey paper as physically brighter
618 than the white.)

By using an apparatus for measuring the amount of inclination towards or away from the light, Katz again showed that the achromatic series is two-dimensional: qualitatively similar colours nevertheless differed in pronouncedness. It may, therefore, be asserted that there are no two object surfaces which are identical in perceived colour when differently oriented with respect to the source of light.

619 : episcotister experiments.]

620 *The standard experiment.*—The apparatus consists of two rotators or colour wheels with disks which may be set to give any desired grey during rotation. The rotators are placed a short distance apart upon a table so that both face the observer (see Fig. 1). There is a screen between them and the illumination is so designed that whereas one rotator (R_1) is directly illuminated, the other (R_2) is shadowed by the screen. The background of both is a neutral grey. The observer is instructed to match the qualityof R_1
621 with that of R_2. Two series of such comparisons are made. In the first a reduction screen is used, in the second this screen is removed.

The shadowed rotator, R_2, is completely white, the illuminated

[1] These differences in pronouncedness (as well as of insistence) disappear, however, if one unifies the illumination conditions (i.e. uses the reduction screen) [p. 614].

rotator, R_1, is varied according to the subject's wishes until the disks seem to him equal. With a perfectly opaque screen between R_1 and R_2 the following values are typical:—

Series I (using reduction screen): When R_1 is 4·2° white and 355·8° black it is seen as equivalent to the shadowed disk, R_2, which is 360° white.

Series II (no reduction screen): When R_1 is 116° white and 244° black it is seen as equivalent to the 360° white R_2.

From these values it can be seen that when the reduction screen is removed (after Series I) the two disks will look very different despite their objective equality. The shadowed disk now seems almost "white". In other words the shadowed disk, when seen without the reduction screen, retains to a considerable extent its character of being white.

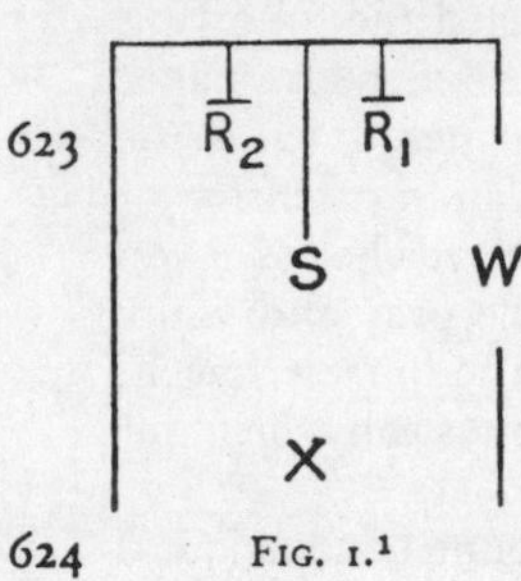

FIG. 1.[1]

623 The differences between the results obtained in Series I and II are diminished when the observer tilts his head to one side or when the two disks are seen in a mirror. A very important role is also played by the observation distance. The farther away the observer moves, the less is the difference between his

624 results for the two series. At a distance of 7–8 m. the difference is almost nil. Also important is the length of observation time. Using tachistoscopic exposures (0·6, 1·1, 1·7, and 3·4 sec.) of R_2 Katz found that with shorter exposures the differences between Series I and Series II were correspondingly diminished. On the other hand, however, even the shortest exposures (0·0017 sec.) did not approach the results typical of reduction screen values. Finally Katz also found that monocular observations decrease the difference between I and II.

[625–629: experiments with chromatic colours. Here the disks used for R_2 were white and variously coloured (blue, red, etc.), and they were seen in illumination of various colours; R_1 also was coloured but was seen in daylight. The differences between Series I and Series II in the several cases were again considerable except where very intense coloured lights were used. In this latter case the constancy of colour upon the rotator R_2 disappeared.]

630 *The Laws of Field Size.*—Common to all of the experiments and observations reported above was the fact that colour constancy

[1] In this drawing S is the screen which shades R_2 from the sunlight entering through the window, W, and falling upon R_1 directly. The observer's position is indicated by an X.

631 was manifested only when an adequate and uninterrupted survey of the existing illumination was permitted. Anything hindering such a survey (e.g. the reduction screen, minimal observation time, etc.) either destroyed or reduced the phenomenon. One of the most important conditions is that the visual angle be large and the field richly articulated.

This relationship has been expressed by Katz in his Laws of Field Size. The first law states that with an increase in visual angle (i.e. an increase of stimulated retinal area) there is a corresponding increase in degree of the colour constancy phenomenon. The second law states that this is also true even when the apparent size of the visual field increases without any enlargement of the stimulated retinal area.

The second law may be demonstrated thus: project a strong negative after-image upon a light-grey, inhomogeneous wall; when the projection distance is increased the image grows in size
632 but it loses thereby in colour and has the impression of a change of illumination within the area of the after-image; at the same time the wall's own colour becomes more and more dominant.

As regards the first law Katz reports the following experiment. Two rotating disks, *A* and *B*, are placed side by side; 2 m. in front of *B* there is a deep-black episcotister with an opening of 10°. The observer's position is varied from 0·5 to 7 m. distance from the episcotister. The *A* disk, which is seen directly, can be changed from white through any degree of grey to black; the *B* disk, which is seen through the episcotister, is white. All comparisons between *A* and *B* are made without the reduction screen. We are interested here in the role played by observation distance. The results of Katz's experiments were as follows:—

Distance of observer from episcotister (in metres)	*Amount of white required in* A *in order for it to match* B (in °W)
7	30·6
6	32·5
5	36·6
4	44·1
3	52·7
2	65·0
1·5	76·3
1	94·0
0·5	108·2

These results confirm the first law by showing that the insistency with which *B*, the white disk, expresses its character of being white *increases* as the observation distance *decreases*, i.e. as the retinal image increases.

[633–639: discusses the "visibility of illumination" and some problems of transparency (both with special reference to shadows); Hering's theory is also discussed.]

640 *Film colours and surface colours.*—No matter in what "mode" colours appear (as surfaces, transparent gelatines, etc., as liquids, reflections, lusters, or glows)—all are reduced to *film colours* by the reduction screen. This Katz calls the "complete reduction of colour impressions". The principal distinction is that made between surface colours and film colours. "Surface colours are those seen normally by the light adapted eye in ordinary perception. They are 'hard', easily localized in any plane, coincide with the shape and position of the object, and usually present a definite structure (microstructure) characteristic of that object. Film colours on the other hand present no microstructure, and always appear to lie in a fronto-parallel plane. The best example of film colour is the colour which is seen in the hole of the reducing screen. The colour does not belong to the surface behind the screen, but seems to come forward and fill out the hole, without at the same time presenting a resistant surface to the eye." [1]

[641–645: omitted. Contents summarized pp. 646–647 below.]

646 *Statement and criticism of Katz's theory.*—The theory originally proposed by Katz [2] to account for colour constancy may be summarized as follows:—

The principal source of colour constancy is to be found in the central factors of individual experience. When we perceive the (surface) colours of objects in illuminations that are quantitatively or qualitatively "not normal", and we are aware of this abnormality, there occurs a *transformation* of the incoming nerve excitations by central factors. This transformation is supposed to
647 take place in such a way that the "physiological" colours (i.e. purely "retinal" impressions) are, in greater or less degree, displaced in the direction of the "actual" or "proper" ["*eigentliche*"] colours which the perceived thing would have in a "normal" illumination for the light adapted eye. Thus the impressions of

[1] [This description, borrowed from R. B. MacLeod, op. cit., is substituted here for pp. 640–642 of the text.]

[2] [This was in *Die Erscheinungsweisen der Farben* (1911); fundamental changes, many of them made with reference to Gelb's criticisms, were made in the revised edition (1930) which was entitled *Der Aufbau der Farbwelt*. The English translation by R. B. MacLeod and W. Fox of the latter publication is called *The World of Colour* (Kegan Paul, Trench, Trubner and Co., London, 1935).]

" proper " or " normally illuminated " colours are assigned by Katz an exceptional status: they are " more primitive or fundamental " [" *ursprünglicher* "] and hence not " problematic " in the sense that the colours perceived in " abnormal " illumination are.

Just as did Helmholtz and Hering, so Katz also makes the distinction between lower (primary) and higher (accessory) processes. His belief that colour constancy is essentially a " psychological " phenomenon is grounded upon this distinction. The principal difference between Katz and his predecessors is his claim that colour *contrast* and colour *constancy* require essentially different explanatory principles. Helmholtz considered them both to be " psychological " in nature; Hering thought they must be " physiological ". Katz attributes contrast to lower, " purely physiological " processes, while constancy he considers the expression of " higher ", psychical functions.

The assumption that colour constancy is due to central psychological processes presupposes (as Köhler has pointed out) a highly developed nervous system by which this transformation may be effected. It should follow from this that the less organized an organism's nervous system is, the less likely it would be that these
648 phenomena would occur. Köhler therefore undertook to investigate the behaviour of apes and chickens (i.e. two species variously remote from human beings) when confronted by achromatic colours of different illumination intensity.[1] Since the results were essentially the same for both species we need here consider only the less complex organisms. The chickens were trained to eat from the whiter of two greys both of which were presented in the same illumination. In the " critical " trials the darker grey lay in full sunlight while the whiter one was shadowed. Physically the former was, therefore, much " lighter " than the latter, but the chickens nevertheless continued to choose the whiter (now shadowed) grey. That is to say, their choice was not determined by the physical light intensity of the two papers. Thus Köhler proved that chickens and apes—and hence not alone human beings—perceive the achromatic colours of objects to a large extent independently of illumination intensity.[2]

649 Let us consider now another part of Katz's theory. The

[1] Cf. *Selection 18*; also W. Köhler, " Die Farben der Sehdinge beim Schimpansen und dem Haushuhn," *Zeitschr. f. Psychol.*, 1917, **77**, 248 f.

[2] Further experiments along this line were carried out by Katz and Révész whose work with chromatic colours gave similar results. (Cf. *Zeitschr. f. angew. Psychol.*, 1921, **18**, 307 ff., esp. 318 f.) Colour constancy phenomena have also been demonstrated with fishes (W. Burkamp, *Zeitschr. f. Sinnesphysiol.*, 1923, **55**, 133 f.).

phenomenon of colour constancy, Katz maintained, can only occur with *surface colours* because only with them is it possible for there to be a separation between illumination and illuminated object.
650 That this view is not wholly admissible, however, was shown by Gelb's study of patients (brain injury) whose ability to perceive surface colours had been lost.[1] For one of these patients the colours of all objects were perceived as film or as space filling colours. They were detached from object surfaces in such a way that the darker they were, the " thicker " they appeared to be. He saw them as " soft ", " spongy ", " downy ". Nevertheless
651 when examined by means of the " standard " technique (above, p. 620) it was found that in both series the patient's results were essentially the same as those of normal persons. This shows that ability to perceive surface colours is not essential in order for the phenomenon of colour constancy to occur.

652 Turning now to Katz's theory of " proper " colours and " normal " illumination and of " reduction " and " transformation ", let us consider the following " paradoxical " experiment. The question is whether Katz's *experiments* justify his distinction between normal and abnormal illumination in the sense that normal colours constitute the norm towards which transformation of abnormal colours takes place. When, in the standard experiment (p. 620), the reduction screen is removed (end of Series I), the subject sees R_2 and R_1 as different even though, as hole colours, they had just before been identical for him. According to Katz this is because the shadowed disk, R_2, no longer appears in its " physiological " colour (i.e. corresponding to retinal excitation), but rather in the direction of its " proper ", " centrally transformed," " centrally whitened " colour. And as a matter of fact it is true that it is chiefly the *shadowed* disk which changes when the reduction screen is removed. That the illuminated disk, R_1, does not undergo
653 any marked change when the screen is removed is due, says Katz, to the fact that *it* is in a " normal " illumination and is displaying its " actual " colour.

But now we ask what the results would be if we reversed the experiment. In the standard experiment both the reduction screen and the observer are in the same illumination as the *illuminated* disk. We now reverse this and place only R_1 in direct illumination: R_2 and all else including the observer are shadowed (Fig. 2).[2]

[1] *Selection 27*, p. 236 f.

[2] [The experiment reported here was first performed (1921) by Max Schlamme, a student of Professor Gelb's.]

Now the results are the reverse of those mentioned above: when the reduction screen is removed (end of Series I) the shadowed disk remains almost unchanged (white) while the illuminated disk appears much too black. One has the impression that the difference between them is due to a radical (subjective) alteration upon the "normally" illuminated side (i.e. in R_1).

When compared with Katz's theoretical assumptions the results of this experiment appear paradoxical because now the non-proper (i.e. shadowed) colour is the one which has remained unchanged while the "normally" illuminated (black) disk has undergone a "central transformation". The results are not paradoxical, however, if we give up Katz's theory that colour experience under "normal" illumination is *not* problematic in the sense in which it *is* under "non-normal" illumination. The experiment shows that it is impossible to rely upon these notions of "normal illumination" and "proper colour" as norms or absolute
654 standards towards which the transformation of "non-normal" illumination proceeds. There is *no* illumination in which the perception of colours is more "primitive" ["*ursprünglich*"] and "simple" than any other.

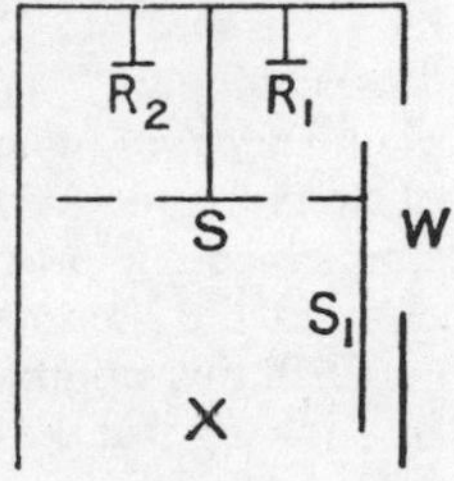

FIG. 2.[1]

655 From this it follows that the difference between reduction and transformation, which Katz claims, must also be rejected. We must entirely abandon the assumption that with vision in "non-normal" illumination there occurs a transformation on the basis of past experience whereby "physiological" colours are caused to approach "proper" colours. It follows also that the significance attributed by Katz to the reduction screen (i.e. eliminating the influence upon vision of central factors) cannot any longer be accepted. What the screen *does* is to reduce both disks to the same conditions of illumination.[2]

656 We have seen that Katz's theory is based upon a distinction between "lower" (so-called "retinally" determined) and "higher" (empirically modified) functions. We have shown why the theory is untenable; this does not, of course, change the validity of his experimental facts. To comprehend those facts,

[1] The daylight entering at the window, W, is prevented by the screen, S_1, from falling directly upon the observer (at X) or upon the reduction screen which is at right angles to S. Thus in this arrangement R_2, the reduction screen, and the observer are all shadowed, whereas in the standard experiment (Fig. 1) only R_2 was shadowed.

[2] [Compare below p. 670 f., esp. p. 676 f.]

however, it is necessary that we view the entire problem of colour constancy in another way. In what follows we shall attempt to suggest how this can be done.

[657–669: the experimental findings and theories of Jaensch and Bühler are reviewed.]

670 *Concluding considerations.*—Despite the variety of theoretical views which have been held regarding colour constancy, one underlying assumption has always appeared. The essentially problematic aspect of the phenomenon has invariably been taken to be the discrepancy between " stimulus " and " colour " reaction. Assuming that retinal stimuli and colour-vision stood in a more or less direct correspondence with one another, any departure from this primitive [*ursprünglich*] and self-evident relationship—i.e. any " discrepancy "—was explained on empiristic grounds. Thus if the discrepancy could not be rendered comprehensible by reference to " physiological " (peripheral) factors alone, " psychological " factors would also be invoked. In this way the phenomena of colour constancy were classified as the *product* of central processes operating upon and reorganizing genetically simpler colour-processes. This type of explanation is especially clear in the theories of Hering and Katz.

672 That this approach is wrong we have demonstrated (p. 654) by showing that the concepts " normal " illumination and " proper " colour (in the sense of fixed norms) are erroneous. With the rejection of these concepts one also abandons the concept of " transformation ". Instead, as we have seen, the perception of surface colours in " normal " illumination is no less nor no more problematic than that in " non-normal " illumination. Neither is more " retinal " than the other, for the fact that surface colours are seen at all (i.e. the separation of " illumination " and " illuminated object ") indicates a type of sensory response which cannot be understood as " merely physiological " in the traditional sense. " *Separation of illumination and illuminated object* " and " *perception of a taut surface of a certain colour* " are simply two sides or aspects of one and the same process.

From this it can be seen that the problem of colour constancy is not one of discrepancy between " stimulus " and " perceived colour " but has to do rather with the general question of how our visual world is constructed. The perceived separation into illumination and illuminated object (i.e. the correlate of having an object-colour) is simply the expression of a certain structural form of our visual world.

673[1] Our visual world is not constructed by "accessory" higher (central, psychological) processes from a stimulus-conditioned raw material of "primary sensations" and sensation-complexes; rather from the very beginning, the functioning of our sensory apparatus depends upon conditions in such a way that, in accordance with external stimulus constellations and internal attitudes we find ourselves confronted by a world of "things", thus or thus, now more poorly, now more richly articulated and organized. With this articulation and organization such aspects of the visual world as "visibility of a certain illumination", "existence of flat colour surfaces" and of "rich articulation of the field of vision" are intrinsically connected, and these aspects are the necessary conditions for the arousal of constancy phenomena.

674 The phenomenon of colour constancy cannot occur unless the visual field is articulated, and this is possible only when at least two surfaces of different albedo are simultaneously present in this field. The following experiment demonstrates this in a particularly instructive manner. In a semi-darkened room a homogeneous black disk revolves upon a colour wheel. The beam of a strong projection lantern is focused upon the disk so that the entire disk and nothing else receives the light from this lamp. When set in motion the disk is seen as a white or very light-grey object appearing in a faintly illuminated room. This impression of white is absolutely compulsory. It does not matter how one thinks about the illumination; it is impossible to see "an intensely illuminated black" instead of "white". Similarly it is immaterial whether the disk be viewed from close range or from a distance. (The light beam itself is seen as a brilliant, self-existent thing in the room-space.)

Now we bring a small bit of really white paper into the light a few centimetres in front of the disk. *Instantly* the disk is "black". The bit of paper is "white" and both are "intensely illuminated". The suddenness of this change is astonishing; there is no impression of a rapid run along the achromatic scale from white through the greys to black. Instead one has the experience that at the place where one *had* been seeing a faintly lighted white there has *now* appeared a brilliantly illuminated black.

675 Simultaneously with this conversion in the disk we observe a change in the appearance of the beam also. Its "thingness" diminishes or disappears entirely. It had formerly appeared as one

[1] [Translation taken from K. Koffka's "Some Remarks on the Theory of Colour Constancy", *Psychol. Forsch.*, 1932, **16**, p. 329.]

of various objects in the dimly lighted room; now one perceives quite clearly that in the "empty" part of the visual field which this beam occupies there is an intense illumination. With the sudden conversion of white into black the entire visual space is reorganized in a specific manner. Now there are subsidiary wholes within the whole visual space, and they display a variety of shades and brightnesses. There has appeared, that is to say, a characteristic articulation or organization into parts of that which formerly was more or less homogeneous.

Now we remove the white paper. The initial impression, as suddenly as it had gone, is once more dominant. One's impression of the illumination is once more unified throughout the entire space; the disk is again white. Modifications of procedure will be observed to give the following results: The same conversion from white to black and the reverse can be observed without the white paper if one stands quite close to the disk and stops and starts the rotator. When the disk is standing still minute particles of dust or irregularities on its surface will be seen to vary in albedo, and homogeneity of the surface is consequently lost. Still another variation of the experiment is to enlarge the beam so that it no longer coincides exactly with the disk. If this is done slowly, the white of the disk will gradually (not suddenly) disappear as the disk darkens.

676 From these considerations we are now in a position to explain the principle underlying the standard experiment (p. 620), and why it is that a (subjective) inequality of R_2 and R_1 is experienced when (end Series I) the reduction screen is removed. When the disks are seen without the screen (Series II) "we perceive", as Katz said, "the entire conditions of illumination." That is to say, we see the *whole* visual space and its *subsidiary wholes*, their various shades and brightnesses, each disk in the quality corresponding to *its* illumination, and so on. When the reduction screen is used (Series I) the two disks appear equal because now the conditions of illumination are subjectively and objectively unified. But it is to be noted that *only unification*—not a reduction to a "more retinal" seeing—has occurred. It is quite obvious that when the reduction screen is used the two disks will be seen as equal, because *now* the impression of illumination is the same for both.

Any substitute for the reduction screen—even an appropriate subjective attitude—will function in the same way if it succeeds in unifying the impression of illumination. Such an "attitude of pure optics " requires, as Köhler has said, that one free one's self from the thingness of objects, i.e. degrade them to the status of mere planes of light.

677 We can now understand also the Laws of Field Size which Katz proposed as well as the reason why the differences between Series I and II varied when observation was direct or indirect, binocular or monocular. It is clear also why tachistoscopic results differed from the others. In all these cases the deciding question is that of richness and specific character of the organization and articulation of the visual space involved.

Selection 17

THE UNITY OF THE SENSES

By Erich M. v. Hornbostel

"Die Einheit der Sinne", *Melos, Zeitschr. f. Musik*, vol. iv, 290–297. [The English translation by Elizabeth Koffka and Warren Vinton, entitled "The Unity of the Senses", which appeared in *Psyche*, 1927, 7, 83–89 of issue No. 28, is reprinted here with permission of the original author and of Kegan Paul, Trench, Trubner and Co., Ltd., London.]

83 I. For the deaf there is no music. The obvious must always be suspect; we should question it—at least a little, tentatively—asking, Why is it so?

A dancer had a dance, "The Lily". Her humanity vanished in the high waving chalice of her veil, a deep violet faded away in spirals, a dazzling white rose up expanding indefinitely. The noises of the suburban music-hall could not spoil this pure music.

Figurative speech? Transferred meaning? I do not pretend to have seen tones or heard colours. I am not deaf, and am fairly musical; I know what is really meant by "music", and was thinking of this very meaning. To call the dolphin a fish may offend the zoologist, but it is no metaphor. A certain negro tribe has a special word for "see"; but only one general word for "hear", "touch", "smell", and "taste". It matters little through which sense I realize that in the dark I have blundered into a pig-sty. In French "*sentir*" means to smell, to touch, and to feel, all together. A child who wants a "bright" trumpet rather than one with a dull tone, spontaneously returns to the original meaning of the word *bright*, which was used only of sound as late as the period of Middle High German. For Germans this use of *bright* now seems "transferred", so natural was its carrying over to light. Nevertheless, everybody knows what "brightness" of sound means—not something corresponding to light, but the same thing.

Here is a tone, here are a number of different grey papers from black to white; choose the one which is as bright as the tone. This one? (Indignantly) "Too dark!" This one? "Too bright!" That one? "Still too bright!" And so on. It can be done quite easily and with great precision; and everyone, except
84 the colour-blind, can find a grey to match the tone. Furthermore,

anyone can find on the piano that tone which sounds as bright as lilac smells. (Generally he thinks the task nonsense at first, but, if he can be persuaded to deal with such nonsense at all, it goes very well.)

So there is a sensuous which is not limited to one single sense. Indeed, looking more closely, the apparent exception becomes the rule, and one must search in order to find the private property of any one sense. It is true that these proprietors themselves are different personalities; the Seen is, as such, different from the Heard; and this is a difference which cannot be made clear to the blind and the deaf. But all the senses have not such clear-cut individualities. There are very few people who know that it is not with the tongue or palate that they taste the aroma of a pineapple, but that they smell it, and that it will disappear if the nostrils are closed. The "five senses" are still proverbial, for it is only in the last few decades that science has split up the skin's sense of "feeling" into a greater number of senses. Warm and cold, however, still appear to us as directions on a single line, linked up by all the different grades of luke-warm and cool, and not as two different species, like seeing and hearing—and this in spite of their having two separate organs. With the finger-tips we can feel which of two vibrations is brighter and which darker, though an interval of only one whole tone lies between them; and an octave chord feels consonant on the skin in contrast to a seventh. Whether fishes hear as we do cannot be decided, though it is possible to train a shad to come in response to a whistle. The "hearing" of the skin, in spite of its relation to that of the ears, seems to call for quotation marks, because it is at the same time related to the pressure-sense. In this double relation of the vibration-sensation, we still feel in our own bodies how an originally single sense splits into two, which only become independent of one another in the course of evolution.

More advanced of all in their specialization are sight and hearing. And really, each of these two "highest" senses has something which belongs to it alone: to the eye, colours, which give variety to the world; to the ear, the music of sounds and tones, a gift beyond life's necessities. Both are late acquisitions, still the least stable of all, and most easily exposed to attack and destruction. Many people—more than know it—are colour-blind or weak in colour-vision; unmusical people are numberless and of all grades. What they lack, more or less, and what animals probably lack altogether, is that which distinguishes tones from other sounds, especially from noises; that which makes a tone so similar to its octave despite their different brightness; and makes the octaves harmonize in perfect consonance.

85 Strange! It is just where eye and ear differ, that their connection has been sought. For colour, like pitch, changes with the wave-length: a fact which misled the physicists. (In reality there is a difference at this very point: brightness in hearing depends on frequency, while brightness in sight depends on amplitude.) Scriabine accompanies his *Prometheus* with colours, which—for him—correspond to the tones. Others would choose otherwise. More often, and with greater confidence, colours are ascribed to the vowels. Everyone who does this thinks his ascriptions the only natural and possible ones. I saw mother and daughter arguing furiously: "E is red!" "No, yellow!" But to both it seemed bright, clear, and sharp.

We pity the colour-blind and the tone-deaf: a world of nothing but greys seems dreary to us. Therefore we easily over-value the individual qualities, colour and tone, which belong to these spheres, and under-value the qualities which they have in common. And yet there is brightness without either colour or tone, but no colour or tone without brightness. He really would be a cripple who had these without brightness.

The painter Troost once papered a bedroom with dark blue velvet-paper. The walls were charmed away, the eye plunged without resistance into a soft, warm, embracing depth. That this depth happened to be blue did not of itself matter; but the blue tended to produce the same effect as the darkness and velvety gloss. Generally speaking, even for the perception of colour, not the colour itself—blue, yellow, or red—is the essential, but all the rest that reaches us by the eye as well as by other senses. When we want to describe this, names come quite easily from everywhere, from the spheres where they happen to be used to-day, and we understand them because we are not using them in a context foreign to their true nature.

So there remains little which is unique to a single sense, and that only incidentally, and only, perhaps, in the case of the higher senses. Nevertheless, the sense which is used will leave its mark on the phenomenon. What is seen, heard, or touched, will, necessarily, we think, have an optical, acoustic, or tactile character. But even this is not necessary.

There are super-sensuous sense-perceptions. Movement can be seen, heard, or touched. It is not necessary, however—as every cinema-goer knows—that it should actually take place. An

" apparent " movement, indistinguishable from a real movement, springs forth from two pictures, sounds, or skin touches following one another at the right spatial and temporal intervals. Now, under certain circumstances, there are apparent movements, communicated
86 through the eye, the ear, or the sense of touch, which, however, possess none of the qualities of the seen, heard, or touched—indeed, nothing of any sensuous sphere. And yet they are movements, normal, and distinctly perceived—not ghosts. Once I dreamed: " It " rushed, raced, past me, around me, though I lay very quietly and neither saw, heard, nor felt anything. But never was a thing more manifest, more real to me, than this " storm-in-itself ".

In ordinary life, it is true, we do not meet any " in-itself ". A movement which we perceive is less real than a movement which we ourselves make. And it is difficult—custom can never quite stop it—not to participate, in some way or other, in perceived movement. And the more it " moves " us, " touches " us, or " carries us away ", the more difficult this is. Again, " movement of feelings ", " course of thinking " are not metaphors, any more than " movement of the air " and " course of a race " ; we simply say what we mean, and incidentally add the immediate specification. (A comparison is only a comparison in so far as it limps ; so far as it hits, it is a simple statement.) But even here the special meaning will not develop until later. The original meaning of a word does not appear from its different applications, but only comes out when the whole range of meanings is surveyed and the various nuances are seen as one. The whole out-growth must be gathered back into itself; only by such a condensation can we regain the pregnant germ. By cancelling out differences, on the other hand, we get nothing but the empty shell (the general concept of Logic).

That such abstract concepts do not occur in natural thinking is very characteristic of primitive people (it is characteristic of us to think this a fault in their intelligence). But this does not mean that primitive man perceives only the sensuous in the sensuous, the perceptible in the perceptible, only experiences the casual in what he is experiencing thus, here, and now. In order to do this, he would have to make abstractions from life, tear objective and subjective from one another, and let the stream of experience crystallize into a material presence—and this is just what he cannot do. In his perception are desire and fear ; his thoughts stand before him, and behave as any of his kind behaves. He does not put soul into things, because soul has not yet been taken out of them. He does not pin names on to things ; does not ask " What are you called ? ", but " Who are you ? ", because everything still is what it is called. And as it is, so it looks, so it sounds, so it feels, so it does to him for good or evil, and so he does to it in turn.

This " so " is heard in speech. The sound paints—and paints
87 more than mere sound. The sense of hollow sounds (like m, mb) is " dull, dark, bitter, blunt, heavy, dense, thick, big, full, round, swelling, deep, tired ", and much more, but all this in one. And now think of the opposites, " bright, sharp, light, blank ", and so forth—how strange it would be for these to say that they were " umb " ! Nobody would believe them. Now speech is not the setting of words one after another, but is a happening in sound. Even isolated single sounds still have a sense—the example was only meant to show that they do have one—but it is less definite than in the course of speech, and often essentially different. It is only the structure of this course, the melody, which transposes the living reality into the sphere of acoustics, at the same time leaving its full sense intact.

To sum up : what is essential in the sensuous-perceptible is not that which separates the senses from one another, but that which unites them ; unites them among themselves ; unites them with the entire (even with the non-sensuous) experience in ourselves ; and with all the external world that there is to be experienced.

II. What is essential in a work of art does not lie in the sensuous-perceptible. The artist will protest against such a disregard of sensuous beauty. (And rightly.) What is essential in a work of art does lie in the sensuous-perceptible. The artists protest still more. (And very rightly.) Both these sentences are wrong. (Now the logicians protest.) Both are right. (" Impossible ! " shout the logicians.) What then ?

The perceptible is not less perceptible because it is more than merely perceptible. Appearances are not only a means by which we get knowledge of something—not otherwise communicable—which stands behind, beside, and beyond. It is not hidden behind the appearance, but is beheld directly therein. We do not hear sounds which someone once put together in such and such a manner in order to express this and that—we hear Mozart. (Busoni, himself a genius, heard that fragment of Heaven which Mozart had within him. He *heard* it, he did not have to work it out.)

What a man is I know by *what* he does and says ; but still more surely and directly, by *how* he does it and says it, and by *how* he looks. But the What is not to be separated from the How ; and even in inanimate nature to change the structure of atoms and molecules

is the same as to transform the substance. I try to show the structure of music by analysis; but I can only show that such
88 parts, so put together, form just this thing. We must hear the "so" of the parts, the "so" of their relation, the "so" of the whole music—this is its form, and at the same time its content. You cannot have this content except in this form.

Hanslick was wrong. Bach was no artificial constructor. To form is not to knead, but to condense.

I may know something, have a clear picture of it, have experienced it myself, and still not remember how it came to me—has someone told it me, have I read it, seen it, or dreamed it, or did it just come into my mind? This could not happen if the mediator mattered.

I find myself in a very definite state of consciousness—"mood" would be too vague—there simply is no term. I cannot say whether it comes from a day in the Black Forest, a picture by Schwind, the work of Möricke, or from the seventy-third bar of Wolf's *Fussreise*. Perhaps from none of these, though each embodies it identically, gives the soul of it. I cannot give an exact account of it or communicate it to others, for I am neither painter, poet, nor singer, and was born a hundred years too late simply to live it out.

Lyonel Feininger, when fifty years old and at the height of his powers, sat down one day and wrote organ fugues. Until then he had only painted fugues. Now the blind also can see his pictures. Even in art the sense-sphere is largely indifferent; transposition from one sphere into another is possible, though not always so completely as here, where (I speak of the pictures) strong linear tensions are pulled tightly together by the clear austerity of the laws of counterpoint.

For there is one real contrast between the eye and the ear. No sound is ever so much an object as is a fixed, visible thing. Even in a constant tone we hear a continual waxing and waning. We say "Be quiet!" when we want to hear no more. A sound may be round, spherical like a ball, to my right or left, distant or near, concentrated or spread out—there does exist a hearing-space, but one in which neither quadrangle nor cube is possible. The eye alone puts before us objects which stare at us, which are as much outside us as we are outside them, and which remain where they are when we go away and are still there unchanged when we return.

To the contrast between the senses there must correspond a contrast between the arts. The arts of the eye form objects, though not for the sake of the objects or for their portrayal. An "object-free" work itself is set free only from material narration, is (to the

annoyance of those who are thirsty for facts) no longer a description; but even it cannot cut off the statics of spatial form. The wood-cutter (of Hodler) holds his arm forever ready for the stroke which
89 through all eternity will never fall, and, as in a watch-spring, the stored up tension gets less and less the longer we wait.

The arts of tone form events—when they will, with an alarming truth to nature. For whether an event develops in the realm of sight or of hearing, in the realm of body or of spirit does not change the way in which it develops. A motif may be beheld as a whole and all at once—as may a space-form—and without temporal development; but what is thus beheld all at once is still a progression with its tempo and its duration, a movement with all its motions. Even Schubert cannot sing "*Ohne Regung ruht das Meer*", but only "*und bekümmert sieht's der Schiffer*". The Egyptians might have caught the vivacity of the long-tailed monkey in the music of the shawm—the grandiose repose of the grey baboon called for stone.

But only in the most extreme cases does the contrast become decisive; its importance should not be over-estimated. And especially so since it has been found (first by Max Wertheimer) that in the stationary space-structure of the contemporaneous—as in the "field" of the physicist—the same play of forces is at work, which, when dynamically discharged, gives rise to movement. And the one as well as the other is preserved by the same "structure" from breaking up into a disconnected conglomeration or sequence. It is the same organizing principle which calls forth organism from mere substance, and which binds the stream of happening into wholes, which makes the line a melody which we can follow, and the melody a figure which we can see in one glance.

Since the sensuous is perceptible only when it has form, the unity of the senses is given from the very beginning. And together with this the unity of the arts. Art unfolded into the variety of the several arts. In the mask-dance, music and painting, sculpture and poetry, are not yet separated from one another; colours and forms are still drawn into the sounding whirl of human action and its cosmic meaning.

To us, alas, sight and sound, inner and outer, soul and body, God and World, have fallen apart. What we knew as children we now must grope for. Only grown-up children—artists and wise men—know this always, radiating life in their glance, listening to the blossoming around.

A dancer had a dance—but this I have said before.

Second Group: Animal Experiments

Selection 18

SIMPLE STRUCTURAL FUNCTIONS IN THE CHIMPANZEE AND IN THE CHICKEN

By Wolfgang Köhler

"Nachweis einfacher Strukturfunktionen beim Schimpansen und beim Haushuhn. Über eine neue Methode zur Untersuchung des bunten Farbensystems" (Aus der Anthropoidenstation auf Teneriffa), *Abh. d. königl. Preuss. Ak. d. Wissen.*, Jahrg. 1918, Phys.-Math. Klasse, Nr. 2. Berlin, 1918, pp. 1–101.

3 Upon what kind of process do the memorial after-effects apparent in learning phenomena depend? An example will illustrate what is meant. An animal has learned to choose one or another of two achromatic colours. One perfectly consistent explanation of what has happened here would be the following: one of the colour processes has through experience acquired a positive, the other a negative, character. Thus the animal not only learns to approach one of the colours but it also learns to avoid the other. In the end these two products of learning will reciprocally aid one another.
4 Such learning has been demonstrated (under other conditions) in experiments performed by Pavlov's methods. It does not greatly alter the results if colours slightly different from those of the learning series are substituted for the original ones. This shows that the memorial after-effect of the original pair holds not only for each specific colour but for a certain zone of adjacent colours. This zone is known as the range of substitution. As long as the colours substituted for the original colour do not go beyond this zone, the theory we shall here examine is able to explain a great number of facts, if one remembers that the substitution value of a stimulus is a direct function of its similarity to the original stimulus.

5 But now let us alter the procedure. The animal is trained to choose, say, the lighter of two greys, $\overset{+}{gr}$, and avoid the darker one, $\overline{gr}$. After this training is completed there is suddenly presented, in a "critical experiment", $\overset{+}{gr}$ and the still lighter grey, $\overset{\circ}{gr}$. If it is true that the positive value of $\overset{+}{gr}$ is attached to the unaltered grey sensation experienced by the animal, then there is no reason why $\overset{+}{gr}$

should lose this value under the new circumstances. The new grey, if sufficiently different from $\overset{+}{gr}$, can have no positive value, for it will then fall outside the range of substitutions of $\overset{+}{gr}$; and it can have no negative value, for it is even farther removed from $\overline{gr}$ than $\overset{+}{gr}$ is.
6 Therefore $\mathring{gr}$ must be "neutral". Since the critical experiment presents a neutral and a positive colour, at least the majority of all choices should favour the latter. On the basis of the theory we

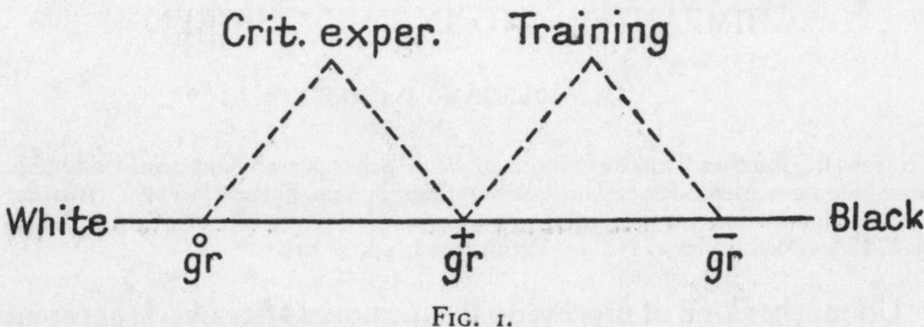

FIG. 1.

are examining it would be quite incomprehensible if the animal were suddenly to choose $\mathring{gr}$ more often than it did $\overset{+}{gr}$.

Let us designate with N the total number of critical trials and with $\overset{+}{n}$ the number of times $\overset{+}{gr}$ is chosen and with $\mathring{n}$ the number of times
7 $\mathring{gr}$ is chosen. If the theory is correct, then

$$\overset{+}{n} > \mathring{n} \text{ where } \overset{+}{n} + \mathring{n} = N.$$

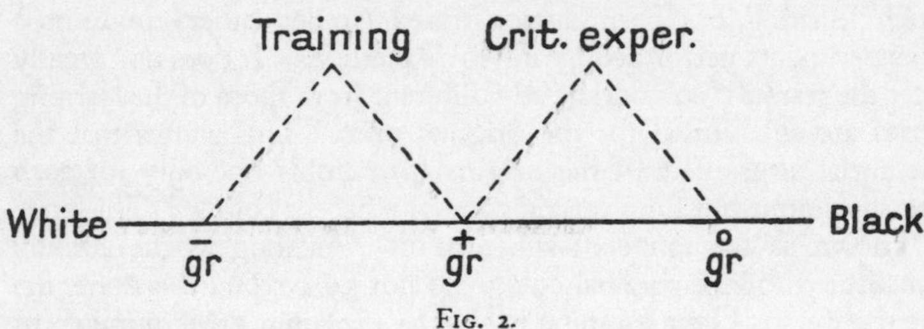

FIG. 2.

If $\mathring{gr}$ were not outside the substitution zone of $\overset{+}{gr}$, the result might be

$$\overset{+}{n} \geqq \mathring{n}.$$

The same reasoning would hold for a case such as that suggested by Fig. 2.

8 *Experiments with chickens.*—A preliminary test with four chickens was carried out in the following way. The chickens II and III were given the training indicated by Fig. 1, I and V were trained

in the manner suggested by Fig. 2. The critical tests gave the following results:

Chicken		$\overset{+}{n}$	$\overset{\circ}{n}$	N
II	W	2	8	10
III	W	9	21	30
I	B	7	13	20
V	B	8	17	25
Totals		26	59	85

9 These results clearly show that instead of being larger, $\overset{+}{n}$ is not even half as large as $\overset{\circ}{n}$. The "neutral" colour (according to the theory) was chosen over twice as often as the "positive" one.

But perhaps the very *newness* of the new colour attracted the
10 chickens more than the positive colour of the training series. Let us test this experimentally. Our principal question is whether the product of training is connected with the individual sensation

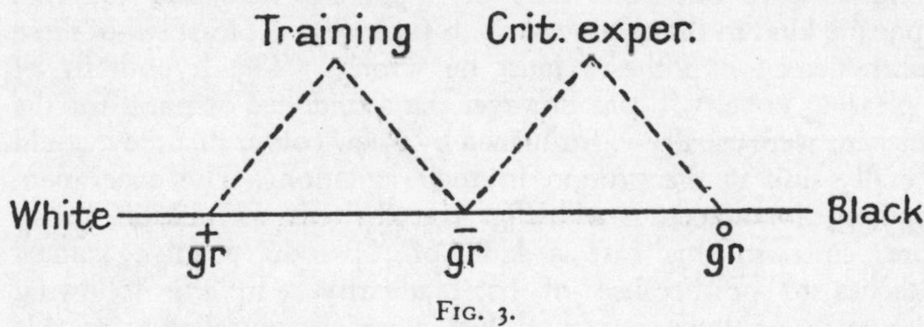

Fig. 3.

processes. Or, more exactly: Does the essential aspect of training lie in the positive value of one sensation process and the negative value of another? We have tested the positive sensation process and found our results at variance with the theory. An analogous test of the negative colour was also carried out in the following way. After the training indicated by Fig. 3 we substituted for the positive colour a new, neutral colour, $\overset{\circ}{gr}$, *darker* than the dark $\overline{gr}$ of the training series. Now the results (to support the theory) must be

$$\overset{\circ}{n} > \bar{n}.$$

That is to say, when confronted by a negative and a neutral colour the chickens ought to choose the latter. The results of our experiment were as follows:

11

Chicken		$\mathring{n}$	$\bar{n}$	N
II	W	3	10	13
III	W	10	10	20
I	B	4	16	20
V	B	9	16	25
Totals		26	52	78

Even though the results of No. III might be the product of chance, the totals show that $\mathring{n}$, far from being favoured, occurred only half as often as $\bar{n}$.

But perhaps this was because $\overline{gr}$ was *familiar* (from the training series) and for this reason chosen in preference to the new and strange colour, $\mathring{g}r$. This explanation can be offered, but it is not permissible to offer one kind of hypothesis here and just the opposite kind in the other case (p. 9 f. above). At least *one* of these contradictory hypotheses must be wrong. The hypothesis of " pleasing novelty " can, however, be abandoned at once, for the chickens were usually so frightened by a new colour that they would literally sink to the ground in their agitation. The experiment reported in connection with Fig. 3 really tells us nothing, therefore, since in this case a kind of " pseudo positive value " attaches to $\overline{gr}$ because of its familiarity. In the following discussion only the results of Fig. 2 will be admitted as reliable evidence.

When a human being looks at the two greys used in these
13 experiments he reports not independent colours, but a togetherness [*Zueinander*] of both. And indeed all investigations of sensation ultimately depend upon this comparison between two things. Studies of " difference thresholds ", for example, are determinations of the point at which a particular kind of togetherness of the presented objects arises or disappears. There are two ways in which togetherness of colours (or any other phenomena) can occur and be effective: *colour-wholes* and perceived *colour-relationships*. It is impossible to explain the former in terms of the latter because the characteristic Gestalt-effect is often at its maximum when nothing

whatever of relations is experienced.[1] The opposite of this is,
14 however, possible, for one can change a whole-experience into an
experiencing of relations: one disintegrates the pair, one "makes explicit" the togetherness. Such active processes are not at all necessary for an ordinary perception of colour-wholes. But these are special problems of human psychology; actually Gestalt- and relation-perceptions have so much in common that, particularly here where we are dealing with animals, we may for the time being ignore their differences.

We may characterize in the following way that which is functionally common to both Gestalt- and relation-perceptions: (*a*) The individual colours appearing in a pair attain an inner union.[2] Their role in this union (regardless of whether this be a Gestalt or a relationship) depends not upon their absolute qualities, but upon
their places in the system they compose. (*b*) If their places with
15 respect to each other are held constant but a variation is made in
their absolute quality, the Gestalt and the perceived relationship will be transposed. Thus if the first pair is $\overset{2}{g}r$-$\overset{3}{g}r$, $\overset{2}{g}r$ is the "brighter side"; but in $\overset{1}{g}r$-$\overset{2}{g}r$ it is the "darker side" and $\overset{1}{g}r$ is now the "brighter side." The role or meaning of $\overset{2}{g}r$ changes as we proceed from one pair to the other. But the essential characteristic of togetherness has not been changed by this transposition: both cases are two-colour wholes: both allow the same judgment of "one colour brighter than the other".

The "inner union" in both Gestalt- and relation-perception
16 depends in either case upon a common basic function. We shall call
it "togetherness" or "structure-function" [*Strukturfunktion*], the term referring to that feature of a perceived Gestalt or a perceived relation which is *common* to both. Differences between them are here intentionally ignored.

Applying this to choice trainings we find that when an animal is trained it may well be that it has learned to choose not "one of the two (absolute) colours", but rather that its choice is of one side of the pair which the colours together compose. If this is the case,
then the results will be such as those reported in connection with
18 Figs. 1 and 2. The terms "positive", "negative", and "neutral"

[1] Example: experiencing a circle is not essentially a process of noting the identical distance of each peripheral point from the centre. A circle whose middle point is lacking may be seen in perfectly adequate fashion, and indeed this perception can be so precise that even very slight variations from the true circle will be detected at once.

[2] The opposite of such inner union would be, say, the external relationship of association by contiguity.

as used above in conformity with the theory we were examining are manifestly meaningless, for in so far as choices are made relative to the presented togetherness, no colour is in itself positive, negative, or neutral.

[19–27: details regarding tests given four additional chickens. Repetitions of the original pair were interspersed among the critical tests (example: in 150 choices the original pair was presented 100 times and the critical pair 50 times). The results are again in keeping with the structure-function theory: i.e. transpositions such as those reported in the foregoing tables occurred. Additional experiments are reported which were designed to study the memorial after-effect of the training series. The function of structure has a much more lasting effect than do absolute qualities. (23): indeed with chickens the effect of absolute colour-training (with the concomitant strangeness of a new colour) disappears in a few minutes after the training series is concluded. Effects due to the function of structure, on the other hand, are much more lasting, and it must therefore be these which carry over from one day to the next during training. (25): one chicken was tested 18 hours after training and chose the structurally correct colour 17 times in 20 choices. Later tests gave even better results.]

28 A more exhaustive comparison between the theories of absolute
and structural choices could be carried out as follows: I. Let
A, *B*, and *C* be degrees of any quality and train the animals to
choose *B* in the pair *BC*. How much additional training with *AB*
is necessary before *A* is preferred over *B*? II. Using *BC*, train
another similar group of animals to choose *B*. How much further
29 practice is needed before *B* is favoured in the pair *AB*? By comparing
the results of I and II one has an index of the relative values of
30 pro-structural and contra-structural learning. III. Use *AB* and *BC*
31 in chance alternation and let *A* be correct in *AB*, *B* in *BC*. IV. Reverse
the procedure: whether appearing in *AB* or in *BC*, *B* will always
be correct. A comparison of the results from III and IV will give
[32–34: omitted] an even more accurate picture of the difference between structural
and absolute values in learning.

35 When we consider, as is to-day becoming more and more apparent, that structural influences are also involved in the accomplishments of higher primates (particularly human beings), it follows that relatively low organisms merit more appreciation than we might otherwise have thought to extend them. One must at least recognize that in conforming closely to its environment the behaviour of such a creature is not so poor and monotonous as it

would necessarily be if there were no structural processes. Nature is
36 richer and more colourful by far than some of the wooden descrip-
tions one encounters would have us believe. There is a tendency to think of structural functions as a kind of process imposed from higher levels of organization upon the lower and more primitive functions. From this we are led to segregate into a higher group those animals which are capable of such functions. This point of view is probably not in keeping with reality.

Between chickens and men there are radical differences both in degree of structural factors and in the level upon which these operate, especially as regards the range of structures and complication of materials involved. A pair of colours is certainly more primitive than the functional structures with which human beings can deal. Nor should we forget that before the bird responds to
the structural togetherness of a pair of greys there has been trial
37 after trial, always with the same material upon which to fasten his
attention. We are not, therefore, proposing a revised hierarchy in which animals formerly classified as lower are to be promoted to a higher place merely because they too are capable of structural responses. Indeed the possibility of such a new classification is more or less ruled out because there is probably no clearly defined lower limit separating those animals which do from those which do not exhibit functional responses. A classification of this kind would presuppose that the behaviour of organisms below a certain level of development would depend entirely upon absolute data (sensation or excitation) and that here togetherness of stimulations or excitations was without any influence at all. This view is probably derived from certain assumptions which may be found in human psychology: viz. that " sensations " are the absolute and mutually independent pieces from which consciousness is made up, and indeed that even the simplest togetherness of stimulations or excitations is secondary relative to these primary constituents. And yet the fact of structural functions in chickens shows how such a point of view errs; and it shows also that quite simple kinds of structural function arise from the elementary properties of the nervous system (or living substance in general) just as readily and just as soon as do the most simple absolute sensations.

If the point of view here maintained is correct—and that it is the more cautious view cannot be doubted—then a classification of the kind just mentioned is worthless. We have not shown that the chicken should be classified on a higher level than formerly; we have proven (by means of a special case) that the forms of

" response to stimulation " are everywhere richer than one might otherwise have realized.

39 *Experiments with apes.*—In view of our results with chickens one is tempted to predict that the function of structure will be even more strikingly demonstrated when apes are used as subjects. This need not, however, be the case, for it is not true that " higher " capacities are required to effect the " greater " accomplishment represented by pro-structural responses. Indeed it would probably be truer to say that only with organisms as capable as the anthropoids might one elicit responses to absolute qualities (i.e. a kind of analysis) even when these qualities are presented in functional contexts. An illustration of what is meant can be seen in the following example taken from human psychology. By adopting a keenly analytical attitude one can reduce the amount of " illusory " effect in the Müller-Lyer illusion. This is accomplished by resolving the long straight line from its context. Much more is required of the observer in this case, however, than when a natural, unconstrained attitude is taken: it is easier to be deceived than not. As
40 regards our present inquiry it is reasonable to assume that a pro-structural response to pairs of colours is easier and more natural than the contra-structural response.

41 The ape Chica was tested with greys as chickens had been. Grey cards 11 cm. square were attached to two boxes 10 cm. apart and were viewed from a distance of 75 cm. Choice was made by placing
42 the end of a stick upon the box desired. Observed from a distance it was clear that the animal was concentrating on the boxes, for she never glanced about until eating provided a slight pause. Chica was given 232 trials and tested when but one error had occurred during the last 75 of these. Twenty critical tests (in two
43 groups of 10 each) were given: two were responded to incorrectly, 18 correctly, i.e. pro-structurally. In the critical tests *both* boxes contained food and the animal was therefore rewarded at every choice whether correct or not. The two wrong choices (i.e. choices of the absolute colour which had been correct during training) were the first ones made. From the animal's behaviour it appeared that the situation was new and strange, and even at the moment when
44 choice was made, the ape could be observed to look at the *other* box. At the third and upon all subsequent choices the formerly chosen (absolute) grey was abandoned in favour of the pro-structural side of the pair which training had emphasized. Since the animal received food even at the first two choices, one might have expected that she would continue to prefer that colour, but the structural influence

was apparently strong enough, once the strangeness of a new pair diminished, to permit the pro-structural response to dominate.

46 A three-year-old child of fairly low vocabulary for its age was next tested in practically the same way as the ape had been. No explanation was given and the only language used was: " Take one ", by the experimenter, and " This " by the child. After 15 training trials no further error was made. The correct side was the brighter of the two greys. After two days of training during which in all 45 selections had been made, the critical experiment was introduced. All 20 choices were made correctly, i.e. the brighter side was selected each time.

47 The results from ape and child are so similar that one cannot but believe that the same basic function was effective in both cases. The extent to which the pair-structure was decisive for the boy is almost beyond an adult's comprehension. Adults deal with more difficult and complicated structures, it is true, but were an adult to be trained for two days with greys *b* and *c* wherein *b* was always correct and then suddenly given *a* and *b*, the chances are that he would not proceed at once (as the child did) to choose *a* with such naïve assurance. The ability to recognize absolute colours is highly developed in adults compared with children, and this fact is not conducive to an unimpeded operation of the togetherness effect. However, if the colours resemble one another greatly or if the test pair is presented (without knowledge) not too soon after the original pair was seen, adults too will, without knowing it, give the same transposition results as those already reported in this paper.

48 It is instructive to note the point at which the subject (child or ape) suddenly begins an almost unbroken series of correct choices. Indicating with *R* and *L* the position of the correct box, and with + and − the correct and false choices, the child's first 25 trials were as follows:

RLLLLRLLLLLLLLLLRRLLRLLLR
\+ − − − + + − − − − − − + − + + + + + + + + + + +
5 10 15 20 25

One can see that at the 15th trial a sudden change occurs and that henceforth every choice is determined by the togetherness of the

49 two colours. The same phenomenon can also be observed with animals. Chica, for example, was trained with two boxes of different size (but identical colour). After a series of 50 haphazard choices a point was reached after which only four errors (in 50 more trials) occurred.

What is the meaning of such abrupt transitions? They are very

like the " genuine solutions " occurring in intelligence tests. As regards the kind of problems studied in this inquiry (" pair training ") it appears that the product of learning is primarily related to the structural function of the two colours. If this is
51 true, then to test the animal (after training) for some absolute recall is beside the point. Nor does one describe the result of such training correctly in expressions such as " The animal has learned to connect one side of the pair with a certain response ". The animal's *real* task during the training series is to discover what it is he is supposed to do. Everything depends upon his observing at some moment during training that there are two colours to consider and that the relationship between them is the clue to a successful choice. This means that he must *see* the *pair*. Whether this event occurs suddenly or comes about gradually is less important. The number of trials needed for training could be greatly reduced if one were only able to tell the chimpanzee " Please take one of the *two colours* there before you ".

[52–55: Chica and Grande were trained with rectangles of 9 × 12 and 12 × 16 cm. and the latter was always correct. In the critical test rectangles of 12 × 16 and 15 × 20 cm. were used. Both made the transposition with but two errors each in 18 and 16 critical choices respectively.]

56 An insightful treatment of the material offered in the training series is one governed by an apprehension of the structural principle of that material. The case of " pair apprehension " is but a special
57 instance of this general problem. Another example: when Sultan fitted one bamboo cane into an opening at the end of another he
58 *never* moved the thicker towards the thinner; one was always passive, the other always active.[1] This process of thrusting one stick into another required that they be treated as functionally different, not as equal in value. Sultan's insight consisted in his recognizing that this difference depended upon the relative size of the two sticks. His behaviour could not be called insightful if success in fitting the sticks together had come merely as a result of fumbling with them. It was insightful if he *saw* which stick could be thrust into the other.

59 However one might wonder if perhaps the animal had merely learned that a stick of a certain absolute size was to be held steady while that of another absolute size was thrust into it. To test this, four bamboo rods of equal length were prepared in such fashion

[1] Observation of this was facilitated by the fact that Sultan always grasped the thicker (passive) stick in his left hand and moved the other towards and into this one.

that 1 fitted easily into 2, 2 into 3, and 3 into 4. Sultan's past experience had been with rods of the sizes 1 and 2. Now, however, when 2-3 were given him the rod which formerly had functioned as the *passive* side of the pair had to become the *active* member. Results: in every case (four trials in irregular order with all combinations) Sultan thrust the smaller rod *into* the other.[1] That he at no time merely fumbled with both or moved them simultaneously towards one another gives positive evidence of his insight into their structural relationship.[2]

[60–101: in another series of experiments chromatic colours were used. These were:—

(*A*) 360° Blue
(*B*) 270° Blue + 90° Red
(*C*) 200° Blue + 160° Red
(*D*) 100° Blue + 260° Red
(*E*) 30° Blue + 330° Red.

Example: Chica and Tercera were trained to choose *B* in the pair *BC* and were given *AB* in the critical tests. Perfect and near-perfect transpositions of the type suggested by Figs. 1–2 above were obtained. Grande and Sultan gave similar results with a yellow-red scale of five colours.]

[1] The sticks were laid side by side in front of him; sometimes one, sometimes the other would be nearest. As a rule he nevertheless picked up the larger stick with his left hand, the smaller with his right. If he did use the reverse hands for picking up the sticks, he invariably changed before fitting them together.

[2] Similar results were obtained with Chica.

SELECTION 19

OBSERVATIONS ON RAVENS

By MATHILDE HERTZ

"Beobachtungen an gefangenen Rabenvögeln," *Psychol. Forsch.*, 1926, **8**, 336–397.

336 The experiments and observations reported in this paper were
337 made on a raven and a jackdaw [1] reared in captivity. The general procedure was determined less by the experimenter than by the birds themselves in the sense that our central question was: How do these birds recognize and deal with the forms and objects occurring in the natural course of their experience? The method of study involved primarily as full and exact a description of the observed behaviour as possible. Every effort was made to avoid preconceptions as to which movements were and which were not important. Instead the aim was to discover from which situation an act arose and to which situation it led.

338 It is not impossible to understand an animal's behaviour. One understands movements of a bird's eyes if, from observing them, one is led to discover the presence of some object which might otherwise have been unnoticed; one knows that the bird is "looking for something" if one can predict that its "seeking behaviour" will at a later moment suddenly change into a rapid movement towards the goal. Every situation in which the animal finds itself may in a sense be considered an experimental situation, and the observer can thus carry out an entire series of actual experiments merely by introducing small variations in the given set-up. It
339 can thus be seen that great quantities of data are available even with relatively few experimental animals. Of course no general conclusions (especially when negative) regarding the entire species can be drawn with certainty; and yet it would be equally incorrect to assume that the principal characteristics of the species are not represented to greater or less extent by the members actually studied. Our attempt therefore was to secure as broad a picture as possible

[1] [The Rabenkrähe (*corvus corone*) is not identical with the common raven (*corvus corax*), but the similarity is great enough for purposes of our present terminology. This holds also as regards the Dohle (*coleus monedula*) whom we shall here call the jackdaw (*corvus monedula*).]

Grateful acknowledgment is hereby made to *Julius Springer*, *Verlagsbuchhandlung*, Berlin, for permission to reproduce the illustrations used in this SELECTION.

of the birds' behaviour. The resemblances between our own method and that used by Köhler are self-evident.

340 *Living conditions.*—The birds were kept in a flying cage 3·65 × 3 m. ground area, and 2·25 m. high (Fig 1). This cage was divided in half (lengthwise); the raven occupied one part, the

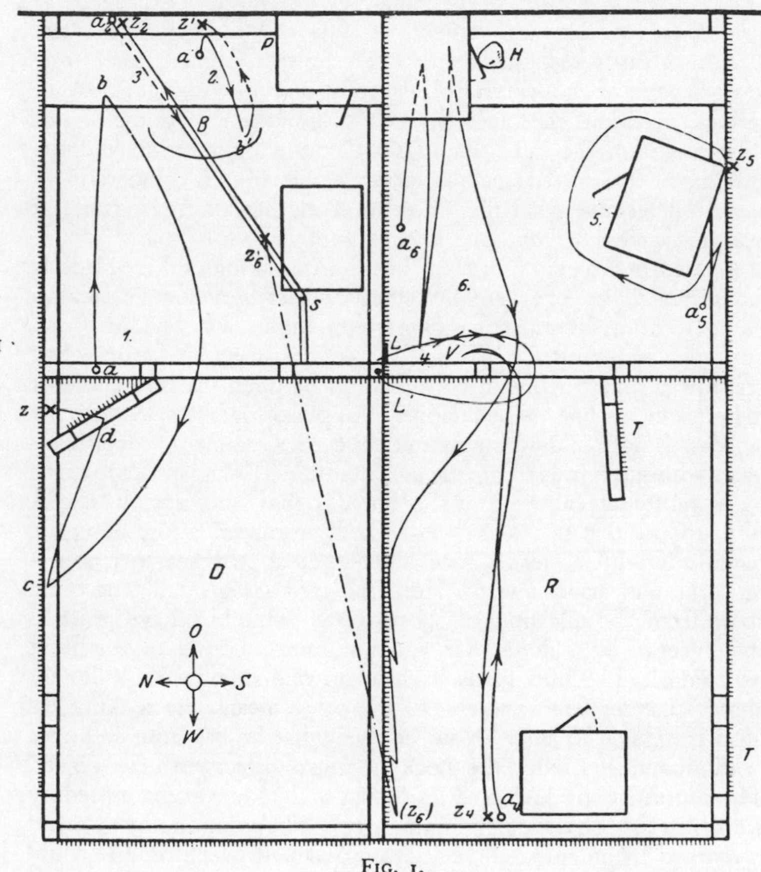

341

FIG. 1.

jackdaw the other. The walls and top were made of heavy chicken wire. The rear part (east) of both halves was covered by a roof and on both sides this part was separated from the forward sections (west) by wire partitions with narrow doors which usually remained open (cf. Fig. 1). There were in all five nesting boxes (dimensions 48 × 43 × 43 cm.; doorways 20 × 20 cm.), two of which remained permanently upon the shelves in back while the others lay upon the ground. These latter served as articulating features of the environment and were also of use in later experiments. Besides the shelves and nesting boxes there were other perching facilities (diagonal roosts, a tree stump, etc.) at various places within the cage.

342 *Expressive movements.*—The most obvious mode of expression in birds of this species is movement. Attack- and flight-situations are, of course, easily recognized but there are many others where one

343 must depend upon a careful observation of eye-movements. With certain exceptions the raven's vision is monocular.[1] In the case of close attention the head assumes an unmoving position and the gaze of one eye is fixed steadily upon the object.[2] It is comparatively easy to determine what this object is if the bird shifts its gaze (by head-movements) from one eye to another.

344 An observer would find no difficulty in speaking of these birds as looking *intelligent* or *stupid*, but since their feathery covering makes

345 the perception of muscular expression impossible one may ask how such an impression arises. For the most part this occurs when one can clearly perceive a continuation between the bird's line of regard and his line of behaviour. Suppose, for example, that the jackdaw is not building a nest and yet carries around a feather in its beak, without, however, paying any attention to it and in fact looking indifferently at other things. Then it *looks* necessarily *stupid.* But suppose that the raven sees something placed before him ; he regards it with a steady gaze and either approaches to grasp it or turns and stalks away. Here the bird *looks* intelligent quite apart from the question of whether he " should " have grasped the object or let it alone. Or, again, consider the case of searching behaviour. The bird turns its head to one side, looks obliquely ahead, changes from one eye to the other meanwhile rocking his head from side to side. Now he sees what he has been seeking: head-movements stop, the beak is aimed directly at the object. The course run by such a series of acts is the same as that noted by Köhler in the behaviour of chimpanzees. The solution of a problem is marked by an energetic, smooth movement which no one could confuse with the irregularity, hesitation, and quick change of direction that characterize uncertainty.

[346–356: no systematic observations were begun until the birds were

[1] [We shall occasionally use the word " raven " as a generic term to designate both birds.]

[2] There can be no doubt about the fact that the raven *fixates* in the full sense of the word.

thoroughly at home in their cage and perfectly familiar with the experimenter; this required several weeks but by this time they showed every sign of recognizing and greeting the experimenter and this continued throughout the entire year of daily observations.]

357 *Food discriminations.*—Because of his fondness for insects the jackdaw was constantly interested in cracks and crevices in the wooden parts of his cage. When perched on my closed hand he would at once begin to peck at the dark crevices between thumb and forefinger; finding nothing further of interest here he would reach up to peck at the nostrils; or, if seated on my shoulder, would
[358-360: omitted] at once busy himself with an investigation of my ear. A nut which was ignored the moment before would be instantly attacked if a crack in it was discovered.

361 Both birds were very fond of cedar nuts (*pinus cembra*) and this proved to be most useful in demonstrating the raven's facility in learning. One day (first day) as I was sitting outside his cage, this bird while attempting to open a cedar nut let it fall through the wire beside me. This was probably an accident, for from other observations it seems unlikely that so esteemed an object would have been dropped out of reach if this could be prevented. I picked up the nut, broke it open and returned it to him through the wire. Two more nuts were then given him at the same place. It occurred to me that with time the raven would probably learn to bring these nuts regularly to be opened.

Next morning (second day) a little pile of six cedar nuts lay at the spot outside the cage where I had been sitting. I gave him three of them broken open. On the following (third) day I had scarcely taken my place outside the cage when two more nuts were brought to be opened. After busying himself with other things for a while he suddenly began a hasty search, found two more nuts and had them opened. Thereupon followed a series of every kind of object
362 he could pick up—sticks, stones, shells, anything. I returned each of these just as it was given to me: this was the last time he ever brought objects of this sort. Next day (the fourth) more cedar nuts were placed in the cage along with his other food and he brought seven of them to be opened. On the day after (the fifth) I sat at a new place outside the cage. He brought the nuts to *me*, not to the former place. After a pause of two days cedar nuts were again among his food. This time, however, I went away immediately and did not return for two hours. All the nuts had disappeared (hidden). A few minutes after my return he turned away from the place where I sat, ran into the rear part of his cage, secured two nuts and brought

them to be opened. (The route, as shown on the right-hand side of Fig. 1, was in this case *a*4 to *V* and back to *z*4.)

363 With but few exceptions (cf. third day) the raven had brought only cedar nuts to be opened. It was also clear that he had thoroughly grasped the relation between the experimenter and the place to which nuts were to be brought. This, of course, does not
364 mean to say that he understood the process by which I broke open
365 the nuts. However, a more intensive series of planned experiments seemed necessary in order to clarify certain questions which these observations had raised. We were struck from the start by the bird's ability to fetch hidden nuts (memory), and by the assurance with which a nut would be recognized even when some distance away (discrimination). As regards the latter our additional experiments were designed to answer the questions: What sort of object will the raven see as "a cedar nut"? What similar forms will he confuse with it?

First series of experiments.—(1) Among other food strewn about in the cage were four cedar nuts which had been coloured by dilute India ink. The surface character of the nut itself was not destroyed by this and under a magnifying glass it was still a striped brown. The raven brought all four nuts in quick succession to be opened. (2) Next day there were again four cedar nuts mixed with other food but two of them were so blackened with India ink that even under the magnifying glass one could see only a homogeneous black covering upon them. The other two, having been stripped of their outer husks, had completely lost their original surface character and were now a light reddish brown colour. In addition the rations also contained two roasted coffee beans which very much resembled cedar nuts. After some time, and then only hesitatingly, the two reddish brown nuts were brought to me. Following another interval one of the coffee beans was brought. He received this back unbroken and succeeded in breaking it open himself. Later in the day
366 he finally gave me the other coffee bean and one of the black nuts; the other had disappeared. (3) Four cedar nuts, one of which had been stripped of its husk, were given; in addition to these there was an imitation nut made from plaster of Paris and coloured (with coffee stain) like the genuine ones. All four of the genuine nuts (beginning with the light brown one) were quickly brought to be opened, and then immediately thereafter he picked up the counterfeit, started with it to the wire but let it drop and did not pick it up again. (4) On the evening of the same day the food supply contained: 4 genuine cedar nuts (1 black and 3 coloured red, blue,

and white with chalk), 1 coffee bean, and 1 reddish brown plaster of Paris ball approximately the same size as a cedar nut. He first picked up this ball but then dropped it at once; then the red, black, and blue nuts were brought to be opened. A little later the coffee bean was picked up but dropped. Then the white nut was brought. After another pause he again picked up the plaster ball and carried it about but showed no signs of intending to present it at the wire. (5) The following objects were used: 2 genuine nuts thoroughly coloured red and blue; 2 imitation nuts of the same colours; there was also a little plaster ball to which cedar nut shells had been attached. For some time none of these was touched. Then the
367 ball with shells upon it was carried almost to the wire, dropped, pecked at (whereby one of the shells came off), and thereafter ignored. Now followed first the blue (genuine) nut; then, after a long pause the blue plaster nut; then the red (genuine) nut; pause; finally the red counterfeit.

Summarizing, we find that for the raven these various objects had approximately the same degree of similarity to the normal nut which they might have for a human being, viz.: genuine cedar nuts of various sizes, form and colour; dark coloured cedar nuts; light brown husked nuts; irregularly marked red or blue nuts; coffee beans; irregularly marked white nuts; thoroughly black nuts; light brown plaster nuts; thoroughly blue or red nuts or imitations; plaster ball with and without shells about it. We may assume that the raven quickly learned that a "cedar nut" may have various
368 appearances, but that other objects (sticks, stones, sunflower seeds, etc.) definitely are "not cedar nuts". Of particular interest in this connection were the cases where a false object (e.g. plaster ball with shells) was taken up but never actually presented to be opened.

[369–372: the raven's proclivity for hiding objects of all kinds (bits of food, nuts, nails, etc.) is commented upon and observations reported. The jackdaw did less of this than the raven.]

373 *Removing obstacles.*—Clearing the way to a sought goal was a common occurrence in the behaviour of these birds. Indeed the heavy beak and strong neck muscles indicate how natural such activity is with this species. If, while they are looking on, one places a small cardboard box over an object which the birds wish to obtain, they at once push it aside: the raven does this with a stroke of its bill, the daw attains the same end by thrusting its beak under the box and thus shoving it out of the way. Objects buried before the birds' eyes are easily retrieved. That quite heavy objects are also attacked may be seen from the following incident.

In winter it was necessary to prevent the jackdaw from bathing in his drinking water, and so a board with stones upon it was placed over the container. Nevertheless he succeeded in a few minutes in rolling aside the stones and reaching the water. Although it may be doubted that the bird possessed any insight into the relation of stones and board, it was clear that he did recognize the obstacle-complex as something to be overcome in order to reach the water.

375 The raven also provided numerous instances of attacks upon obstacles encountered while retrieving objects which he had hidden. Thus once, when unable to grasp a morsel of food which he had thrust under a small shovel, he caught the shovel in his beak, flipped it over, and then proceeded to eat the food.

376 Adding to the foregoing the fact that the birds had become quite familiar with the small doors of their nesting boxes, it was but a step (aided by a chance discovery) to the formulation of the following problem.

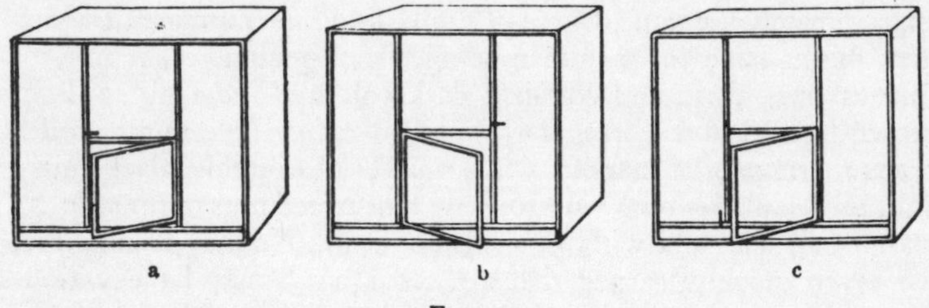

FIG. 2.

377 *Second series of experiments.*—Assuming that the raven would not be able to open the latched door of a nesting box (Fig. 2) which rested on the floor of his cage, I once left a supply of food there when called away. Returning shortly afterward I found the door open and the food gone. This had doubtless resulted from chance movements during play, but thereafter I gave him several opportunities to repeat the performance and in a few days he was able to unlatch the door with complete assurance and intention. But that he had not *understood* the latch was clear from the fact that he still gave his first attention to this even when the closed door was not actually fastened. And, that he was not certain about the sequence of steps necessary to open the door was also apparent when the door, though latched, was allowed to show an opening crack: in this case his first efforts were to pry at the door and it was only when this failed that he attacked the latch.

378 After the game of opening nest doors was well learned and
practised (one-half year), I changed the latch from right to left
(Fig. 2b). The raven was at first nonplussed, but he did not attempt
to force open the door from the (now) wrong side; instead he
turned and went away. I opened and closed the door a few times
with him looking on. Not immediately but after a time he returned,
noticed the new location of the latch, and taking hold of it turned
379 it so that the door came open. Some days later and with the latch
[380- now at the position shown in Fig. 2c the raven again succeeded,
381 :
omitted] after an initial hesitation, in opening the door.

382 In a later experiment an additional obstacle was added: Food
having been put inside the regular nest box a large flat stone was
placed in front of its latched door. An obstruction prevented the
stone from moving more than 5 cm. (cf. Fig. 1 *H*). The raven
approached, opened the door in the usual way, and then began
struggling to pull it wider. He seemed not to notice the obstacle.
(Stones were frequently lying upon this shelf at other times.)
383 He even braced himself against the stone in order to tug still harder
at the door. The bird had already stopped once or twice only to
renew his struggles when a sudden change occurred in his behaviour.
He began tugging now at the lower part of the door, then quickly
abandoned this and attacked the stone with great force. In this
way the stone was first shoved a little to one side, then was tipped
over and so off the shelf. The raven sprang down after it before
returning to the door which he once more attacked with unnecessary
vigour. As the door now moved quite readily he ceased this exertion,
opened the door in the usual way, and secured his food.

In evaluating this achievement it would be incorrect to assume
that more than partial insight into the situation had been involved.
384 But, as Köhler has remarked, "With but little insight it is still
possible to accomplish much that would never have arisen from
mere chance." [1]

385 *Detours.*—It was clear from observing their behaviour that
"detours", far from offering difficulties for these birds, often
constituted the preferred mode of approaching their goals. Triangular flights, for example, were made on numerous occasions:
if an insect was seen on one of the rafters, the bird would fly to a
half-way station at one side, then to the prey, and then back to the
starting point. It is possible that this mode of approach is due to
the position of the eyes: visual direction and behavioural direction
do not coincide for the raven. Nevertheless a "triangular"

[1] W. Köhler, *The Mentality of Apes*, p. 214.

approach enables the bird to maintain a constant watch upon his goal during the approach. For the purposes of experimentation, however, this means that no ordinary type of detour problem would constitute a " problem " for these birds.

Nevertheless a few genuine detour problems were presented as the following case will show. The daw was sitting at the point *a* (left-hand side of Fig. 1) when I thrust a piece of paper through the wire at *z*. The door between front and rear sections of his cage was ajar and fastened in the position shown in Fig. 1. The direct distance from *a* to *z* was approximately 20 cm. For a moment the bird stared at the paper, then turned and flew to the point *b* (shelf). From here he flew at once (through the doorway) to *c* and then to *d* upon the upper edge of the door; he then scrambled down to the paper at *z*.

[386–389: descriptions of other routes shown in Fig. 1 are given. (387–388): when food was available at the end of a strip of cloth hanging from a roost the jackdaw proved himself much the better angler, for he held down the hauled-in slack with one foot while reaching to make another haul; the raven never learned to do this.]

390 *Play.*—Throughout our observations we were constantly struck by the interest both birds exhibited in objects which had little or no connection with food. Any moving object as well as anything which appeared in contrast to its surroundings was sure to be pecked at. Their preference for thin, isolated parts of objects was shown, for example, upon their first experience with cherries, for instead of attacking the fruit itself they were much more attracted by the long thin stems. But quite in general the initial mode of examining any new object was to see if it could be broken up, and since pieces of paper were easily torn they continued throughout the entire period of observation to exhibit a great preference for this material. Indeed when fed from a paper bag they often showed more interest in the bag than in the food which it contained.

391 The acuity of their discriminative abilities could be readily observed in connection with play activity. Once, for example, I gave the raven a bright stone about 6 cm. long; he carried it about, hid and retrieved it, then dropped it in the outer section of his cage. I put another, almost identical stone in the hiding place he had used and called him. He came, took up the new stone but dropped it at once (" as if it were hot ") and began searching for the former one. Although there were 40 or more stones of almost this same size in his cage he ignored all of them until he had found the original which he then picked up and brought to the hiding place.

392 In view of the raven's ability to discriminate individual objects it was all the more noteworthy that he should also be able to recognize resemblances within groups of objects. This he showed in the following manner. If I tossed a pebble to him he would not only pick up this stone but would then begin collecting all small pebbles in his vicinity. If one nut shell happened to attract his attention he thereupon devoted himself to all the nut shells he could find. When I would pretend to remove a shred of paper, he at once gathered and hid all bits of paper which might be lying about.

394 *Summary of results.*—One of the most outstanding characteristics of these birds was the vigour and extent of their responses and the persistence of their desire (quite apart from a search for food) to
395 investigate everything around them. Their behaviour was guided almost entirely by vision, and it was evident from the beginning that the environment was for them organized into concrete " things ". The contours and boundaries of objects were constantly observed and attacked with the beak ; whatever could be broken up was broken, and whatever could be moved was moved.[1] In general their ability to discriminate (e.g. the same stone) seemed not noticeably inferior to that of human beings. As regards similarities among objects (e.g. cedar nut experiment) we again found a rank ordering which would correspond roughly to that which a human being might have made. For the raven the decisive consideration was apparently the surface character of objects ; he seemed indifferent to " identical qualities " as such.

396 The major part of their time was spent in activities dictated by circumstances ; in addition, however, there were occasions when new situations were responded to in ways which must be described as insightful. Their best accomplishments of this type were achieved in connection with search- and obstacle-behaviour. Within the range of their understanding these birds showed an excellent memory and great learning ability.[2]

[1] In this they differed greatly from Köhler's apes for whom visually stable objects were often absorbed into and became a part of their environment with the result that for the apes they became " immovable ".

[2] [This study is concluded by an article entitled " Weitere Versuche an der Rabenkrähe ", which appeared in Vol. **10**, 1928, pp. 111–141 of the *Psychologische Forschung*. By providing several openings of different sizes in the wire of their cage and supplying the birds with nuts which also differed in size it was found that they could discriminate size relationships very accurately : the bird on each occasion used the opening whose dimensions most nearly corresponded to those of the nut he happened to have picked up. In repeating the " barrier " experiment a wooden bar was laid upon two bent nails across the doorway of the bird's nesting box (within which food had been placed). After an initial fright he succeeded in removing this and upon a later occasion removed two such barriers in succession.]

Selection 20

FIGURAL PERCEPTION IN THE JAY BIRD

By Mathilde Hertz

"Wahrnehmungspsychologische Untersuchungen am Eichelhäher," I., Zeitschrift für wissenschaftliche Biologie, Abt. C., *Zeitschr. f. vergl. Physiol.*, 1928, 7, 144–194.

144 One of the most striking natural activities of the jay bird (even
in captivity) is its hiding and retrieving of food. Since the bird is
practically without a sense of smell, this achievement is especially
remarkable because an object once hidden is thenceforth quite
145 outside the bird's perceptual field. Only memory can be relied
upon to rediscover a hiding place.[1] But how does the bird recognize
the critical place where food has been cached and how does it distinguish the particular objects which hide its prize from other
similar objects in the vicinity?

We can attack this problem only by presenting simple test
146 situations resembling the bird's normal, biological conditions. It
should then be possible to infer how the bird's perceptions are actually organized. The most practical test is for the experimenter himself to "hide" a bit of food (with the bird looking on) and then observe how it is found. If the bird is capable of doing this, we know already that the search was guided solely by vision and memory functions—not by some literal mechanical repetition of a process which he himself had performed at an earlier time.

Procedure.—Before the bird's eyes a bit of food is placed under a small flower pot; the bird approaches, moves the covering aside, and grasps its food. Success here means that the bird has apprehended the covering as an obstacle to be removed, i.e. one which must be dealt with as an intermediate goal before the real goal can be reached. A natural complication of this situation is to add one

[1] It would be false to speak of a "memory image" or "presentation" as i comparison or recognition required these. The "comparison partner" of a presen perception is not the memorial image of an earlier perception; instead it is a physiological, usually non-conscious residuum left by that earlier experience.

Grateful acknowledgment is hereby made to *Julius Springer*, *Verlagsbuchhandlung* Berlin, for permission to reproduce the illustrations used in this Selection.

147 or more additional flower pots. This provides an opportunity to test the bird's discriminative ability as regards characteristics of the presented situations.

It is customary in testing discrimination to present *two* objects and require a positive choice of one. The number of correct choices may be greatly increased, however, if but a single positive object is used together with several negative objects. If there is but one positive and one negative object, the result is an equilibrium of the situation which, while not necessarily inducing a confusion as to their critically distinctive characteristic, may nevertheless increase the number of false choices because it confuses the *relationship of these characteristics* to goal and "non-goal". When, on the other hand, one positive object is presented along with several negative ones, situational equilibrium is disturbed (if the objects are at all distinguishable), the positive object "stands out" from the complex and a correct choice is almost sure to follow. Moreover positive choice is of much greater significance when the chance value of the positive
148 object is, say, 1 : 5 than when it is 1 : 1. The experimenter is thus requiring that the bird shall resolve the situation into a critical object (i.e. the intermediate goal or flower pot under which food was placed) *and* a general remainder. By varying different characteristics of the situation the experimenter can then discover which properties of the total complex are crucial for successful behaviour on the bird's part.[1]

149 *Experiments.*—The study was made with two jay birds (*garrulus glandarius*) approximately six months old. Both "worked" excellently throughout the investigation and at no time showed any interest in the various experimental materials apart from actual efforts to secure food. The flying cage in which the experiments were conducted had a ground area of 8 × 2·5 m. The flower pots were 4·5 cm. high, 5 cm. in diameter at the opening and 3 cm. diameter at the base; they were never in the cage except for the purpose of an experiment. The birds were not, however, wholly unfamiliar with these objects since even before our experiments began the pots had been stored in an adjoining space where they could be seen if not touched by the birds.

150 The tasks were presented as follows. First the various "negative" pots were placed upon the ground; then a peanut kernel was set down in full view at the point where it was to remain; after a brief pause the "intermediate goal" was placed over the

[1] Although differing in outer form, this method is the same as that used by Köhler in his study of chimpanzees. Cf. *The Mentality of Apes* (Appendix).

kernel. This was done with manifest emphasis.[1] The experimenter
151 always withdrew 1–2 metres immediately after arranging the pots. The bird usually waited from 10 to 30 seconds before flying from its roost. The experiments in any one series followed one another at intervals of one or two minutes.

152 *First series.*—The first problem was to determine whether the birds could select the correct flower pot when several similar ones were also present. If a bird is predominantly correct in his choices, then various rearrangements of the pots can be made until a point is reached where he is predominantly wrong, and *vice versa*. The first arrangement was of three pots in a row, 10 cm. apart (Fig. 1).

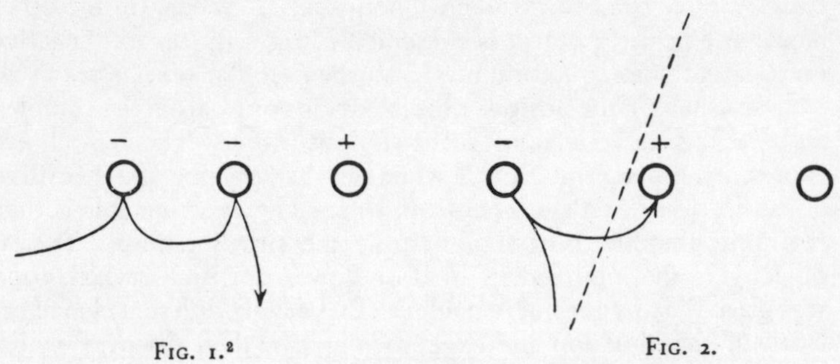

FIG. 1.[2] FIG. 2.

It can be seen from this drawing that the correct choice was not made. Upon repetition of this set-up a correct choice occurred.

Fig. 2 shows the second arrangement and behaviour: the intervals in this case were 15 cm.

153 After thirteen repetitions it was apparent that nothing but chance could have been responsible for the results. Everything seemed to depend upon the direction of approach, for the bird would merely knock over the pots in the order he happened to come upon them. At nc time were more than two pots approached; if the second proved foodless he walked away (see Fig. 1). On the other hand, if the first pot was the correct one, then neither of the other two was approached. The reason for these failures was apparently

[1] [This method of "showing" the intermediate goal was used for the first 10–12 trials of a series. In cases where such "training" resulted in consistently positive choices one or two trials would then be given without emphasizing the intermediate goal. Here the critical object was not the last one to be put in place nor was this object given any particular emphasis when put down over the kernel of food.]

[2] A plus sign indicates the correct flower pot; the minus signs designate incorrect pots only when they were approached and turned over. A dotted line marks the route of flight while a solid one traces the path where the birds walked.

an inadequate grasp of the total complex. Evidently the intermediate goal possessed no fixed and unequivocal place among the several pots. Better results could be expected only if this difficulty were removed.

154 A series of trials was therefore given with the two negative pots placed open-end up, the positive one upside down. A typical arrangement is indicated in Fig. 3. The distances between pots were 25 cm. in one trial, 10 cm. in two trials, and 6 cm. in two other trials. All results were positive (as shown in Fig. 3). Correct choices also occurred when triangular arrangements (intervals 50–30 cm. in various trials) were used. With intervals smaller than this the consistency of positive choices was lost.

When four pots (placed bottom-side up and 20 cm. apart) were arranged in the form of a square, all three incorrect pots were turned over before the correct one was reached (Fig. 4).

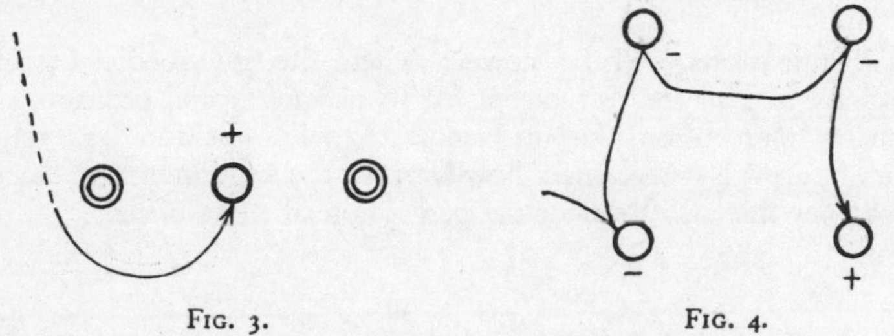

FIG. 3. FIG. 4.

155 It can be seen that when all of the pots were turned bottom-side up and with intervals of 30 cm. or less, no reliably positive results could be obtained. The reverse was true of tests made with arrangements such as that of Fig. 3, for every choice was correct when all but the intermediate goal were hollow-side up. In other words our results thus far show that the birds can easily discriminate between the pots in these two positions.

Second series.—The experiments of this series were designed to discover whether the birds could locate the correct pot when it differed from the others in *colour*. A white flower pot was used
156 as intermediate goal; the others were brown as before. The result was that in each of eight trials a correct choice was made even though the arrangements were the same as those with which the birds had previously failed (cf. Figs. 1, 2, 4). Also the intervals used (10 cm.) were here much smaller than those formerly necessary for successful choices.

157 *Third series.*—Our experiments thus far have shown that the birds can resolve a complex into an intermediate goal and a general remainder (1) when there is a difference in form (hollow- *v.* bottom-side up), and (2) when there is a difference in colour (white-brown). The next problem is to discover whether their

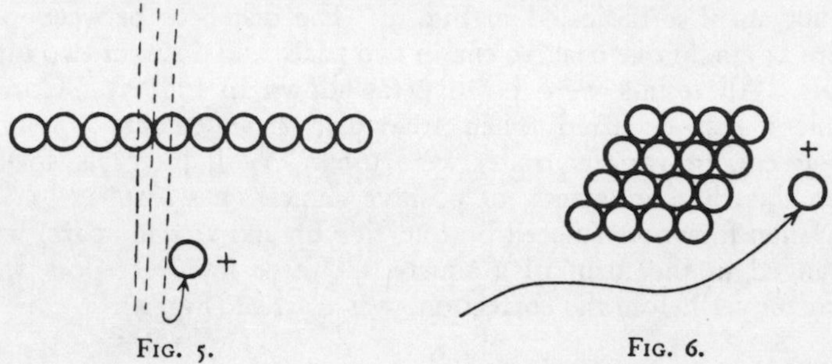

FIG. 5. FIG. 6.

discriminations will be correct when the intermediate goal is exactly like all the rest except for its unique spatial position. For human perception the intermediate goal's position *was* unique (cf. figures); it remained, however, for the experiments to disclose whether this also held for the perception of these birds.

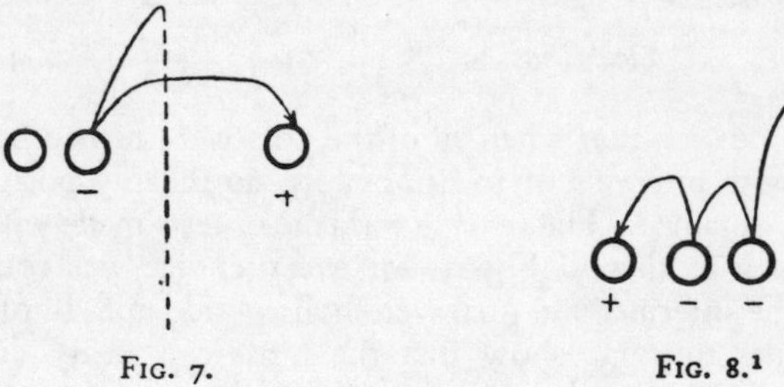

FIG. 7. FIG. 8.[1]

We began with an arrangement such as that shown in Fig. 5. The positive object stood 10 cm. removed from the row of ten negative ones. As can be seen from this drawing, the results were positive. A correct choice was also made when the arrangement depicted in Fig. 6 and several similar ones were used.

158 If the number of negative objects was reduced and their internal

[1] The interval between incorrect pots here was 2 cm.; the correct one stood 3 cm. from its neighbour. Evidently the former did not constitute a single compact object over against the intermediate goal.

unity made less compact, errors increased and the chance results
159 of Figs. 1–2 reappeared. Compare Figs. 7 and 8 where it can be seen that incorrect choices by the birds began when (for human perception also) the contrast between a group on the one side and an individual object on the other was no longer very striking. Conversely, when closure of the negative group was strengthened

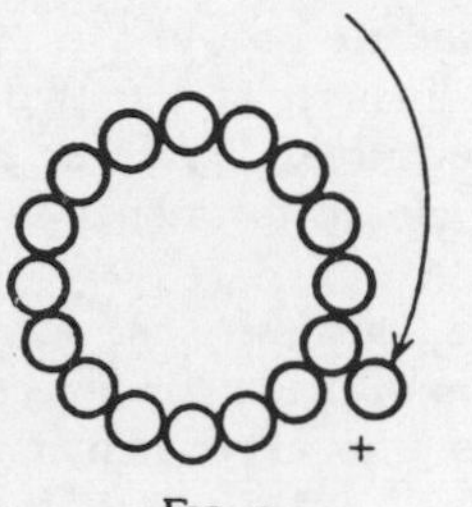

FIG. 9.

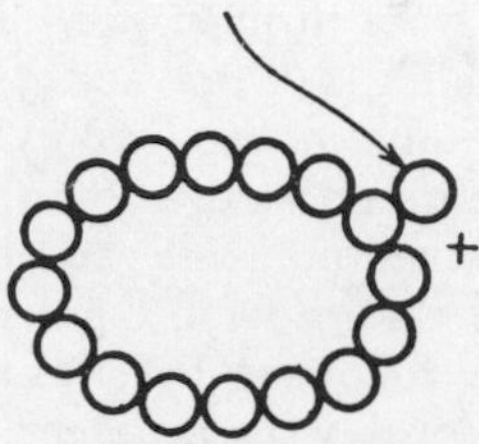

FIG. 10.

160 (as in Figs. 9 and 10) it was possible to reduce the interval to zero
161 and nevertheless obtain consistently positive results. It must not be assumed from this, however, that correct choices were always made when a large number of negative objects was given. The results in Figs. 11 and 12 were distinctly negative.

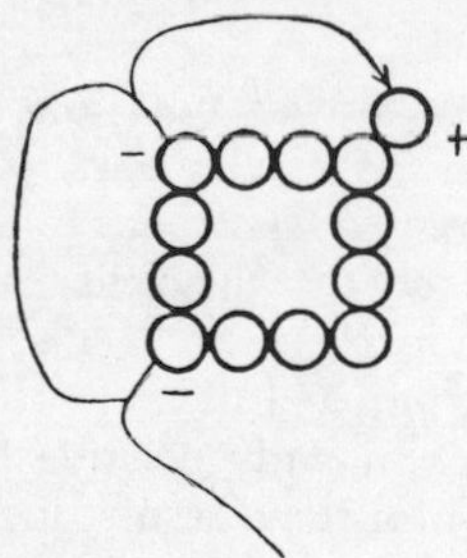

FIG. 11.

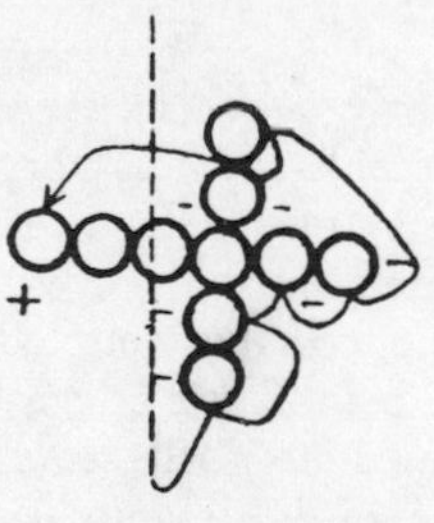

FIG. 12.

But there is a decided and important difference between them. The arrangement of Fig. 12 elicited only hit-or-miss trials and it is evident that the bird had no clear orientation towards its goal. With Fig. 11, on the contrary, there was a definite orientation toward the *corners* of a *square*. It is unnecessary to speculate as to whether the corner objects were confused with the intermediate goal or whether the most distinctive parts of the entire form were its " corners ". In any case it is evident that the bird's behaviour was determined by the whole-figure as such, for he reacted to significant parts *of* that figure. In the arrangement of Fig. 12, on the other hand, the intermediate goal must have vanished into the total complex and therefore could not be visually resolved from this whole.

162 *Fourth series.*—We may now raise the question whether successful choices can be made when the critical object occupies no distinctive place and resembles the others in form and colour but differs from them in *size*. The intermediate goal in this case was 5 cm. high, 5·7 cm. and 3·5 cm. in diameter at the two ends.[1] The results in Figs. 13–15 were all positive. Those of Fig. 16,
163 on the other hand, show that with a closed form such as this no discrimination could be achieved.

The results with Figs. 13–15 were, however, *not* positive on the day following the first introduction of the larger object. This was probably because the birds, like the experimenter herself,

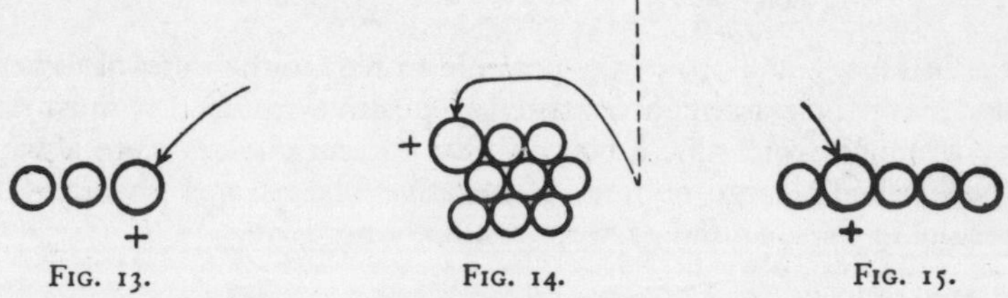

FIG. 13. FIG. 14. FIG. 15.

evidently grew accustomed to the new flower pots and ceased to perceive them as very different from the smaller ones. On the first day the difference in size had seemed enormous; later it appeared much less obvious. It seems likely that the birds may have experienced this same change.

164–165 : using large pots as the negative group and a very small one as intermediate goal the results were predominantly positive for one of the birds, less so for the other. From these results it appears probable that the jay bird's vision (like that of human beings and of chimpanzees) exhibits the phenomenon of *size* constancy. If this were not the case—i.e. if objects appeared different in size proportionately with different sized retinal images—consistently correct choices when size alone was the distinctive difference would have been impossible. The bird in such a case would have seen the more distant pots as small and closer ones as large—and their sizes would have been constantly changing with every movement (flying, walking). From the fact of predominantly

[1] Dimensions of the other pots were, as before, 4·5, 5, and 3 cm.

correct choices, however (one of the jays never failed in this situation), we may conclude that size constancy probably prevailed.]

166 *Fifth series.*—Let us now ask whether the birds can choose
correctly when with *every* trial a new colour is used for the inter-
[167– mediate object. (In all other respects these experiments are the
169: omit- same as those of the second series.) We found that with the
ted]
170 exception of reddish-brown, every colour was readily distinguished
from that of the unpainted negative pots. From this it is clear that the colour (reddish-brown) which most resembles the pots for human vision did so for the birds as well. Moreover the results also show that the choices were determined by the principle "isolated in colour". In every case the intermediate goal was different in colour from all the rest and if this could be distinguished at all, the correct object was invariably chosen. The choice was not determined by a specific sensation but by the colour structure of the whole complex.

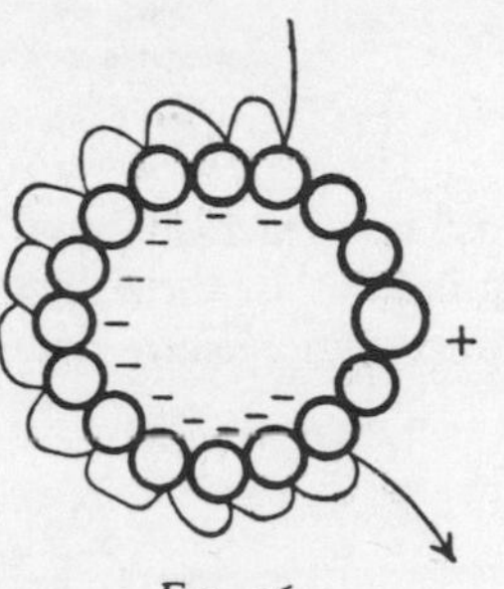

Fig. 16.

Sixth series.—All experiments of the last four series required the bird to resolve a complex of similar objects into an intermediate goal and a remainder. The complexes were such that the required
171 meaningful resolution corresponded with
their perceivable organization. The intermediate object was always isolated from the rest in a distinctive way so that (assuming a corresponding discriminative ability on the bird's part) it stood out "of its own accord" from the homogeneous remainder. The task will undoubtedly be more difficult when, in this and the following series, *ambiguous* organizations of the material are employed. By an "ambiguous organization" is meant one which may be resolved in more than one way. The bird's task will then be to carry out only that particular resolution which actually does distinguish the intermediate goal from the remainder.

172– Three types of results were obtained, and it would appear
174 that they correspond closely to what might (from a human point
of view) be called three degrees of ambiguity in the presented arrangements: (1) examples of the least ambiguous organization are shown in Figs. 17–19. In these cases the birds showed great assurance and made no errors; (2) of quite another kind were the results obtained with arrangements such as those shown in

Figs. 20–21. Evidently the critical object in these cases was almost completely lost in the presented complex; (3) finally, there were several instances in which the bird, although it began incorrectly,

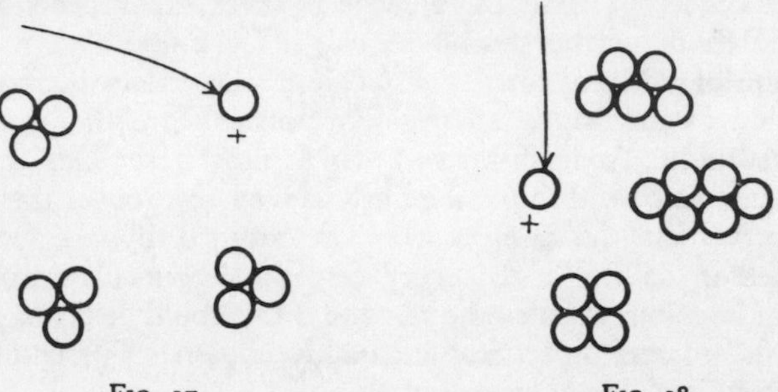

FIG. 17.
Intervals 15 cm.

FIG. 18.
Intervals 4–6 cm., intermediate goal 6 cm. from the groups.

did not reach the goal merely by random trials. The intermediate goal was in these instances the object of a specific, if apparently uncertain *choice*. Examples are given in Figs. 22–23.

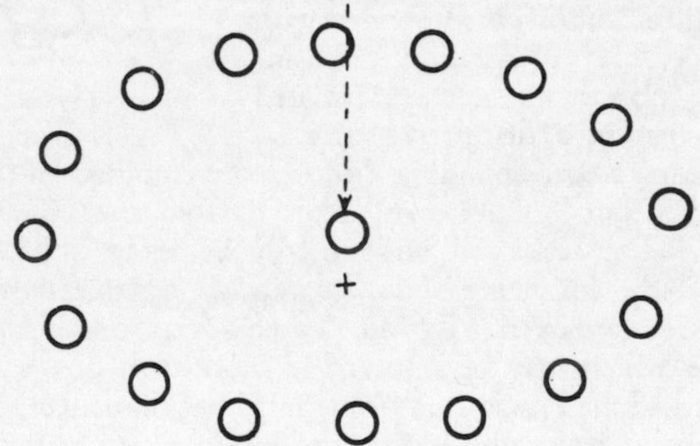

FIG. 19.
Intervals in the ellipse 6 cm., intermediate goal 15 cm. from rim.

175 *Seventh series.*—Again we shall present situations which permit of *more than one* perceptual organization. In this case every flower pot differed in colour—but in no other respect—from every other pot and the bird's task, therefore, was to note and remember the
176 specific colour of the critical object. A typical arrangement is

shown in Fig. 24. The results for both birds were nearly perfect
177 (no errors in twelve trials by bird *A*, one error in seven trials by
B). When colours closely resembling that of the intermediate
178 goal were used in its immediate vicinity the number of errors
naturally increased considerably. At no time, however, was the
behaviour one of random trials.

179 *Eighth series*.—Combining some of the factors already used in these problems we will now present situations in which the intermediate goal is without any distinctive characteristic except that it is located beside another object (the large white pot) which is different from all others. As can be seen from Fig. 25, which exemplifies a number of different arrangements, the bird's first task, therefore, is to see the intermediate goal *together with* its immediate environment as a subsidiary group distinct from the general remainder (average interval 8–10 cm.). Its second task, then, is to select the critical object from within this group.

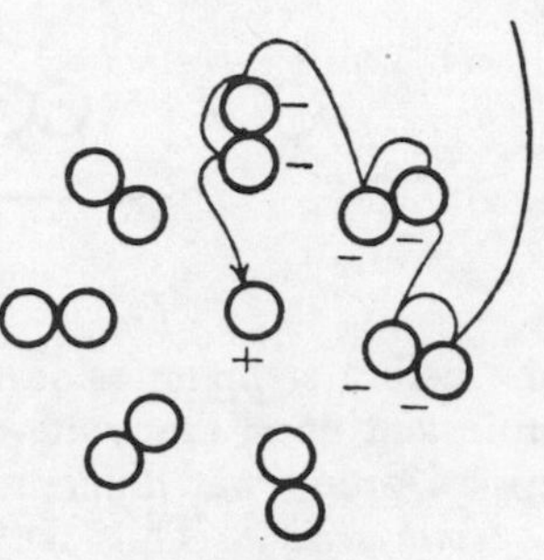

FIG. 20.
Intervals approximately 6 cm.

The arrangement shown in Fig. 25 consisted of twelve flower pots of the kind used in most of our earlier experiments, and one white pot 6 cm. in height. The first trial resulted, as may have been expected, in an immediate attack upon this larger pot. Bird *A* repeated this behaviour twice and was each time shooed away immediately after
having turned over the white flower pot. On the third trial he
180 chose the intermediate goal and secured his food. A fourth trial
was also successful. Bird *B* merely upset a few outer pots and
showed no particular interest in the critical group.

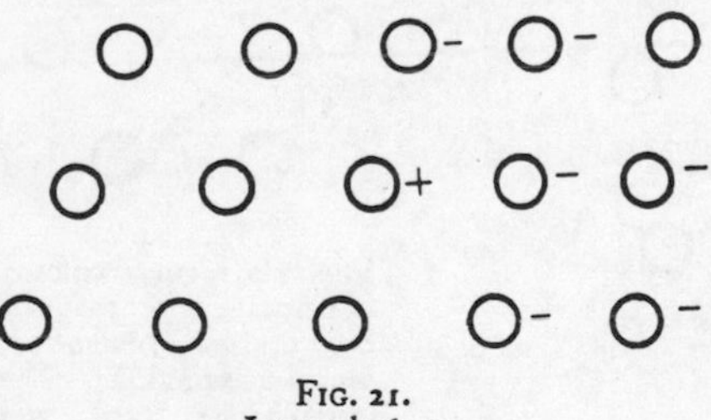

FIG. 21.
Intervals 6 cm.

When fourteen smaller pots were used, both birds succeeded in selecting the intermediate goal. On another occasion, however, *B* again attacked merely the outside ring of pots. *A* had nine trials of which the last seven were all correct; *B* tried three times

181 and failed twice. Finally an arrangement was presented in which the negative pots were brought somewhat closer together (7–9 cm.)
182 and the positive pair moved a little farther away from any of the others. The results in this case were predominantly correct (even for *B*) despite the fact that the intermediate object was not " shown " to the birds and the only designation of the white pot was that

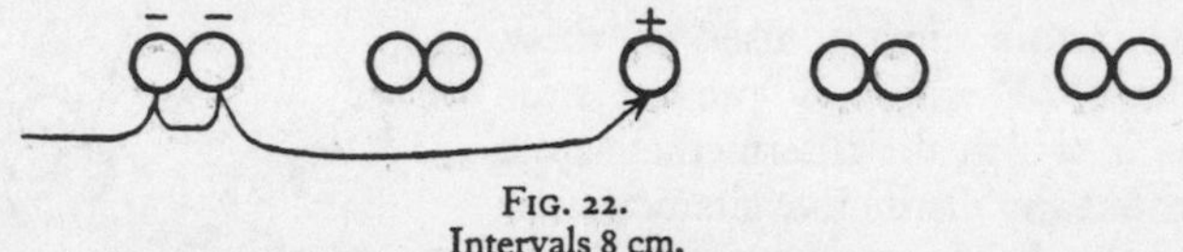

FIG. 22.
Intervals 8 cm.

just before stepping aside the experimenter placed her finger for an instant upon the white object. (Obviously the location of the critical group was different in each trial.)

Ninth series.—Thus far the objects used in these experiments
183 have been all alike in general form. Now, however, we shall introduce a variation of this factor also. Fig. 26 shows the kind

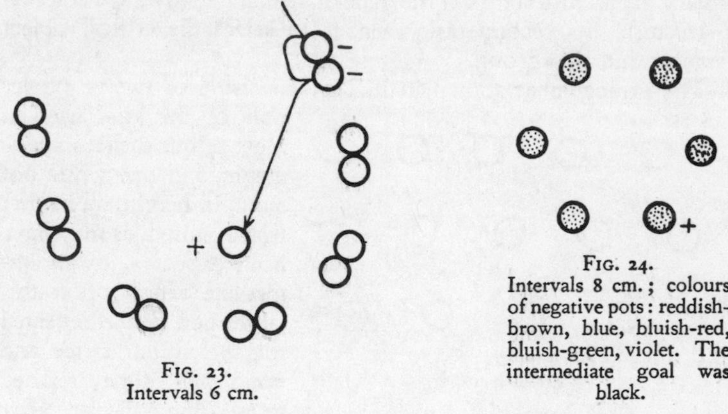

FIG. 23.
Intervals 6 cm.

FIG. 24.
Intervals 8 cm.; colours of negative pots: reddish-brown, blue, bluish-red, bluish-green, violet. The intermediate goal was black.

of objects used. These were made of grey cardboard and were approximately 4–5 cm. in height. (There were always *two* of the negative objects, but for convenience only one is shown in this and subsequent drawings.) As can be seen in Fig. 26 the only difference between these objects was the triangle or disk mounted upon the cylinder. The results were predominantly negative and we therefore concluded that under the present circumstances form discrimination (i.e. triangle *v.* disk) was not possible.

184 It will be recalled how readily the birds discriminated "hollow" from "closed" in Series I (Fig. 3). We therefore repeated this problem with the present objects and presented situations such as those shown in Figs. 27–29. The intervals between them were 5–7 cm. The results were almost all positive even when (as in *all*

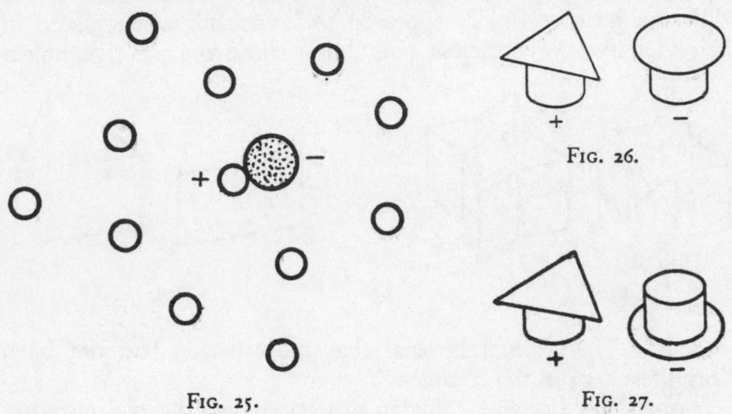

FIG. 25. FIG. 26. FIG. 27.

cases hereafter) the intermediate goal was not "shown" to the bird and was not the last object to be put in place.

185 To test this ability in discriminating "hollowness" from "solidness" we performed a series of experiments using a variety of identical objects such as those pictured in Figs. 30–31. No

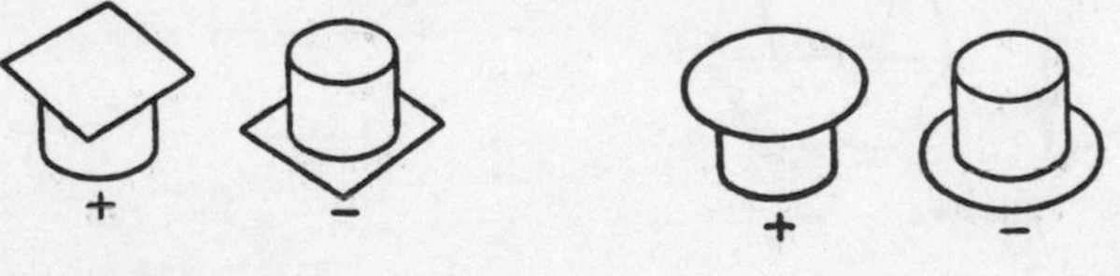

FIG. 28. FIG. 29.

difficulty at all was apparent: both birds chose the correct object in every test. Our next task, therefore, was to discover if possible
186 by what criterion the birds were being guided. Possibly something else besides "hollowness" might be serving as the real criterion. It might, for example, have been a difference in illumination conditions. The solid surface reflected light, the hollow opening naturally had a much less brilliant appearance. By reversing the relationship (hollow object strong in light reflection, solid one not)

we can test this hypothesis. As may be seen in Fig. 32, the positive object now had but a small upper surface and fairly steep walls, the walls of the negative objects were less steep and the opening much larger. When seen from above the negative objects thus reflected more light than did the positive one. The two hollow objects seemed to the experimenter to be "filled with light", while the positive object appeared to "vanish" when placed in their vicinity. Nevertheless both birds chose the positive object

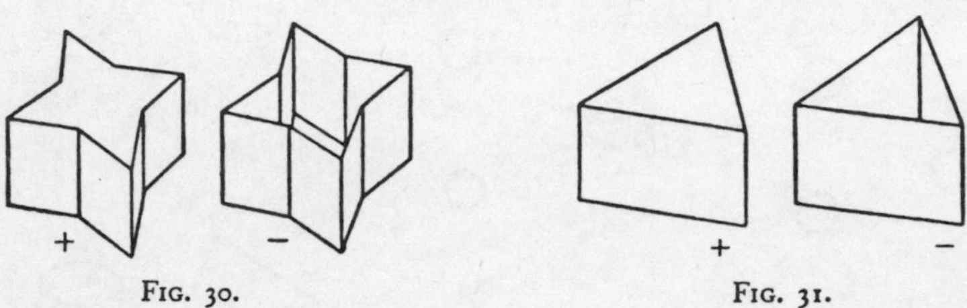

FIG. 30. FIG. 31.

at once. Therefore it is clear that the criterion had not been "brightest spot in the complex".

It might be, however, that in this latter case the real criterion was that of slope: the sides of the positive object converged from below upward, those of the negative object converged in a downward direction. Our next test (Fig. 33), therefore, reversed these
187 features. Despite this, both birds again chose correctly.

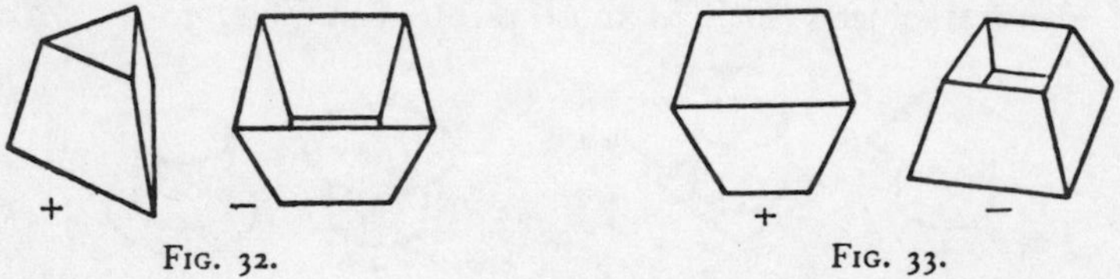

FIG. 32. FIG. 33.

From these results we therefore know that the inclination of the lateral surfaces was not serving as criterion. One factor, however, has remained constant in all tests: the positive object always had a horizontal surface above the ground. It is possible that *this* may have been the criterion. To test this possibility we presented objects such as those shown in Fig. 34. For the first time *A* made an error on his initial trial. It seems possible that the criterion "horizontal surface above the ground" was playing a part in determining the choices.

188 Further experiments using objects of other shapes were, however,

positive in their results and we may, therefore, conclude that this criterion was not alone crucial. There seems to be no other conclusion than the one originally suggested, namely that the birds were guided by the difference between an "open" and a "closed" form.

[189 : in constructing the models a strip of grey paper somewhat lighter than that of the cardboard was pasted *inside* each of them as a means of fastening together the overlapping edges. When the negative objects were turned hollow side up, this seam was visible while

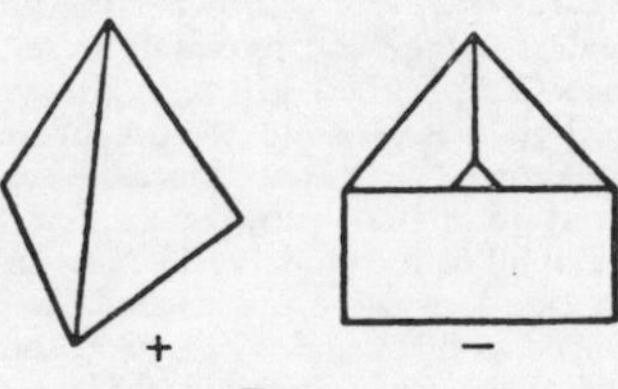

FIG. 34.

not visible on any of the positive objects. Reversing this situation did not, however, change the results. Therefore it may be concluded with even more assurance that "hollow" *v.* "solid" constituted the real criterion.]

190 When cardboard models such as those shown in Fig. 35 were

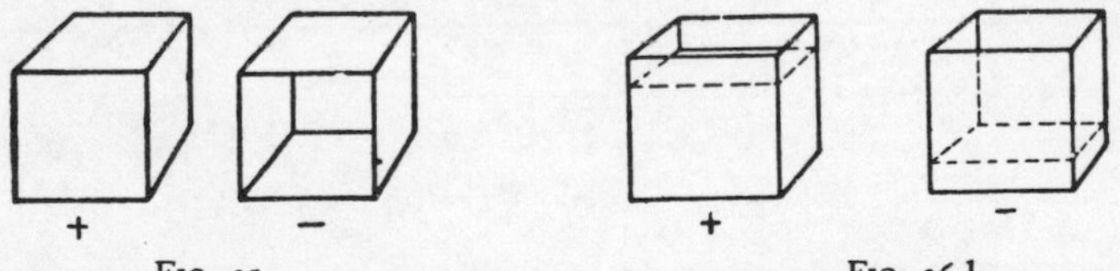

FIG. 35. FIG. 36.[1]

192 used the birds seemed confused and made several errors. With
193 objects of the type depicted in Fig. 36 every sign of assurance was again apparent. We may, therefore, reaffirm our former conclusion with this slight modification: that, namely, the birds selected as intermediate goal the *most convex* object presented in any given experiment.

194 To characterize in a single statement the results of our present

[1] Three hollow cubes were used. Seven cm. from the top a floor parallel with the ground was inserted. As may be seen from the drawing this surface was at the upper end of the positive object while the negative objects were placed with the floor partition 7 cm. from the ground. Seen from above the positive object, therefore, appeared nearly filled while the negative ones seemed more empty or hollow.

study we may say that the perception of these birds is manifestly much nearer that of human beings than one might at first have thought probable. There seems every reason to believe that the organization of their perceptual field is essentially the same as our own.[1]

[1] [" Wahrnehmungspsychologische Untersuchungen am Eichelhäher II " (*Zeitschr. f. verg. Physiol.*, Abt. C. der *Zeitschr. f. wissen. Biol.*, 1928, 7, 617–656) concludes this study of the behaviour of the jay bird. Small prisms made of cardboard were used instead of flower pots and the birds readily distinguished the positive prism when arrangements similar to those reported above (p. 152 f.) were presented. In these experiments the birds were not " shown " the intermediate goal. When cardboard models of cylinders, cubes, and pyramids were used as negative objects the birds successfully chose a (positive) prism model even when no positional preference was given it. This was possible because of a few initial trials during which the prism had been " shown " to them. Since the negative objects in this case presented—when seen at certain angles—surfaces identical with those of the prism the positive results show that all of the models had been seen as three dimensional by the birds. Using but one " negative " and one " positive " object, 16 cards (upon which various patterns in black and white had been drawn) were presented in assorted pairs. A record of the card spontaneously preferred in each trial showed that in every pair where a brightness difference could be discriminated by human eyes, the birds exhibited a decided preference for the *brighter* of the two patterns. Several coloured cones (negative objects) and one grey cone (intermediate goal) were arranged in haphazard order. After a few preliminary trials when the positive object was " shown " they succeeded thereafter without this assistance and chose the grey cone from among others of red, yellow, blue, and purple. There were signs of uncertainty only when bluish-green cones were used.]

Selection 21

FIGURAL PERCEPTION IN BEES

By Mathilde Hertz

"Die Organisation des optischen Feldes bei der Biene," I., Zeitschrift für wissenschaftliche Biologie, Abt. C., *Zeitschr. f. vergl. Physiol.*, 1929, **8**, 693–748.

693 There are at least two ways of explaining the bee's orientation. This paper reports a series of experiments whose results, by clarifying the distinction between these explanations, shows the inadequacy of one while serving to justify the other. An explanation such as that of association theory or the doctrine of conditioned reflex assumes that the insect's behaviour is governed by a system of fixed
694 couplings of the stimulus-response type. This approach would be proven wrong, however, if it were shown that changing spatial arrangements of the perceived stimulus objects are grasped and evaluated by the insect's nervous system without the aid of a special mechanism and irrespective of which place on the retina is stimulated. Since with insects, even less than with vertebrate animals, "intellectual" processes cannot be assumed which might effect this organization of sensory and memorial data, the processes must be physiological just as the processes of perception are physiological. We are thus led to the consideration of another type of explanation: viz., one assuming the operation of physiological processes such that an immediate organization of the sensory field is effected. Here instead of many independently stimulated centres, either *rigidly* connected with or insulated from one another, an excitation-field analogous to a physical field is assumed.[1]

695 The question whether forms played a part in the bee's orientation
696 was first studied systematically by v. Frisch in 1913. He concluded that the bee was able to recognize certain forms if they resembled flowers, but not otherwise, Later H. Baumgärtner repeated the
697 experiments and stated that *colour* and not form was the decisive characteristic for the bee. In a series of preliminary experiments
698 the present author found that bees were able not only to distinguish very faintly coloured objects but that discriminations were possible

[1] Cf. *Selection 3*.

Grateful acknowledgment is hereby made to *Julius Springer*, *Verlagsbuchhandlung*, Berlin, for permission to reproduce the illustrations used in this Selection.

(1) even when forms were used which were unlike flowers, and (2) even when the same colour (achromatic as well as chromatic) was used for both objects. The experiments reported below represent a systematic inquiry into this question.

699 *Apparatus and procedure.*—A pane of glass ¼ m. square was placed on a table not far from the hive. A white paper of the same size was placed under the glass and upon this variously shaped black figures (two at a time) were laid. A watch glass containing a small amount of sugared water was placed near one of the black figures.[1] In a short time one or two bees would appear, drink up the water and fly to their hive where they would transfer the liquid to other members of the colony, and return—usually with several more of their kind.[2]

700 After each departure the pane was washed and dried and the black figures shifted in irregular order to new positions relative to one another. The table, also, was turned about from time to time. In general every precaution was taken to make *only* the figures crucial. A new dish of sugar-water was used for each flight. A decisive result was recorded when the swarm descended as one mass upon one of the figures.

701 *Experiments* 1–2. *Figure and ground.*—Figs. *a* and *b* of Fig. 1, separated by a distance of 20 cm., were presented in the manner already indicated.[3] The reward lay 1–2 cm. to one side of the star. In the first critical experiment the swarm descended upon *b*, and

[1] [At first a somewhat different technique had been used. During the initial trials with any given pair of figures one watch-glass (filled) had been placed beside the "positive" figure; another, empty one, was laid beside the "negative" form. At the critical tests both watch glasses were empty. This method was later abandoned, however, because it was found impossible to be sure that both glasses were equally free from bee odours, and also because the glasses glistened in the sunlight and thus served as an unnecessary disturbance. In reduced illumination they were probably not perceived anyway (cf. below pp. 721–724). In a later experiment ("Die Organisation des optischen Feldes bei der Biene" II., ibid., 1930, **11**, 107–145 : pp. 110 and 112 f.) the spontaneous and uninfluenced preferences of the bees were studied and in this case several food dishes were used simultaneously. The bees ignored these entirely and settled instead upon the preferred figure at each trial. Cf. also, in the present paper, pp. 701–702 below, where it is shown that the swarm descends upon the *figure* only. In no case was the food dish upon, but always 1–2 cm. to one side of, the positive figure; yet *the bees alighted first upon the figure itself* and then found their way to the sugared water.]

[2] [By marking certain of the bees with a spot of white ink it is possible to determine the frequency of visits on a given day. Having given up their "cargo" they usually return for more within 2–3 minutes so that within an hour the same bee visits the experimental table from 20–30 times. Rarely did the swarm number 100 bees; usually fewer.]

[3] In this and all subsequent cases the figures were from 5–10 cm. in diameter. The difference can be estimated from the drawings (given here) where the sizes are proportional to those of the figures actually used in the experiments.

in the second *a* ; in the third, fourth and fifth, *b* was again chosen. Although no preference for either figure was marked, the experiment shows that the bees were at least able to distinguish both figures from their white background, for in each swoop *only* one or other of the figures was visited. This shows that the distinction between figure and ground with which we are familiar in human psychology is also present in the perception of these invertebrates.

Because of the great theoretical importance of this question (figure-ground discrimination) the following experiment was also car ied out. The background was a yellowish green and the figure

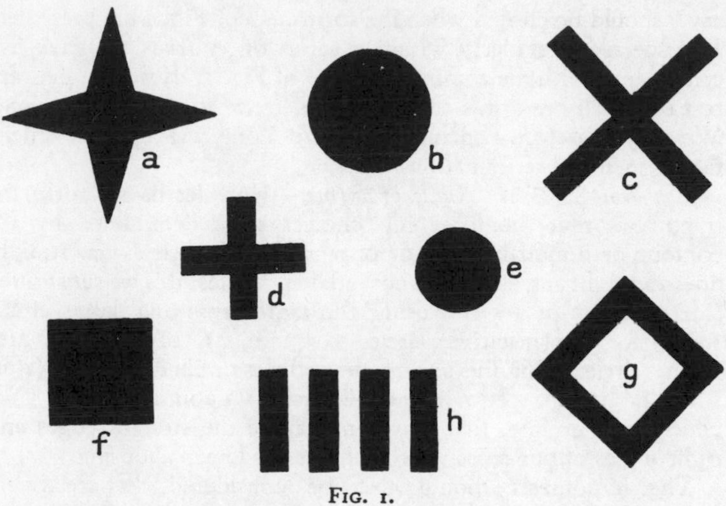

FIG. 1.

a blue circle 6·5 cm. in diameter. Some 2·5 cm. from the figure a
702 watch crystal of sugared water was placed. No previous training
with blue had been given. After each visit of the bees the blue
circle was shifted under the glass pane to a new position 15 cm.
distant from the last. In every case the swarm flew straight to the
blue figure.

Experiments 3–5. *Form and size.*—In the next experiment we
703 used *b* and *c* of Fig. 1 and placed the reward beside *c*. In the 38
critical tests almost all were positive (i.e. *c* was chosen) and none
absolutely negative.[1] Since, however, the preference for *c* might

[1] [For one reason or another the swarm sometimes divides and some bees go to each figure. In the critical tests reported below only those are designated as positive (or negative) where the entire group settles upon *one* figure.]

have been due not to our training but to some biological factor,
705 we reversed the procedure and rewarded *b* instead of *c*. In the 39 trials which were then given about two-thirds of the swoops fell on *b*.

Before we may safely conclude from these results that the bees had really distinguished the form-characters of our cross and circle we must test whether or not secondary differences between them had served as criteria. The cross, *c*, is a larger figure than the circle, *b*, even when their areas are the same; its arms, on the other hand, if taken individually, are smaller than the circle. If the criterion had been that of size, and the larger figure was preferred, then the *circle* should be chosen when the forms *d–b* of Fig. 1 are presented.
706 Interspersed irregularly within a series of 37 trials we gave five critical tests with the combination *d–b* of Fig. 1. Results: in every test the small cross was chosen in preference to the (larger) circle. We may therefore conclude that size alone was not the crucial factor in the discriminations.

Experiments 6–8. *Kinds of forms*.—Now let us set forth the hypothesis that the foregoing choices were determined by the contour or boundary lines of our cross and circle: viz. straight lines and right angles *versus* a curved line. To test this we substituted (in the midst of a series using the large cross and large circle, 1*c*–1*b*) for the (negative) circle, a square, 1*f*, of the same area as the circle. But the swarm nevertheless still descended (after
707 some hesitation, yet without dispersing) upon the *cross*. We conclude, therefore, that it was not alone the straight edges and right angles of our cross which the bees had been choosing.

The hypothesis should also be considered that relatively independent [*selbständiger*] parts (e.g. the beams) of the cross may have served as criterion. To test this we presented, together with the cross, a figure (*g* or *h* in Fig. 1) composed of the same parts as the cross. Results: in the first case the bees chose *g* rather than *c*,
708 and in the second they chose *h* rather than *c*. It thus seems very probable that the choices before had not been made relative to the entire appearance of our figures, but that a single part (viz. a beam of a definite size) had really been serving as criterion.

This conclusion can be tested in two ways. First let us re-introduce the whole figures (cross and square) used before and determine whether or not a transposition can be made from a small cross and small square (Fig. 2, *a–b*) to a large cross and large square (2*c*–2*d*). Secondly, let us use a single beam of the larger cross (2*e*) together with the large cross itself (1*c*) and, again, together with the

square, *f*, shown in Fig. 1. If the hypothesis is correct that relatively independent parts (e.g. a single beam) had served as criterion before, the bees should be clearly disoriented in the first case, and should, in the second, choose the single beam in preference to its accompanying form. The results, however, were just the reverse of this.
709 There was no disorientation when the larger pair (2*c*–2*d*) was substituted for the smaller pair (2*a*–2*b*); nor was there any preference shown for the single beam (2*e*) when presented together with the large cross (1*c*). In the pair 2*e*–1*f* (beam-square) they chose the square even though, in the trial just preceding this, the square had been avoided.

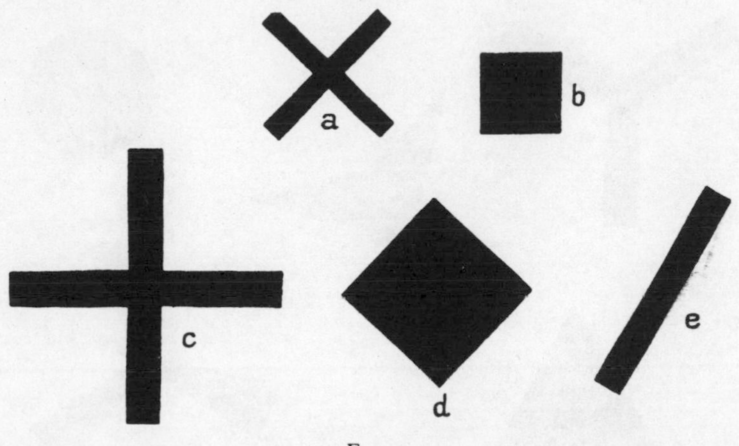

Fig. 2.

From this we are led to conclude that, after all, the bees' choice (here and before) was determined by some character of the whole figures which did not appear in parts of those figures. The character common to our crosses and to 1*g*–1*h* also is lacking in our circles and squares and also in the single beam. The only characteristic consistently present in the preferred figures and consistently absent from those which the bees rejected is that of openness and articulation. The preferred figures in all the foregoing experiments have been those richest in contrast; the others are all comparatively closed structures with but little contrast.

Experiments 9–12. *"Open" and "closed" forms.*—Our investigation now turns to the question of degree of articulation which the bees can distinguish. When the figures *a* and *b* of Fig. 3 were

presented, and the watch crystal food dish placed beside the former,
710 the bees discriminated between them and settled on *a*. After five trials with this pair *c* was substituted for *a*. During several trials with this new pair (*b–c*) the bees seemed disturbed and uncertain.
711 The results were also irregular when the pair *a–c* was given. From this it may be assumed that the bees found *c* less different from *a* or *b* than these were from each other.

The procedure just described was used again: *a–b* for several trials and then the triangle, *d*, substituted for *b*—thus giving the
712 pair *a–d*. The bees chose *a*, which shows that under the conditions of this experiment *b* and *d* were both negative relative to the cross,

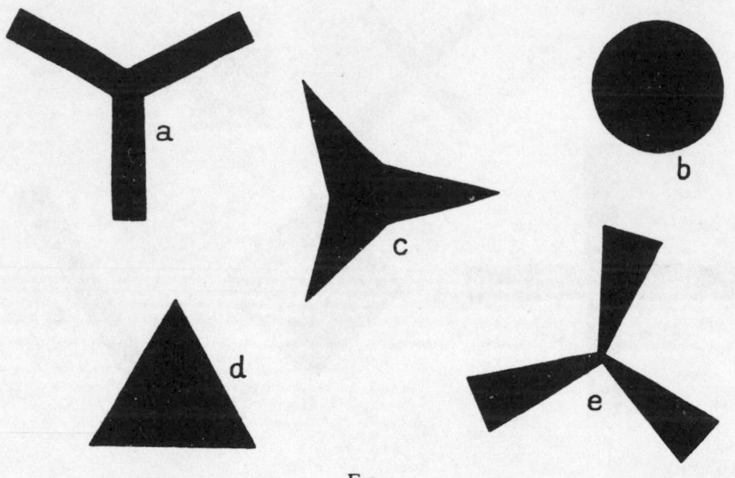

FIG. 3.

a. After 12 more trials with the pair *a–d* we substituted *e* for *a*—thus presenting the pair *d–e*. The bees chose *e* without hesitation.
713 These results greatly strengthen the probable validity of our hypothesis that "openness" is the criterion by which the bees were guided. Recapitulating, we find the bees to have indicated by their choices the following (increasing) scale of articulation values: circle, square, triangle, 3-pointed cross, 3-armed cross, 3-armed propeller blade (Fig. 3*e*), and the 4-armed cross. Undoubtedly a human being would have arranged these forms in the same order.

714 *Experiments 13–15. Degrees of openness.*—We have thus far used figures which differed not only in openness but in other respects as well. How similar may they be when only differences of openness

distinguish them? The bees were given 9 trials with the pair *b–c*, shown in Fig. 1. In practically every case *c*, the (positive) cross,
715 was chosen. At the 10th trial the figures *a* and *d* of Fig. 4 were used. Result: *a* was chosen immediately. The pair *b–c* of Fig. 1 was then resumed for several more trials during which *c* was chosen in all but one instance. Then the pair 4*b*–4*d* was introduced. Result: 4*b* was chosen. This was repeated with 4*c*–4*d*, and 4*c* was chosen. Thus we see that 4*a*, 4*b*, and 4*c* all differed from 4*d* (i.e. 1*b*) in being *open* figures while differing among themselves only in degree of openness.

In another experiment also designed to study degrees of openness we began with the pair 5*a*–4*d* (i.e. eight-arm cross and solid circle).

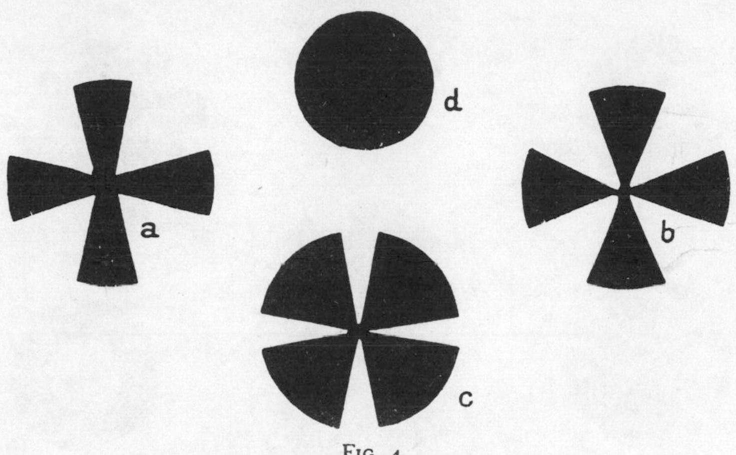

Fig. 4.

716 There was an obvious preference for the cross. At the ninth trial 5*b* was substituted for 5*a* (thus yielding the pair 5*b*–4*d*, i.e. cogwheel and solid circle). In all of the nine trials with this pair the cogwheel was chosen. The experiment was resumed on the following day: the pair 5*a*–4*d* was again presented for five trials (in all of which 5*a*, the eight-arm cross, was chosen). On the sixth trial 5*b* was substituted for 5*a* (as before) and 5*c* was substituted for 4*d* thus yielding the pair 5*b*–5*c* (i.e. cogwheel and large solid circle). The eight trials all resulted in choices of the cogwheel, 5*b*. Similarly, when the pair 5*c*–5*d* was used the bees chose 5*d*; they also descended at once upon 5*e* when the pair 5*e*–5*f* was presented.

In some of these pairs the differences in amount of openness were comparatively slight, but correct choices persisted nevertheless.
717 One may therefore wonder if the bees were not perhaps relying upon some criterion other than openness. In order to test this

Fig. 5.

we presented the pair 5*b*–5*g* (cogwheel–star). Result: there
718 was no decisive preference for either figure. In the first three trials the cogwheel was chosen, then the star, then both together (dispersal of swarm), and so on. The results became increasingly

less distinct as additional trials were given. One must conclude, therefore, that the two forms (5*b*–5*g*) were not markedly different for the bees, and hence that their criterion in the earlier trials cannot have been the kind of angles appearing in the preferred figures.

After several trials using the pair 5*b*–5*c* (cogwheel and solid circle) we substituted 5*h* for 5*c*: thus giving the pair 5*b*–5*h*. The bees continued to choose the cogwheel, 5*b*. Then the pair 5*b*–5*i*
was presented. Results: 5*b* was still chosen in nearly every case,
719 but it was clear that this combination did not contain for them a
strong distinction between degrees of openness in the two figures. Our experiments have shown that the bees' choices were determined by the relative continuity or discontinuity of contours.

Experiments 16 *and* 18. *Transpositions.*—(1) Having discovered by what criterion the bees were able to discriminate between our figures and, further, that they were able to distinguish degrees of this quality, we shall now submit these findings to a further test. By repeated presentations of a certain pair we shall train the bees to select one of the figures (the "positive" figure) and avoid the other. In the critical experiment we shall substitute for the figure
which had been negative during training another of a character
720 still more positive than the originally positive figure.

Proceeding in the manner described by Köhler, we trained the bees (nine trials) with 5*c*–5*d*, to choose *d*. In the critical test 5*k* was substituted for 5*c*. Thus *d*, the figure to be ***chosen*** in 5*c*–5*d*, became, in 5*d*–5*k*, the one to be ***avoided***. The bees chose 5*k* and continued to choose it at nearly every one of the eleven trials with this pair which followed. These results not only substantiate our earlier interpretation regarding degrees of openness but show also that the decisive characteristics of the positive object (training series) were not its absolute qualities but its place relative to the
other partner in the pair.

[721–724: *Experiment* 17. How much can the brightness distinction
between figure and ground be reduced without disturbing positive results? Figs. 5*b*–5*c* were used. These were cut from greys of varying brightnesses and presented one after another until the bees were no longer able to respond correctly. The background was white filter paper; the greys were numbered from 30 (practically black) to 2 (almost white). It was found that the grey No. 5 was the last which could be used and still have the figures clear enough for successful discriminations between them to occur.]

725 (2) If articulation was effective in the figures already used, will
it also prove the decisive quality in arrangements such as those in

726 Fig. 6? Using the pair *6a–6f* for training, it was quickly seen that our question could be affirmed and that *a* (the positive figure) was distinctly open in the sense already discussed. Thus when *6b* was substituted for *6f* (the pair was thus *6a–6b*) *a* was still chosen:
727 this time in preference to *b*. Similarly when the pair *6a–6c* was introduced during a series of trials using *6a–6f*, *a* was chosen. These results show that *a* was undoubtedly experienced as more richly articulated than either *b* or *c*, and we are therefore able to use these designs in transposition experiments. Again the question is whether the bees will learn to react positively to a given figure because of its absolute qualities or because it is more richly articulated than the other member of a pair.

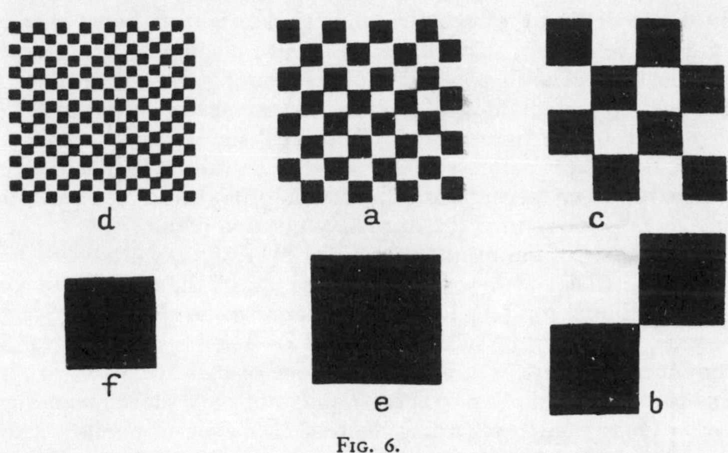

FIG. 6.

728 The bees were trained with the pair *6a–6c* and *a* was positive. After a number of trials with this combination, the pair *6a–6d* was presented (i.e. *d* was substituted for *c*). The swarm descended immediately upon *d* although during training *a* had always been chosen. Five more flights to this pair (*6a–6d*) were allowed and then the pair *6a–6c* once more introduced. This time *a* was chosen without the slightest hesitation. Again five flights (with *6a–6c*). Then *6b–6c* was used. The bees flew at once to *c*. After five trials with this pair *e* was introduced in the place of *c* (i.e. the pair *6b–6e* was given) and this time *b* was chosen. During five more flights *b* continued to be preferred instead of *e*.

The results of this series of transpositions are so unequivocal

that comment is unnecessary. In every case the relatively more
open figure was chosen despite its having been negative and
avoided in the pair just preceding. Or, when we proceeded from
6a–6c to *6a–6d* the figure which had before been positive and
729 preferred instantly became negative and was avoided. There can
be no doubt that the bees had learned the relative rather than the absolute qualities of the material used, i.e. they had throughout responded to properties which occur only when the figures are partners in a total set-up.

731 *Discussion.*—There can be no doubt that bees are capable of reacting to form and that they distinguish relative differences within pairs of figures such as we have used. At the beginning of this paper reference was made to two types of explanatory concepts. An
example of the first may be seen in the following (by v. Kühn):
732 " All orientational responses of multicellular beings are made up
out of reflexes. Upon the definite stimulation of a definite sensory spot a definite activity of the movement apparatus is released by the nervous system." Our experimental results conclusively disprove this hypothesis. Instead they substantiate Köhler's [*Selection 18*, p. 37] conclusion that " quite simple kinds of structural function arise from the elementary properties of the nervous system just as readily and [phylogenetically] just as soon as do the most simple absolute excitations."

Unlike human beings the bee is unable to discriminate simple closed forms (circle, square, triangle) nor does it distinguish between a cogwheel and star, nor between arrangements such as those shown in Fig. 1*c*, *g*, *h* (beams forming a cross, hollow square, parallel row). These results can in no sense be interpreted, however, merely as failures in the face of tasks which for some unassigned reason proved more difficult than the others. *The organization of the bee's visual field is entirely different in principle from that of the vertebrates.* Our results show that for the bee visual units depend upon and are distinguished by the relative continuity or discontinuity of their contours.

[733–748 : omitted.]

THIRD GROUP: THOUGHT

SELECTION 22

NUMBERS AND NUMERICAL CONCEPTS IN PRIMITIVE PEOPLES

By MAX WERTHEIMER

"Über das Denken der Naturvölker, Zahlen und Zahlgebilde," *Zeitschr. f. Psychol.*, 1912, **60**, 321–378; reprinted (with new pagination) in Wertheimer's *Drei Abhandlungen zur Gestalttheorie*, Erlangen, 1925.

322 It is not enough to ask which numbers and operations of *our* mathematics are used by the peoples of some other (especially a so-called primitive) culture. Instead the question must be: *What* thought processes *do* they employ in this domain? *What* are their problems? *How* do they attack them? *What* are the results? *Our* categories of thought—number, cause, abstract concepts—are to greater or less extent a part of *our* social structure and heritage. The tendency to consider primitive thinking a mere preliminary stage, a vague, rudimentary and perhaps relatively incomplete form of our own thinking is sure to do little more than obstruct genuine inquiry.

323 Counting, for example, in the sense of repeated additions of unity does not constitute the only factor in the genesis of numbers. The ideal of universal transferability (i.e. abstractness) of thought structures is not necessarily the aim of all thinking in this sphere. There are structures [*Gebilde*] which, less abstract than our numbers, nevertheless serve analogous ends or can be used in place of numbers. These structures do not abstract from their natural context and natural relationships; they may occasionally be abstract with regard to the form or arrangement of materials, less often, however, with regard to material itself. Here are a few examples:—

324 A hut is being built and posts are needed. One can count the number required and fetch them, *or* one can simply know, without counting, that the framework depends upon " posts " and although the number is neither specified nor counted, " these posts " are intrinsically involved in the idea of the hut. Or again, while we may say that a mast is braced by three stays, a shipwright does not think of how *many* stays are required. His problem is to brace the mast. His ideas have to do with what a "braced mast" *is*, what the

arrangement, form, and direction of the stays must be. Or, a large family sits down for dinner and someone observes, " There is somebody missing." There was no need to count those present; one merely sees that a member of the group is absent.

The " five and five " of one's hands can be applied to *other*
325 things beside hands. Here the material is variable. But these structures are not transferable without more ado as numbers are, for their essential character is that they constitute two groups-of-five. When I recognize a square it is not from thinking about the " four-ness " of its sides and corners. The possibility of experiencing such wholes does not stop with the limit of our direct grasp of number [1] because form, arrangement and organization are also involved. This is clear in the case of polygons; also in the ideas we have of " aggregates " whose " number " is unknown.

Groups of this sort are " natural groups "; eyes are two, a plate and table are not. Our " pair " is one such natural structure. The " pair " structure is based upon symmetry (pendants), use-relationships (eyes, shoes), biological relations (married pair). It does not express the union of identical objects but of any two things which *belong together*. Two trees here and another at some
326 distance are not so much 3 as they are a pair of trees and another over yonder.

327 *Numbers* are applicable to anything and everything, to any arbitrary objects, arrangements, or groups, and they themselves are in all cases the same. *Structures*, on the other hand, are relevant only to natural groupings or relationships between parts and their whole. Two eyes, two beams, thumb and forefinger, two warriors, etc., constitute different kinds of pair-structures, though all may be spoken of *as* pairs. This does not hold, however, of mother and son nor of man and horse. Indeed many languages have no plural form of the word " mother ". Even with us the plural " mothers " is comparatively rare. The relevant biological relationship is of mother to child, not of a plurality of mothers.[2] As regards man and horse: notice how only under very special conditions is a human being ever *paired* with anything except another human being. A perhaps somewhat extravagant way of expressing this: 1 horse + 1 horse = 2 horses; 1 man + 1 man = 2 men—but 1 man + 1 horse = *a rider*.

[1] In general such apprehension extends to 5.

[2] It is typical of a certain kind of thinking that in it concepts are not formed so as to function in any arbitrary (logical) operation, but with regard to their biological relevance. *Our* " logical " concepts are conceived to be such that any one of them may appear in any operation of formal logic.

328 Generally speaking, the execution of a numerical or other intellectual operation whose meaning is not rooted in actuality is almost if not entirely impossible for primitive peoples. Evidences of how remote from actuality *our* thinking often is can be obtained when one sets for a primitive man some task carried over from the world we consider quite matter of fact and obvious. For example, an Indian school boy was told to translate the sentence, " The white man shot six bears to-day." He not only refused but clearly showed himself incapable of performing the task because, he insisted, no white man could have shot six bears in a day. To this topic belongs also the well known story: how many dumplings did you eat? If you had three more what would you have? A stomach ache!

329 To us it seems a great advantage to be able to abstract from the natural relationships of things. It is this facility of thought which we must thank for many technical achievements in our civilization. But there are others whose thinking may be described thus: Wherever there is no natural relationship, no vividly concrete and relevant connection amongst things themselves, there is also no logical connection, nor is any logical manipulation of these things possible. In contrast to this stands our kind of thinking whose logic tends in this direction: " Everything can be counted ", and " All things can be combined in and-summation." The difference between these ways of thinking appears clearly in such cases as the following. Suppose I talk with a child or a primitive man and say, " What are both X and Y?" [1] I am given several answers in which the two things together are classified just as they would be by a civilized adult. When, however, in the course of questioning, one chances to mention something like " dog and cat ", very often the *other* kind of thinking will suddenly appear, and instead of " pets " the answer given is " enemies ". It does not bring us nearer to a solution to label this a case of " inferior mental ability ". Nor does it help us if someone names it a case of association by familiarity. As a matter of fact answers of this kind, arising, as it were, by a kind of " clicking over " from one thinking process to the other, often indicate (even by their rejection of abstract thinking) rather good sense.

330 An arrangement of items can be arbitrary: five apples may lie before me in a pile, e.g. four together on the table and one on top. Of course I can see them in any number of different ways or arrange them differently, a row or a pentagon or the like; or the arrangement may be quite irrelevant. Out of all this arises a kind

[1] [E.g. what are " horse and cow "? Answer: domestic animals. Etc.]

of " type " characteristic of all the various arrangements. In general
every " Gestalt " evinces a certain variability or, as one says in
logic, a certain " latitude ". A quincunx lends itself to a great
many changes of intervals, proportions, resemblances amongst the
material parts, etc., without losing its original quincunx character.
But certain of these variables often function together more
adequately than others. A particular arrangement has degrees of
stability and of precision according as some and not others of the
variables predominate. It is not true, however, that there arises in
this way a general " concept " (i.e. through logical elimination or
abstraction of differences) which is poorer in content, i.e. with
331 narrower connotation, than its species. Instead there is a complex,
general " concept-analogue " of five-ness in various (but not
unlimited) arrangements. And it is the same with the rectangle.
To perceive a rectangle we do not need to observe its right-angled-
ness and four-sidedness. Instead one perceives the type " rectangle "
whether the particular figure is long or short, broad or narrow,
vertical or horizontal.

332 Conceptual structures of non-quantified plurality (i.e. of the
kind excluded from mathematics) are very important for everyday
life. Thus we speak of a herd, a school, a flock, a troop, a handful,
a load, etc. The farmer, shepherd, hunter, cook or huckster knows
very well the use of such terms. And semi-numerical group
structures are also abundantly illustrated in everyday speech. We
say, for example, " He is a man in his thirties " or " X died in the
333 twenties of the last century ". Nor do we necessarily mean exactly
12 when we refer to " a dozen people ", for the term includes the entire group, say, from 11 to 14 indifferently. The same type of approximation holds in practical usage for the terms battalion, squadron,
army, etc. To characterize such structures as inadequate, inexact,
or vague merely because of their numerical variability would be
334 wrong. There are occasions where numerical exactitude is meaningful only up to the limit assigned by those occasions themselves.
In business, for example, it would be meaningless to carry one's
calculations to decimal places beyond which the merchandise itself
could be divided. In physics decimal places indicating operations
335 beyond any possibility of experimental verification are also meaningless. Approximate-numbers from a certain magnitude onward,
and within a considerable range of variation, also occur in everyday
life (e.g. around 15 it is often immaterial whether exact quantities
are expressed or not, and *one* central number can thus represent
the entire region).

336 Of a similar character also are the words "much" or "many"
337 and "little" or "few" in many of their uses. We speak, for example, of many people, a large number, a huge assemblage of people, and so on. Again, in place of "much and many" we sometimes name a particular number (or its plural): hundreds of people were present.

In contrast to the wide range of approximation attending the usage of "much", etc., as one extreme, we find as opposite extreme
338 the cases where certain fixed, *unique amounts* are used to designate what we may call "almost numerical" quantities. Our round numbers are examples. Sometimes even the very *name* of a quantity shows how that quantity is represented by some unified whole (e.g. the hand). Again, sign languages contain instances as when 10 = *mfundiko* = "clasping" (i.e. of the hands), and 9 = *mfundiko imó* = "clasping one."[1]

339 With material objects this type of representation also appears in our languages. An extreme case is the Czech *nádavek* ("something tagged or added on": I buy 5 and get 6, I pay for 20 and am given 21). A long dozen or baker's dozen is really not 13 but a dozen and something to boot—and as for 11, one simply does not buy 11 pieces of anything. This is a general function of unique amounts which shows itself also in the rounding out of prices and in stepwise increases of values. In this connection belong also notions such as those of "good weight", and "good, ample, bare" in measurements, distances, durations, etc.

340 From the foregoing it is clear that the goal of numerical structures is not that of being variable in their own right. There can be many numerical structures in which natural groupings rather than unity of system prevail. Here, instead of abstraction (and hence unification within the numerical system) there arises an abundance of variety among group- and combination-structures.

When we consider the case of counting by units it is clear that here a factor is involved which generally operates in the direction of a unified numerical system. Upon the basis of counting there arises a new kind of generality, with the result that numerical structures become less rooted in naturally given groupings. And
341 yet even in operations with money—a field one might suppose to be quite remote from reality [*wirklichkeitsabstrakt*]—natural structures do not completely disappear. And the same can be observed in gradations of value (e.g. gradations of relevancy, natural wholes, approximate structures, etc.)

[1] [References and numerous other examples are given in the original text.]

Our numerical system is constructed according to a uniform
plan whose principle allows of no variation. It arises from the
multiple application of one unique quantity. This is not, however,
an absolute necessity, for cases may be cited where the various
factors operative in the construction of number-analogues are also
operative in determining numerical series. In New Guinea, for
example, one counts 1–5 on the left hand, 6–10 on the right hand,
342 11–15 on the right foot, and 16–20 on the left foot. Such number-
analogues and group-structures of groups, lacking the universal
applicability of our abstract numbers, remain longest attached to
material objects. Even where higher numbers are reached by
multiplicational operations, their relations to material objects nevertheless remain relevant. In general there may arise quite different
objects to be counted or numbered. Certain South Sea languages,
for example, have different ways of counting fruit, money, animals,
and men. The strong tendency towards uniformity of monetary
343 values is not always present in primitive peoples. Different
[344-345: omitted] monetary materials are sometimes used for purchasing different
articles, and indeed there are even cases where three non-exchange-
able kinds of money exist side by side.[1]

346 The conditions and functions already discussed apply not only
to the formation of quantitative structures but also to *operations*
upon and with such structures. This is shown in progressions
towards larger structures analogous to those attained by our own
abstract methods of addition and multiplication. Thus several specific
structures combined together yield specific (not arbitrary) larger
structures. Similarly with division. The parts of a larger structure
are not abstract in arrangement and organization of material and
the material itself is divisible only in such a way as to conform
with its natural properties and with natural requirements. Certain
arrangements predetermine through their form *certain* divisions.
347 This can be seen most clearly in the division of geometric
figures.

Identity of parts is not the universally decisive factor in division. Instead it is on the one hand predetermination within the Gestalt of the whole (e.g. the cleavage plane of crystalline structures), and on the other the tendency (not necessarily conscious) to maintain even after the division certain naturally unified wholes (Gestalten). The division of triangles is an example. It is but a psychological fiction to assume that all divisions are arbitrary and hence on the

[1] Cf. Schurtz, *Grundriss einer Entstehungsgeschichte des Geldes*, Weimar, Faber, 1898, p. 83.

same footing with one another. Instead we find that objects themselves imply certain specific divisions. It is possible to divide objects without regard for these factors, but such divisions belong in the class of operations which are " remote from reality " [*wirklichkeitsabstrakt*].

348 But let us consider another aspect of division. If I break a stick,
349 ordinary calculation says that I then have " two ". But when I break
a spear I do not have *two* spears. In the first case " two " is abstract;
I began with one unity, later I had two. In the other, more concrete
instance we have a structure in which the parts still depend for their
character upon the whole from which they were derived (e.g. one
is the head-piece; the other, part of the shaft).

The difficulty of teaching children the use of transferable numbers
is often due not to their lack of intelligence but to the strength of
such natural factors in their thinking. There are aggregate objects
which, although they *can* be apprehended as summations, are nevertheless themselves unified forms (e.g. a *thing*, such as a family).
350 On the other hand there are aggregate objects which are incapable
of having any other unity than that of their abstract sum (e.g. 7, 8, 9
gourds). Mathematics employs only the latter type of aggregates.

Operations with the two kinds of structures display differences which may be illustrated in the following way. Suppose that a chain of 8 links is to be divided. The divisions and their results for abstract and concrete thinking may be sketched thus :—

Abstract.		*Concrete.*
8 links	1 chain . . .	a chain.
4 ,,	1 half . . .	half a chain.
2 ,,	1 quarter . . .	a quarter of a chain?
1 link	1 eighth . . .	no longer a chain but a single link or ring.

With the third division there occurs a leap which for primitive peoples and children (following the process in the concrete way) constitutes a genuine shift; the result of the third division simply is not equivalent to that of the first.

352 We spoke above (p. 338) of certain spheres of relevancy. This
concept applies not only to amounts but also to location within
a number series: a kind of quasi-localized predetermination, we
may call it. Thus the additional unit in 101 is in the vicinity of 100
and the same holds for what is added " to boot " to a dozen. The
353 number 50 is a middle number and 51 is one beyond the middle.
354 Localization in such cases does not mean strictly spatial but rather
a more logical orientation. Thus certain quantities have a place

relative to some unique quantity: 25 is a quarter and 25 + 25 is the
first quarter plus the second quarter (in 100). Nor is $a \times b$ always
355 identical with $b \times a$: a huge amount occurring a few times is not
the same as a small amount occurring a great number of times.
And similarly with additions.

357 It is not true that all (meaningful) counting consists in the
addition of 1 more, as Locke claimed. A person may add + 1 for
a great while and still not understand the numbers he has been
counting. He would know only that any given number was one
more than its predecessor. A comprehension of the process is
358 possible only if he possesses at least some idea of the *amount*
of + 1, + 1 . . . which has been added. He must have some idea of
how far he has proceeded from the original 1. Better still would be
a knowledge of how any attained number stood relative to some
definitely unique amount. But best of all would be the ability to
organize the attained quantity into known unique amounts.
Without structural group-apprehensions or a readiness for quasi-localized specification (even though merely in approximation), no
meaningful concept of quantity is possible.[1]

It is probable that not counting, but natural group- and quantity-structures relative to real biological relationships constitute the genetically important origin of numerical concepts. The primary structures are probably not such concepts as 1 and continued additions of 1 but conceptually analogous individualized structures. Plurality is not genetically a quantity of identical items but an articulated whole.

360 The biological importance of numbers may lie in the fact that
quantity is a measure of the effectiveness or value of groups, and
that all operations, i.e. divisions and arrangements of all kinds,
can be carried out for a given group of numbers and then carried
over to the actual material group itself. The enormous technical
361 advantage in such cases is that operations performed upon the
numerical quantity are valid forever afterward and need only be
applied to new cases as they arise. But one must not assume that
amount *always* parallels value or effectiveness. In the first place
minute modifications of amounts (e.g. drops of water, grains of
rice) frequently have no influence at all upon the value or effectiveness of large quantities. Secondly, not every mathematically

[1] A good teacher of arithmetic places the principal emphasis upon comprehension (i.e. a survey) of problems. His pupils are taught to get an idea (even if only in general approximation) of what a problem is about. This is the opposite of mechanical mathematics where perfectly meaningless results (due, say, to an oversight in placing the decimal point) may be accepted by the pupil without questioning.

meaningful division is also biologically meaningful (e.g. half a pot, one-fifth goose). I can divide 4 arrows into 4 arrow-heads and 4 shafts, not into 3 and 5. Thirdly, numerical increase does not always signify a parallel increase in value. Consider in economics the Law of Diminishing Returns. Indeed values sometimes so change with amounts as to pass from positive through neutral to negative. In
362 everyday life 1 + 100 has a different meaning from 100 + 1, and in 1 + 2 the 2 is not at all the same as in 100 + 2, for whereas in the former case 2 is very much, in the latter it is scarcely appreciable.

[363–378: (363–366): comments regarding size. (367–369): questions are addressed to the anthropologist. Example: How do the members of a primitive tribe proceed in cases where *we* would rely upon operations with abstract numbers? (370–378): specific problems for investigation are suggested.]

Selection 23

THE SYLLOGISM AND PRODUCTIVE THINKING

By Max Wertheimer

"Über Schlussprozesse im produktiven Denken," *Drei Abhandlungen zur Gestalttheorie*, Erlangen, 1925, pp. 164–184.

165 When one attempts, in actual thinking, to use the *modus barbara* [1] of traditional logic, a curious discrepancy may arise. Like so many of the examples in textbooks of logic the *barbara* often appears empty, inadequate, and sterile. No wonder the *modus barbara* has been styled a *petitio*, or a merely classificatory device.[2]

And yet this is not invariably the case. Much clever thinking occurs in terms of this modus; very often one has the feeling that one's thinking *has* advanced. *What is really involved in such processes? How does it happen that the same logical operation can yield such diverse results on different occasions?*

Our aim here is to inquire into the nature of thought processes as they occur in actual affairs (not, as is customary, with regard merely to logical validity).

I

The syllogism should—on this everyone is agreed—lead in
its conclusion to a "new" proposition. The extreme case of this
166 requirement is expressed in the rule that the conclusion must not
appear as a premise. This requirement is obviously justified, for
if the conclusion merely repeats in a new way (i.e. as a kind of
recapitulation) what was already known in the premises, the result
is "meaninglessness". But what are the conditions imposed by
the requirement?

In its essentials the situation before the process is this: I possess, somewhere in my knowledge, the judgments that are to be used as premises; I do not yet possess the judgment which will appear as conclusion. Later I do possess this.

[1] All men are mortal . . . M—P (Major premise)
Socrates is a man . . . S—M (Minor premise)

Socrates is mortal . . . S—P (Conclusion)

[2] Some logicians—notably John Stuart Mill—have maintained that the major premise is really an induction in disguise.

Now how does this apply to Socrates? If the syllogism is to fulfil its essential conditions I must not know in advance whether Socrates is mortal or not. I write: S?P and then I proceed as follows. Somewhere in my knowledge I encounter the proposition that all men are mortal; elsewhere, that Socrates is a man. . . . Both of these *without* knowing whether or not Socrates is mortal. But is this possible? Are there really such cases?

The requirement of which we have been speaking sets forth that neither MP nor SM may, taken alone, provide any knowledge regarding SP. Neither may I know of Socrates that he is a man *because* he is mortal, nor that the mortality of "all" men would naturally include that of Socrates. The former condition is easily
167 fulfilled. Of the latter, however, one is at once suspicious, for it is not true that I know about the mortality of *all* men; of many, yes, but not of all. Actually the major premise here is not universal but is an induction in disguise.

Now let us take an example which *does* satisfy both requirements. Socrates goes to pay his taxes. He inquires at the central office which sub-office he should visit. The attendant asks to which Tax Zone Socrates belongs. Socrates does not know; how should he? "Well," answers the other, "you must know the street where you live! . . . Good, you live in X Street (*SM*); and X Street is in Zone 426 (*MP*)—therefore . . . ."

The fact that Socrates lives in X Street does not trespass upon the fact of this street being in Zone 426, and hence the conclusion
168 regarding Socrates is not gratuitous. The major premise asserts a civil regulation, not a piece of "knowledge"; it is an ordinance of the city government that for all cases having the property *a*, the property *b must* follow. Nothing is said about Socrates himself one way or the other; for purposes of the *ordinance* nothing need be known regarding any properties peculiar to Socrates. Indeed this is universally true and therefore holds also in cases where the major premise is a verbal definition or where it states something at least temporarily conceived of as subject only to human specification—e.g. an hypothesis tentatively set forth as presumably a law of nature. This was also accepted by Mill.

Everything seems to depend upon having the major premise universal without thereby presupposing any knowledge of *SP*. This brings up the ancient question of how knowledge can be universal without a prior determination of all particulars. Although this question is undoubtedly very important it may nevertheless be left outside our present considerations. I specify: *P is* known in all its particulars; the major premise *is* universal. Does it follow then that every syllogism is a *petitio*, a mere recapitulation of things already known? Are the foregoing requirements then impossible of satisfaction?

Let us consider how the requirement applies to the minor premise. Before the syllogism comes into being I must already possess SM but *not* SP. So far as SM is concerned the properties
169 contained in P must be irrelevant. Thus neither S nor M in my minor premise may contain the property P. I can know a thousand things about Socrates, but I must not know that he belongs in Tax Zone 426. The formula, then, is that although any number of *other* characteristics may be contained in S, those appearing in the major premise must not appear in S.

It is a genuine question to ask: *How* does Socrates enter the syllogism? Do I mean here the Socrates who possesses *all* the possibly true characteristics (known and unknown) of the "object" designated by that name; *or* do I mean the Socrates whose *known and directly determinable characteristics* are actually given?

The same holds for M. In the most simple case S is introduced as involving but one certain characteristic; S is defined, then, through *characteristic* [1] 1. Then to Sc1 there is added c2 [i.e. M], and this is the significance of the minor premise. Neither c1 nor c2 may contain anything of c3 [i.e., P] which appears as predicate of the major premise.

170 The major premise asserts (according to our formulation of its role, p. 168) that *all* instances of c2 are instances of c3 [i.e. all M is P]. But to assert anything of *all* c2's naturally involves asserting this of S [since all S is M]. Does this lead to a *petitio*? Not necessarily. Let us not overlook what has just been said regarding Sc1 and regarding the difference between the properties of S before and after the process carried out by the syllogism itself.

That there is such a difference seems obvious, and yet it is upon this basis that the charge of *petitio* is founded. This is particularly true in cases where S is defined by denotation, for then S is placed within a class in such a way that the *entire* S with all its characteristics, known and unknown, is thereby assigned its logical (denotative) locus. But if S already "contains" everything that could possibly pertain to it, then no "new" knowledge about it is possible. It is into this *impasse* that the traditional logic is predestined to fall. Such a logic is suitable only for one who

[1] [Hereafter the word "characteristic" as used in this connection will be designated by the letter c.]

already knows everything and needs only a system of classification; for a genuine advance in knowledge it is useless.

171 When, however, the foregoing is taken into consideration, an advance in knowledge *is* possible. What does it mean to say that S has already been examined with regard to P? The object S, yes, but is this already Sc1? Must I already know, must it be already stipulated that the given object (it is, namely, one of those containing c2) contains c1? Is it identical with the S which contains c1? As an object containing c2, S has necessarily already been examined. There is, however, *no* necessity that in this examination I should have established or known S *as* Sc1.

Here is the occasion upon which a genuine (and sometimes astonishing) advance in knowledge is possible—viz. when Sc1 reveals itself *as* a member of the group c3, which is already thoroughly known.

Two determinations are involved: I, that all cases having the property c2 also have the property c3; II, that Sc1 is a member of the group characterized by c2. If I specify that determination I takes place in such a way that no recourse is made or can be made to c1; and, likewise, that in determination II there shall be no reference to c3, then I have a pure case in the desired sense.

Changing our example of the tax payment slightly we may illustrate this situation as follows. Suppose that each taxpayer is given a number and that all numbers between 1–1,000 have been entered in the ledger as paid. That such entries have been made has nothing to do with the fact that Socrates, who happens to be No. 43, is thereby involved. Conversely, the fact of *Socrates's* being No. 43 is not involved in the entry procedure.

172 In science, too, this form of procedure plays its role. Completely pure cases are not easy to find, however, since pure determinations are seldom available. An example, however, may be suggested. I investigate a liquid of unknown composition. I am interested in the relation between low specific gravity and low boiling point. I heat the liquid and note which gases are discharged. The first is yellowish, the second bluish, the third greyish. I observe that in the end the yellow gas floats on top.

> The first gas to be discharged is yellowish
> The yellowish gas comes to the top
> ———————————————
> The first gas to be discharged comes to the top.

(I.e. the material of relatively lowest boiling point is also relatively lowest in specific gravity.)

II

173 But we must consider examples of a different sort if the significant aspects of our problem are to be discovered. A busy lawyer is in the habit of destroying the papers of cases so-and-so many years past. Consequently the records of Case A were recently burned. One day he is looking for a certain receipt connected with a current Case B. He looks in vain. He stops to think: what *was* it the receipt referred to? Suddenly he recalls that the *contents* of the receipt had to do with Case A—and the A papers have been destroyed! Now, expressed as above, we find: in the determination of the major premise the papers referred solely to Case A; not S and not Sc1, but Sc2. But Sc1 is a receipt referring to Case B. Their simultaneity does not of itself give rise to the conclusions, for in addition there must be a "click", so to speak, which snaps them together into the kind of inner relationship which *is* the conclusion.

Or to take another example. Peter and Paul have for a long time been members of the executive committee of their club. The committee meetings are dull and uninteresting and they have given up attending—except for the principal meeting once a year, when the annual Statement of Accounts is presented. One day
174 Peter returns from a journey and finds a letter telling him of a decision unanimously reached in a recent committee meeting. He is incensed and starts to phone Paul when he reads further and finds: "The decision was reached at the annual Accounts meeting which was held earlier than usual this year. The Statement of Accounts was accepted on motion of Mr. Paul Brown."

It is from examples of this sort that one sees how S can suffer a radical upset. For a moment the premises are side by side, then suddenly there is a "click". A decision distasteful to Peter was reached; an Accounts meeting has been held. Suddenly they snap together. (What! Paul was there!—Paul too—is that *possible*! ——aha—ha—*so*—.) The whole concept S (Paul) suddenly undergoes a complete reorganization.

Such processes frequently occur in a study of history. Fundamental changes in one's judgment of an historical figure are often due to the discovery of some new facts about that person. The whole character is suddenly re-centred.

175 The objection might be raised that our examples of Socrates and his taxes or of Peter and his club raise only nominalistic issues, i.e. that the same object merely appears twice under different names. While not false, this objection is actually quite unimportant.

One need merely consider the example of the lawyer in order to appreciate this fact. Here it is not true that the same object appears under two names; instead they are *logically different objects*: a memorandum among the papers of Case A is logically quite different from a receipt used in Case B. And viewing the matter in this light we see that the same applies to Peter and Paul. An abyss sunders the Paul of before and after the syllogistic process. The concept I have of a thing is frequently not only enriched but changed, improved, altered, deepened by the process itself.

176 Let us consider some further examples. We shall choose more modest illustrations whose determinations do not require so strenuous a purification in order to render clear the thought process involved.

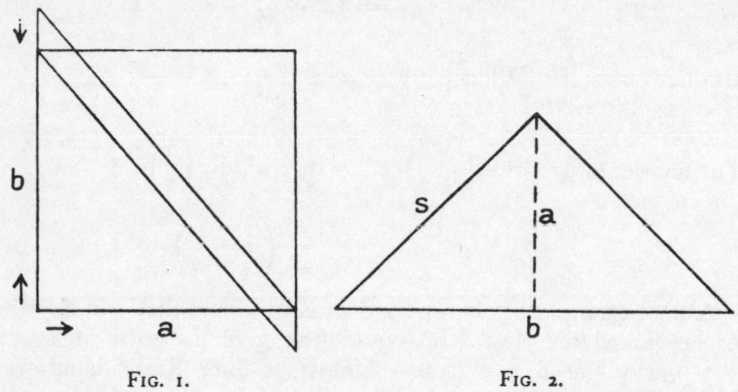

FIG. 1. FIG. 2.

In this square with a parallelogram strip across it (Fig. 1) the lines a and b are given. Find the sum of the contents of the two areas. One can proceed thus: The area of the square is a^2, in addition that of the strip is . . . ? But suppose instead that one hits upon the idea:

[Sc1 =] (square + strip) = (2 triangles, base a, altitude b) [=Sc2]

$$[\text{Sc2} =] \ldots\ldots\ldots\ldots = \left(2\,\frac{ab}{2}\right) = ab\ [= \text{P}].$$

The solution has thus been attained, so to speak, at a single stroke.

177 Or, to take another example. Suppose, in the isosceles triangle of Fig. 2 the equal sides are given and the angle between them is 90°. Find the area. One could work out from this what a and b

are, divide them by 2 and solve the problem. On the other hand, however, one might *see* that this isosceles triangle is tipped over—its base is really s; its altitude is also s. It is therefore nothing but half a square. Area $= \frac{s^2}{2}$.

Or again: Is 1,000,000,000,000,000,000,008 divisible by nine? The answer:—

$$(1{,}000{,}000 \ldots + 8) = (1{,}000{,}000 \ldots - 1) + (8 + 1)$$
$$\ldots\ldots = 999{,}999 \ldots\ldots\ldots + 9.$$

Similarly: Is $a^2 + ac + ba + bc$ divisible by $(a + b)$? The answer: $a^2 + ac + ba + bc = \overline{a.a + a.b} + \overline{a.c + b.c}$
$$= a(a + b) + c(a + b)$$

Another example: What is $\sqrt{a^2 + \frac{b^2}{4} + ab}$?

The answer: $\sqrt{a^2 + \frac{b^2}{4} + ab} = \sqrt{a^2 + \left(\frac{b}{2}\right)^2 + 2.a.\frac{b}{2}}$
$$= \pm\left(a + \frac{\;}{2}\right).$$

178 A final example. It is reported of Karl Gauss that one day the teacher asked his class who could first give the total of 1 + 2 + 3 + 4 + 5 + 6 + 7 + 8. Almost at once Karl's hand was raised. When the teacher asked how he had done it, Karl answered, "If I had had to add 1 and 2 and 3, it would have taken a long time; but 1 and 8 are 9, 2 and 7 are 9, 3 and 6 are 9, 4 and 5 are 9—four 9's, the answer is 36."

179 In general we see that in S?P the object (S), whatever it be, is given *as* Sc1—but there is no direct route from Sc1 to P. Upon further inspection, however, S proves amenable to a "recentring" away from c1—and in Sc2 I find the route to P opened. Now this procedure is enormously important in science, particularly in mathematics. It frequently occurs that the needed c3, exhibiting the required relationship to P, is only *possible* when Sc1 has been *re*-formed, *re*-grasped, *re*-centred in a specific way. And it is not
180 less frequently the case that to effect this process *a deeper penetration into the nature and structure of S is required.*

Although illustrations of the steps which thinking involves

are particularly obvious in geometry, we are dealing here with phenomena of a more general character. The hierarchy of properties in a concept may be subjected to the same treatment as has been suggested in the foregoing examples, for here too are involved certain structures and structural principles. And the same holds also for combinations of concepts. We are dealing no less in these cases than formerly with re-centring and the other operations already mentioned.

The history of science has provided many examples: comprehension of the nature of stellar movements ("falling" toward one another); the theory of the screw (i.e. seeing the screw as a wedge); the history of the conception of inertia. Until recently such accomplishments were thought of as essentially the results of "imagination", or "chance", or "the intuition of genius". But it is not these alone. *Formal* determinations, expressible in definite laws, are also involved. Crucial to many such cases is the fact that *certain* moments or characteristics of S are emphasized and brought into the foreground. In other cases the crucial step consists in a certain combination of factors.[1] In still other cases the essential process may be one of *centring*, where the important point is:
181 *from the point of view of which part shall the remaining parts be seen?* Thus centring leads to a penetration into the essential content and hence to an apprehension of the concrete inner structure and inner necessity of the whole with which one is dealing. Manifestly there are other cognitive operations besides subtraction, abstraction, and classification.

In this connection it can be seen that neither the determination Sc2, nor the step Sc1 : Sc2 is *arbitrary*. It is formally not a matter of indifference which of several possible reorganizations shall be employed, for the determination is carried out relative to the question "?P". We are dealing with S and P not as disparate juxtapositions; instead, they enter the operation as parts integrated according to definite formal determinations. Given S?P and no direct route leading to P, then the question arises: What is there in Sc1 (or, better, in the general range of things known about S) which is related to ?P? On *what* aspects of S must I concentrate? Or: *How must I apprehend* S sub specie *the task here before me?* How must I alter my former concept of S if I would see it in terms
182 of ?P? Expressed more formally: not everything in S, not every view nor every reorganization of S is equal with regard to ?P.

[1] Example: a + b + c + d . . . may also be seen as [a + b] + [c + d] . . . or, again, as a + [b + c] + d . . .

There are, in other words, determinations of S which *themselves* point to the required solution.

The question of how Socrates combed his hair would be *meaningless* when we are interested in his mortality. Socrates *too* must be considered *sub specie* the question (of mortality) raised by P.
183 And thus we come to the most important question of our entire study: When is the process meaningful, when meaningless? For the *modus barbara* we may say that over against S?P we have $S \searrow M \nearrow P$ in which M serves as a bridge. There are two extreme forms:—

In the *first*, M has no other formal relationship than that of its *bare co-existence*, on the one side with S, and on the other with P. These are two relationships which merely involve general validity of the formal syllogistic procedure.

In the *second*, M is a bridge in the sense that its bridge-character is *meaningfully demanded* by the question S?P itself. Here M (i.e. Sc2) stands *sub specie* S?P and it possesses certain formal relations within the whole process or situation.

In the first extreme form M is on principle *arbitrary*, and the most meaningless examples of M are (formally) as good as any
184 other: All persons whose names end in *tes* are mortal, Socrates's name ends in *tes* . . . and so on. In the second form M is much more than a mere indicator of co-existence, and whereas the first form, asserting an empty fact of co-existence, leads to mere classification, the second accomplishes a genuine advance in knowledge.

Fourth Group: Psychical Forces

Selection 24

WILL AND NEEDS

By Kurt Lewin

"Vorsatz, Wille, und Bedürfnis (Mit Vorbemerkungen über die psychischen Kräfte und Energien und die Struktur der Selle)," *Psychol. Forsch.*, 1926, 7, 294–385. [The two articles appearing on these pages of the *Psychologische Forschung* were also published, with slight alterations, as a separate off-print, Berlin, 1926. The pagination followed in our summary is that of the latter publication.]

12[1] Part I. *The Psychology of " elements " and activity- or process-Gestalten.*—In the fields of perception and thought we may to-day assume that strict elementarism has, at least in principle, disappeared. Not so, however, as regards theories of will and emotion. Here we still find psychologists intent upon discovering the independent elements out of which these phenomena are presumably compiled.
13 Their next concern is to see how such elements may be combined (additively and piecewise) to form the wholes of experience. Although usually more adequate, the point of view to be suggested here has been almost ignored: viz. that the so-called " elements " of volition and emotion depend for their nature upon the whole in which they occur.

This point of view does *not* propose, however, that the entirety of mental processes be considered a single, closed unity.[2] The problem, rather, is to inquire in each case whether a unitary whole (in the sense of a Gestalt) is involved; and if so, whether it be a " strong " or a " weak " Gestalt.[3] This is the *macroscopic* as opposed to the microscopic procedure, a procedure which leads at once to consideration of the outer and inner fields in which behaviour takes place.[4] In *writing*, for example, both the materials

[1] [Text pp. 1–11: preliminary comments on the nature of psychological laws and on the relation between practice and theory in psychology.]

[2] Cf. *Selection 3*, p. 153 f.

[3] *Selection 3*.

[4] [The expression " outer and inner fields " refers to the psychical field of behaviour. For convenience we shall here use the English term " environment " for the outer field, but with the understanding that this does not refer to the *physical* environment in the sense of physical properties. The outer environment, constituting the psychological milieu, is at best " quasi-physical ". The terms " *psychisch* " and (often) " *seelisch* " will as a rule be expressed here by the English word " psychical ". When necessary " *Seele* " will be rendered by our word " soul ". It will be clear from the text that no parapsychological implications are intended in either case.]

14 used (outer conditions) and the purpose (inner conditions) will materially affect one's procedure. Consider the difference between a letter where the message is the principal concern, and an exercise in penmanship. It would be meaningless to examine any one piece of handwriting in isolation from the total circumstances and conditions in which it occurred.

Moreover such processes are also *temporally* extended wholes of a structural type as yet very little studied. Thus they may have the character of continued repetition, or of direction towards a goal: they may merely encircle this goal (as often occurs, for example, in musing on a thing), or may consist in renewed onslaughts from various sides; or they may have the structure of a step-wise approach, and so on. Finally, activity units often display striking initial and end characteristics (e.g. a sigh of relief, putting down the finished work with an emphatic gesture, etc.), which serve to mark off the boundaries of a temporally unified field.

15 But temporal articulation is not the only factor to be considered. The structure of the behaviour as a whole-of-processes (operating together on levels of different depth and with varying weight) is fully as important. There will be certain processes in a total of behaviour-acts, for instance, which naturally belong together; others which do not. The *specific situation* analogous to the field in optics and acoustics, will undoubtedly play a role of the greatest importance in experiments designed to study these phenomena. Hence the results of individual experiments cannot be submitted to statistical treatment where the assumption prevails that preceding and succeeding trials are identical in kind. Instead each trial must be treated as a separate, *concrete* event, i.e. in an essentially non-statistical way. The *specific place* which a given trial occupies in a temporal series of trials will thus have to be considered with the greatest care.

Nor should we overlook the question of *energy*, in the following sense: Suppose a certain act has become intolerable. By changing the situational background a repetition of the act can easily be secured without the subject's finding it in the least " intolerable ". In one experiment a single word was written over and over until the subject declared he *would not* write it again. " Very well," said the experimenter, " we shall stop; by the way, please write that word on the back of the sheet so that I can remember which experiment this was." This the subject did without difficulty.
16 In general we may say that when the source of energy is changed, often the whole manner of behaving changes with it.

Accomplishment concepts.—Emphasis upon end-products or accomplishments as opposed to the *process* whereby such results were reached has seriously obstructed the recognition and study of
17 Gestalt phenomena in behaviour. The practice curve, e.g. in typewriting, rises gradually to a plateau, proceeds there for a time, rises again, this time with something of a jump, and so on. The concept " practice " lumps all of this together as " typewriting ". Actually, however, the typing of an experienced stenographer is not that of a highly trained beginner (i.e. quantitatively " more "), but something entirely different *qualitatively*. The beginner's caution and groping care characterize a searching process; the finished stenographer is not one whose " searching ability " is more highly trained than the beginner's.

Considering the general principle illustrated by this example one can see that *psychological processes subject to none but the " product " type of definition are not amenable to description in terms of psycho-*
18 *logical laws*. Instead our procedure should be to study concrete, individual cases regarding which the specification of type and general law may be made according to the structure of the cases themselves.

The concepts of phenotype and genotype.—" Psychologists in the past were constantly confusing the phenomenal and the conditional-genetic sides of acts. Two acts can be phenotypically quite different and genotypically identical—or the reverse. Thus an embarrassed child may exhibit its shyness in blushes and confusion, or it may become loud-voiced and assertive—the two modes of behaviour are genotypical equivalents. On the other hand the play-acting of emotion and real emotion may be said to resemble each other phenotypically, although genotypically quite opposite." [1]

The prominence of " elements " in psychology has brought about an over-emphasis upon questions of phenotype which, though important, should not obscure the problems of causal dynamics (genotype). Both physics and biology have recently shown that phenotypical similarity does not imply similarity of causal dynamics, i.e. of origin and effect. Botany once arranged plants in groups according to the form of leaves, petals, buds, etc.—i.e. phenotypically. It became evident, however, that a
19 plant's appearance will vary according as it grows in the flat lands or in hilly country. Biologists for their part have definitely added to the descriptive vocabulary of their science concepts which

[1] [Borrowed from J. F. Brown's " The method of Kurt Lewin in the psychology of action and affection," *Psychol. Rev.*, 1929, **36**, 200–221.]

we may call *conditional-genetic*. The result is that biological structures are no longer defined in terms of momentary appearance, but rather with regard to the entirety of their modes of behaviour. They are characterized with reference to a range of possibilities such that when a specific complex of conditions is given the *specific* phenotype may be determined.

What holds here for other sciences holds also for psychology. Questions of origin and disappearance, of cause and condition, etc., cannot be exhaustively answered merely by the specification of phenotypical characteristics. Cases arise also in psychology where close phenotypical kinship may obtain between two phenomena of extremely different genotypical origin. Thus, for example, genetically intense purposes may be *experienced* as weaker than certain genetically more powerful intentions. And the same holds also for emotions. A feeling of pleasure and a joyful mood may seem phenotypically to be closely related, yet their origin may be completely different. Again an affect may cause excessive activity
and felt excitement although in itself relatively superficial and of
20 low energy content. Or one may, despite some deep and strong
emotion, be perfectly calm both within and without. In saying this, of course, no suggestion is implied that careful observation and exact investigation of phenotypical factors should be omitted. Indeed in a sense phenotyoical determination must precede the genotypical.

21 *Regarding the causes of mental happenings.*—In earlier experimental psychology the basic notion regarding the *cause* of psychical events was almost universally of the type of *adhesion*, and the most obvious employment of this relationship was made in the concept of association: the events *A* and *B* having been coupled together by earlier contiguity, this union now *causes* the reproduction of *B* on the appearance of *A*. Even theories which went beyond associationism nevertheless retained concepts of the adhesion type: to the stimulus there adheres a certain reaction, and so again the *cause* of behaviour was attributed to adhesion.

Psychology considered such couplings as rigid, mecnanical connections. The reaction against this theory of rigid connections began, however, when the thought arose that behaviour consists not in a sequence of bits or elements, but (as a rule) in temporally extended wholes (e.g. of the melody type) whose moments or phases are explicable only in terms of the wholes themselves.

It is unfortunate that the approach adopted by Gestalt theory in this instance should have been improperly understood in certain

cases. Misinformation has it that what Gestalt theory is saying is this: No adhesive connection obtains between *A* and *B but* when *A* is a dependent part of an inclusive whole, the occurrence of *A* carries along with it the occurrence of that entire whole—
22 and hence also of *B*. There is no chain-like coupling of elementary parts, yet the union of these parts in the given whole " causes " the event to run the particular course it happens to pursue.

That this interpretation is quite erroneous has been demonstrated by experiments which show that in no sense can the coupling established by a habit be considered *as such* a kind of motor in the service of psychical activity.[1] Indeed the interpretation would be at error even if the essential characteristic of habitual processes lay not in the construction of piecewise associations but in their modification and creation of certain action unities. *Instead* the necessary prerequisite of all psychical behaviour is that there be psychical *energies* (which can usually be traced to a pressure of the
23 will or of some need)—i.e. to psychical *tension* systems. Mere *connection* never " causes " any process no matter where or in what form we may find it. In order for the connected parts to engage in any process (and this holds even for purely mechanical systems), energy capable of doing work must be released. It follows, then, that *in any instance of a psychical process we must inquire after the origin of its actuating energy.*

To deny that connections can supply the energy of processes does not involve denial either of connections as a fact nor of their importance. Although connections are not themselves sources of energy the *type* of connection greatly affects the course which processes take.[2]

24 Let us turn now to the question of psychical energy. In some cases (to a certain extent in optical processes) stimulation itself serves as a source of energy. In most cases of behaviour and emotion, however—as when, upon receiving a telegram, one departs on a journey—the physical intensity of stimulation plays no significant part. Hence the analogy has been proposed of " *release* " comparable to the explosion of a powder magazine by a releasing

[1] [The reader is referred to K. Lewin, " Die psychische Tätigkeit bei der Hemmung von Willensvorgängen und das Grundgesetz der Assoziation," *Zeitschr. f. Psychol.*, 1917, **77**, 212–247; " Das Problem der Willensmessung," *Psychol. Forsch.*, 1922, **1**, 191 ff.; ibid., **2**, 65 ff. Also to Julian Sigmar, " Über die Hemmung bei der Realisation eines Willensaktes," *Arch. f. d. ges. Psychol.*, 1925, **52**, 91–176.]

[2] It is an open question whether these concepts of *energy*, *force*, *tension*, and *system* may eventually be traced to physical forces and energies. The concepts themselves are fundamental principles in the logic of all dynamics.

spark. Two fundamental amendments to this view must be considered :—

First we should observe that the perceptual world is not one of sensory elements but of meaningful " things " and " events ". Hence perceptual stimulation (e.g. the distorted face of a wounded soldier) cannot be assessed in terms of physical intensity but in terms of its *psychological reality*. Such perceptions can, of course, directly arouse new intentions or desires, and alterations may
25 thus occur through which energy capable of doing work is set free.
But the quantity of energy in a psychical process does not as a rule come from the perceptions of any given moment.

Secondly the foregoing has not admitted " release " of the type given by a spark in a powder magazine or the throttle of a steam engine. Let us consider the following: (*a*) A child tries to get a piece of chocolate that is out of reach. If an obstruction is encountered the child makes a detour. We observe that his behaviour is governed by the forces of the entire psychical field.[1] *These forces determine the flow of events, and the events themselves in turn*
26 *bring about changes in the forces*. It is in this manner that behaviour
is *steered* by the perceptual field. (*b*) The objects sought (e.g. the chocolate) should be viewed primarily in terms of their ability
27 to steer behaviour. But in addition to this they may serve as
occasion for the arousal of a desire from which, as reservoir of energy, the activity follows. If the child were already satiated with sweets, the entire behaviour would never occur. To this extent the chocolate thus fulfils here a second function. It is therefore of the first importance whether such a reservoir of energy is present or not, for the forces which might otherwise have served to govern behaviour are without effect if there are no sources of psychical energy. (*c*) With attainment of the goal (e.g. the chocolate) there occurs an important change in environmental forces. Satiation involves not only a change in locus of these forces, but also a decided change in the psychical tension which had underlain the goal-seeking behaviour.

The perception of an object or event may thus (1) give rise to a
28 certain psychical tension (e.g. a desire), or (2) it may communicate
with a state of tension already existing (as a result of some intention or need) in such a way that this tension system thereupon assumes

[1] In psychology as in physics we find no unequivocal relation between the strength of such *forces* and the amount of *energy* in the process which occurs. If the field is appropriately arranged it is possible for relatively small forces to control relatively large amounts of energy; or, again, large forces and tensions may go hand in hand with minute energies.

control over motor behaviour. In such cases we say that the object in question possesses a "valence" [" *Aufforderungscharakter* "]. (3) Valences act as environmental forces "steering" subsequent behaviour. Finally (4) this behaviour leads to satiation or to a resolution of tension so that a state of equilibrium is approached.

29 *Psychical energy.*—There is in psychology to-day a tendency to oppose *atomism* by emphasizing the *unity* of the soul. We are not interested here, however, in the wide complex of problems suggested by the term "unity of the soul". Instead we propose to examine merely one problem: viz. the problem of psychical energy. But first let us make the following observation. It is particularly necessary that one who proposes to study whole-phenomena should guard against the tendency to make wholes as all-embrasive as possible. Especially must one realize that the real task is to investigate the structural properties of a given whole, ascertain the relations of subsidiary wholes, and determine the boundaries of the system with which one is dealing. It is no more true in psychology than in physics that "everything depends upon everything else".[1] What may have happened twenty-five years ago—whether I went to school that day or not, played in the garden, was late for lunch—cannot have more than a relatively insignificant influence upon the details of my present behaviour. It *may* have, but one cannot say that each and every aspect of earlier experiences
30 necessarily *does* have such influence. Every past experience may "in some way or other" exert an influence upon contemporary events. But in most cases this influence can be compared with that of the fixed stars upon physical occurrences here in my room. Such influences are so small as to be almost nil.

And what thus holds for temporal relationships, holds also for simultaneous occurrences. I look out of my window and see smoke coming from a smoke stack across the street. This *can* in a special case have a strong influence upon me; but in general these thousands of "minor experiences" have little or nothing to do with other psychical processes. My behaviour would not be different (or only "unnoticeably" so) if many of my experiences were different from what they are. Nor is it true that very intense experiences are, because of their strength, necessarily related to all else in my psychical processes. Mere strength alone does not effect such relationships. Instead one's activities, emotions, intentions, wishes, and hopes are ***embedded in specific psychical units***,

[1] *Selection 3*, p. 156. [In general, *Selection 3* should be borne in mind throughout the present discussion.]

personality spheres and behaviour wholes. The question whether or not, and how two psychical events influence each other depends upon whether they are embedded in the *same* or in *different* whole-processes: or, otherwise expressed, it depends upon the relation between these psychical whole-processes. Sometimes, for example,
31 the dynamic relationships may be so constituted that satisfaction of *one* desire will more or less carry with it the satisfaction of some other desire. But it must be obvious that these communications are not subject to generalization, for what may function with one person as a closely knit unity may with another (or with the same person under different circumstances) enjoy no such unity at all. Indeed if it were true that all psychological processes were in equal communication with all others, organized behaviour would be impossible.

32 The question regarding the *unity of consciousness* is not identical with the question regarding the unity of the whole range of psychical structures and processes whose *totality* one can designate as the *soul.* It is also possible that that which we call the "ego" or self is only *one* complex or functional part within this psychical totality. Expressed in terms of strong and weak Gestalten we may say that psychological unity is that of a weak Gestalt comprising a number
33 of "strong Gestalten". We are dealing here not with one undifferentiated system but with a great number of such "strong Gestalten" which in part are in communication with each other, in part disclose no genuine unity at all.

The tendency towards equilibrium.—Psychological processes—no less than biological, physical, and economic—may often be deduced from their tendency towards equilibrium. The transition from a state of rest to a dynamic state, or the modification of a stationary process occurs when systemic equilibrium has been upset. There results a process in the direction of a new equilibrium. But, whereas this is true of the system *as a whole*, it is nevertheless possible for partial processes to act in the direction opposite to that pursued by the whole system. (This is a matter of considerable
34 importance for the theory of detour behaviour in psychology.) It is therefore obviously of great importance to determine *what* the whole-system is in order to discover the concrete course of events.

Systemic equilibrium does not, of course, mean an absence of *tension* in the system, for equilibrium may also be attained in a state of tension (e.g. the spring of a watch or a container filled with compressed gas). But the occurrence of such a system presupposes for it—not in a spatial, but in a functional sense—a more or less rigid *boundary* and factual *separation* over against its surroundings.

In psychology we encounter tension systems of this sort very often. Sometimes they press towards an immediate resolution of the tension; often, however, the whole-situation is such that resolution (e.g. through gratification of a wish) is not possible
35 at the moment. In such cases there arises a stationary tension system which can, in extreme instances, involve widespread psychical strata. A child who throws himself upon the ground when something is denied him often remains for some moments in a state of general tension which only later resolves into some more specialized tension system. With many such specialized tensions, even if not resolved by gratification of the desire or completion of the interrupted activity, a gradual resolution will nevertheless occur. This may result from satisfaction by substitution or simply by leakage (i.e. diffusion into the surrounding field) when the functional enclosure of the system is relatively weak. Very often, however, the tension of such specialized systems will persist throughout long periods of time.

With adults there is as a rule a plurality of relatively segregated tension systems which constitute reservoirs of energy. The possibility of organized behaviour depends upon a relatively complete segregation of these various systems. Indeed that psychological phenomena do not comprise a unity without differentiation has been demonstrated experimentally.[1] If several tasks are given and certain of them are interrupted before the subject has finished, there results not a *general* tension system (whose resolution might occur in *any* arbitrary manner), but specific tensions specifically related to particular (interrupted) tasks. Only in extreme cases
36 does the state of tension in one system spread to and affect the
[37-39 : omitted] state of neighbouring systems.[2]

40 PART II. *Purpose, Will, and Needs.*—In introducing this topic
41 let us turn first to the question of "discipline" in schools. The rules of classroom conduct are to-day far less rigid and restrictive than formerly. Children are taught to govern themselves and not merely to obey blindly a set of fixed rules authoritatively imposed upon them. The school is no longer an institution sharply distinct from everyday life, but has established much closer relationship with affairs outside the classroom. The break between what is

[1] *Selection 25.*

[2] In this connection it may be remarked that one such relatively segregated systemic region within the total psychological field is that of the Ego. (Cf. above, p. 32.)

learned in school and practiced elsewhere is thus gradually diminishing. Self-control, for instance, cannot be instilled upon a background of cringing obedience to fixed rules. The teacher can shape psychological drives and teach a genuine self-control only if the current of these processes is actually in flux. Hence the aim of
42 education is to tap genuine drives and sources of energy in order that control of them may be *gradually* transferred from the teacher to the child himself. Hence we see that an about-face in pedagogy has been made: self-control is not sought via obedience and purpose, but the reverse—obedience and purpose are derived from self-control. In attacking the problem of will it seems likely that
43 a similar reversal of procedure may prove necessary. From this point of view *control* will assume primary importance for our study while purpose and decision are assigned but secondary places.

The influence of time upon the effect of purposes.—It has been customary to consider *the process of intention or purpose* [1] as the fundamental type of all acts of will. The " phases " of this process may be catalogued thus: (1) conflict of motives, (2) choice or selection, (3) consummation. The second of these has been considered the genuine core of all psychology of will. In this connec-
44 tion there arises the question of temporal interval between decision and consummation. Does the influence of an intention gradually diminish in the way associations disintegrate (i.e. the forgetting curve)? Suppose I intend to mail a letter; the first mail box I encounter stands out prominently in my visual field. I deposit the letter. As soon as this act is performed subsequent mail boxes are perfectly indifferent to me.

45 The theoretical question here is whether or not we should think of intention, and ideas of completing the intended act, as *associatively* united. If they were, then placing a letter in the first mail box should strengthen the bond so that at the next box there would be a still greater tendency to repeat the process, and so on. Nor is this merely a case where a greater time interval (before the second box is encountered) can be thought of as weakening the " coupling ". If one were affixing posters to each mail box, those following the first would *not* go unnoticed. In the case of posting the letter, however, there appears to be a sudden exhaustion of forces acting to bring about the performance.

46 *The role of opportunity or occasion for consummatory actions.*—Custom has it that the basic type of process of intention or purpose

[1] [This is J. F. Brown's translation of Lewin's *Vornahmehandlung*, op. cit., p. 206.]

[*Vornahmehandlung*] is that in which the intention itself designates the *precise occasion* upon which a *specific consummatory activity* is to occur—after the manner of the simple " reaction experiment ". It is not true, however, that every intention involves specific determination of occasion and mode of consummation. The actual process of carrying out an intention may at first remain quite undecided: one intends to persuade a person to do something without at all knowing in advance which arguments will be used or how they will be expressed. Indeed one may merely go walking with the person, get better acquainted, and so on, without even mentioning the subject at hand. One's intention to avoid being struck by a ball *may* involve a specific readiness to leap to the left, but it need not imply any such specific plan of action. Instead—here as in other cases—one does what the situation itself requires.

And it is the same with the *occasion*. Indeed the most important decisions in life (e.g. choice of a particular profession) are often made without the intention itself containing any precise implication as to the specific occasion for consummatory activity. But not
47 only this. Even when a specific occasion *has* been set forth in the original intention it is nevertheless possible for some totally unanticipated occasion to serve instead. Examples: I intend to send my friend a postcard as soon as I reach home this evening. During the afternoon I am at a place where a telephone is available; it reminds me of the message and I phone my friend. Or, I plan to mail a letter; a friend calls to see me and I ask him to post it. In such cases we see how an entirely different experience (e.g. seeing the telephone) can nevertheless call into action the forces originally set to be released only by some other, specifically intended occasion (viz. coming home in the evening). A consummation has occurred which—from the point of view of the original intention—must be designated as a substitute-act, or, better, as an equivalent act, i.e. one that is " relevant ". If one proceeds in
48 terms of a " *coupling* " between the intention and occasion for its execution, it is incomprehensible why such *substitution-acts* should abolish the tendency to perform the intended act even when the originally intended occasion *does* present itself. That there *is* a resolution of the original intention is clear, for, having telephoned, one neither writes nor feels any desire to do so, i.e. the response (writing) which " should " have been elicited by my coming home in the evening does not take place.

A coupling theory of the relation between occasion and consummatory action encounters still greater difficulties in cases of the following type. I want to tell my friend something and plan to do so when he visits me to-morrow evening. The visit is cancelled, i.e. the expected occasion does not present itself, but the influence exerted by my intention does not disappear; indeed one *seeks* a new opportunity. In all of which it is clear that a tension system is present which presses from within towards resolution by means of appropriate activity.

49 *The resumption of interrupted activity.*—Pursuing the foregoing from another point of view let us consider the following: A task is interrupted before the subject is able to complete it. Now if the "coupling" between performance and occasion were the essential factor, nothing further should happen unless the occasion were repeated. A series of experiments was undertaken to test this. The subjects were given rather uninteresting tasks such as modelling a figure from clay, laying out playing blocks in certain forms, etc. Yet despite this lack of interestingness, all subjects showed considerable reluctance to obey when told to stop before they had finished the work assigned them.[1] Moreover, when a second
50 activity, interrupting the first, had been completed there appeared at once a strong desire to *resume* the first, unfinished task.

Two types of interruption were used: "*accidental*" (e.g. the light would go out, due apparently to a short-circuit), where the experimenter seemed to have no hand in the matter; and *intentional*, in which the subject was assigned another task. No subject failed to resume his original task after an "accidental" interruption; almost every subject returned to the original task after intentional interruptions, even when nothing in the perceptual situation recalled the first task.

51 Resumption of the original act rarely occurs when the subject is interrupted with instructions to complete the act in some other way. If a child is relating a story and is interrupted with the request to draw a picture of the ending, the likelihood of his returning afterwards to the verbal form is very slight. We may call this a case of substitution fulfilment.

52 *The forgetting of an intention.*—Two types of forgetting must be distinguished. One is inability to recall something formerly experienced, or to reproduce a technique learned at some earlier time, etc. The other type of forgetting is that in which an intention is not carried out even though one could (if called upon to do so) recall exactly what the intention had been. This latter type is often called "forgetfulness".

[1] *Selection 25.*

53 In an experiment designed to study this kind of forgetting the subjects were told to sign each paper upon which they had been working and hand them to the experimenter. It was found that conditions could be established in which very few or very many cases of forgetting to do this would occur. Thus if six *similar* tasks were followed by one of a different character, the subjects usually forgot to sign their work before turning it in. When a pause of a few minutes was introduced between tasks, the signature requirement was usually forgotten; with a pause of *a whole day*,
54 however, it usually was not forgotten. This shows that time alone is not the decisive feature in "forgetfulness". The importance of the occasion was shown when, say, white paper was used in a series of five or six experiments and an experiment was then introduced where coloured paper was used: in such cases the percentage of forgetting would be greatly increased. The white-paper-situation had been one thing, the coloured paper tended to establish a new
55 situation and was, as such, very likely to *lack* a "signature requirement" for the subject. When the task required that the subject design and reproduce monograms of his own name, forgetting the signature was almost universal. The task itself apparently served as a substitution fulfilment. Obviously this cannot be explained by the principles of associationism, for if frequency and associative bond were the effective factors, the more often one signed one's name (or drew monograms) the more likely it should be that this would be done again (i.e. signature) upon turning in the work. In *group* experiments the percentage of forgetting to sign was relatively low: due, i.e., to the need for an identifying mark upon one's own work.

57 The intensity of an intention is no criterion of likelihood that consummation will occur. In the study of forgetting it was found that vigorous intentions were frequently less effective than those which were calmer and less emotional. One may ask: Under what circumstances does an act of intention (especially when very intense) come about? A somewhat exaggerated saying has it that "What one intends, one forgets". This means that an *act of intending* occurs when there is no genuine *need* for the intended activity—or when there is even some genuine counter-need. If the intention is not based upon a real need, it has little chance of succeeding. But it is in just this situation that one is most given to intensifying the act of intention. Paradoxically: either the intention was not necessary or it is doomed to failure. As Wilde said (in *Dorian Gray*): "Good resolutions are useless attempts to interfere with

scientific laws. Their origin is pure vanity. Their result is absolutely *nil.*"

Quasi-needs.—The foregoing examples have shown intention
to be a force whose operation does not depend upon some specifically anticipated opportunity or occasion. Instead there is an inner
pressure, an inner tension demanding that the intended act be carried
58 out—whether by pre-designed means or not. We have seen, in
other words, that the "motor" of consummatory activity is not
of the type implied by mere coupling, but is rather a state of
tension. It is on this basis also that one may understand how, when
an opportunity is lacking, some other is sought or even created.
It is clear also why the activity ceases when satisfaction has been
59 attained. In all these respects intention resembles the psychological
forces which we ordinarily call *needs*.

Thus we find that natural drives (e.g. hunger) show the same
qualities as those we have been considering: here too the occasion
plays a fundamental role; also in the sphere of natural drives we
find certain things or events possessing "valences". We live in a
world of things and events, not of visual, auditory, and tactual
sensations. Psychology has gradually come to recognize the truth
of this and we customarily think of many objects in terms of
emotional emphasis: unpleasant, delightful, and so on. But going
a step beyond this we must emphasize here the further fact that
60 things and events have properties for us in our capacity as behaving
organisms. This holds not only as regards their ease or difficulty
of manipulation; many things which we encounter display
in greater or less degree a will of their own—they challenge us to
engage in certain activities. A lovely day "calls for" a stroll;
the stairsteps invite a young child to climb up and jump down,
toys entice it, and so on. As regards such relationships between
ourselves and objects two varieties of valence may be distinguished:
things which attract—a concert, an interesting man, a pretty girl—
possess *positive* valence for us; those which repel—something
disagreeable or dangerous—do so because of their *negative* valence.
61 The valence of a thing is *not*, however, a constant; it depends,
rather, both in kind and degree, upon the inner and outer *situation*
prevailing for the person at the time: i.e. it depends upon the part
which that thing can play in promoting the satisfaction of a need
or desire. Indeed to a certain extent the statements are equivalent
when we say "there is such and such a need" and "such and such
a range of things possesses a valence calling for such and such
behaviour".

63 However, the relation between needs and valences is not such that a certain need may be once and for always correlated with a certain valence. It is instead frequently the case (especially with newly acquired needs) that there can be a wide range of possible
64 valences. Once more, then, we encounter a resemblance between intentions and genuine needs, for the former of these also disclosed cases of indefiniteness both of occasion or opportunity and of the means for obtaining satisfaction. Intentions we may therefore call "*quasi-needs*". Both needs and quasi-needs reveal themselves
65 in the fact that certain things or events assume, by virtue of these needs or quasi-needs, *valences* calling for certain activities. They agree also in showing the inability of couplings or bonds to explain the causes of behaviour.

[66–81 : (66–71) : specific things sometimes acquire "fixed" valences so that they alone are capable of satisfying certain needs. Example: a *certain* doll is preferred above all others. (72–74) : examples of substitute satisfaction. (75–79) : intention differs from mere wishing in that it (like genuine needs) involves *activity directed towards* satisfaction. (79–81) : omitted.]

82 *Conditions for the occurrence of intention.*—The *act* of intending does not occur in everyday life as often as one might suppose. Getting up in the morning may require an act of this sort, but in dressing, having breakfast, leaving for work, etc., little or nothing of intention can be detected. And this is typical also of the entire day. The rarity of manifest intention is not due, however, to the habitual character of these acts. Consider a group of children at
83 play. Even though new situations are involved, acts of intention are infrequent. Instead transitions from stage to stage, etc., in the play seem to proceed "through their own impetus", i.e. what we ordinarily call "unintentionally". This does not mean, of course, that all behaviour not preceded by manifest intention is "impulsive". In conversation the speakers may have no specific intentions (such as lying or seeking to hide something), but their behaviour is not for that reason to be called "impulsive". From these and other considerations, too ramified for treatment here, it appears that purposive behaviour cannot be considered the fundamental instance of willing. The issue is not whether a certain act has or has not been temporally preceded by some other act; rather, the behavioural process itself must be relied upon to inform us what type of process is involved.

Under the term impulsive behaviour [*Triebhandlung*] we ordinarily mean behaviour guided by forces which are *not under*

84 *the control* of the individual. On the other hand, a sudden response to some stimulus situation is often the sign of an *un*controlled reaction. In this way, then, " compulsory " [*triebhaft*], " unintentional ", " impulsive " have taken on a second meaning as being the *opposites* of behaviour preceded by a specific act of intention. What we wish here to emphasize is the fact that genuine processes of intention or purpose are by no means always strongly controlled by the individual. The customary simple reaction experiment is as a rule an excellent example of such uncontrolled behaviour despite the fact that the subject's first response was, of course, a genuine process of intention or purpose. Let us therefore make the following distinction: (1) " controlled " *versus* " uncontrolled ",[1] and (2) " intentional " behaviour—and by the latter is meant behaviour following upon an act of intention regardless of *how* the behaviour itself proceeds. This much is certain, that the mere fact of having an antecedent intention does not tell us whether the behaviour will be controlled or uncontrolled. Hence the essential aspect of an intention lies in the *preparation* which it accomplishes: the result of an intention is that the psychical field assumes a character (and this applies to future as well as to present happenings) different from what it would otherwise have been. In other words certain things or events now have valences which would otherwise have remained neutral.

[85–87: discussion of intention as modified by prospects of success and by the character of the act of decision.]

88 *Quasi-need as a conditional-genetic concept.*—Since quasi-needs may often be satisfied in a variety of ways the specific behaviour necessary to resolve the tension will not be determined until a concrete situation is encountered. In biology, as we have seen, it is customary to define organisms " genotypically ", i.e. an organism (or an organ) is defined as an entirety of capacities [*Anlagen*] which in their turn are characterized as an entirety of modes of behaviour each of which is co-ordinated with and depends upon the occurrence of some definite situation. One and the same genotypical structure can thus lead in Situation *A* to the pheno-
89 typical structure *a*, in Situation *B* to phenotype *b*, and so on. In the same sense a quasi-need cannot be defined as a tension

[1] Synonymous with " uncontrolled " would be " field-behaviour ", i.e. behaviour directly co-ordinated with the forces of the field in which it occurs. Of course controlled behaviour is also subject to psychical field forces, but controlled behaviour does not draw the entire person into the behavioural field; there remains always a certain reservation, a certain independence and one has the situation more completely in hand.

invariably leading to the same fixed behaviour; it is rather to be defined in terms of an array of possible behaviours such that different situations necessarily call forth one or another of these behaviours.[1]

And this holds also for the origin of quasi-needs. The same quasi-need may arise through processes which are *phenotypically* quite different. The concrete process is not determined phenotypically until the *need* and *the situation for the expression of that need* are actually together.

[1] Example: an intention (quasi-need) which cannot be satisfied in the manner originally planned is satisfied in some other manner.

Selection 25

ON FINISHED AND UNFINISHED TASKS

By Bluma Zeigarnik

"Über das Behalten von erledigten und unerledigten Handlungen," *Psychol. Forsch.*, 1927, **9**, 1–85.

3 An intention implies not so much a predetermined opportunity for its realization as it does a need or quasi-need whose dynamic state of tension *makes* opportunities.[1] Therefore it may be asked whether such a need functions only to accomplish this task or whether the state of tension also influences other aspects of the person's behaviour. In the present study we shall investigate the influence of such tensions upon an achievement of *memory*. Specifically we shall seek to answer the question: *What is the relation between the status in memory of an activity which has been interrupted before it could be completed and of one which has not been interrupted?* We suspect that an unsatisfied quasi-need probably does influence even purely memorial retention.

4 The experiments reported here were conducted with 164 individual subjects (students, teachers, children), and in addition there were two group experiments (47 adults, 45 children).

Procedure.—The instructions were: "I shall give you a series of tasks which you are to complete as rapidly and correctly as possible."[2] The subject was then given from 18 to 22 tasks one at a time—but half of these were *interrupted* before he could complete them. The order and type of interruption was such that no one could suspect the reason. For example, two tasks would be interrupted, then two allowed to reach completion, one interrupted followed by two completed, etc.

Following the last task the experimenter asked, "Please tell me what the tasks were upon which you worked during this experiment."[3] No time limit was imposed during the subject's report. A record was kept noting the *order* of recall. Very often a number

[1] See *Selection 24*.

[2] In no case did the subjects know what the problem really was in which the experimenter was interested.

[3] Before this information was requested the table was cleared of all tools, pencils, paper, etc., which had been used during work. This was done not as if it were part of the experiment but casually and with some incidental remark about "tidying up".

of tasks would be mentioned, and then a pause would occur during which the subject tried to remember what other tasks he had
5 had. The quantitative results given below refer to the number of tasks recalled *before* this pause.

After the experiment was over, introspective reports were requested. Following this the subjects were asked to tell which tasks had been the most and which the least interesting, pleasant, etc. In addition to these data the experimenter also made notes of all spontaneous remarks occurring during the work period.

[6–7: omitted] The tasks themselves consisted of manual work (constructing a box of cardboard, making clay figures, etc.) and of mental problems such as puzzles, arithmetic, and the like. The time required for
8 most of these was 3–5 minutes. The tasks were divided by the experimenter (without the subject's knowledge) into two groups, *a* and *b*, and half of the total number of subjects completed all of the *a* and none of the *b* tasks; the other half completed all of the *b* and none of the *a* tasks. Hence our data refer to memory for *each* task both as completed and as interrupted.

Results.—Let us designate those tasks which were *interrupted and recalled* as IR, those which were *completed and recalled* as CR. If the memory for both types was in any given case the same, then $\frac{IR}{CR}$ would equal 1. Should there be a case in which $\frac{IR}{CR} = 1{\cdot}5$, this would mean that the interrupted tasks were recalled 50 per cent better than the completed ones. If $\frac{IR}{CR} = 3$, the superiority
10 of interrupted over completed tasks would be 200 per cent. If $\frac{IR}{CR} = 0{\cdot}8$, then recall of the interrupted tasks was 20 per cent worse than that of the completed ones.

The results obtained from our first 32 subjects indicate an average memory advantage of 90 per cent enjoyed by *interrupted* tasks (i.e. $\frac{IR}{CR} = 1{\cdot}9$). The extremes extend from a 500 per cent advantage with one subject to a 25 per cent *dis*advantage
11 with another. Summarizing, we find that of the 32 subjects, 26 remembered interrupted tasks best; 3 remembered the completed and interrupted ones equally well; 3 remembered the completed better than the interrupted. That interruption of a task greatly improves its chances of being remembered can be seen from this survey: of the 22 tasks used, 17 were remembered best

when interrupted, 2 were equally well recalled regardless of interruption or completion, 3 were better recalled when completed.

So far as amount of time is concerned, the advantage *should* lie with completed tasks since a subject who completed a task naturally spent a longer time with it than one who did not. That, however, completed tasks were not the best recalled can be seen from the foregoing figures.

As regards the order of recall we find that the interrupted tasks were mentioned first three times as often as were the completed
12 ones. The same holds almost as decisively for the second task to be mentioned. (Somewhat later in the recall there is a reversal of this: completed tasks are then mentioned more frequently than the interrupted ones.) This shows that the memory advantage of interrupted tasks is also apparent as regards priority of recall.

The foregoing experiment was repeated with a *new* set of tasks and 15 *new* subjects. The results were an almost exact duplicate of
13 those already reported. In this case the recall advantage of interrupted tasks was 100 per cent (i.e. $\frac{IR}{CR} = 2$).

14 *Group experiments.*—The next two experiments were given to groups of 47 adults and 45 school children (average age of the latter, 14 years). There were 18 tasks; the material for each was presented in a separate envelope. An additional envelope contained a questionnaire for the report.[1] At the word "Begin" each subject opened the first envelope, noted the instructions for that task and began work. As soon as he had finished, or immediately upon being told to stop, the entire contents were returned to the envelope. All subjects began each new task at the same time. Because some worked faster than others the instructions to stop (interruption) were given when approximately half of the group had completed a given task.

15 The results show a memory advantage enjoyed by interrupted tasks of 90 per cent ($\frac{IR}{CR} = 1{\cdot}9$) for adults and of 110 per cent ($\frac{IR}{CR} = 2{\cdot}1$) for children. Of the 47 adults, 37 remembered the interrupted task best, 3 remembered both equally well, 7 recalled the completed ones best. Among the 45 children, 36 were best in recalling unfinished tasks, 4 were equal, and 5 remembered the finished tasks best.

[1] Each subject himself indicated by a line the point at which a pause occurred in his recall (cf. above, p. 4).

17–19 *Discussion.* 1. *Additional data.*—Three " types " of subjects could be distinguished. The first were those who sought to perform as instructed because they wished *to please the experimenter.* Another, the ambitious type, strove *to excel as if in competition with others.* The third type was *interested in the task for its own sake* and sought to solve each problem in the way the problem itself demanded. In keeping with these differences the experimenter did not preserve a fixed mien and method with all subjects. Those of the first type were allowed to see the experimenter's pleasure when a task was well done. Work done by the second group was inspected with the air of an examiner, while the third group was allowed to work unmolested, the experimenter in this case remaining passive.

Those tasks which the subject was allowed to finish were brought to an end by the subject alone: he was never disturbed until he himself declared the work done. Where an interruption was to be made, the experimenter would say, " Now do this, please," and
20 lay the new task on the table. The reasons assigned for this by the subjects themselves (in subsequent report) showed that but very few had been able to guess *why* they had been interrupted. The most common views were: " You wanted to see if I had really been concentrating," or " You interrupted me as soon as you saw I was on the right (wrong) track ". Finding a plausible explanation for the interruption did not, however, mean satisfaction with the fact of being interrupted. On the contrary. The subjects objected, sometimes quite strenuously, and were loath to stop even when the experimenter insisted upon it. Some subjects even showed affective reactions.

Since the real meaning of an interruption is realized only when it is *felt* to be an interruption, the experimenter always chose a time when the subject was most engrossed in his work. As a rule this occurs when the subject has just discovered *how* the task is to be done but has not yet envisaged the ultimate result. Example: the subject is moulding the clay figure of a dog; he has reached
21 the point where something four-legged and " dog-like " is appearing, but there is still grave danger that his " dog " will become a " cat " before he is through. The fact that most subjects were quite willing to talk while working served as one guide in selecting the correct moment for interrupting.

2. *Possible explanations.*—We turn now to the question of why interrupted tasks were recalled best. It might be suggested that in the case of interrupted tasks the " shock " of being disturbed served

to emphasize *these* tasks, thus enhancing the attention paid them, and in this way greatly improved their chances of preservation
22 in memory. And therefore, according to this view, the interrupted tasks enjoyed a superior opportunity for retention because even during the work period special emphasis (strong affective colouring) had been given them.

To test this hypothesis it is necessary to change our procedure so that both interrupted and completed tasks will be given the same "shock"-value during the work period. This was done by interrupting some of the tasks and then re-presenting these for completion before the work period was over. According to the hypothesis, these interrupted-resumed tasks should be remembered as well as the genuinely interrupted ones since both will have had the same "shock" emphasis during the work period. Indeed they should be recalled best of all because, having been presented *twice* during the experiment, their repetition value will thus be double that of any other task.

23 The experiment was conducted with 12 new subjects; 18 tasks were used and of these 9 were interrupted and resumed, while 9 were interrupted but not resumed. Our results thoroughly disprove the hypothesis: memory for tasks interrupted but not resumed was 85 per cent better than for the interrupted-resumed (i.e. $\frac{\text{IR}}{\text{I-nR}} = 1{\cdot}85$). Moreover, of the 12 subjects only 1 recalled the interrupted-resumed tasks best. We conclude, therefore, that the memorial advantage enjoyed in our earlier experiments by the interrupted tasks cannot have been due to the emphasis they received from the interruption itself.

24–25 The experiment was repeated with 12 new subjects to whom 18 tasks were given. The subjects were divided into three groups, A, B, and C, of 4 each; the tasks were likewise divided into three groups of 6 each: (*a*) completed, (*b*) interrupted and not resumed, (*c*) interrupted-resumed. In this way each group of tasks was given to each subject in the manner *a* or *b* or *c* and hence our results refer to each task as completed, as interrupted and not resumed, and as interrupted-resumed. The findings were as follows. The average memory advantage of tasks which were interrupted and not resumed, *b*, over those which were interrupted-resumed, *c*, was 90 per cent (i.e. $\frac{b}{c} = 1{\cdot}9$); the superiority of interrupted and not resumed, *b*, over completed, *a*, was 94

26 per cent (i.e. $\frac{b}{a} = 1{\cdot}94$). It is apparent therefore that *c* (interrupted-
resumed) and *a* (completed) had practically the *same* value. The
validity of our earlier conclusion is thus substantiated.

But if our earlier results were not due to affective emphasis during
the work period, perhaps the following hypothesis is more
adequate: The subject thought that certain tasks were interrupted
momentarily but would be resumed later during the experimental
hour. In order to take up the work where it had been interrupted
he therefore made a special effort to remember these tasks. If the
27 hypothesis is correct, and if at the time of interrupting we assure the
subject, "*This task will be resumed later*," then these tasks should
be remembered better than those for which no such assurance is
given. And conversely, if interruption is accompanied by the remark,
"*You are not to work on this task any more*," then these tasks should
be remembered less than the others.

Our results show, however, that the hypothesis is wrong. In the
first case [1] ("This task will be resumed") the hypothesis would
have predicted an even higher value for $\frac{IR}{CR}$ than had been found in
our earlier experiments. Instead the result was $\frac{IR}{CR} = 1{\cdot}7$, whereas
28 in the earlier cases it had been 1·9. In the second instance [2]
("... will not be resumed") where, according to the hypothesis,
there should be no memorial advantage enjoyed by the interrupted
tasks, the results were $\frac{IR}{CR} = 1{\cdot}8$, which is almost as great as the 1·9
of our earlier experiments. We conclude, therefore, that the earlier
results were not due to the subject's believing that interrupted tasks
would be re-presented some time later during the work period.

Since neither of the hypotheses is satisfactory we must look elsewhere for an explanation. The memorial advantage of uncompleted
tasks lies not in any experience accompanying the interruption but
rather in the forces existing at the time of recall. The relevant
29 distinction is that between a state of completion and one of incom-
pleteness, and we must therefore seek to discover the psychical
difference between *completed* and *uncompleted* tasks as it exists at the
moment of recall.

When the subject sets out to perform the operations required by one

[1] Twelve subjects, 20 tasks; none was really resumed despite the promise to that effect.

[2] Twelve new subjects, 18 new tasks.

of these tasks there develops within him a quasi-need for completion of that task. This is like the occurrence of a tension system which tends towards resolution. *Completing* the task means resolving the tension system, or discharging the quasi-need. If a task is not completed, a state of tension remains and the quasi-need is unstilled. The memorial advantage enjoyed by interrupted tasks must be due to this continuation of the quasi-need.

The tension leading to gratification of a need can therefore be seen to operate not only towards completion of the task; it also improves the chances of later recall in cases where such completion has been obstructed. Hence recall serves as a sign indicating the
30 existence of such a tension system. In consequence the improved recall-value of interrupted tasks depends not upon experiences occurring at the moment of interruption but upon the totality of forces prevailing at the time of recall. Naturally this totality includes other forces besides those given by the tasks themselves. The experimenter's instruction to recount the tasks certainly constitutes an important factor in this total situation. As a result of this request there arises in the subject a desire or quasi-need to recall *all* of the tasks. Dynamically expressed, the situation at the time of recall may be described as follows: A quasi-need to report all tasks has been established by the experimenter's request; in addition, however, there are quasi-needs leading to recall of the unfinished but not of the finished tasks. Just how strong the tension favouring recall of unfinished tasks is will depend upon the *relationship* between these two fundamental factors. If, in accordance with instructions to report *all* tasks, the desire to do this is overweening, the relative advantage enjoyed by unfinished tasks (IR) will be diminished and IR will approximately equal CR. On the other hand, if this desire is not excessively strong, the advantage enjoyed by IR will be determined almost entirely by the unresolved tensions of the interrupted tasks.

[31–55: (31–39): experimental evidence is reported which shows that the recall-value of unfinished tasks improves as desire to obey instruction (" report *all* tasks ") sinks in importance. Since in the main experiment IR has a value nearly twice that of CR, it is evident that desire to report all tasks was as a rule much weaker than the tension systems of the unfinished tasks. (40–55): careful study of the tasks themselves reveals that the per cent of recall varies not so much with what an onlooker might consider " finished " or " unfinished " but rather with the subject's *own* feeling. The subject may *seem* to have finished a task but may himself consider the result inadequate and the task far from completed and vice versa. Comparing the introspective reports with other data collected from such a subject one finds that tasks of this sort often enjoy as much advantage in memory as those actually interrupted by the experimenter. As regards tasks with clear-cut goals and those that could conceivably go on *indefinitely*, a decided difference in result was found. Interruption of the latter plays a far weaker role in the matter of tension and memory than when the former are interrupted. Example: if the task is one of marking X's on a sheet of paper this is presumably an endless undertaking and therefore interruption means not so much leaving the task unfinished as merely calling a halt. Hence there was no marked difference in memory advantage in this kind of task.]

56–58 3. *Some factors governing recall.*—(*a*) Time of interruption. What part does the place of interruption play? If we compare the results of 38 tasks interrupted in the middle or towards the end, with 45 interrupted soon after the task was begun, we find that whereas the former were 90 per cent, the latter were but 65 per cent better remembered than completed tasks had been. It will be recalled (p. 20) that the experimenter intervened when the subject seemed most engrossed in his task. Records of the experiment show that this was predominantly toward the end of work. Why is it that absorption and (hence) greater memory advantage of the task comes late rather than early? As everyone knows it is far more disturbing to be interrupted just before finishing a letter than when one has only begun. The desire to complete a task may at first have been only a quasi-need; later, through "losing one's self in the task", a genuine need arises. The goal which at the start perhaps had little or no valence [1] now possesses a *positive* drawing power.

59 (*b*) "Ambitious" subject. Since the subjects frequently commented upon their work, the nature of the task, etc., it was relatively easy to distinguish those who were motivated primarily by a desire to succeed in what they did. Exclamations such as "What is the matter with me . . . !" or "I wouldn't have believed I could be so stupid", marked the "ambitious" subjects quite clearly. The recall advantage enjoyed by unfinished tasks with these subjects was 175 per cent as against the general average of 90. It appears that although mere intention gave no particular impetus for recall (p. 26 f.), the extent to which a subject was immersed in his work

[1] Cf. *Selection 24*, p. 28.

did make a decided difference. In behaviour of the latter type, to
solve the problem has become a genuine need whereas in many
cases it could not be considered more than a quasi-need related to
60 nothing more fundamental in the person himself than just what the
experimental procedure sets forth. Again, just as the *recall* advantage
of unfinished tasks was especially marked with these subjects, it
was also observed that they *forgot* completed tasks much more
readily than did the average subject.

61 (*c*) The question of attitude. The results of our main experiment
will not occur in cases where the subjects feel themselves at the
mercy of the experimental situation. A group of 10 high school
pupils, for example, was sent by their teacher "to visit the psychological laboratory". While highly interested in being shown a psychological experiment, they took no interest in the tasks themselves
but submitted to them only as a kind of school discipline. They
behaved like soldiers under command, not like individual persons.
They admitted afterward that they had repressed their own wishes
62 and had merely done as they were told. When asked whether
he had wanted to continue the interrupted tasks one of them
answered: "I did not care . . . it would have been entirely different
if I had had the task at home, but here I simply did what you told
me to do." With these subjects there was no memorial advantage
of unfinished tasks ($\frac{IR}{CR} = 1{\cdot}03$).

63 Nor was the attitude of another group, although very different
in character, any more conducive to repeating the results of our
main experiment. This group of 5 subjects was primarily interested
in learning what went on in a psychological laboratory. They
constantly sought to ferret out the "meaning" of the experiment
and looked upon the individual tasks as utterly incidental. Indeed
they considered the tasks a mere cloak designed to conceal some
recondite significance which they had not yet uncovered. Performance of the tasks was therefore itself dominated by a *single* need:
to unmask the secret which lay behind them. For these subjects
the separate tasks were integrated parts of a single whole whose
real nature they were so anxious to fathom. They did not look upon
64 each task as a separate entity, and, therefore, to complete a task or
to leave it unfinished was for them but a phase in another total
process: either would mean proceeding another step towards
completion of the whole series. Hence with these subjects there were
few if any distinct tension systems corresponding to the several

tasks, but only a general tension relative to the experiment as a whole. The results were $\frac{IR}{CR} = 1{\cdot}12$.

65 Evidently to have $\frac{IR}{CR} = 1$, a separate state of tension must be established for each task. If the boundaries between these systems are weakened, no more memorial advantage should accrue to interrupted tasks than to those which have been completed. In addition to the evidence contained in the two preceding examples we tested this hypothesis again with 8 new subjects by telling them *in advance* all the tasks that were to be solved during the hour. In this case $\frac{IR}{CR} = 0{\cdot}97$—which signifies no difference between interrupted and completed tasks.

(*d*) Fatigue. It was found in the course of these experiments that with fatigued subjects memorial advantage lay on the side not of
67 the unfinished but of the *completed* tasks. To study this phenomenon somewhat more closely, two groups of subjects were given a special series of tests as follows. The 7 members of Group I performed the tasks while tired and were questioned after 13–15 hours rest. The 8 subjects in Group II did the tasks when fresh and were questioned that evening after a hard day's work. The results show that with Group I (tired-fresh) the *completed* tasks were remembered best ($\frac{IR}{CR} = 0{\cdot}61$) while with Group II (fresh-tired) memory for
68 both kinds was practically the same ($\frac{IR}{CR} = 1{\cdot}06$). If the tension system of an unfinished task is to persist until the time of recall, it must have a sufficient " firmness " [" *Festigkeit* "] in order to withstand self-dissolution. In a state of fatigue the subject is too " slack " ; the medium is too " loose ". The tension cannot
69 persist.[1] And this is why, at the time of interruption, no separate, persistent tension system can be formed for the individual tasks.

It is interesting to note, however, that on the other hand, memory for completed tasks is not worse but *better* than in a normal state. To explain this we must now introduce a matter of essential importance for our entire experiment. Finished tasks differ from those which have been interrupted not only because with the former no quasi-need is present, but also because finished tasks present

[1] A state of tension in any loosened, relatively fluid medium is very difficult to maintain.

completed, stable forms in contrast to the unclosed, somewhat more indefinite, instable character of uncompleted processes. If this is so, then the results of our main experiment attain an added importance. They show, namely, that recall-value is enhanced far more by a dynamic state of tension of the relevant quasi-need than by the closure of stable forms. Likewise we can explain our results with tired subjects. In a condition of fatigue unstable systems (being, as they are, under a tension pressure) cannot maintain themselves. On the other hand, systems which lack this tension pressure (viz. those of the finished tasks) will, if they already possess a stable, closed form, persist even though the subject be in a state of fatigue.

71 (*e*) Delayed recall. It may be supposed that even without fatigue
the separating walls of tension systems such as these will in time
become weakened. To test the influence exerted by an interval of
72 time between performance and recall, certain groups of subjects
were not questioned until the following day. The memorial
advantage of unfinished tasks declined in these cases to a bare
14 per cent. Eight of these people were *also* used as subjects (some
of them 6 months before and some 6 months after the " delayed
73 recall " experiment) where immediate recall was requested. With
these 8 subjects the average recall-value of unfinished tasks *reported on the following day* was 13 per cent ($\frac{\text{IR}}{\text{CR}} = 1{\cdot}13$) while for the *immediate* report it was 110 per cent ($\frac{\text{IR}}{\text{CR}} = 2{\cdot}1$). Another group (17 subjects) was asked to report immediately after the last task (result : 100 per cent advantage favouring interrupted work) and *again* on the following day (result : only 40 per cent advantage of unfinished work).

74 Nevertheless diminution of tension is not due to time as such, but depends rather upon the significant events which take place *during* the interval. If our earlier considerations are correct, a radical change of situation and special modifications of pressure within the psychical field should greatly accelerate equalization of the individual tension systems. We undertook to test this by creating decided changes of situation immediately after performance of the tasks themselves, and before recall was asked for. We found in this way that a delay of but 10–30 minutes often sufficed to eliminate the memorial advantage usually enjoyed by unfinished tasks. An example of this is the following. Immediately after his last task one subject was called to the telephone, being told that Mr. X had

just called. This announcement was particularly exciting since an important message from X was expected. But there was no one on the line; he called out "Hello! Hello!" several times. There was no response. Meanwhile the experimenter and messenger who had followed, now began laughing. Soon the dupe of the joke laughed also and continued laughing for some time. Thereupon a report of which tasks had been performed in the experiment was demanded.

"What? Oh yes. Why I don't know at all; it's all a muddle now. I have forgotten the whole thing."

It was only with difficulty that an answer could be obtained.
75 Result: the finished tasks were recalled best. Six subjects were tested in this way and in each case the *finished* tasks were remembered better than the unfinished ones.

In two other groups the intermission between tasks and report was of two different kinds. Group I (4 subjects) was interrupted but in a manner permitting an easy return to the experimental situation. For example a discussion about some recent book would be introduced between the last task and a request for the report. Here *unfinished* tasks were recalled 50 per cent better than the completed ones. Group II (3 subjects) was distracted during the intermission in a way calculated to make return to the experimental situation much less easy. Suppose the subject was a colleague also doing experimental work in the same laboratory. It would be agreed that immediately after A's experiment (i.e. the one reported here) in which B was subject, A would perform as subject for B. As soon (10–15 min.) as A saw that B was thoroughly absorbed in the *new* relationship of experimenter-subject, the report was demanded. In these cases *completed* tasks were recalled best.

77 (*f*) Repressed tasks. It often occurred that a subject would be given a task which he "could not do". He felt that the task was beyond his capacity. Should this task be interrupted, such a subject frequently assumed that the experimenter had detected his "inferiority" and had withdrawn the task for that reason. Such tasks were usually forgotten when the report was made. An example is the following. Although most boys were poor at knitting, they nevertheless remembered this task (if interrupted) very well. Girls, on the other hand, who were inept at this task very often forgot to mention it in their report even though it had been interrupted. We should not assume, however, that tasks which were (but "should" not have been) poorly performed left no tension system when interrupted. Instead we must think of them as subject to

the special forces of *repression* which caused their recall to be unusually difficult.

78 4. *Individual differences.*—The range of values obtained in the main experiment extended from 500 to −25 per cent memorial advantage for unfinished tasks. The question naturally arises: Was this spread due to chance or did it depend upon genuine individual differences between the subjects themselves? To study this more closely the experiment was repeated (new tasks being used) with 14 subjects after an interval of 3–6 months. The correlation between results from the earlier and later experiments was 0·9—which, as an answer to our question, clearly shows that the spread of results in the main experiment was due almost entirely to consistent individual differences between the persons acting as subjects.[1]

79 Further insight into the matter of individual differences may be gotten by comparing the results obtained from children (average memorial advantage of unfinished tasks 150 per cent) with those of the adult subjects (average 90 per cent). It was characteristic of children, for example, that they sometimes recalled *only* the unfinished tasks. They took the experiment much more seriously than did the adults. By comparison with older subjects, the children's attitude towards these tasks was far more *natural.* In consequence, each task assumed for them decided lineaments of its own. If an adult could not recall the name of a task he would perhaps content himself with some such designation as, "Well, and then there was that folding task." Not so with the child. If he could not recall its name, he would reproduce the task in pantomime, describing it in detail as he proceeded. And the tone of voice was also noticeably different. Never did any child speak
[80-81: in a "superior" manner about the tasks. One could see that with
omitted] children there had been a genuine *need* to complete the tasks given
82 them and not infrequently they would beg to continue the interrupted tasks even two or three days after the experiment was over.

83 This attitude of earnest concern for the work given them was not, however, wholly confined to children. Adult subjects who let
84 themselves go were also to be found among the members of our principal group. Comparing the results of these subjects with those of the very staid adults one finds that whereas with the latter unfinished tasks had a memorial advantage of only 10 per cent

[1] This does not assert, of course, that the percentage of memorial advantage would remain unchanged for the same subjects under varying experimental conditions.

$(\frac{IR}{CR} = 1{\cdot}1)$, its value for the " child-like " subjects was 190 per cent $(\frac{IR}{CR} = 2{\cdot}9)$.

Summary.—The experiments reported here have shown that *unfinished* tasks are remembered approximately twice as well as completed ones. Neither affective colouring nor other special characteristics of the tasks themselves will account for this. Nor will reference to the " shock "-effect accompanying interruption provide grounds for an explanation of this finding. Instead the recall-value of unfinished tasks is high because at the time of report there still exists an unsatisfied quasi-need.

This quasi-need corresponds to a state of tension whose expression may be seen not only in desire to finish the interrupted work but also in memorial prominence as regards that work. Prominence of the quasi-need to recall unfinished tasks depends upon the intensity and structure of the tension system, and also upon the strength and kind of quasi-need set up by the experimenter's instructions to report all tasks. If the subject considers the request a test of his memory, interrupted tasks will enjoy no particular recall-value. If he makes a free and untrammelled report, these tasks will be far better recalled than the others.

85 A quasi-need persists if the task has not been completed *to the subject's own* satisfaction regardless of whether this is equivalent to what may seem from another's inspection to constitute " finished " or " unfinished ". Tasks with whose solution the subject is not content will function in his memory as " unfinished " even though the experimenter may have classified them as completed tasks, and vice versa.

With ambitious subjects inner spheres of the person himself are more involved than is ordinarily the case. In consequence the recall-value of interrupted tasks is higher than the general average.

It is essential for the memorial advantage of unfinished tasks that the tension systems be sufficiently isolated from one another. When the individual tasks lack separate lineaments for the subject, there develops only one large tension system in place of several. This was the case with subjects who had been told beforehand what the tasks were to be ; it held also for others who considered the tasks merely incidental to some hidden meaning lying behind them.

When fatigue diminishes firmness in the total field, the development and maintenance of tension systems is greatly impaired.

Excitement or some radical change of situation will also weaken or destroy the walls separating these systems.

The strength with which such tension systems arise and persist evidently varies greatly between different individuals but remains very nearly constant with the same individual. Strong needs, impatience to gratify them, a child-like and natural approach—the more there is of these, the more will unfinished tasks enjoy in memory a special advantage over those which have been completed.

Fifth Group: Studies in Pathological Phenomena

Selection 26

ANALYSIS OF A CASE OF FIGURAL BLINDNESS

By Adhémar Gelb and Kurt Goldstein

"Zur Psychologie des optischen Wahrnehmungs- und Erkennungsvorganges (Psychologische Analyse hirnpathologischer Fälle auf Grund von Untersuchungen Hirnverletzter, I.)," *Zeitschr. f. d. ges. Neurol. u. Physiol.*, 1918, **41**, 1–143.

2 The war brought to the attention of science a large number of cases where young and healthy men were suddenly transformed by brain injury into patients of a type only rarely encountered in times of peace. It is the purpose of this and the immediately following *Selections* to report some of the investigations undertaken with several of these patients.[1]

[3-4: omitted]

5 We have concerned ourselves less with what the patients could *not* do and have been guided more by a desire to learn how normal apprehension is modified by brain injury as well as to discover if possible the real character of these modified forms. Our purpose has been to determine what was contained in the consciousness of these patients. As a result we have relied heavily upon naïve reports and descriptions as given by the patients themselves. From data such as these we have tried to understand the structural idiosyncrasies of their experiences.

[6-8: omitted]

9 *Case history* (Sch.).—This man was 24 years of age when our study began. Before the war he had been a labourer, had never been ill, and had had an average education. He was wounded 4th June, 1915, by mine splinters and was unconscious for four days. The diagnosis of 10th June: two wounds at the back of the head, one clearly penetrating into the brain, the other (just above the left ear) possibly less deep. About one and one-half months later the wounds had closed and were beginning to heal. His physical condition improved rapidly and although there were dizziness and buzzing in the ears, he suffered no headaches at this time. He did not associate with other patients in the hospital. On the

[1] [The practical side of this work was governed by the need for helping the patients regain a place in the world of normal affairs—frequently the specific interest was to discover what they could do and secure work for them in this field.]

29th of December he was operated upon and a small iron splinter removed from the back of his head.

Headaches were troubling him and the dizziness and buzzing still persisted in February, 1916, when he was transferred to the Hospital for Brain Injury, Frankfurt am Main. His ability to speak was not disturbed; he was also able to read. He was easily fatigued and
10 excitable, particularly when reading. Otherwise his behaviour was fairly normal. The patient was orderly and quiet; his attention seemed normal and he followed with interest the experiments we conducted. His visual perception was not normal and was classified as psychical blindness. Line drawings were unrecognizable and it was found that in reading he had to trace each letter of every word with his finger (see below p. 18 f.). Although not completely colour blind at the time he reached the Frankfurt hospital, the patient said that immediately following his injury he had seen everything as colourless.

Meanwhile he had begun to learn the leather goods trade and
11 succeeded very well, especially in learning to guide himself by the sense of touch.[1] The experiments we shall report here were made between June, 1916, and June, 1917. In general we found no reduction of intelligence in this patient.

[12: the visual field of both retinas was greatly reduced. (This topic is discussed below, *Selection* 28, p. 130 f.)]

13 *Word Blindness.*—The customary tests for visual acuity did
14 not show exceptional disturbance. When *words* were presented *tachistoscopically*, however, the patient failed completely. This led us to make a long series of tachistoscopic tests using words, groups of letters, pictures, figures, etc. With exposure time of 100σ his only report would be: "That was too fast" or, "That was like a flash." Even when the exposure was increased to 1–2 sec. he declared: "Nobody could read that, it is like shorthand."

16 These results were the more puzzling because the patient could read and draw (unusually well) and was also able to recognize and describe objects in his ordinary environment (compare, however,
17 p. 117 below). And yet this same patient accomplished in tachistoscopic experiments *much* less than other patients had who displayed marked inferiority to him as regards continuous exposures. We concluded therefore that his difficulty was purely visual, yet in some fashion which did not appear under ordinary circumstances. A more exact inquiry left no doubt that the patient's failure came from some serious incapacity to *grasp* purely visual presentations.

[1] [He was later given employment as a purse maker.]

We were dealing, that is to say, with a kind of disturbance which
has been named "psychical blindness". We began our study,
therefore, by investigating the patient's ability to read.

18 Although with longer words he sometimes required as much as
10 secs., the patient was nevertheless able to read almost any text
given him. This convinced us that *time* was the critical factor in
his apprehension of the presented material. Careful observation
eventually disclosed that his "reading" was accomplished by a
series of minute head- and hand-movements—he "wrote" with
his hand what his eyes saw. He did not move the entire hand as if
across a page, but "wrote" the letters one over the other, meanwhile "tracing" them by head-movements. An especially interesting aspect of the case was the patient's own ignorance of using this
19 method. Even after our discovery we found it difficult to persuade
him that his procedure was not the customary one. He showed
very clearly that he considered it inevitable for people to "read"
in this way.

20 Our next step was to study the relationship between the patient's
"reading" and the corresponding head- and hand-movements
21 which he made. Our findings may be divided into the following
groups:—

(*a*) If prevented from moving his head or body, the patient could read nothing whatever.

(*b*) His movements led to reading only if they corresponded to
normal writing movements. If required to trace a letter the
"wrong" way, he was quite at a loss to say what letter it was.
23 When given a word in script he would trace through (sometimes
with great rapidity) from beginning to end and say the word
immediately.

(*c*) If a few cross-hatching marks were drawn across the word,
he followed these when he reached them and consequently lost all
sense of what the word was (see below p. 53 f.). This showed us
24 that when proceeding through the word he had been following
each line as he encountered it—and this in helpless dependence
upon the lines themselves, for the word as a whole was not present
in his perception. It was like following a path or track; the scratches
"derailed" him and he was unable to rediscover the correct path—
25 i.e. he failed to read the word. If the scratches were made with a
different coloured pencil, no difficulty was encountered; the same
held for very thick letters and very thin scratches.

26 Nor was the patient able to read various samples of script
equally well. He could decipher only the most plain and regular

hand-writing and became quite confused if asked to read a word or
[27–30: omitted] letter in any other than the familiar script. His own writing was the
easiest of all for him to read.

31 *Other visual perceptions.*—Even circles had to be "traced"
33 by head-movement before the patient could say what they were.
But because of their symmetrical or unequivocal character his tracing of circles and a few other figures might start at any point,
proceed in either direction and nevertheless yield a correct result.
With other objects the situation was frequently not so simple.
34 If compelled to trace a letter in the reverse of or in any other manner
different from that in which it is ordinarily written, he was wholly
at a loss to say what the object had been. Or, as sometimes happened,
he would report one thing if his tracing had proceeded in one
direction, and something different if in the other. Very often he
would cease the tracing process as soon as he believed he could name
35 the object. An H with an additional, oblique line between the
uprights was reported merely as an H; the oblique mark was not
mentioned. It may be said that his tracing was quite "planless",
if by a plan we mean guidance based on an antecedent grasp of the
structure of the object to be traced. If the drawing given him for
tracing were, like a circle, of such a character that he had but one
route to follow, the result was always successful. Not so, however,
with drawings where several lines led away from a single point.
Usually nothing but chance decided which of these he would follow.
If an incorrect line was chosen, he became completely disoriented.
36 The line drawings of an ordinary picture book were extremely
difficult and *all* drawings in perspective were utterly meaningless
for this patient. A circle tilted away from him was invariably
37 described as an ellipse.

39 Such behaviour as this will be comprehensible only after the
[40–42: omitted] qualitative composition of his actual visual experiences has been
determined.

43 *Discussion.*—Our experiments thus far have sought to discover
how this patient arrived at some understanding of visual objects,
and we have reported the significance for him of motor responses.
That the patient "sees" cannot be doubted, but this statement says
no more than that he does have some kind of visual impressions;
it tells us nothing regarding the phenomenal character of these
impressions. Are his present experiences essentially the same as
before his injury?

[44–50: review and examination of the literature on psychical blindness.]

51 Our first attempt to clarify these problems was naturally the

most direct and obvious conceivable: we showed him drawings
52 of various kinds and asked what *visual* experiences he had when looking at them. If no "tracing" movements were permitted, he invariably declared that he did not know what had been shown him. Actually (as we later discovered) the patient failed so completely here because he thought we wished him to say what the object itself was. This he naturally could not do. In cases where movements were allowed the object became clear to him only *after* it had been "traced". He could not say, however, whether or not he saw the object more clearly after he had traced it.

53 Are there in normal experience any "derailment"-situations comparable to those encountered by this patient (cf. p. 24)? It would seem that there are, for if asked to trace the hidden figure in
54 a puzzle picture, a normal person is almost sure to be "derailed" at some time during his first attempt. He "sees" the lines but he does not grasp their meaning; the strokes objectively outlining a hidden figure are not "separated" for him from those which do not compose it. The differences between his perceptions before and after solving the puzzle are really the differences between a jumble of meaningless lines and a unified, self-contained and clearly organized figure.[1] In the former case no line is better than any other, and when observed by one who knows already what the figure is, the subject is seen definitely to get himself "derailed" at various points. But for the subject, as yet ignorant of the hidden organization, this is not "getting off the track", since as yet there is no "track", i.e. his procedure is truly planless.[2]

55 Similarly the patient is derailed because he has not visually *grasped* the *whole* to be traced nor is the presented object (for him) so constituted as to guide his tracings in a correct and unequivocal fashion. The comparison holds also for those instances where the patient does trace correctly. There is no reason to believe that he
56 experiences visual wholes in this case any more than in the other. He succeeds if the object is itself unequivocal, yet his procedure is here as planless as before since in neither case is it guided by any visual grasp of the spatial figure to be traced.

It seems likely that our patient had lost the ability to experience
57 compactly organized visual impressions. A normal person hears melodies and sees spatial forms, both of which are composed objectively of successive or spatially separate parts. Were one, however,

[1] For our present purposes it is immaterial how this difference occurs; we emphasize merely that phenomenally such differences do exist.

[2] Compare the relation of *a* and *b* figures in *Selections 9a* and *9b*.

to describe a melody or a rectangle as consisting of such parts,
58 one would be stating their *objective*, not however their psychological
character. As *experienced* these phenomena are normally not
" sums " but unitary, self-contained wholes.

60 *Experiments with negative after-images.*—In order to discover
just what his visual impressions were and in how far our assumption
was correct (viz. that " tracing " movements were indispensable)
we undertook to establish conditions calculated to exclude *all*
possibility of tracing movements on his part. We wished to obtain
61 observations from him which were wholly uninfluenced by such
movements. This we accomplished by means of negative after-
62 images. After a little practice the patient was able to see " some-
63 thing reddish " when a green triangle (2·5 cm. high) was used as
initial presentation. He reported the after-image to be approximately
the same in size as the presented object but was unable to describe
its form. With further practice he could report that the presented
figure was more clear-cut than the after-image, but he was still
65 unable to say what the figures were. The after-images, according to
his reports, were neither round, cornered, nor any other assignable
shape.

66 How is it possible that the same patient who formerly required
a tracing process before the presented object became clear, could now
(despite accurate fixation at the centre of a presented figure) refer to
a difference in *clarity* between the presented object and its hazy
after-image? Our real question here as above was: What is the
67 patient's phenomenal equivalent of a presented object? At last
he himself understood the problem and reported that no more as an
initial presentation than as an *after-image* had a figure ever been for
him " round, cornered, or any other determinable shape ". It was
[68-69 omitted]: experience with after-images which had, so to speak, provided him
with a vocabulary for his phenomenal impressions in general.

70 *The perception of dots, lines, and figures.*—Just as the patient
71 failed to see contour and surface figures, so also was he unable to
grasp discontinuous arrangements of dots. Any normal person can
see ∷ as a square or multiplication mark.[1] The patient " saw "
one or other of these only when allowed to move his head. Further
study along this line revealed him to be wholly lacking in ability
to grasp or apprehend groups of objects. The consequence of
this was that he could obtain no idea of how many points even the
simplest figure contained except by *counting* them. Unlike a normal

[1] [See illustrations in *Selection 5*.]

person he was without any immediate apprehension of whole-forms as such.

Furthermore he even lacked direct apprehension of straightness
and curvature. When shown a line 5 cm. long he could state its
72 direction, but (even with head-movements) had no impression of
it as "straight". A cradle-shaped curve was for him merely
"something extended, narrow and black" but he saw no "curved
object" and reported simply, "On both sides [of the fixation point]
73 something extends upward." He could not grasp characteristic
structures, yet his visual impressions of triangles, squares, circles
and rectangles did differ from one another somewhat. Though he
saw no "triangle", the "blot" which this figure was for him was
not the same as that of a square. A triangle was something "wide
below and narrow above"; a circle or square was "nearly equal
in all directions". Similarly he could, even without head-movements,
discriminate a straight line from a sharp curve because the latter
extended above or below his point of fixation.

74 It is clear now, of course, why this patient failed completely
75 when first shown the tachistoscopic exposures. We were more
successful in this on later occasions of which the following is an
example. A black triangle 17 cm. high and with a base of 20 cm.
was exposed on the wall 1·5 m. away.

1. Exposition (1 sec.)— "I saw light and a large point." ("What was its shape?") "I cannot say."

2. Exposition (*c.* 1½ sec.)—"An upward stroke on the right [gesture]."

3. Exposition (*c.* 2 sec.)— "It goes up one side and down the other [gesture]." ("What is below?") "I do not know that."

4. Exposition (c. 2 sec.)— "A triangle."

Beginning with the second exposure he had been "tracing" the figure from the lower right-hand corner upward, downward and across. The *movement* had thus eventually produced for him a triangle.

76 Summarizing thus far, we may say that that which the patient
experiences visually lacks all specific characteristic structure. His
impressions are not organized like those of normal people; he
77 lacks, for instance, the characteristic stamp of squares, triangles,
straight or curved lines, etc. He experiences "blots" from which

he obtains only the most crude impressions of properties such as altitude and width and their relationship.

78 *The " tracing " process.*—We have spoken thus far of the tracing process only as regards simple geometric figures, letters, and numbers. Very complicated contour drawings could not be " traced " both because there were too frequent opportunities for confusion and *also* because with these objects the tracing technique itself is impaired. This fact may be taken as further substantiation
79 of our belief that his tracing was not guided by any grasp of spatial forms. If he *had* had this ability, then simple parts (triangles, rectangles, etc.) of the more complicated drawings should have been traced with the same speed and assurance now as they were when encountered alone.

At first even very simple objects had required considerable care; later he traced these figures quite easily. The question therefore arises as to how and by means of what processes he had learned to do this? In answering this, one must remember that triangles, for example, were for him in some way " different " from squares and circles, even when head-movements were prevented. His skill in tracing the few simple figures was the result of remembering and recognizing some peculiarity of each: " wide below and narrow above " was, for instance, a sufficient warning that here the tracing
80 process appropriate for triangles would be needed. Indeed he even skipped part of the total outline in such cases—with the result that quite often a considerable speed in " tracing " could be attained.
81 Naturally this same method was also used in reading. Not only whole letters but even words themselves would be skipped if he could guess from the text what they must be.

[82–89: an account is given of the patient's tracing of German letters (see drawing on p. 82 of original text). His " tracing " did not follow every line but consisted of marks sometimes differing considerably (as in the case of his S which resembled an English capital G) from the presented letter. These marks constituted for him, however, a motor " alphabet " by means of which he was able to read. (86 f.): it was found that he could trace straight lines better than curves. A curvilinear spiral proved more difficult to trace than one composed of straight lines. This was because with the latter he had no reason to worry about changes of direction until a corner was reached; with the curved spiral it was necessary, since the direction was constantly changing, to be always on the alert else he might lose the path.]

90 *Visual perception of movement.*—It has been shown on the basis

of experimental studies with normal persons that visual perception of movement depends upon central processes. An investigation of our patient with regard to movement perception should, therefore, prove especially enlightening in view of the place and nature of his
91 injury. Moreover if it is true, as Wertheimer has maintained, that the perception of movement is essentially a Gestalt perception, this patient should fail entirely in such a test. Experiments were made
92 both with objective and with apparent motion.

(1) Objective movement such as a rapid straightening and bending of the arm was not seen by the patient at all. He could see the arm in one position and then in the other, but between these two he saw nothing. If a very slow motion was used, he could follow the
93 moving hand with his eyes—but here also he saw no movement but only a series of isolated places in space. Similar results were obtained when, in the dark, a moving flash light was shown to him.

(2) Using two alternately exposed illuminated strips (separated, in different trials, by 11, 18, 25, or 30 cm.; observation distance 2 m.) we found it impossible to awaken in this patient any impression of movement.

The patient could not even understand what we meant by visual perception of motion. He was able to experience tactual movement
[94-96: omitted] without difficulty but he saw no analogy between this and visual movement.

97 *Surface figures, pictures, and objects.*—In general the patient "recognized" surface figures more quickly and better than he did contour figures. This is understandable because with normal people also a homogeneously filled surface usually stands out from its environment much more easily than a corresponding contour figure. And it was observed that whereas he traced most contour figures bit by bit he was able with surfaces to abandon this ultra-careful procedure. He saw the surface in such cases as a unified "blot" and this served, even if indirectly, to assist the tracing process.

It was noteworthy that when given a drawing he would at once try to find some surface figure in it. This sometimes led him into error as on occasions when he would conclude that some purely incidental background feature of the drawing constituted a meaningful figure.

[98–100: results obtained with the Müller-Lyer and other illusory figures are discussed.]

101 In his descriptions of pictures such as landscapes the patient relied greatly upon processes of inference. In one such picture, for example, a winding road proceeded from foreground into the

distance. He discovered that there were trees on either side and a gap between. From this he was able to say of the opening: "It may be a road coming out of the forest because it is brighter [than
102 the surroundings]". This is, of course, but one example among the many which we collected during this study. All agree, however, in showing the marked prominence of inference and guesses.

[103–106: examples, protocols and discussion of his descriptions of pictures.]

107 The customary tests showed him to have no difficulty at all in guessing what everyday objects were. Dice, for example, he "inferred" from black dots on a white surface. He did not see the corners of these objects, but from the facts of their size and the dots he reached the conclusion "dice".

Indeed it was remarkable how relatively unhampered he was, even where vision was of crucial importance, in the affairs of everyday life. When walking in the park, for example, he declared that he had no trouble in orienting himself. He could identify various objects
108 (trees, bushes, pools, buildings, animals, shadows, leaves, etc). But the criteria upon which his inferences were based may be seen in the following conversation:—

"How do you distinguish men and vehicles?"

"Men are all alike—narrow and long, vehicles are wide; one notices that at once. Much wider [spreads out his arms]."

The shadow of a large tree: "What is that?"

The patient looked up at the tree then down at the shadow. "That is a shadow." ("How do you know?") "Well, there is a tree and there it is dark."

109 These and many other accomplishments were noted only towards the end of our study. He was by no means so sure of himself at the start. On the other hand, his characteristic failures at the beginning were as decided later as they had ever been. He had, however, learned during this period to make the most of non-visual cues just as he had previously learned how to read by means of tracing-movements. It would be false, therefore, to conclude merely from the results of "abstract" tests that a psychically blind person would
110 be helpless in everyday affairs. Our patient could not visually grasp the properties of straightness or curvature in lines, he could
[111–112: omitted] not experience movement, yet he was able to learn a new trade and do well at it. His was, in other words, an excellent example of adaptiveness.

113 *Mental imagery and drawing.*—When asked, "What does a lion

114 look like ? " he replied, " It has a yellow coat . . . The male has
hair on its neck ; the female is vicious."

115 It would be quite erroneous to conclude from this that the
patient's answer indicated the presence of memory images. It
could have been, and in all likelihood was, merely a verbal reproduction of some description which he may have learned in school
116 or elsewhere. Moreover, the patient himself disclaimed *any* visual
images. Nor is there anything in his replies which would justify
117 one in assuming that he must possess such imagery. He asserted
that his correct answers (such as the above) depended upon other
aids than visual imagery. He was quite unable, for example, to
form any mental picture of a well-known room, although he could
by purely verbal reproduction give an account of its contents.
Nor could he see before him the image of a close friend or relative.[1]
One day he was questioned shortly after a conversation with another
[118–119: omitted] man and gave an accurate account of all that had been said—but he
could not give even the slightest account of how the man had
looked.

120 In conclusion we may mention the enormous part played by
" types " in this patient's drawings. Despite his lack of memory
121 images, he could nevertheless draw pictures very well. That he
could not, however, *copy* them was shown by the fact that when
specifically instructed to do so, he was incapable of drawing a single
line. His procedure was of a very different order : having " traced "
the presented object in his accustomed way (head-movements)
[122–142: omitted] he would then draw a picture of his own of that type of object.
He did not reproduce the *particular* object shown him, but rather its
class or type. He drew *a* boot, not *the* boot that had been presented.

[1] Thus showing that even affective colouring was insufficient to produce imagery.

Selection 27

A DISTORTION OF "SURFACE COLOURS"

By Adhémar Gelb

"Über den Wegfall der Wahrnehmung von 'Oberflächenfarben' (Psychologische Analyse hirnpathologischer Fälle auf Grund von Untersuchungen Hirnverletzter, IV.)," *Zeitschr. f. Psychol.*, 1920, **84**, 193–257.

In the foregoing *Selection* we reported a case of figural blindness resulting from brain injury. The patient to be discussed here, while also exhibiting characteristics of psychical blindness, differed,
194 however, in several important respects from the other patient. Our present report will deal primarily with problems of colour vision with special emphasis upon the distinction made by D. Katz between film and surface colours.[1]

195 *Case history* (W.).—The patient was 25 years of age. Before the war he had been an electrician; colour vision had been normal. On 7th September, 1915, he was wounded by shrapnel, the injury being located at the rear left side of his head.[2] Immediately after the injury he lost all ability to perceive colours; vision itself improved soon thereafter but there remained a total colour blindness. The visual apprehension of objects was difficult if not impossible. In March, 1917, he was sent to the Frankfurt Hospital for Brain Injury.

196 In making campimetric measurements it was discovered that when a dark pointer upon a white ground was used his visual field
198 was 20–30° larger than when a light pointer upon a dark ground had been employed.[3] As regards memory for colours he was unable to recall anything of what these had looked like before his injury. He "knew", of course, that corn flowers were blue, that blood was red, etc., but he could not awaken within himself an image of such colours.

[1] Cf. *Selection 16*.

[2] Report of March, 1917: scar indicates injury in the region of the lobus parietalis inferior and of the lateral occipital area, left side.

[3] [Pp. 195 f. and 235: perimetrically determined visual fields are illustrated but with the proviso that, having been obtained by the use of a white object on a black background, they give no reliable picture of the actual fields.]

Grateful acknowledgment is hereby made to *Johann Ambrosius Barth*, *Verlagsbuchhandlungen*, Leipzig, for permission to reproduce the illustrations used in this Selection.

[199–201: further reports are given concerning the initial examination of this patient; also the case history of another patient is reviewed. We shall here omit all reference to the second patient as the results obtained from him are essentially the same as those of W.]

202 *The perception of surface colours.*—In connection with our routine examination of the patient's visual disability we discovered something
203 which at first proved very puzzling. If we placed before him a series of achromatic colours graduated in steps from white to black which the normal person could just distinguish, the patient saw only *four* steps or degrees of brightness. He volunteered the information, moreover, that these four steps were for him sharply separated from one another: "It goes to there, then suddenly something else begins." This result reoccurred every time no matter how often we repeated the experiment or how varied the conditions of illumination.

204 This and further investigation soon led us to realize that for this patient all visual objects had lost the character of *surface* colours and assumed instead the character of *film* colours.[1] They were seen, that is to say, as "spatial" in the sense that they themselves seemed
205 to occupy or fill the space. This will be clear from what follows.

(*a*) Localization of colours. The first distinction which Katz makes between film colours and surface colours refers to their relative specificity of *location*. A film colour, he points out, can usually not be localized as occupying so precise a position relative to the observer as, say, the colour of this page. This latter appears to be at the same place as the paper itself. The distance of a film colour, on the other hand, can be stated only with some indefiniteness. Turning now to the reports made by our patient, we find him unable to specify the exact location of colours. He was shown a haphazard arrangement of coloured (chromatic and achromatic) papers upon a table and given a pointer with instructions to place its tip upon various colours. More specifically the instructions were to indicate the *place* where these colours appeared. In every case
206 his pointer came to rest at a position some little distance *above* the coloured paper and he would say, "About here is where the colour begins." But this interval was not the same for all colours. At an observation distance of approximately 1 m. the pointer would be placed 10–15 cm. above the black or blue papers while with white or yellowish green the distance was 2–3 cm. The interval between pointer and paper was, with other colours, somewhere between these extremes according to their relative brightnesses. When the

[1] [The reader may recall the definitions of these terms as given in *Selection 16*, p. 640.]

observation distance was increased (up to 3 m.) the other distances
increased also. When describing what he saw the patient spoke of
the darker colours as " thick " compared with others which were
in varying degrees " thinner ".

207 (*b*) Texture of colours. Katz has pointed out that whereas the
texture of film colours is loose, that of surface colours is stiff or taut.
One seems to be looking *into* a film colour, while one looks *at*
surface colours. Here again the patient showed very clearly that
the world about him, even in his everyday life, consisted of filmy,
swimming regions where other people see fixed surfaces. He commented, for example, upon the " thickness " of a blackboard which
we once used while experimenting with him, and when he picked
208 up a black card he had the feeling that his thumb was sunk into a
thick object.

209 (*c*) Orientation of film colours relative to the line of regard.
210 When seen foveally and straight ahead a film colour always appears
vertical to the line of regard. The surface colour of a piece of paper,
on the other hand, may occupy any position relative to the eye,
for here the colour itself lies in the surface of the paper. When our
patient looked at a piece of coloured paper held up in front of him,
he saw the colour as vertical *even* when it was tilted forward or
backward from the vertical position. If a coloured disk was shown
him and then tilted, he would report that the circle had become
an ellipse but that the coloured object still appeared vertical.
211 Eventually as the angle of inclination increased he would be able
to see that the object occupied a tilted position. This angle had to
be greater with dark coloured objects than with lighter ones.

(*d*) Adherence of colours to the surfaces of objects. The surface
of a body may be flat or curved and its colour, will, of course, appear
in the corresponding position. A film colour, on the contrary,
212 exhibits no marked curvatures whatever. As a means of testing
this characteristic of colours in the case of our patient, we laid
parts of a black cloth into deep folds while leaving the remainder
smooth. He saw no folds whatever. Instead he described this
part of the cloth as consisting of " darker and lighter stripes ".

From this evidence there can be no doubt that our patient had completely lost the ability to experience surface colours. Every spatial characteristic which Katz has suggested for film colours held also for the manner of this patient's entire colour perception.

213 *Vision without surface colours.*—The everyday life of this patient
was by no means an easy one. His shoes seemed thick and filmy;
he could not tell whether his hair was properly combed except by

214 feeling it with his hands. If he wished to pick up something he had to move his hand to feel his way before grasping; he frequently broke glasses and dishes because he would let go of them too soon. The result was, of course, that he was forced to depend greatly upon touch in guiding himself.[1] He commented in this connection
215 upon the difference between visual and tactual impressions and said,
[216-222: omitted] "The things I see are always hazy and soft; what I touch is usually firm and hard."

223 *The question of transparency.*—As mentioned above (p. 208) the patient felt upon touching a black object that his finger penetrated for some distance into the colour before encountering a resistant surface. This does not mean that a lighter coloured object was seen to cleave through the darker colour, but rather that the otherwise opaque colour appeared at this point to be
224 *transparent.* The lighter object seemed to lie "within" and to be tinged by the darker one. Thus the arrangement of black and white areas shown in Fig. 1 was seen by the patient as a white submerged in black. The black itself was "transparent" where it covered the white but elsewhere it was opaque.

FIG. 1.
Outside dimensions 30 by 30 cm.; white 20 by 20 by 5 cm.

225 Obviously the degree to which a white band would appear submerged in (and tinged by) black depended upon the width of the band. With a white strip wider than 1 cm., for instance, the sides bordering on black would be tinged by a black
226 which became fainter towards the middle of the strip. By widening still further the objective gap between the black borders (i.e. increasing the width of the white) a cleavage between them could be achieved. An example of this may be seen in the following.

Two dark grey cards of equal size and brightness were placed upon a sheet of white paper so that they covered it entirely. When the cards were slowly drawn apart the gradually widening strip of white between them appeared to the patient to be "within" the dark colour of the cards. In other words the grey closed over the
227 white. As the cards were drawn farther apart the middle of the strip between them became brighter. Finally the grey ceased to extend across the gap and a pure white was suddenly visible for the first time; only the outer edges of the strip were still tinged by grey. Now the patient saw: thick, thin, thick (dark, light, dark).

[1] [The latter observations were more characteristic of the other patient than of W., but the principle is the same. (See above, pp. 199–201.)]

228 This result obtained for a *spatial* arrangement may be compared with that of the *temporal* succession of light stimuli in apparent motion experiments. As has been shown by Wertheimer, the impression of movement arises only when an optimal range of speed is maintained for the successive exposures. The analogy lies in the fact that in one case an optimal speed, in the other an optimal interval, is necessary before the result (movement in the one case, separation of white from grey in the other) can be achieved. It appears also that our present results, no less than those obtained in experiments with apparent movement, are due to the operation of specific central processes.

Moreover the analogy may also be drawn as regards degrees of *Prägnanz* in which the end-result appears. There are " good " movement impressions and others which the observers described as " bad ". Similarly here, for between the patient's " good " impression of a closed, transparent mass and that of a " cleavage " there was an increasing " tension " in the middle of the transparent grey.

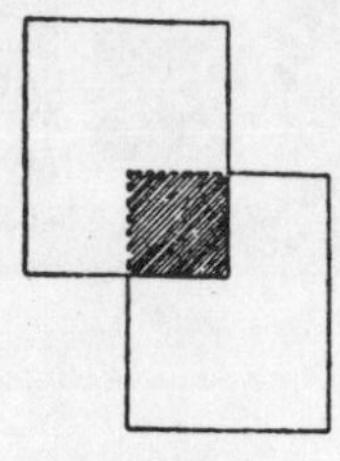

Fig. 2.

229 The results obtained in the following case were not unlike those just reported. One corner of a white card was moved diagonally across one corner of a red card in the manner suggested by Fig. 2. The patient's initial impression was of an unbroken red partly covered by white. Evidently this is an instance of the " completion phenomenon " discussed in *Selection 29*. The
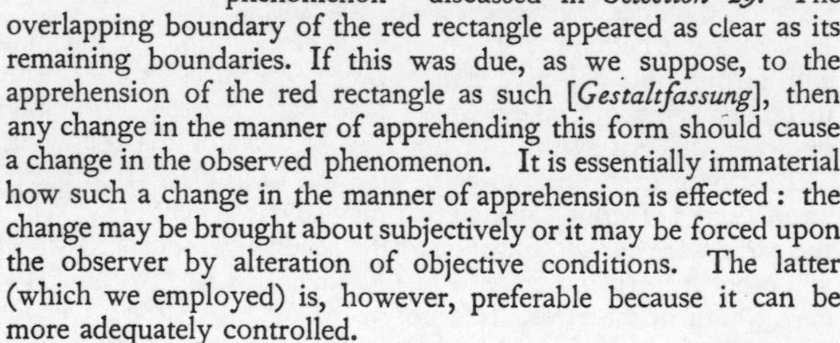
overlapping boundary of the red rectangle appeared as clear as its remaining boundaries. If this was due, as we suppose, to the apprehension of the red rectangle as such [*Gestaltfassung*], then
230 any change in the manner of apprehending this form should cause a change in the observed phenomenon. It is essentially immaterial how such a change in the manner of apprehension is effected : the change may be brought about subjectively or it may be forced upon the observer by alteration of objective conditions. The latter (which we employed) is, however, preferable because it can be more adequately controlled.

We discovered, namely, that when the white card was moved so far across the red as to destroy the latter's rectangularity, the " completion " phenomenon disappeared. That is to say, a point would be reached where a sudden transformation [*Umschlag*] of the apprehension occurred. No longer was the white bounded in a definite manner ; the red quickly became lost above the white and the patient was unable to describe its appearance in this region with any assurance.

[231–235 : miscellaneous observations. (231 f.) : when small bits of medium grey paper were placed upon white and black backgrounds the patient's report was the opposite of that which a normal person would give : for him the grey on black was *darker* than the grey on white. Evidently this was because for him the grey on black appeared submerged in and could not therefore be isolated from its dark background. (234 f.) : in a relatively subdued illumination the patient was shown a piece of black cardboard upon which a word had been written with chalk, and a piece of white cardboard with the same word written upon it in charcoal. The word in white upon black was illegible. This was because black " closed over " the narrow white lines thereby rendering recognition of the word impossible. Conversely, the charcoal lines were more than ordinarily easy to read because of the relief-effect with which they stood out for him from their background.]

236 *Colour constancy without surface colours.*—Even when seen in an intense light, a piece of black paper will look darker than white
238 paper in subdued light.[1] It has been thought, however, that this phenomenon—of " colour constancy "—was possible only with surface colours. Since our other tests showed him to be without a perception of surface colours, we should have to infer that the
240 phenomenon of colour constancy would not be experienced by our patient. To test this we employed the same apparatus and procedure
241 described in the " standard experiment " of *Selection 16* (p. 620 f.) : one variable colour wheel was placed in a shadow and another in direct illumination ; after an equation of their perceived brightnesses had been made with a double-aperture reduction screen, the screen was removed and another equation made.

The results were not at all what might have been expected, for when the reduction screen was removed the patient almost invariably found the two colour wheels to be *unequal.* This is typical of normal experience also. Before he could see them as equal without the screen it was necessary (just as with normal observers) for the experimenter to *add white* to the wheel in direct illumination.[2]

242 *Therefore we must conclude that ability to perceive surface colours is not necessary for the occurrence of the phenomenon of colour constancy.*

But, even more striking, therefore, was our patient's failure when

[1] Cf. *Selection 16*, p. 596.

[2] A typical pair of equations : (i) (with screen), 38·5° white, 20° yellow, 301·5° black ; (ii) (without screen), 176° white, 20° yellow, 164° black.

confronted by the following situation. When the shadow of a cane was cast upon any light or dark surface he described the shadowed
[243–245: omitted] region as "darker" than its surroundings. He never saw this area as a *shadow* and this was also true of his everyday experience.

246 In seeking an explanation for this discrepancy between the results of our colour constancy and shadow experiments we were reminded that for this patient the colours of objects were apprehended *as* the colours of *objects* even though they were experienced as film colours. They lacked the spatial qualities of surface colours but were nevertheless seen as being carried by concrete objects. Of course, when looking through the aperture of a reduction screen
247 the patient saw film colours without any carrier; when the screen was not used he saw film colours with their carrier. He was conscious, ordinarily, that a perceived colour was the colour of some object and this sufficed to establish for him a difference between situations with and without the screen. The surfaces of objects had, of course, lost for him their taut form—this was shown by the discrepancies between visual and tactual impressions—but he was nevertheless still conscious of them as concrete objects.

249 The conditions given by our shadow experiment were quite different from those of the "standard" demonstration of colour constancy. In this latter case one does not experience the shadowed colour wheel as "shadowed"; it is merely seen in "a poorly illuminated space". In the shadow experiment, on the contrary, positive results depend upon a clear apprehension of the shadow *as* a shadow. In order to experience this impression it is essential that one be able to see taut surfaces. Naturally our patient was bound to fail in this case.

250 Summarizing, we find that the phenomenon of colour constancy is possible whenever *object*-colours are perceived. The specific manner in which these objects appear to be coloured is not important. In a "shadow" experiment, however, the extent to which a colour carrier is structured will be of crucial importance as regards the question whether or not the shadow will be seen *as* a shadow.

[251–257: restitution of colour vision. (251 f.): gradually the patient's localization of colours (cf. pointer experiment, p. 205 f.) became more exact until finally the "thickness" of bright colours disappeared entirely and he could experience them as surface colours. Darker colours followed later. He also reported the ability to see a foveally fixated point as a surface colour although everything peripheral thereto appeared increasingly "thick" the farther removed it was from this central point. (254 f.): omitted.]

Selection 28

PHENOMENAL DISPLACEMENT IN VISUAL FORMS

By Wilhelm Fuchs

"Untersuchung über das Sehen der Hemianopiker und Hemiamblyopiker, I. Verlagerungserscheinungen," *Zeitschr. f. Psychol.*, 1920, **84**, 67–169.

69 The purpose of this and the following two papers is to report a series of experiments with patients suffering from partial blindness due to brain injury.

Case history (*D.*).—This patient was twenty-five years of age, a machinist, and was wounded in the back of the head on 20th November, 1917, by bomb splinters during an air attack. The immediate consequences included a temporary sinistral hemiplegia and homonymous reduction of the optical range on the left side.
70 As the wound healed, the paralysis was gradually overcome. He was transferred to the Hospital for Brain Injury at Frankfurt am Main in April, 1918. The patient was at this time frequently too ill for psychological study and complained of headaches, dizziness, etc. Nevertheless his mental condition seemed sound and he could remember events before and after the injury.

71 As may be seen from Fig. 1, the first perimetric examination revealed an almost total homonymous hemianopsy on the left side. The lower left quadrant was completely eliminated; the upper left
72 quadrant (shaded area) though not invisible was amblyopic. Some months later the patient's vision began to improve and certain sections that had formerly been hemianopic became amblyopic.

73 The present report will deal only with errors of localization [*Verlagerungserscheinungen*] in the functionally competent and amblyopic regions. The apparatus, observation distance, etc., for tachistoscopic presentation of the stimulus objects may be seen in Fig. 2.

74 *Errors of localization.* 1. *Amblyopic region alone.*—Using the tachistoscope [1] we presented a series of disks 2–10 cm. in diameter

[1] P. 77: expositions of 85σ were used; eye-movements were therefore impossible.

Grateful acknowledgment is hereby made to *Johann Ambrosius Barth, Verlagsbuchhandlungen*, Leipzig, for permission to reproduce the illustrations used in this Selection.

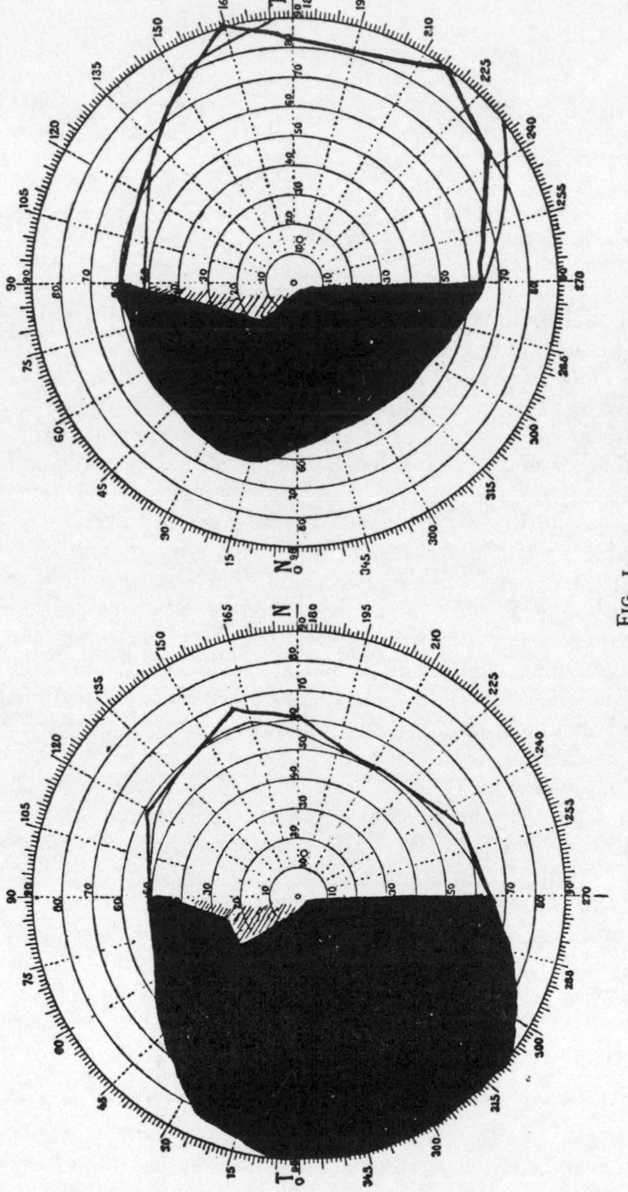

Fig. 1.

This drawing depicts the patient's objective field of vision (not the retinas). Single objects falling wholly within the darkened areas were invisible.

in the injured region (Fig. 3). Although the patient was aware that
something had been presented, he could not describe its form.
When asked to show where the object had appeared, he indicated
a point (on the frosted glass) several centimetres to the right of and
usually above the actual place of projection. Errors of localization
75 did not occur when the object was presented in the functionally
competent region—i.e. rightward of the fixation point.

76 A 10 cm. disk was exposed 3 cm. below and (*a*) 2 cm. or (*b*) 14 cm.
to the left of the fixation point. These alternate expositions were

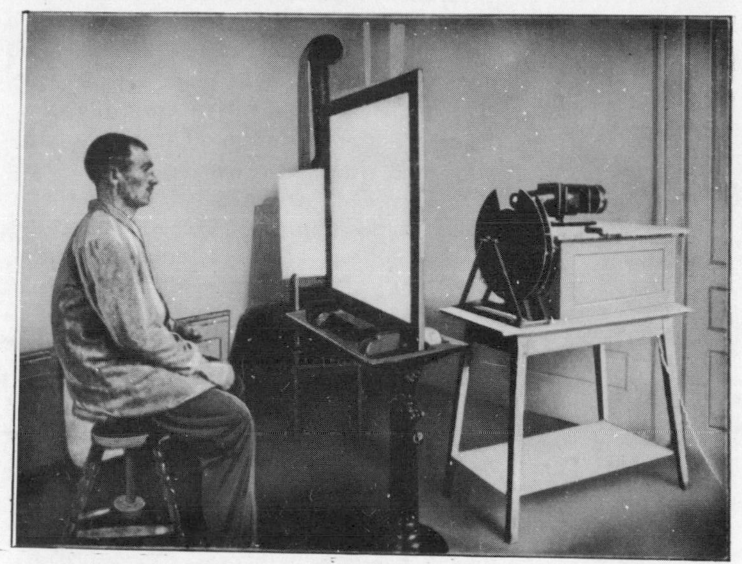

FIG. 2.

made several times and the patient was instructed to report on their
position and clarity. The results were very surprising, for he
invariably localized the more *remote* disk closer to the fixation point
77 than he did the objectively nearer one. The more centrally placed
disk was clearer and brighter than the other, and his localization of it
was very nearly accurate. These results led us to carry out additional
experiments in which the more eccentrically situated disk was
objectively brighter than the other. In this way it was possible to
equalize brightnesses while varying the peripheral distances of the
two disks. Since identical localizations for both disks were now made,
one can see that in the first case the amount of error was due not

to differences in distance from the fixation point but to brightness differences between the two disks. When a disk was exposed alternately at 14 and at 7 cm. left of the fixation point the patient noticed no brightness differences—but also none as regards position either. With both exposures he localized the disk as being just below and to the left of the fixation point.

78 2. *Amblyopic and functionally competent regions together.*—Will errors of localization occur when both sides of the retina are stimulated simultaneously? As the earlier experiment had shown, objects presented in the sound half were not mislocalized. As a first attempt to answer our question we used a narrow strip 15 cm. long and 1·5 cm. wide. The angle of exposure is shown in Fig. 4; fixation was at the centre. The patient local-
79 ized this strip some distance to the *right* and *downward*. When the strip was shown in a new position (Fig. 5), he localized this to the *right* and *above* the correct position. The second exposition in both cases yielded an almost correct localization.

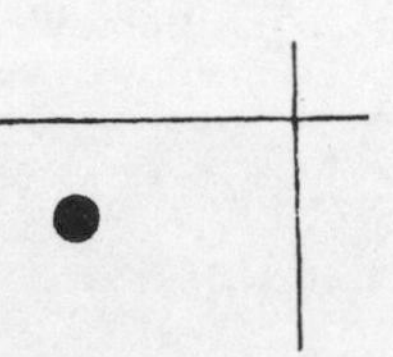

Fig. 3.
Distances: 9·5 cm. left and 4 cm. below the fixation point.

The results of the two initial expositions show that with a *unified figure* falling simultaneously in both regions, even the competent zone will be affected. The error of localization occurring in these cases is, in other words, a rightward displacement of the entire figure. That this effect was probably due to a unitary whole-process embracing both visual areas seems the most likely explanation of these results. If this were not the case, i.e. if the injured and uninjured parts of the visual cortex had functioned independently, two separate "localizations" should have occurred: viz. erroneous localization
80 in the one area and correct localization in the other. The initial expositions resulted in localizations determined by impressions received in the amblyopic side of the retina; in the second expositions the localizations were governed by the competent area. *Both* are instances of whole-processes.

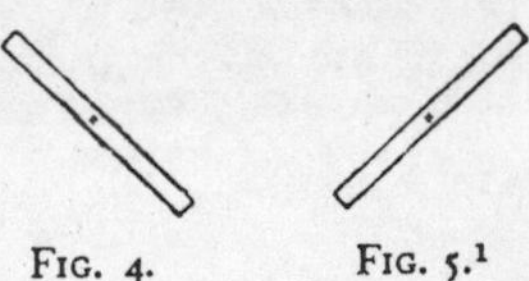

Fig. 4. Fig. 5.[1]

We asked whether errors of localization will occur when both sides of the retina are stimulated together. From the results just

[1] Here the lower end of the strip falls directly in the amblyopic part of the retina.

reported it is evident that with a solid strip, the patient's localizations (whether erroneous or correct) are of the figure as a whole.
81 For this to occur, the patient's apprehension of parts falling in the two retinal areas must have been of a single, unitary figure. If now, the same type of result occurs with figures composed of *dots*, we may conclude that they too will have been apprehended as organized wholes. The first object to be used (Fig. 6) was a reproduction of Figs. 4–5 except that it consisted of five dots (1·5 cm. diameter, interval 2 cm.). The fixation point was at the middle dot. Result: the upper left-hand point was entirely invisible, but the remaining four were displaced to the right and downward as a single row or line. When the
[82–83: omitted] row was presented at the reverse angle (as in Fig. 5) only the three upper dots were seen.

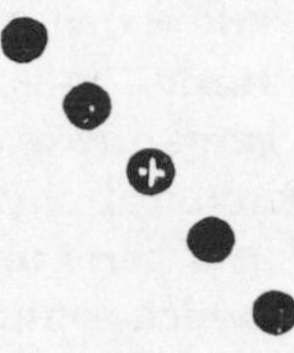

FIG. 6.

84 When the constellation shown in Fig. 7 was exposed, the patient's perception of it was that given in Fig. 8 (his own drawing). This again shows how dots lying in the competent area suffer a mislocalization provided they compose with those in the injured zone a unified figure. The patient did not see the constellation of Fig. 7 as a group of four parts; he saw two separate entities—a single dot and a line.

Occasionally, however, Fig. 7 was seen correctly and in drawing

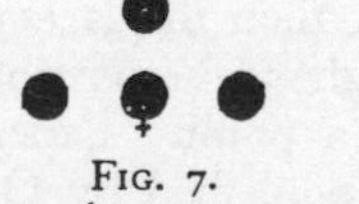

FIG. 7.
The leftmost dot was 3·5 cm. from the point of fixation (indicated here by the small cross).

FIG. 8.

85 the picture he reproduced our own arrangement of it. In these cases the position of the left-hand dot—*which when presented alone was always displaced to the right*—was now determined by the line to which it belonged. That is to say, dominance by the right-hand side of the line overcame the tendency of the left-hand dot to shift downward. Sometimes this dot succeeded in dominating the entire line—and then the error of localization shown in Fig. 8 resulted. Sometimes it failed, whereupon a correct localization was made.[1]

[1] In the former case we may assume that the four dots were seen as 1 + a row (of 3); in the latter instance, however, it is evident that a triangle such as that shown in Fig. 7 had been apprehended.

[86–113: additional examples are given of displacements towards the functionally competent side. In studying another patient, however (p. 110 f.), instances were observed where the error of localization was towards the injured side. Comment upon this type of displacement is given below (pp. 126 f.).]

114 *Theoretical considerations.*—These displacements *towards the fixation point* resemble a condition also found in normal vision and called by Helmholtz "concentric shrinkage of the visual field".[1] An example is this: if one attempts to indicate the centre of a line one of whose ends is fixated, the peripheral "half" will be made too large. That is to say, the other end will be displaced towards the fixation point. Is this, as Hering thought, because of anatomical-physiological differences between the peripheral and
115 central parts of the retina? Is an amblyopic part of the retina one
in which optical values are inferior and their significance for
116 localizations therefore lessened? If it can be shown that errors
of localization can be educed even in normal persons in a direction *away* from the centre of clearest vision, it will follow that anatomical-physiological inferiority of the peripheral zones is not the direct cause of "concentric shrinkage". It is this problem which we now propose to treat.

The point of regard is usually the centre of maximum attention. Let us set forth as an hypothesis that errors of localization occur in the direction of this centre (usually the fixation point and its immediate vicinity). If this is true, then displacements towards other positions in the visual field ought to be possible if attention centres elsewhere than at the fixation point. Experimental sub-
117 stantiation of this has already been published by O. Lipp[2] who
found precisely what our hypothesis states: displacement of a
118 presented object occurred not towards the fixation point, but
(when their location differed) towards the *centre of attention.*
Moreover the attended portion of the field exhibited a marked
119 *clarity*. In a word Lipp found that displacement proceeds towards
that part of the visual field which is attended, viz. towards the
120 object of greatest clarity. In view of this we shall classify errors
of displacement as instances of confluence phenomena [*Angleichungserscheinungen*].[3]

For normal vision, errors of localization proceed toward the *macula lutea* because this region is usually also the centre of attention.

[1] Helmholtz, *Physiol. Optik*, vol. i; cf. also E. Hering in Hermann's *Handbuch der Physiologie*, iii, p. 372.

[2] *Archiv für die ges. Psychol.*, **19** (1910).

[3] Cf. *Selection 7*.

This does not assert, however, that superiority of the macula is solely one of anatomical-histological factors; its superiority derives primarily from central factors (as D. Katz has pointed out). The functions ordinarily performed by the macula can be taken over by peripheral parts of the retina.[1]

121 In experiments performed by the present author (using Lipp's method) it was found that the more *clearly* one apprehended the attended area, the *greater* was the displacement occurring towards that centre.

122 Returning now to abnormal cases, we find that objects presented in the amblyopic region are unclear and hazy in appearance. The functionally competent region (and especially the fixation point)
123 is by comparison much clearer than this injured area. In view of what has already been said, therefore, errors of localization such as those reported above are readily understandable. It sometimes happens that after becoming aware of his visual defect a patient will seek to compensate for it by localizations away from those he would otherwise have made. In many cases a pro-
[124–125: omitted] cess of adjustment may occur which results in a gradually improved mechanics of localization.

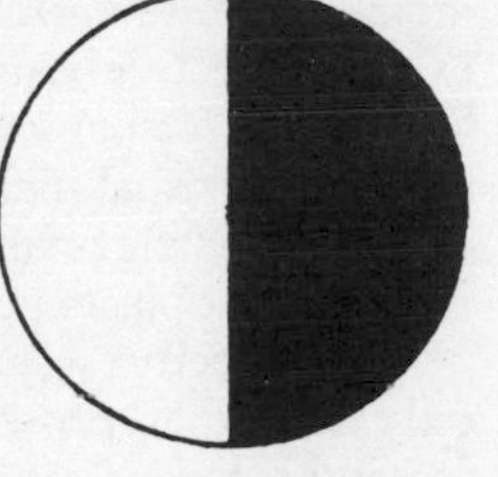

FIG. 9.
This diagram represents a spatial field in front of the patient. He experiences only the uncoloured half; the other half is invisible.

126 *Displacements of the median plane.*—The
127 errors of localization reported above were made towards a definite centre (usually the fixation point), and may, therefore, be classified as instances of *relative* localization. But in studying hemianopic and hemiamblyopic patients one also encounters cases where the entire *visual*
129 *space* is shifted to right or left. These are disturbances of absolute localization. In such cases a point slightly to one side of the patient's line of regard will be *seen* as "straight ahead", and this may occur (depending upon the nature of the brain injury) either towards or away from the unseen area.

130 What psychological factors are involved in such displacements of the median plane? Let us assume a theoretical case of complete right-sided hemianopsia (suggested by Fig. 9). Here the visible area lies entirely leftward of a foveally fixated point. If the visual field of a normal person is artificially restricted in this way, he will observe that the point of equilibrium of the perceived field lies

[1] Cf. the account of vision in the "pseudo-fovea" (below, *Selection 30*).

131 within the semi-circular (visible) area—i.e. leftward of the vertical boundary. One's attention is "distributed" over the entire visible area, but *one* part of this restricted field will possess a special character—viz. that of an anchoring point for attention and hence as the centre from which attention "radiates" evenly in all directions. The importance of this point (or centre of gravity) is that the visible area is "organized" with regard to this centre. This does not mean that the fixation point (situated as it is at the vertical boundary) need lose its character of nuclear point, i.e. of being "straight ahead".

From these considerations one may readily understand how the hemianopic patient too might apprehend the restricted area coming
132 within this purview. We must not, however, confuse the subjective visual field [*Sehfeld*] with the objective visual field [*Gesichtsfeld*]. The former is the field consciously perceived at any given moment, i.e. the *perceived*, not merely the *perceivable*. In speaking of the subjective visual field one refers not to something potential but to the actual experience of any given instant. Hence the subjective visual field is not constant, for as perceived events change it changes also. Its modifications depend upon the kind and size of objects perceived, one's purposes, etc.[1]

The objective visual field of our hemianopic person would be only half that possessed by a normal person. This does not assert that his *subjective visual field* (i.e. that which is psychologically present) is half that of a normal person's—e.g. that it will be experienced as only a "left side" (Fig. 9).

133 In hemianopsia the subjective visual field is organized around a functional centre just as "naturally" as it is with a normal person whose vision has been artificially restricted (cf. p. 130). In neither case is it *necessary* that the median plane should be displaced. But the fact that this does occur so often is evidence that with hemianopic vision (unlike the normal) the nuclear point and the centre of gravity within the perceived field are usually one and the same. This is readily understandable because for these patients the injured side is a "blank". A patient will himself report that his subjective visual field is extended in all directions, that it possesses a left and a right, an above and a below—all in terms of a definite
134 centre or mid-point. And the patient believes himself to be looking squarely at this new centre; it constitutes for him the direction "straight ahead". It is that which is "right in front of me" and hence determines the subjective median plane. The result,

[1] Cf. below, p. 141 f.

as may be seen from the diagram in Fig. 10, is that the *objective* median plane is displaced towards the unseen area and the patient's entire visual space shifts (in the case depicted in Fig. 9 above) rightward.

In Fig. 10 the patient's eye is indicated by *P*. The fixation point, *F*, is objectively straight ahead; the point *A* lies to the left a distance measurable by the angle *AKF*. For the normal person *F* would also look "straight ahead" and *A* would appear on the left. Now suppose that *A* is the centre of gravity of our patient's field of vision, then *A* (being projected on a peripheral retinal point) will look "straight ahead" and correspondingly *F* (whose image falls on the fovea) will appear shifted towards the right (i.e. the blind half) through the angle *AKF*.

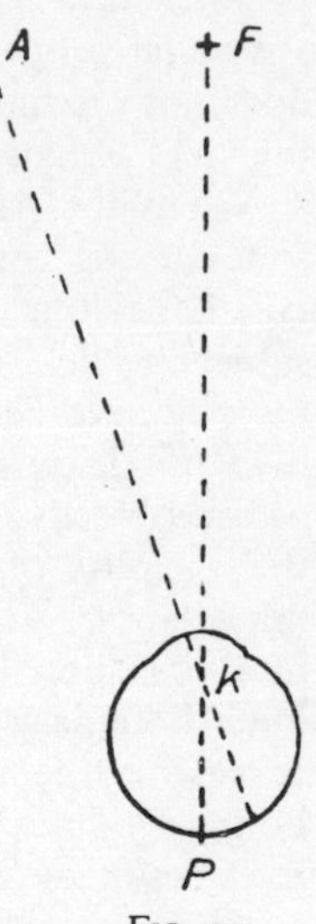

Fig. 10.

Most hemianopic patients are not even aware that their eyes are affected in this way. Sometimes years will elapse [1] before they discover
135 the nature of their defect. They may complain of reduced vision in *one eye* (hemianopic side), but say that they can see quite well with the other. The subjective visual field in such cases so nearly resembles the normal that they do not notice the difference themselves. The perceived area is *never* experienced as "half a visual field" consisting, say, of only a left or a right side of the objective field. Unlike an artificially restricted normal vision (cf. p. 130) the patient's subjective field of vision does not possess a nuclear point (which determines his "straight ahead") *and* (to one side) a centre of gravity. Instead his visual field is organized relative to the nuclear point itself—i.e. this is also the centre of
136 gravity. Hence the visual mid-point, the "centre of attention" and the nuclear point fall together in one. Here, as long as he remains naïve, he places his attention. And indeed all this can be said of normal vision also. In both, apprehension is of the total visual space relative to its centre and in ordinary seeing this mid-point is identical both with the point of fixation and also with the place where attention centres.

137 We go one step further and ask: How does it happen that with hemianopic patients attention is disposed in such a way as to cause

[1] [Reference is here made to pre-war studies by other investigators.]

a displacement of the entire visual space? The answer to this question is already contained in our foregoing sections, for the locus of attention is here determined by "structural functions" (i.e. Gestalt properties) of the visual field itself. In hemianopsia the peculiar form of the objective field elicits a correspondingly peculiar *organization* of the subjective field, and this is responsible for a definite distribution of the patient's attention. This holds true only so long as he is unaware of the defect; it is, therefore, in no sense a product of inferences made regarding visual data. His responses relative to the remaining field of vision are necessarily pro-structural.[1] Attention is "focused" or "directed" by structural properties of the visual field, not vice versa. Attention does not organize the subjective visual field; the organization of this field assigns the centre of attention.[2]

138 When the patient becomes aware of his defect the naïve and spontaneous organization of his visual field usually disappears. His behaviour and the former pro-structural responses of his subjective field undergo severe changes. With the discovery that his objective field is only one-half the normal size, the subjective field of vision begins more and more to approximate the shape of the objective field. The region nearest the injured side (i.e. in the vicinity of the boundary line) now assumes an increased importance. The former "mid-point" of the perceived area now loses its special significance; attention shifts more toward the inner boundary of this region. A new distribution of equilibrium comes into being. In this transformed field of vision the vertical boundary line (Fig. 9) serves as anchoring place for attention. As a result the median plane is no longer displaced.

[139–169: as recovery from hemianopsia proceeds, the formerly blind side becomes amblyopic and the median plane is now displaced towards the functionally competent zone. This may be due either to the increased attention now devoted to the faintly perceived area, or (which seems more likely) to a condition such as that already suggested regarding D.'s errors of localization (p. 78 f.), viz. objects falling in both regions are seen as wholes and appear to be shifted towards the side of clearest vision. This latter is a case of *relative* displacement (cf. p. 127). . . . Additional experiments (p. 141 f.) are reported which show that the centre of attention is determined by the place and size of objects exposed in the visible area. The larger the object or the more peripherally it is exposed, the farther away (eccentric) from the fixation point will

[1] Cf., for example, *Selections 5*, p. 329; *9b*, p. 29. [2] Cf. *Selection 30*, p. 179.

this centre be [cf. *Selection 30*]. This shows that the centre of attention is not anatomically fixed; it shows also (cf. p. 132) how the subjective field of vision varies in organization from case to case. These results also prove (cf. p. 137) that attention is not a *deus ex machina*; it does not arbitrarily determine the centre of vision (e.g. fixation point). Organization of the visual field normally occurs not as a product of the patient's arbitrary "intention", but of its own accord relative to the objects offered for perception. (156 f.): the pseudo-fovea, or new centre of vision, does not lie at the geometric mid-point of the functionally competent region; it is the "centre" of the subjective, not the objective field of vision. (158–169): omitted.]

Selection 29

COMPLETION PHENOMENA IN HEMIANOPIC VISION

By Wilhelm Fuchs

"Untersuchung über das Sehen der Hemianopiker und Hemiamblyopiker, II. Die totalisierende Gestaltauffassung," *Zeitschr. f. Psychol.*, 1921, **86**, 1–143.

3 The preceding *Selection* has reported errors of localization when
the exposed stimulus object was in the area of reduced vision alone
and also when both regions were involved (pp. 74 f. and 79 f.).
The latter cases show that the displacements were of whole-figures,
since stimulus objects falling only in the functionally competent
region were never displaced. The displacement of dot-figures
provided still further evidence that the entire constellation of dots
had functioned as a single unity. The processes occurring in such
4 cases must, therefore, have been whole-processes. The " totalized
whole-apprehensions " or, as we shall more frequently designate
them, " completion phenomena," to be reported in the present
5 paper are additional instances of such whole-processes. The
term " completion " will be used to designate cases where, in
view of the objective conditions, the patient sees *more* in the
6 blind or amblyopic area than he " really " can see. . . . Our
results with hemianopic, hemiamblyopic, and normal vision will
be treated separately.

The totalized whole-apprehension: 1. In hemianopic vision.—
There are some hemianopic cases where completion never occurs.
This is especially true when the patient has the experience of seeing
" black " or " darkness " in the blind region. Our report deals
only with cases where completion of some kind did occur. A
typical example of this was B. [case history omitted]; the following
7 report of his results will reveal the general nature of completion
phenomena. B. was unable to see anything on his left side, yet
8 when shown (tachistoscopically) a disk, outline circle, or ring in
such a way that it encircled the fixation point, his partial blindness
seemed completely overcome.[1] This was true also of solid squares

[1] [Pp. 16–17: the patient experienced thoroughly unified figures and his impressions in the blind area had in nearly every case the same character as those of the competent region.]

Grateful acknowledgment is hereby made to *Johann Ambrosius Barth, Verlagsbuchhandlungen*, Leipzig, for permission to reproduce the illustrations used in this Selection.

and both solid and outlined ellipses. With outlined squares there was no completion. Figs. 1 and 2 were readily seen in their completed form when exposed so that the vertical line passed through the fixation point.

9 If the hemianopic area is really blind (as perimetric and campimetric examination would tend to show), these completions must be due to central processes. If, however, the area were only amblyopic, then the completions might have been due to excitations occurring in the injured part of the retina. To check this we introduced certain irregularities in that part of the circle falling in the injured region or even omitted part of the circle. Nevertheless
the patient reported having seen a full circle in all these cases.
10 Indeed it was possible to omit as much as half of the figure without
11 disturbing the patient's impression of a total circle. If more than
half was left out, the circle was not completed. Nevertheless a partial completion occurred even here, for when the patient drew

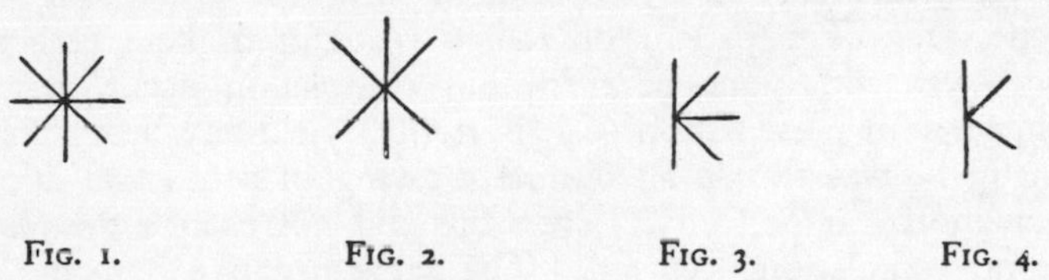

FIG. 1. FIG. 2. FIG. 3. FIG. 4.

a picture of what he had seen he indicated more than had actually been presented. In no case, however, was less than half a circle fully completed.

Figs. 3 and 4 gave particularly interesting results. If exposed so that the vertical line passed through the fixation point and the arms extended into the perceived area, the figures would usually be seen as Figs. 1 and 2 respectively, i.e. completed. If presented with the arms passing into the blind area, the patient saw only a vertical line and nothing more.

Within certain limits totalized whole-apprehensions do not depend upon the size of the stimulus object. When half or, better,
more than half of the figure was given in the competent area, B.
12 completed circles of a diameter up to 30 cm. (observation distance
1 m.). In connection with this study of size we made the following discovery. With the observation distance constant we presented first 4 cm. of a 10 cm. circle and then 20 cm. of a 30 cm. circle. The latter was completed, the former not. Of the former only 6 cm. had been lacking while the latter was 10 cm. short of objective

completeness, yet completion of the smaller circle was impossible because not *enough of the figure* had been given. In other words, completion depends far less upon the absolute *size* of the circle than it does upon the condition that enough figural impetus be given on the uninjured side. Absolute size is important only as regards surveyability: circles of over 30 cm. diameter were not completed even when a relatively small piece (e.g. 10 cm. from a 35 cm. circle) was missing. Neither was it possible to improve these results materially by increasing the observation distance. It was never possible to secure completion of circles three times or even twice as large merely by lengthening the observation distance from 1 to 3 metres. Optimal surveyability evidently depends not upon the size of the retinal image, but upon the *apparent* size of the circle—and this was not materially altered within the limited
13 range of observation distances which we used.

To study the influence of familiarity with the objects presented we performed a series of experiments using *pictures*: dog, face, bottle, etc. The patient obviously recognized these objects at once—yet with none of them did completion occur, nor did
14 symmetry of presentation (e.g. butterfly) yield any better results. Finally he was shown an outline drawing of a fish and allowed to memorize it perfectly. Even this did not change the results, for no completion occurred. The same negative outcome held also for letters and words.

The question of "simplicity".—From our results thus far it might be concluded that only very "simple" figures can be completed and that the meaningful pictures were too "complex". And in a certain sense this is correct. It is not true, however, that the "simplest" geometrical figure—a straight line—is more readily
15 completed than any other. A straight line extending from the visible into the injured area is *never* completed; it always *stops* approximately in the region of the fixation point. The reason for its non-completion may be easily seen from our foregoing reports. That portion of the line falling in the competent area requires no "completion", for it already possesses the appearance of something complete as it is. This does not, however, contradict the results of our star-shaped figures which were themselves composed of "straight lines". A single, isolated line is phenomenally quite different from the (objectively) same line in a star such as those of Figs. 1–2.

A horizontal line presented with the fixation point in the centre —×— or one falling only in the uninjured area ×—— will not be

completed. This holds also for diagonal lines  and  or 
and  . It will be seen that when the vertical line is added we
have here the geometric elements of Figs. 1–2. The results show,
16 therefore, that that which is completed is not a group of independent lines, but the star. When the *star* is seen these lines no longer have the character of " lines ". Through participation in the star figure their independence is lost and their role in the perceiver's consciousness is changed. [The question of simplicity is discussed again below, p. 81 f.]

18 *The influence of a critical attitude.*—In connection with these studies it was discovered that if the patient's attention became more critical, the completion phenomenon was disturbed or would even disappear altogether. Specific investigation of this was not carried out with B. but with another patient, Th. (right-sided hemianopsia).

19 The phenomenon of completion was with Th. as clear-cut as
20 in the case of B., already reported. When, however, the patient was asked whether he had really seen the entire object, he replied in the affirmative, but added that the question had made him more " critical ". Thereafter he reported the right side as not exactly seen; then that he merely " supposed " the figure must extend on into the right side; still later he reported that he " could not say for sure ". Finally he ceased reporting any completions.

[21–25 : it is evident from this rapid upset that the phenomenon can be considerably influenced by the type and manner of instructions given. To investigate this phase of the problem it was necessary to use a new subject. The patient Gr. (right-sided hemianopsia) observed in this series. The completion phenomenon was clearly exemplified. The " attention " technique was repeated and the phenomenon disappeared. After several weeks it reappeared for circles.]

26 2. *In hemiamblyopic vision.*—It is ordinarily assumed that any
27 vision in the amblyopic region will be due to retinal stimulation. We shall show, however, that at least part of the perception occurring in this region is a completion phenomenon of the central physiolo-
29 gical processes. The first patient was Br. whose peripheral vision
[30-32 : omitted] of objects to his right was inadequate; anything at rest in this region was invisible. He was unaware of the defect.

33 A circle tachistoscopically exposed and falling within the injured
34 area was invisible. When, however, presentation was such that

the fixation point was *within* the circle (rightward periphery 6–7 cm. from fixation point) the completion report followed at once. But the same figure which was thus complete when exposed tachistoscopically was once more incomplete (on the right side) when shown continuously for several seconds or minutes.[1] Even
35 with the tachistoscope it was necessary that the centre of gravity should lie within the seeing area. In this our amblyopic patient exactly resembled the hemianopic cases (p. 10 f.). Thus we found
36 that if a 6 cm. segment of a 10 cm. circle fell in the affected area, the entire figure would be dim and indistinct; if the same amount (6 cm.) of a 15 cm. circle penetrated the amblyopic region, the figure was clear and bright throughout. In the *latter* case the circle's centre of gravity lay in the seeing region, in the former it did not.

When a vertical line crossed the right-hand side of a circle presented for completion, it would not be noticed (although a completed circle was reported) if its position was more than 5 cm. to the right of the fixation point. If 5 cm. or nearer, the chord would be seen and a reversed-D figure—*not* a full circle—would
37 be reported. Since a vertical line only a short distance from the fixation point was never seen when presented alone in the right-hand area, it is evident that the circle had effected an enlargement of the visible region. How? The results here would seem to indicate that vision farther rightward from the fixation point than 5 cm. is due to a *central* completion phenomenon, and not a result of retinal impressions.[2] When the chord *was* seen, it formed with the visible part of the circle a new figure (reversed-D) in which the chord played a meaningful role: hence there was no reason
38 why the circle should be completed. The leftward part of the circle was now not part of a " circle " despite the fact that no objective change had occurred in it. It was now an integral part of the reversed-D figure and as such needed no completion.

[39–42: a small circle, *a*, discernible just inside the amblyopic region became invisible when another small circle, *b*, was exposed anywhere in the functionally competent area. When, however, *a* and *b* were connected by curved lines so that they became geometric parts of a ring, "*a*" was readily seen simultaneously with

[1] This difference is, of course, true of normal persons also. Julius Wagner has shown, for example (*Zeitschr. f. Psychol.*, 1918, **80**, 1–75), that whereas up to twenty letters can be seen tachistoscopically, only six or seven will be seen if one looks at them steadily.

[2] [That this is not to be taken as a final conclusion is shown below: p. 43 f., esp. p. 47.]

"*b*" and all the other geometric parts of this circle. Indeed, "*a*" was now lively and bright, which it had not been before.]

43 From the results of our first chord experiments (p. 36) it appeared that completion of the circle could not have been due to impressions from the more eccentric portion of the retina. This conclusion is not, however, wholly justified. Let us consider the results of the following experiment.

A blue circle 13 cm. in diameter was so presented that the right side was 5 cm. from the fixation point (patient Br.). Although with steady gaze the right extreme was invisible, with tachistoscopic exposure the entire circle was seen and both sides were bright
44 blue. We now added a black dot 4 cm. in diameter (Fig. 5). The patient failed to report this and still failed even when told to notice the right side very carefully. Nor was the dot visible when moved to the position of Fig. 6 (1 cm. from fixation point). Instead a full, bright blue circle was reported at each exposition. We showed Fig. 6 again and let the patient inspect it carefully

Fig. 5. Fig. 6.

(head- and eye-movements). He still did not see the dot when we again exposed the figure tachistoscopically. Finally the dot was
45 moved to the fixation point so that its left side could be seen. Now he reported that a contact had been established between the fixation point and the right-hand rim of the circle. He did not see anything filling this region but nevertheless reported that it was not empty. After several more expositions the black dot seemed to extend all the way to the rim of the circle.

Comparing these results with those of the chord experiment we find that whereas the narrow line (chord) was seen even when situated as much as 5 cm. from the fixation point, the much larger and more conspicuous [*reizstärker*] dot could not be detected until juxtaposed with the fixation point. What bearing has this on the general question of thresholds? The completion process
46 of the larger circle was not disturbed by the concurrently exposed dot. When the chord was shown (within 5 cm.) completion of the *circle* failed to occur and a reversed-D was seen instead. Under the conditions of these two experiments the chord became a figural part of the circular line (leftward), the dot did not. Expressed with

special reference to the question of thresholds (in normal as well as the present cases) our results may be formulated as follows. The absolute threshold for peripheral stimulation or for stimulation in the amblyopic zone can be lowered by appropriate figural cohesion between the eccentrically and the centrally exposed parts of a figure. By a suitable figural apprehension it is possible to reduce the threshold (and increase the clarity of vision) of a peripheral area even below (above) that of the central region.

In view of these results it is difficult to say whether the rightward part of the circle was " really " seen (i.e. as a consequence
of *retinal* impressions, cf. above p. 39) or whether it was a completion phenomenon in the central physiological processes (cf. above
47 p. 27). It is possible that the right side of our blue circle *was*
" really " seen even though objects *within* the right-hand side of
that circle remained below the threshold. However, acceptance
of this possibility need not exclude the assumption that central
completion processes may also have been involved. The area of
reduced vision was very low in colour sensitivity, yet under the
influence of the circle's figural cohesion both this defect and that
of the amblyopia were completely overcome. We are forced,
therefore, to conclude that central physiological factors were at
least partially involved in bringing about the reported results.

48 Thus far we have not submitted conclusive evidence either for
a theory of retinal impressions or for one of central completions
as alone responsible for our patient's reports.[1] Real vision and
totalized whole-apprehensions cannot be sharply differentiated,
49 for they are connected by transitional phases which frequently
make it impossible to determine where one leaves off and the other
begins. There can be no doubt, however, that central processes
are alone responsible for the completion phenomena in cases
(already reported) where irregularities are not observed or omitted
parts are supplied.

[50–64: similar results were obtained with another patient, Tho. A series of experiments using the patient Prz. (left-sided hemiamblyopsia) as observer is also reported (pp. 52–64). When a small dot (triangular in shape) was presented leftward of an outline circle whose left side fell in the amblyopic region the circle was seen as complete and the dot was localized as being *within* the left side of this figure. The circle itself, however, was *not* displaced. There was, in other words, a displacement of one (the dot) yet not of the other—though the areas involved were identical.

[1] Cf. below p. 52 f.

Evidently the central processes corresponding to these two impressions must themselves have been separate and relatively independent. Such processes must therefore occur in two different parts of the brain or, if at the same place, in specifically different ways.]

65 *Inadequate explanations of the completion phenomenon.*—Is this
phenomenon a result of "imaging" the presented object as
complete? Are our completion results due to the patients' filling
in the "unseen" parts by images based on residua from earlier
67 experiences with the same object? Such an explanation would have
to rely on the principles of association, i.e. it would have to
assume that the parts falling in the injured and uninjured areas
had long been *associated* and that experiencing one now reproduced
68 the other. But, if this were true of the circle and star figures, it
should hold also for the pictures of a face or dog (p. 13). Nor did
symmetry of the meaningful object improve its chances of completion, for the butterfly picture also yielded consistently negative results. The outcome was also negative when the "simplest" possible figure (a straight line) was used. It became negative when a critical attitude was suggested. From these findings we cannot but conclude that a theory of associations between images is incapable of explaining the completion phenomenon.

Nevertheless, instead of drawing final conclusions from these
data let us submit the theories to experimental tests. Using the
69 patient Br. as observer and proceeding first to determine the
influence of "residual factors" we presented a dot-figure to be
memorized. That he had succeeded in this was guaranteed by his
ability to draw the figure from memory. He was then told that
this figure would be shown tachistoscopically in such a way that
70 part of it would fall in the amblyopic area. Despite this he failed
to see any more than when the figure had been tachistoscopically presented before the memorizing. The experiment was repeated several times with different figures and the results were always the same. It seems evident that the completion phenomenon cannot be due to a residuum left by "previous experience".

71 Our next experiment was designed to test the influence of
[72–73 omitted]: frequency of experience. We chose letters of the alphabet as being
forms with which the patient had undoubtedly had a great deal
74 of experience. The fixation point was located within the letter,
about two-thirds of which fell in the competent area. The results
were negative. Everything 1–1·5 cm. to the right of the fixation
75 point was invisible. Yet in the midst of our series a circle, extending

7 cm. into the amblyopic region, was seen at once as both clear and complete. We combined these and presented a letter inside the circle. The letter was seen only in the competent part, the circle in its entirety. Concentrating his attention upon the right side of
77 the letter did not change the results at all. With pictures of everyday objects (face, etc.) the results were similarly negative and the patient himself called attention to the following fact. He recognized *what* the objects were but could see only their left side. Of circles,
78 star figures, etc., on the contrary, he knew that he had actually *seen* the right as well as the left sides. From these findings we conclude
[79–80: omitted] that frequency cannot be the essential factor in completion phenomena.

81 Once more it is apparent that totalized whole-apprehensions (" completions ") are possible only with certain characteristic and hence coercive figures: viz. those whose " really " seen part (i.e. the part falling in the competent region) conveys within itself the law of the *entire* figure [. . . *bei denen der in die gesunde Feldhälfte fallende und daher " wirklich " gesehene Teil bereits das Gesetz des Ganzen in sich trägt*]. Our experiments have shown that only " simple " wholes are completed. But by " simplicity " is not meant the *geometric elements* of a figure such as the stars shown in Figs. 1–2 above. The geometrical components (lines) of these star figures (if presented alone) were never " completed even though the patient reported an entire *star* at each presentation of *that* figure. Completion can and does occur only if the " seen " part implies a *whole* of which it is a *part*—i.e. whose law it already contains. The straight line is autonomous, it is not a " part " referring to a " whole ". The tendency towards wholeness exhibited by an incomplete *part* is a tendency towards simplicity or *Prägnanz*.[1]

82 We have shown that completed wholes are not necessarily those with which the subject had had a great deal of earlier experience. Certainly the stars of Figs. 1–2 had not been more frequently experienced in the past than letters of the alphabet. Nor can it be said that the true circles of our experiments had been seen before more often than the other (non-completed) drawings.

[83–125: the completion phenomenon does not depend solely upon the condition of tachistoscopic presentation. With hemiamblyopic patients totalized whole-apprehensions were also obtained in after-images. This occurred, however, only with figures whose tachistoscopic presentation had also yielded completion reports. Example:

[1] [Generally the German word " *Prägnanz* " cannot as here, however, be translated by the English " simplicity ".]

the patient Prz. (left-sided hemiamblyopsia) was shown (for 20 sec.) a red disk 14·5 cm. in diameter. The left side was invisible; in the after-image a completed green disk was seen. Then a 2 cm. segment at the left was blocked off with black. The after-image was nevertheless complete and the patient reported that "both sides were equally clear". As mentioned above this type of result must be due to central processes alone. That completion occurs only when the "seen" part is apprehended as a part (cf. above p. 81) is demonstrated experimentally. (Pp. 114 f.): two contour circles (diameters 9 and 14 cm.), known to give positive results alone, were presented concentrically. Now only the larger circle was completed. With circles of 12 and 14 cm. completion reports—of a "ring"—were obtained. Thus by inducing the patient to apprehend the smaller circle as part of a figure (of which the larger circle was also a part: viz. a ring), completion of the "smaller circle" was obtained also.]

126 3. *In normal vision.*—The general phenomenon of completion is not limited to cases of brain injury; it is not a pathological occurrence. The same kind of phenomena have long been known through studies of vision in the region of the blind spot. (A hemianopic patient who does not see "black" in the injured area simply has a large "blind spot" on one side.)

127 Let us first notice what previous investigations have disclosed
about the blind spot. (*a*) It is not ordinarily experienced: when we
look at a large, evenly coloured surface there is no "hole" in it
corresponding to the retinal blind area. (*b*) When looking at a
printed page the blind area appears filled. (*c*) A straight line running
from one side to the other of the field of vision and passing through
the blind spot is not seen as broken at that point. If the line is
actually broken within the blind area, it nevertheless is seen as a
continuous line. (*d*) Similarly a circle whose perimeter passes
through the blind spot will be seen as a complete circle. Helmholtz
observed [1] that a small disk falling squarely in this zone and only
128 slightly extending beyond it will be experienced as a unified coloured
130 surface. Our case of a straight line which was not completed
(p. 15 f.) resembles a phenomenon commonly observed in studies
131 of the blind spot: if the *end* of a line enters but does not continue
through the blind spot, that end will not be seen.

132 As mentioned in (*b*), one does not experience an hiatus
corresponding to the blind spot when looking at a page of printed
133 matter; but neither can one read the words at this spot. This

[1] *Physiol. Optik*, 3rd ed. (1910), vol. iii, p. 175.

illustration is important because it shows in what sense completions occur. The page appears as a unified greyish surface, and neither words nor letters are read. The completion occurring in this case is that of a greyish surface. There is, however, another type of apprehension: we see the printed lines as dark stripes across the page separated by brighter spaces of light grey. It is impossible to read words in the blind region, but the *stripes* are completed. Now suppose that certain words in the seeing area become clearly visible as individual objects of attention. One now experiences a number of thoroughly independent forms which have nothing to do with a greyish surface or with stripes. "Reading" of the words or letters can now take place. That is to say, "reading" inevitably causes a disintegration of the surface and of the stripes. It is for this reason that the letters which fill the blind spot cannot be read.[1]

134 Inability to read anything falling in the blind spot does not prove that perception in this region is impossible. Still less proof is contained in the fact that when attention is concentrated upon the blind spot one sees "nothing" in that area. It is possible, by attending very carefully to the straight lines of a Müller-Lyer figure to destroy the illusion. But this is no guarantee that a naïve glance encompassing the whole figure will not reveal an illusory difference in length between the two arrows. "Attention" had destroyed the whole-figure, and the illusion was entirely dependent upon a whole-apprehension of that figure. And the same may be said of concentrating attention upon the blind spot: completion occurs
135 when the greyish surface or the stripes are seen; attention destroys these in favour of other forms.

Were one to argue for the priority of "sensations" it would be incomprehensible how anything could be perceived for which there was no corresponding stimulation to arouse the necessary "sensation". If, however, perception, as a whole-process is primary, then sensations are but the products of analysis—an analysis, namely, which disintegrates the originally available [*ursprünglich*
136 *vorhandene*] whole-process.[2] Specifically: a "good" figure composed of geometric elements, e.g. dots, will be seen entire, without a missing element even when one of its "elements" falls in the blind area. Moreover, the impression at this point will not depend upon impressions being received in the immediate

[1] It is, of course, possible to "read" a word only part of which falls in the blind spot: the entire word is often understood though only part of it is actually seen.

[2] [There are two kinds of analysis: in one a whole is divided into subdivisions already given or implied by the whole itself; in the other an arbitrary principle of division is imposed upon the whole.]

vicinity of the optic disk. The experiment establishing this was performed by K. L. Schaefer.[1] He divided an ordinary writing slate into squares 6 mm. to the side and laid bits of white paper in each alternate square of one horizontal row. Observing this row from a distance great enough to permit all of it to be seen at once he had the impression that it was unbroken (although some of the dots fell in the blind spot). When viewed at an observation distance so chosen that only one square fell in the blind spot, the colour of this region was like that of the remaining (slate) background, i.e. no white square was seen at that place.

137 On the basis of our foregoing discussion these results may be explained as follows. An image of a white bit of paper in the blind spot will arise only when there is a clear and coercive figural impression of " a row of squares ". This impression is really clear only when an observation distance is chosen from which one can survey all or nearly all of the row. At a closer distance the row disintegrates into separate figures. Under these conditions an isolated square falling in the blind spot will not be seen. Physiologically the success of this experiment depends upon the occurrence of a single whole-process for the entire row. The more readily a whole-apprehension takes place, the more easily will lacunæ be filled up. Schaefer used a figure (straight line) which for his purpose is not the most favourable even though it is considered very " simple " in form. A circular arrangement of the dots would probably have yielded much better results. Possibly also a tachis-
138 toscopic exposure would have been better.

In connection with Schaefer's work it may be remarked that in twilight, foveal vision is like that of the blind spot in ordinary light. Vision under these conditions is governed by the same figural laws as those set forth above for the blind spot. These instances (blind spot and twilight vision) do not, however, exhaust the possibilities of completion phenomena in normal vision. If a
139 broken line (black on white) is apprehended as continuous, the hiatus will often be completed by a dark connecting piece not only when the break falls in the blind spot but even when it appears elsewhere in the field of vision.[2] Because of the white ground, however, the completing piece does not attain equality of colour
140 with the line itself. Similarly when two sides of a triangle are presented one will perceive the interior as greyish (compared with the white ground) if the lines are apprehended as enclosing the

[1] *Pflüger's Archiv*, 1915, **160**, 578.

[2] This experiment was first performed by F. Schumann.

affected area, and this grey will be found to stop at the " line " which would connect the other two to form a triangle. This experience disappears when one apprehends the two lines not as sides of a triangle but as constituting a " hook ". From this it is evident that the greying effect was due to an apprehension of the enclosed area as a surface figure. The central physiological completion occurring in this case, while only partial, is essentially the
same as that in the blind spot with normal persons or in the blind
142 area with hemianopic patients. The phenomenon is less vigorous
in normal vision than with our patients (or in the blind spot) because
143 the region in which completion occurs is also sensitive to stimulation from without. For this reason the examples just cited must be thought of as stages merely antecedent to the more pronounced completion phenomena discussed above.

Selection 30

PSEUDO-FOVEA

By Wilhelm Fuchs

"Eine Pseudofovea bei Hemianopikern," *Psychol. Forsch.*, 1922, 1, 157–186.

158 It was mentioned in *Selection 28* (pp. 114 f., esp. p. 129 f.) that with some hemianopic patients a new centre of vision—a pseudo-fovea—was found. In such cases clarity of vision diminishes in all directions from this point—even towards the anatomical (injured) fovea which now functions as a peripheral point. The new centre of vision does not occupy a fixed place upon the retina, but
160 is rather a *functional* centre. The experiments reported below were designed to determine the laws governing the place occupied
161 by this pseudo-fovea. The patient, W., who served as observer was completely hemianopic on the right side.

A new centre of vision.—The patient explained that he had formed
162 the habit of looking to the right of things in order to see them most clearly. He was nevertheless able to fixate " straight ahead " when
163 requested to do so.[1] When a horizontal row of letters was shown him (observation distance 1 m.) the clearest letter proved to be one lying about 6 cm. left of the fixation point [at the same time the total subjective field of vision (measured on the plane upon which the letters appeared) was approximately 12 cm. wide]. At an observation distance of 2 m. the point of maximum clearness was 6·6 cm. left of the fixation point [subjective field of vision approximately 13·8 cm. wide]. The subjective field of vision (measured in the same way) was not greatly increased at observation distances greater than these. At 3 m., for example, the total subjective field of vision was 14·5–15 cm. wide with the point of maximum clearness some 6·8 cm. left of the fixation point, i.e. again approximately in the centre of the field. Had the point of greatest clearness been dependent upon the angle of vision, it should have been, for the latter observation distance, not 6·8 but 18 cm. left of the fixation

[1] Although the patient did not understand the concept " fovea ", anatomical foveal-fixation was nevertheless possible because everything right of the fixated point was black for him : thus fixation was controlled by allowing only half of the fixation point to fall in the seeing area.

Grateful acknowledgment is hereby made to *Julius Springer*, *Verlagsbuchhandlung*, Berlin, for permission to reproduce the illustrations used in this Selection.

point. Thus it seems quite evident that the pseudo-fovea is not anatomically fixed.

164 When the observation distance was held constant (1 m.) and the size of letters varied, the pseudo-foveal point was found to vary in the following manner. With small letters it was nearer the anatomical fovea (fixation point); with larger ones, farther away. With very small letters the point of clearest vision was but 1 cm. left of the fixation point; with large ones it was 6 cm. to the left.

165 We next studied the difference between small letters at an observation distance of 1 m. *versus* large ones at 3 m.—the retinal images being thus identical in size in the two cases. Results: the pseudo-foveal point was not at the same place in both instances. With large letters (at 3 m.) it was farther left than with objectively small
166 letters at 1 m. When taken together these data conclusively prove that the point of clearest vision is determined not by the angle of vision and not by the objective size of the stimulus, but by its apparent (i.e. "perceived") size. That is to say, the pseudo-fovea varies from place to place in the seeing half of the retina relative to the structure of the object seen.

[167–170: tachistoscopic experiments gave results harmonious with those just reported. (169 f.): visual acuity in the pseudo-fovea was found to be better than in the anatomical fovea.]

171 *Clearness in the pseudo-fovea.*—If a letter was seen with maximal clearness, moving it to one side (the original fixation being retained) caused it to become unclear and hazy.[1] When a small letter was thus moved from *its* clearness centre and into the region known (by the experimenter) to be the centre of clarity for *larger letters*
172 it became hazy and dim or even disappeared entirely. It thus appears that every object (within reasonable limits) has in the competent area its own region of maximum clarity.

If large and small letters were presented together in such a way that each occupied its own centre of clearest vision, *both* were clear and distinct. Efforts to alter the centre of clarity by voluntary shifts of *attention* (i.e. by "active" attention) were without noticeable success. Evidently the point of greatest clarity is determined primarily not by active attention but by the figural properties of presented objects.

173 The question naturally arises whether passive attention might not be able to alter the pseudo-foveal centre. As a means of investigating this, two letters were chosen whose point of clarity lay,

[1] When the letter was moved towards the anatomical fovea it either became unclear or, with but slight loss of clearness, disintegrated (cf. below, p. 175).

for the smaller 1·5 cm., for the larger 3 cm., left of the anatomical fovea (cf. Figs. 1 and 2). Our question was whether the smaller letter (ordinarily indistinct at 3 cm.) could not be made to *share* the larger letter's clearness at this distance. The results were negative: the larger letter was sharply contoured and its lines a saturated black; the smaller one appeared hazy, dim and blurred. Thus one can see that clearness in the visual field is a function of figural relationships, not of the direction of attention.

The same result was obtained when the small E was enclosed by a rectangle (Fig. 3). The small letter was merely a diffuse blot or was not seen at all. In other words it had no figural part in the surrounding rectangle and hence did not profit by the clarity of that figure. If diagonals were drawn from the corners of the rectangle to the letter, its centre would usually be seen, but not as an E. If visible at all, it was seen merely as a (somewhat blurred) juncture of the diagonals. Indeed these results persisted even after

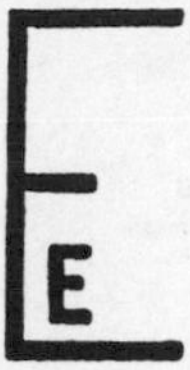

FIG. 1.  FIG. 2.  FIG. 3.

the patient had been permitted to inspect the figure carefully (head- and eye-movements). This shows that neither knowledge of the objective relations nor residual effects left by the inspection were able to increase the clarity of E in this case. Apparently even the diagonals did not suffice to establish a sufficient figural connection with the rectangle, i.e. the E still remains a foreign body not belonging to the rectangle. Thus the condition stands: either E is a mere blur, or, in functioning as intersection of the diagonals, it vanishes entirely. If the rectangle is lightly drawn (pencil) while
175 the E is boldly set forth with ink, they will be seen as equally grey, but although the rectangle appears sharply contoured the E figure is not seen as an E but only as a diffuse blot.

If a *large* letter was exposed beside a clearly seen *small* one, it sometimes appeared dim, sometimes not so much so. But in the latter cases the letter disintegrated and became, instead, a number of small lines or " strokes ".

176 These experiments show at the same time that for small objects

the patient's subjective (and objective) field of vision is more limited than it is when large objects are presented.[1] In other words when looking at a small object the patient's visual space was narrower than when large objects were seen.

177 In order to investigate more closely the influence of figural factors upon clearness we used a design such as that shown in Fig. 4. Notice the angle-lines of the corners and centre. When the figure was presented in its own area of maximum clearness an E was seen. When a small (extraneous) right angle was added (Fig. 5) *it was not* seen. A small right angle such as this can be seen under the present conditions *only* when it appears as an integral part of the large E. Since the centre of maximum clearness for small objects lay approximately 1 cm. left of the fixation point, the small vertical line of our E (Fig. 4) was invisible when exposed

FIG. 4. FIG. 5.

178 2·5 cm. to the left. When, however, the remaining lines were added, the entire E was clearly seen. The patient saw the E as we do here (i.e. composed of short lines with gaps between) and hence (*now*) the small upright line also. The same small line which before had been blurred or even invisible became, now, by virtue of its integral membership in the E-figure, perfectly clear. That which no amount of concentrated attention could accomplish was effected with ease by the larger figure.

179 Now suppose we more or less reverse the procedure. With the large figure clearly seen the patient is requested to concentrate his attention upon the small line. The result of thus segregating the line will sometimes be so pronounced as to render it almost invisible.[2] If the small line does disappear from view, the patient's
180 impression is of a *hole* in the larger figure. Thus we see that attention can cause a clearly perceived, sharply contoured object

[1] A smaller object becomes invisible sooner, i.e. nearer to the pseudo-fovea, than a larger object.

[2] That this should be the consequence of focusing attention upon the small line definitely shows that *attention* is not the source of clarity in these experiments. (Cf. above, p. 172 f. and *Selection 28*, p. 137 f.)

(viz., here, the small line) to vanish entirely. The reason is that over-emphasizing the small line destroys its union with the (larger) figure in which and through which alone the smaller line's clearness was possible.

181 The experiments thus far reported have shown that a small line
falling at a place peripheral from its own centre of clearness will be
clear only when it belongs to and functions as an essential part of
that larger figure. That the presence of other short lines in its
vicinity was not responsible for the clearness or haziness of the
critical line was shown by the following experiment. The patient
was shown a haphazard group of 12–15 small lines; these were for
him a complete blur except when he succeeded in seeing "a large
figure" composed of some of the small lines. When this occurred
the large figure thus seen was perfectly clear; other of the small
lines not included in this figure remained invisible or extremely
182 diffuse. With one assortment of lines, for instance, he saw certain
of them form an ellipse; all the remaining lines were hazy and
183 blurred. These results show that in a chaos of lines such as we have
described only *those* will be clear, saturated, and sharply contoured
184 which together compose a stable figure. And, conversely, it may
happen that a well organized arrangement of such lines becomes
disintegrated: whereupon the lines themselves become blurred.
Obviously there are many possible arrangements in which an
(objectively) irregular assortment of lines can be seen. But of these
the only ones seen clearly are those which may be apprehended as
parts of a stable (*prägnant*) figure. The *size* of an object and its
distance from the fixation point will, of course, play a part
in determining whether or not it is seen clearly; but this is not the
essential condition governing clearness. Not everything of a certain
size will be clear at a certain distance from the fixation point. Only
that will be clear, sharply contoured and definitely formed which
belongs to a *prägnant* figure; all else, despite optimal size, will
be indistinct.

Selection 31

AN APPROACH TO A GESTALT THEORY OF PARANOIC PHENOMENA

By Heinrich Schulte

"Versuch einer Theorie der paranoischen Eigenbeziehung und Wahnbildung," *Psychol. Forsch.*, 1924, 5, 1–23.

1 *Theories of paranoia.*—Numerous theories have been advanced to account for psychoses with delusions of self-reference [*Eigenbeziehung*]. One such theory emphasizes *intellectual* factors: the patient suffers from delusions; or, his memorial imagery is deranged; or, his critical faculties are insufficient; or, such a patient ignores all other modes of interpreting his environment except those referring to his own person.

Another theory stresses *emotional* factors. The most important
2 causes of paranoia according to this view are suspiciousness, uneasiness, a tense expectancy, uncertainty. A third explanation holds that the primary cause of paranoia lies in a pathological intensification of the *ego-functions*, abnormal over-emphasis upon the ego, a heightened self-consciousness. Finally we may mention a fourth theory, viz. that of characterological traits: certain types of people are constitutionally predisposed to paranoia and any shock or injury may bring it about.

It is characteristic of all such theories that the symptom which each stresses is thought of as the primary and irreducible cause, and that all others must therefore be considered secondary and derivative. Yet despite these claims there is no single theory from which one could derive all of the principal symptoms. The present paper is an attempt to formulate such a theory.

Outline of a general theory.—(1) *Some situations demand a "we".*
A situation in which several people are continually together in
3 a restricted space and are engaged there in some common and interrelated enterprise (such as work toward a common goal; or one in which they are subject to a common fate, e.g. soldiers in a dugout) demands [*intendiert*] a "we" rather than a sum of independent egos.

(2) *In certain situations a person is not present as an "I" but as a characteristic part of a "we".*—This means that he feels, acts,

thinks, and behaves not as an ego over against other egos, but as a member of a group. His work and thought, indeed even his perceptions, are determined by this membership.

(3) *The demand for we-ness is not equally effective for all people.*—(*a*) The *situation* may for one type of person (e.g. primitive man) demand we-membership, while for another (e.g. the energetic, self-confident, strong-willed) it may contain no such demand. Or, (*b*) *irrespective* of the we-demands of a situation, certain types of people (e.g. the hysteric suggestible) will tend very easily towards
4 we-membership. The opposite type of person (self-centred, eccentric, malcontent, suspicious) habitually finds group membership difficult and inhibited; with him there is an "insufficiency of we-fitness".

(4) *The situation may demand a "we" and yet the person be incapable for some reason of complying with this demand.*—He cannot feel and act as a member of the "we" even though the claim of group membership is strongly upon him. This may be characterized as "we-crippledness". The we-cripple is poignantly drawn towards genuine group membership, yet he cannot or does not achieve it. Among the sources of this condition the following may be mentioned: (*a*) External cause: the situation may demand a we-group (compare, e.g., (1) above) and yet the person (hereafter designated as A) be unable through some extraneous cause (e.g. he does not speak the same language) to participate. Or perhaps the group is organized around some interest which in its nature precludes A. (*b*) Internal cause: the demanded "we" may have a goal or common task too complex or specialized for A's intelligence; he tries to play the game but fails.

(5) *A state of chronic we-crippledness is for some people unlivable.* There is a continual urge towards membership in the "we", yet it remains as continually unrealized.

(6) *Since this state is unlivable, there develops the following process:* (*a*) A becomes preoccupied with the "chasm" between himself and the group. The attention which in a we-group would be devoted
5 to their common activity focuses now upon this chasm, this incompatibility; and now it is this which becomes vital. It is impossible to be indifferent to such a condition for any length of time. (*b*) There now results a new relationship: "I am no longer 'with-the-others'" in a common union: "I am 'beside-the-others'." (*c*) In a person thus isolated there arises a genuine "I—over against the others". Now one's behaviour and feelings are processes of one's own self—a self with its own appearance, its own goals and ends. (*d*) This is, however, not an ego which stands

firmly, calmly, and self-assuredly in the presence of its environment. Its relation to the demands of we-membership, and the fact of a chasm may be compared to a wound which nature seeks in *any* way possible to heal. The process moves now towards transforming the unlivable into something livable. The following procedures are possible: (i) The ego may be more strongly consolidated. There are people who can, when we-membership fails, learn to stand alone; they mind their own business, think and feel with " objective indifference ". A reaction of this kind exhibits a decided achievement and appears to be always accompanied by intensification of the ego. (ii) Some people, if intelligent and energetic enough, will flee and save themselves by joining another circle. (iii) If neither of the foregoing is possible, a livable state can be achieved by means of a purely subjective reorganization in which actually nonexistent relations are being posited, meanings reinterpreted, etc. The fabrication of this surrogate equilibrium proceeds as follows: (α) The chasm is of such great significance, and influences the person's everyday behaviour so completely, that no ordinary
6 " explanation " for it will suffice. The only satisfactory resolution of the chasm-problem is some kind of union which *does not contain this chasm*. (β) The indifference and preoccupation of the others is now seen in a new light. Even the most unimportant occurrences, the most trivial acts are utilized in closing the wound, and their meanings transformed accordingly. Indifference by another is now interpreted as intentional avoidance. Thus from " I and the others " there has now developed a kind of " with the others " in the sense that " the others are against me." Whereas the others act without any concern for him, he interprets their actions as directed towards, i.e. against him, and in place of the desired but unattainable " we " there is now at least this union of antagonists. Self-reference has thus accomplished a surrogate togetherness. (γ) The most important characteristic of this surrogate equilibrium is its abolition of the chasm, for now the behaviour of the others is intrinsically related to A's we-crippledness. Their " enmity " establishes the genuine union of pursuer and pursued.

(7) *The new relationship is further elaborated into a phantasied system.*—The new apprehension of relations organizes at first, however, only one *part*; an organization extending into and anchored in the past, which is characteristic of all realities, has not yet been accomplished. The new and decisive factor does not yet co-ordinate with A's former attitude in his thinking, feeling, and acting. He must therefore reorganize and reconstruct his entire

world picture. Thus arises the delusional system. But as he becomes more and more absorbed by this process of system-building, A's abilities in all other respects suffer accordingly. Eventually nothing else engrosses his attention so strongly as this.

(8) *By this process a livable state is established in which the person has a genuine function.*—The duration of the period before a delusory system is finished and the nature of this system will, of course, depend upon the kind of situation in which it occurs as well as upon the character and intelligence of the person involved.

7 The foregoing theory refers solely to psychical processes, but one may also view the problem from another side. Just as "we-insufficiency" can in certain situations bring about a paranoic reaction, so also may certain physiological conditions involve an insufficiency for physiological stimuli. The abnormal reactions necessary to overcome this condition probably resemble, in inner organization, the type of psychical reactions outlined above. If one assumes a parallelistic point of view and postulates for psychical processes a series of co-ordinated physiological processes, one can view this or that determining factor in the whole constellation as somatic in character. Seen in this way the distinction between psychical and somatic factors would in a certain sense lose its
8 meaning. What is it, however, that in many cases despite the plausibility of a psychological theory gives us the feeling that the fundamental cause of the disease is organic? This persistent problem seems to obstruct all attempts at the formulation of a psychological theory. It appears to be an argument against our mode of approach that, in the attempt to survey and grasp the essential factors in their relation, it should be in principle immaterial whether one proceeds from the psychical or the somatic side (or from both together). That cases are possible in which the same or similar symptoms will result from a psychical or from an organic cause is true. Would one not expect in such cases that though roughly speaking they yielded the same results, they would nevertheless be different in many important details? Thus, a purely somatic disturbance will often have a more crass, brutal, undifferentiated appearance, and take a more relentless course than would the intrinsically corresponding psychical influence. An individual may, for example, behave in a certain way as a result either of bad news, a sudden fright, etc., or as a result of some toxic influence. In the latter case the effect may very well appear more "brutal" and "undifferentiated". But the effect of somatic brain injury will differ qualitatively from the influence of alarming news *not* because one is physical and the other

psychical, but merely because the physiological effects are cruder and more rigorous than are the psychical.

9 *Examples illustrating the foregoing theory.*—The central factor in our theory is " we-insufficiency ". This concept signifies that psychological comprehension of paranoia with its ideas of reference and delusions can be attained only in terms of the unity of a " we " or group. As the following examples will show, the most significant factors are not arbitrary or purely accidental changes of relationship ; instead the question is what role the person played in human groups, how he fitted in as a part in the we-structure of his associates. It is possible from this point of view to render the traditional concept of insanity much more concrete : not just any derangement relative to the environment, not just any reorganization and recentralization within the individual personality, but something much more definite, something dependent upon the group as a whole and therefore exacted by the chasm-phenomenon in the manner already described.

During the war a wounded Tartar was taken prisoner and placed in a hospital where no one could understand his language, nor he theirs. In a few days he began to have delusions of persecution. He believed that he was being pursued by his ward companions and that his life was threatened. And the ordinary occurrences in his environment were interpreted accordingly. Occasionally he even
10 grew anxious over the fate of his relatives too. These psychotic phenomena disappeared, however, as soon as an interpreter was found who could re-establish language communications with him. The constellation may be interpreted thus : this man had been in intimate contact with his fellow soldiers (camp, trench, etc.). Suddenly he was torn away and found himself, wounded and apart from all his comrades, in an enemy hospital, yet not treated as an enemy. A real " all against me " was lacking, but a real companionship with his new neighbours was also impossible. The conversations of these others served to isolate him still more. His energy and intelligence were insufficient for him as an individual to gain control of this we-exacting situation ; the persistent demands of the present " we " could not be realized, and flight to another was impossible. The conditions for an unlivable situation are thus satisfied, and the result was a surrogate equilibrium established by means of delusions. Now, instead of " all of them " and " I " there did develop a " they against me ". In effecting this delusion he not only interpreted their words and acts but invoked acoustic hallucinations as well. Indeed, not even this sufficed and he therefore developed fears for the welfare of his relatives also.

[11–14: deafness and similar defects which inhibit ease of social relations will sometimes be a contributing factor in bringing about the paranoic process.]

15 As another example we cite the case of a man whose native disposition was decidedly unsocial. His early family life had been unsatisfactory and he himself was mistrustful, self-centred, vain, pedantic in his work, and very ambitious although not unusually capable. He had served in the army and was then a minor clerk in the War Office.

His delusions began on the day war was declared in 1914. Certain of the documents with which he had to work were checked with red pencil when they reached his desk. This was an accusation signifying that he was a socialist. There followed a vehement self-defence and soon all colours conveyed special meanings for him.[1] Then followed a phase of specific phantasy regarding his colleagues. By whispering, clearing their throats, and sly observations they were seeking to interrupt his work in order to hasten the time when he would be pensioned. When, in 1917, this did occur there began a general transference of his delusions to other things. He imagined that he was accused of arson, of homosexuality, etc. Finally he decided that his brother-in-law was responsible for all the calumny which pursued him.

This is a typical case of we-insufficiency. Ambitious and vain, he strove to establish his position as an isolationist, and in this way he had achieved a livable state for the narrow range of his everyday life. But with the advent of war a wave of universal we-feeling ran throughout the country. Suddenly there was a chasm between himself and his fellow men, for with him no " we " was possible. A strongly consolidated ego was beyond the powers of his character and intelligence; flight to another circle was equally impossible. The result was an unlivable state and to establish another equilibrium, therefore, became imperative. As we have said, it is not enough that the chasm be recognized; the situation must be resolved in some unity which does not contain this chasm.

16 It is at this point that reinterpretation of meanings sets in. Formerly a red mark on the margin of some document had meant that he was to examine the items occurring at that place. On the day that war was declared these same remarks meant that his superiors were calling attention to his socialism. For him this conclusion bore all the marks of a logical certainty; it was the

[1] A black cloth indicated his approaching death, white testified to his innocence, blue dresses signified that he was stupid.

sudden discovery of a real and inner meaning.[1] Whereas earlier the particular *colour* of the marginal check was a purely arbitrary attribute, now it occupied the central place in his judgment. The next phase in his delusion, it will be remembered, was to ascribe special meanings to all colours. Thus the chasm was bridged. But only one part of the whole constellation had now been newly organized. How does the process go on from here in order to bring about the whole new organization? (Cf. (7) above.)

The colour phase soon passed and the patient had no memory of its ever having occurred. This shows that the colour factor was not intrinsically related to the newly developing phantasies; it was merely a means of emotional discharge. Soon, therefore, another focusing point for the surrogate picture was found; a centre, namely, which served much better in bringing about a meaningful transition to the "against me" necessary for we-union.
17 This phase took the form of imagined harassment by his colleagues. Eventually the various delusions which had arisen were organized (with strict consistency) into a logically developed system centring around his brother-in-law.

Critical examination of our theory.—There are cases of paranoia whose development can be shown to conform with our theory. There are others where, from lack of data, this cannot be done. Are there, however, paranoic phenomena which do not fall within the pattern we have sketched? The following crucial questions may be raised.

(1) Often incipient paranoia is first manifested by a vague feeling that the environment has mysteriously, enigmatically, indefinably changed. This feeling may precede any recognizable symptoms of reinterpretation. Yet our theory would seemingly say that reinterpretations (particularly of human behaviour) are the first symptoms of the bridging process. This is not, however, a contradiction. Indeed it is not a rare occurrence for a psychical conflict which has not yet been concretely grasped to express itself in this way. The chasm as such need not be immediately sensed for "something" about the environment to seem different. Indeed it seems quite plausible that a preliminary state consisting of the mysterious and indefinite should precede the stage of actual manifestation. When it does occur this preliminary state gives way after a shorter or longer period to one of concrete reinterpretation.

18 (2) Why does the paranoic reinterpret not only human acts, gestures, etc., but also the meanings of inanimate things? The

[1] Cf. *Selection 23.*

answer is that reinterpretations of inanimate objects refer not to those objects as such but to the motives of human beings responsible for them. There is no difference between reinterpreting the way a person acts and reinterpreting an object which he places in such and such a position (cf., e.g., the marginal check marks). There appear to be no cases of a paranoic's reinterpreting inanimate objects which are beyond human control.

(3) Are there not some reinterpretations which do not serve to eliminate the chasm-problem by a surrogate structure? Are not objects and human acts reinterpreted which have nothing whatever to do with the "we" to which the person could not belong? There are, surely, but not at first. Reinterpretations of this kind occur only after the surrogate structure has come to occupy the centre of attention. In the process of system construction anything may now be drawn in and used.

19 (4) In cases such as our example of language isolation there is a clearly defined we-situation, but how may one account for less definite instances? Must one in every case seek out the we-situation no matter how vague? The real problem here lies not with our theory but with the inadequacy of psychological knowledge regarding we-structures in general. It is at present impossible adequately to determine the nature of we-phenomena; yet it is known that very few human beings can continue a healthy existence without some kind of "we" association.

(5) [omitted].

20 (6) Is it necessary that reinterpretation should always proceed towards an imagined "they are *against* me"? No, it is also in keeping with our theory that, indicated preliminary conditions being satisfied, paranoia might fully as well develop in the direction "they are *for* me". The reinterpretation may be as complete in this case as in the other, and hence as regards the formation of a surrogate picture there is no difference. A young man may love a girl who ignores him completely. For him the situation of "I and she" (separately) may be intolerable. If, now, he interprets insignificant acts on her part as being in reality directed towards him, he establishes delusional relationships that do not otherwise exist. The result may be surrogate equilibrium in which "she loves me".

(7) Is our theory able to account for delusions of grandeur? It is very possible that delusions of grandeur may arise, in some cases at least, as a result of steps such as our theory sets forth.

[21–23: omitted. In this concluding section Freud's theory of paranoia is examined and rejected.]

III. REPLIES

Selection 32

REPLY TO V. BENUSSI

By Kurt Koffka

"Zur Grundlegung der Wahrnehmungspsychologie. Eine Auseinandersetzung mit V. Benussi," *Zeitschr. f. Psychol.*, 1915, **73**, 11–90.

Introduction.[1]—In his studies of the Müller-Lyer and other illusory figures Kenkel found that with stroboscopic exposure objectively *equal* lines in these figures would be seen to expand and contract (α-movement) just as two similarly exposed objectively *unequal* lines will do (β-movement). Moreover it was found that the α- and β-movements were commensurable in the sense that they can be added (algebraically) to each other; also that the influences exerted by fixation, attention, length of observation period, etc., were the same for both; and, finally that with each the stages of succession, optimal movement, and simultaneity could be demonstrated. In the theoretical conclusion to this paper Kenkel argues that these results show the α- and β-movements to be *functionally* as well as descriptively the same. With this Benussi [2] takes issue. It is the purpose of this paper to examine Benussi's theory and compare it with that which Kenkel's inquiry supports.

14 In criticizing Kenkel's studies Benussi maintains that apparent differences between his own theory and ours are merely the result of misinterpretations of his doctrine. In order, therefore, to distinguish between these theories experimentally it is first necessary to juxtapose the two theories themselves, particularly as regards their respective positions in formulating experimental problems.

15 *Benussi's production theory.*—What kind of experiences are those in which Gestalten are apprehended? Benussi holds that they are presentational, i.e. experiences in which we are able to apprehend an object or thing with complete sensory freshness and clarity. Hence it is impossible to discover by introspection whether any

[1] [Based on pp. 70 f., below; the reference is to F. Kenkel, "Untersuchungen über den Zusammenhang zwischen Erscheinungsgrösse und Erscheinungsbewegung bei einigen sogenannten optischen Täuschungen," *Zeitschr. f. Psychol.*, 1913, **67**, 358–449.]

[2] "Referat über: Koffka-Kenkel, 'Beiträge zur Psychologie der Gestalt- und Bewegungserlebnisse,'" *Arch. f. d. ges. Psychol.*, 1914, **32**.

given presentation is a Gestalt or a sensation. In opposition, however, to this descriptive similarity they do differ from one another genetically. The difference lies in their relation to the external stimuli, in the following ways: (1) Gestalt presentations have, strictly speaking, no stimuli [i.e. they are *reizlos*]; (2) compared with the stimuli which indirectly release them, these presentations are characterized by *ambiguity*; and (3) *inadequacy*. Moreover, in addition to sensory activity a Gestalt presentation involves a
16 process known as *production.*[1] It is the function of this process to work up or organize the contents of sensory activity.[2] Thus the
17 arousal of a Gestalt presentation, according to Benussi, requires that there be "inferior presentations" (usually sensory contents) which are then brought into dynamic relation [*Realrelation*] by a unique kind of added psychical process.

As regards the role played by inferiora in the superior presentations, three possibilities must be considered: (1) they occur beside the superior; (2) they disappear in favour of the superior; (3) they remain, more or less modified, in the superior as its com-
18 ponents. Benussi rejects the first two of these and retains the third. As analogy for the latter he refers to the chemical relations of H and O in H_2O. With reference to the question of inadequacy he maintains that inferior presentations are completely adequate and that it is due to an anomaly of the production process that inadequacy appears in the superior presentations. It is one of Benussi's cardinal theses that super-sensory inadequacy comes about only through the apprehension of a Gestalt.

Sensations precede the production process which organizes
19 and changes them. Benussi further elaborates this point by reference to his concept of ambiguity, by which he means that *different* Gestalt presentations may be determined by the *same* stimulus object. But not only are the stimuli from the object constant, so also are the *sensory contents*. Thus again we see that Benussi's theory of Gestalt presentations demands the presence of sensations. It may also be observed that these sensations exemplify the so-called "constancy hypothesis" as defined by Köhler: viz. that the stimuli alone determine sensory contents.[3]

[1] This process is variously designated by Benussi as a psychical operation, a psychic activity, an intellectual process, a psychic accomplishment, an event defying description but resembling a process of synthesis. [Here, as elsewhere in this paper, the statement of Benussi's theory is in every point substantiated by references to his writings, twelve of which are listed in the bibliography.]

[2] The operation, Benussi says, frequently requires a noticeable interval of time.

[3] "Über unbemerkte Empfindungen und Urteilstäuschungen," *Zeitschr. f. Psychol.*, 1913, **66**, 51–80, esp. p. 52.

The argument advanced by Benussi for his theory that Gestalt
presentations have no stimuli runs as follows: There are objects
which have no reality ("ideal objects") and cannot therefore act
20 upon our senses. Their "basis" is in real objects and they are
therefore given the name superiora as against inferiora. Thus a
melody is called a superior relative to the individual tones from
which it is composed. But since ideal objects cannot affect our
senses and we nevertheless have presentations of them, they must
be due to some psychical process other than sensory activity. It
is the function of the senses to provide the inferior contents for
this process to organize. If stimuli corresponding to the tones *c*
and *g* affect our auditory organs, there are, as regards our inner
experience, three possibilities: our thought may be directed towards
the tones *c* and *g*, or towards the interval (fifth), or towards the
21 tonal distance. In the last two cases, Benussi says, our thought
is undeniably directed towards something *more* than the two tones
c and *g*; and he asks: does there correspond to this enrichment
an added sensory process or even an added stimulus? Are there
physical *stimuli* which correspond to the *interval* and *tonal distance*
such as those corresponding to the tones *c* and *g*? Certainly not.
It follows that the apprehension of such ideal objects is only
possible by means of such presentations as are completely
independent of all sensory activity because their objects have no
co-ordinated stimuli. It is the process leading to such presentations
which Benussi calls *production*.

We turn now to Benussi's ambiguity argument. The fact that
a line may appear longer or shorter than it "really" is (Müller-
Lyer illusion) seems important to Benussi because, he says, this
must be due to something outside the sphere of purely sensory
activity and apart from the constant stimulus object. Thus in
22 reporting his study of a typical black-white pattern which may
be seen as a black figure on white ground, or vice versa, Benussi
contrasts the equivocal presentations occurring in such cases with
the unequivocal apprehension one may have, say, of a piece of red
paper. There must be, he concludes, another process, X, which
23 takes place between the sensory impressions and the presentation
of figures, else it would be impossible for these presentations to
change while the sensory impressions remained constant. But not
only this. It is often possible for the observer in some measure to
[24–25: omitted] control the presentational process. The sensory material remaining
constant, he can at will apprehend the figure or largely prevent this
Gestalt presentation from occurring.

26 *Criticism of the production theory.*—Let us first examine the criteria by which Benussi distinguishes between sensory and super-sensory presentations.

1. *Ambiguity.*—We reject Benussi's claim that in ambiguous Gestalt presentations there is constancy of sensation during the changes which the presentation undergoes. Benussi says that it is possible for Gestalt presentations to change despite constancy not only of stimulation but also of sensory data [*Empfindungsmaterial*]. He cannot, however, offer direct evidence to support this contention, for if direct observation of Gestalt presentations were able to yield evidence of constant sensory data [*Sinnesvorstellungen*], this would mean that Gestalt- and sensory-presentations were as such and simultaneously accessible to introspection, and this Benussi denies.
27 Thus we see that the production theory cannot be supported by direct observation. Moreover, if constant sensory contents cannot be observed directly, yet are necessary for the occurrence of Gestalt presentations, they must be assumed as *unnoticed*. But that grounds for this assumption are just as undemonstrable as they are for the constancy hypothesis has been too clearly shown by Köhler [1] to require repetition here. The sensory contents (sensations) of Gestalt presentations, which the production theory claims, are therefore merely hypostatized; there is neither evidence nor any
28 possibility of evidence for the relationship between stimulus and sensation which is here postulated. It would seem better, therefore, to abandon this part of the theory entirely. Only then can one attain a recognition of self-sufficient Gestalt experiences.

Nor will ambiguity serve as a rigid criterion to distinguish sensory- and Gestalt-presentations. Benussi says, "I show a piece of red paper [to a number of people] and ask, 'What colour is this?' The answers are quite free from contradiction." But the answer "red" is by no means unambiguous: the red may be dull or
29 brilliant, it may be of a loose or firm texture, be more or less yellowish or bluish, it may be more or less warm, more or less impressive. None of this is expressed nor can it be expressed in a manner enabling one to conclude that all of the answers are really the same. It is possible that under the same external conditions the red may be seen now in one way, now another; and it is very probable that certain properties occur together: e.g. dull and cold, firmly textured and but slightly impressive, brilliant and warm. This ambiguity of contents with the same stimulus object might be explained in terms of the production theory thus: (1) we may

[1] Ibid., pp. 58 f. and 78.

consider *one* mode of appearance to be sensory, all others are super-sensory; or (2) we may say that they are *all* the result of production. The first assumption supplies no criterion by which to distinguish the uniquely sensory mode from all the others; the second would have to invoke red-sensations which lacked the qualities we have mentioned, but in doing this it would necessarily transcend all characteristics of red which can be experienced.

Of course minute differences such as these are far less marked than
30 are those between ambiguous Gestalt presentations, but if any ambiguity can be shown to occur in sensations, the criterion of ambiguous-unambiguous which Benussi employs has been proven inadmissible. Indeed the relatively minute ambiguity of sensory data is sometimes very important. One may, for example, select from a scale of greys three which will be perceived in this way: $a=b$, $b=c$, but a does not equal c. If one retains the doctrine that sensory contents are unambiguous, one is forced to explain the results here as due to unnoticed differences. But this hypothesis exactly resembles that of unnoticed sensations in also being undemonstrable.

31 The reliability of Benussi's ambiguous-unambiguous criterion may be further impugned if certain presentations which he would undoubtedly classify as super-sensory are found to be unambiguous. When, on a cloudless day, one looks from a mountain top at the sky directly overhead, one sees an unambiguous expanse of blue. Yet according to the theory all surfaces are produced presentations (spatial order). But more than this, the Gestalt presentations whose ambiguity Benussi has reported were themselves composed of Gestalt presentations (lines, angles, etc.), not of simple sensations. Yet the perception of these inferiora, he says, contains no illusory effect. This clearly shows that for him these inferiora are unambiguous so long as they do not enter into some larger Gestalt presentation. We must conclude, then, that it is not characteristic of all sensations to be unambiguous, nor of all Gestalt presentations to be ambiguous.

33 2. *Without stimuli.*—We turn now to the questions raised by Benussi's claim that Gestalt presentations are without stimuli. In characterizing a real object as a *stimulus* we do not refer to any absolute property of that object, in and by itself, but only to the object's relation to a living organism. The question whether or not there can be stimuli for certain processes in the organism cannot be decided therefore solely by a physical examination of the objects. Instead the inspection must be extended to cover the relations of

these objects to the organism. Such an inquiry clearly reveals that
34 there are " Gestalt stimuli ". The same object can be for the same organism at one time a " sensation stimulus " and at another a " Gestalt stimulus ", depending in each case upon the state of the organism.

In his example of the tones *c* and *g* (above, pp. 20–21) Benussi says that one's experiences may change even though the physical data remain constant. He proceeds then to ascribe to the *stimulus* a constancy which actually holds for nothing but the physical data. This would be legitimate only if the constancy hypothesis were valid. But the definition of stimulation as given above rules out that hypothesis entirely. And the same holds for Benussi's argument that it would be a hopeless undertaking to look for the stimuli (analogous to those for tones) underlying such a presentation as " difference ". The search would be hopeless only if, having committed one's self to the constancy hypothesis, one sought exclusively among external physical objects. The question regarding the existence of stimuli can be formulated thus: Are there physical processes which are functionally related to conscious processes? Even though one might find (or believe) that there are only " and-summations " in the physical world, one could not conclude from this alone whether or not there were stimuli for Gestalt presentations (which are more than mere and-syntheses). Hence even if there were no physical Gestalten, there might nevertheless be stimuli for Gestalt presentations. Every psychologist knows that the number of variable moments of an air vibration does not tell us the number of attributes a tone sensation will have. Yet no psychologist would think of saying that the " more " of sensation attributes relative to the stimulus moments was *without stimuli.* In our present case the principles are exactly the same: to say that Gestalt presentations have no stimuli corresponds to saying that tonal attributes are without stimuli.

36 The claim that there are no real Gestalten asserts that physical reality contains nothing but and-summations. Whether or not this holds for physics may be left aside; [1] our problem has to do with the processes of the central nervous system which we may think of as correlated with Gestalt presentations. Benussi himself admits that there must be some physiological correlate of produced presentations, but he declines to speculate about their nature. For our own part it appears fruitful to make this attempt, and our first suggestion is that these processes are not to be viewed as sums

[1] Cf. *Selection 3.*

of individual excitations, but as organized whole-processes. In
this way one avoids all notions of Gestalt presentations as bizarre
37 and unique phenomena. We may in fact place the *experiencing*
of Gestalt presentations squarely beside that of *creating* Gestalten ;
to sing or play a melody, dash off a sketch, write, etc., are not cases
where one sings or plays *tones*, or where one draws or writes *strokes*.
The motor act is an *organized whole-process* ; the many individual
movements can be understood only as *parts* of the process which
embraces them, and it is indeed only thus that they attain their
particularity.

[38–56 : an examination and rejection of Benussi's theory of adequacy-inadequacy as applied to sensory and Gestalt presentations.]

57 *An opposing theory.*—The theory we shall advance in opposition to Benussi's may be compared with that of American Functional Psychology since in both cases the principle of a fixed relationship between stimulus and sensation (Structural Psychology) has been discarded in favour of a biological point of view : the organism in its environment.

Descriptively this theory holds that the objects of experience (both simultaneous and successive) are not typically summative, composed of and decomposable into elements ; instead, " experiences are usually organized wholes whose parts are co-ordinated in a hierarchical system around a central point. Such structures (Gestalten) are in no way less immediate than their parts ; indeed one often apprehends a whole before anything regarding its parts is apprehended " (Wertheimer). For this reason a pure description of one's experiences cannot be oriented towards the concept of sensation ; its point of departure is, rather, that of the Gestalt and its properties.

Functionally the theory rejects sensations (psychophysical
definition) as the typical connection between stimulation and experience. Just as Gestalten are descriptively no less immediate
than their parts, so are they functionally no less primary. Attempts
to derive the whole from its parts or to erect it upon them are very
58 often futile, wholes not being created by combination of pieces
but being direct experience-correlates of the stimuli ; thus the
relation between a whole-presentation and a stimulus-pattern is of
the kind which traditional psychology reserved for the relation
between sensation and stimulus. Since purely summative (piecewise) changes in the stimulus object can bring about qualitative
changes in one's experience, one cannot predict merely from a
knowledge of the stimulus object what the experience will be.

Finally, a further complication of the stimulus-experience relationship is that one factor in it is the state of the entire nervous system. It follows that the traditional type of psychological analysis is thus ruled out, because in shifting one's attention for this purpose one continually changes the state of the nervous system and hence also the experience. There is no proof, therefore, that the "sensations" found by such analysis were present in the original perception; indeed sensations, appearing now as a product of analysis, arise under conditions which favour a destruction of the original whole-process. In this both outer and inner conditions may be effective.

Physiologically the theory will treat the brain process correlated
with an experience not as the individual excitation of one brain area
plus association, but as a whole-process with its whole-properties.
59 When we see a figure there are no "founding sensations" and in
addition to these an accessory "Gestalt"-excitation, but rather
the entire process is specifically different accordingly as we
experience Gestalten or "sensations". The essential aspect of
Wertheimer's theory is not, as Benussi claims, "a physico-physio-
logical short-circuit analogy", but a recentring of the entire question.
Whoever is not interested in the physiological aspects of the theory
may leave this part out of consideration; for even without it the
new apprehension of the functional relation between stimulus
and experience is still possible.

Let us now apply the foregoing to the production theory. If, as
we have said, a Gestalt is descriptively no less immediate and
functionally no less primary than sensations, and if its physiological
correlate is a whole-process and not a sum of individual processes,
there is then no reason to postulate unambiguous sensations as
underlying ambiguous Gestalt presentations. Moreover the classificatory significance of ambiguity cannot be maintained because,
as has been shown, there is no boundary functionally between the
60 two classes of experiences (Gestalten and sensations). *All*
experiences are alike in that they depend not only upon stimulation
but also upon the state of the nervous system.

[61–90: a further examination of Benussi's theory of adequacy-inadequacy discloses the *relativity* of these concepts and thus justifies their rejection as criteria for distinguishing between Gestalt and sensory presentations. 70–90: omitted (see "Introduction" footnote above.]

SELECTION 33

REPLY TO G. E. MÜLLER

By Wolfgang Köhler

" Komplextheorie und Gestalttheorie, Antwort auf G. E. Müllers Schrift gleichen Namens," *Psychol. Forsch.*, 1925, **6**, 358–416.

389 *Introduction.*—On the basis of his own [associationistic] theory of whole phenomena in perception G. E. Müller launches a vigorous attack against the methods of working which characterize the Gestalt theory.[1] The polemic is unduly simplified by Müller's failure even to mention some of the essential doctrines of his opponents while at the same time falsely attributing to them assumptions which they do not themselves make.

The question of part-whole relationship.—Müller denies that Koffka's statement, " Gestalten are in no way less direct

[1] [A résumé of Müller's book, *Komplextheorie und Gestalttheorie*, and a criticism of it are given on pp. 358–388 of the present paper. No summary of these pages is given here because a further condensation of the material could not be made without doing an injustice to both authors. The theory : Müller maintains that the perception of wholes, whether simultaneous or successive, is accomplished by a process of collective attention in which the elements composing these wholes are associatively combined. Since this process occurs below the threshold of consciousness we are not aware of the elements themselves and the group enters consciousness as a unified complex. The criticism : (i) Müller's theory throws no light on the problem of which elements will be combined, and under what circumstances. Indeed his theory would tend to exclude the possibility of this question being raised. (ii) He also fails to define the term " attention " which in his theory plays so important a role. (iii) The theory demands the impossible accomplishment that mutually exclusive processes shall occur simultaneously : e.g. letters are composed of elements and must be apprehended collectively ; they, however, compose words, to apprehend which in turn also requires a collective process. (iv) The theory errs in fact when it argues that " collective " (Gestalt) apprehensions are more difficult to achieve when one is fatigued. (v) It lies outside the province of this theory to distinguish between genuine *parts* of a figure and the " parts " or pieces which make it up geometrically (see below pp. 390–395). (vi) The associationistic doctrine set forth in Müller's theory is incorrect in holding that the " parts " of a whole are the same whether they appear in this whole or not. (vii) The argument by which this theory attempts to account for the specific whole-properties of a complex is circular : the whole-properties of a complex are given by its relations, but relation-experiences (when they occur at all) are due to the whole-properties of the complex. (viii) The term " collective attention " undergoes an unexplained shift of meaning in the latter half of Müller's book. (ix) The argument is again circular when, despite his insistence that wholes and their whole-properties arise as a result of collective attention, Müller nevertheless says that collective attention itself is determined by the whole-properties of the observed object.]

[*unmittelbar*] than their parts " contains anything novel. But if this is really so obvious to him, how can Müller base an entire book on the opposite point of view? In Müller's theory the collective attention takes parts and combines them into complexes, and this means that these parts *precede* the complex. For him attention builds up wholes out of parts just as a mason builds a wall out
390 of bricks. If a mason cannot build the wall until bricks are provided for him, so also can there be no theory such as Müller's unless prior elements are presupposed. It is indeed a great pity if Müller's theory cannot accommodate itself to the fact he considers so well known. As a matter of fact, in what sense is this fact known? One often hears that a complex may be grasped before its parts are grasped, yet with many psychologists (of whom Müller himself would be one) this observation has as yet brought about no change in point of view. Instead the fact is quietly passed over by saying, for example, that though the parts are all present, they are not equally noticed, etc. But if this way of speaking merely conceals the assumption that wholes are composed of parts, are erected upon them, are created by a unification of them, etc., the question still remains as to how a whole can be clearly present *before* its parts are clear. How could a whole as a clear, unequivocal structure be determined over and above parts which are not themselves apprehended? How could one create an organized whole if one had attentively to unite parts which were unnoticeable?

Müller seems to overlook entirely that for a view beginning with whole-phenomena the word *part* has an entirely different meaning from what it had in the past or has now in his own usage of it. We find that (if it occurs at all) the articulation of a Gestalt into its *genuine* parts is an essential factor in the nature of the Gestalt-formation itself. Normally a circle, for example, has no natural parts. With the number 8 parts might be distinguished: not just any geometric pieces, however, but if at all, then, the upper and lower halves. Nor is ⌇ a Gestalt part of R. At best the vertical line might be considered a part of this letter. It is primarily the properties of the whole stimulus configuration which determine what the *relatively* separate " natural parts " of a figure shall be. Thus the vertical line in an R is not a " natural part " under all circumstances and in any arbitrary whole. And conversely, ⌇ might in *another* whole become a natural part.

391 According to Müller about the only concrete consequence of Gestalt theory is that an interaction between visual excitations

influences the local conditions of excitation and thereby the local phenomena; this effect, however, does not exist, since the "parts" of a whole retain approximately the same appearance even when apprehended in isolation (subjectively or objectively effected) from that whole. But if he can say this, Müller must be completely unacquainted with the distinction between "natural parts" of a whole (which alone are phenomenally real as *parts*) and arbitrary "pieces". A simple classroom demonstration of this is as follows. One draws on the blackboard an easily apprehended figure and then, while the students seek to hold this figure, one adds a few appropriate lines and the original design disappears.[1] Müller, however, takes as his example the number 10 and finds the appearance of its 1 and 0 but little changed when they are presented alone.[2]

Functionally, also, Müller says, the excitations aroused by a part in a complex are not essentially different from the excitations caused by that part in isolation. He reports that when the subjects in an
392 experiment were instructed to note the occurrence of a certain letter in syllables shown to them, the proper letter seemed to "leap" towards them whenever an appropriate syllable appeared. This would have been impossible, Müller holds, if the excitation caused by the letter had been different when it appeared in the syllable from what it was when seen alone. Certainly, but he commits the error of drawing a general conclusion from this very special case. The parts (letters) investigated in this experiment were themselves relatively separable parts; if he had continued the experiment and used more closely organized figures rather than syllables, and if his "parts" had been *unnaturally* dissevered pieces, he would have seen that nothing would leap out since the critical "part" of such figures would not be present at all.[3] The special case cited by Müller is incapable of substantiating a theory and polemic such as his, particularly when he closes his eyes to the Gestalt problem raised by individual letters themselves: here Müller's conception of "parts" would have no validity at all.

[1] [Cf. the drawings in *Selections 9a* and *9b*.]

[2] [P. 375 f. In choosing a complex such as the number 10 to illustrate his theory Müller selected one in which the parts are very loosely knit. But if he stipulates no principle according to which parts must be chosen for such examples, then ||| may also be taken as (geometric) "parts" of 10. The difference is, of course, that whereas 1 and 0 are genuine parts of 10, the lines ||| are not. (P. 391): it is significant that Müller should, as a matter of fact, choose natural parts to illustrate his argument. Müller himself was determined in this by Gestalt principles even though his theory denies them.]

[3] [The experimental evidence underlying this discussion is given in *Selections 9a* and *9b*.]

But even when parts remain recognizable in the natural articulation of a whole, they may nevertheless be definitely affected by their inclusion in the whole—as is proved by optical illusions. Indeed illusion phenomena are continually present (although usually not detected as such) in everyday life. Fuchs has reported, for example, that even the colours of parts are strongly determined by the whole in which these parts occur.[1] It has also been found that the constancy of colour in an enclosed field is a function of the
393 illumination relationships in the vicinity of that field.[2] And again, that apparently the phenomena of simultaneous contrast are also determined by whole-conditions of the stimulus field.[3]

The outcome of this point of view would be, Müller says, that a visual area would be differently excited in accordance with differences in the colour of its immediate neighbours. He raises the objection that this necessary conclusion has not been drawn by the present writer. The objection is inadmissible, however, for on p. 210 of the *Physische Gestalten* [4] there occurs the sentence: "The colour-quality of a perceived surface will depend upon Gestalt factors". The conclusion cannot be attacked if experience shows that such influences do actually occur. That such is true, Müller himself extensively maintains. The only difference is that he believes the phenomena to be due to an activity of attention.

394 It would be an inexpedient device, Müller argues, for our sensations of isolated parts to be different from those which these parts would call up when appearing in a complex. The struggle for existence requires that a part shall be able to remind us of its whole. In answering this we must first reject the notion that Gestalt phenomena are due to any special "device". Nor should a question of fact be set aside by the issue of "expediency". Müller's argument here suffers from the same misconception as the one above: a part will suggest its whole only if it be a genuine part; if we unnaturally dissever from a well organized whole some arbitrary piece, no reproduction of the whole will be suggested by this "part". And indeed it is biologically advantageous that this should be so. Is it not good that we fail to see the D or P in an R, the F in an E, the x in a Q, etc.? What would become of us if any arbitrary "part" (D, P, F, x) were really to reproduce its whole?

395 Müller's attacks are directed against a "Gestalt theory" which, as he interprets it, says merely that interaction among pre-existent pieces causes changes in those pieces. But, he concludes, since such

[1] Cf. *Selection 7*. [2] Cf. *Selection 16*. [3] Cf. e.g. *Selection 8*.
[4] *Selection 3*; cf. also ibid., pp. 211 ff.

changes can hardly be demonstrated, the theory is bound to fail in the face of all important problems. How can a complex as a whole have specific reproduction effects? "Gestalt theory" could not possibly explain this, he maintains, since the individual and essentially unchanged pieces comprising a complex cannot have lost their own definite, prior associations. But it is precisely this problem which Gestalt theory has been attacking from the beginning. It was the Gestalt theorists who proposed the view that the specific structure of wholes, far more real than any "element", cannot be understood in terms of pre-existent parts; it is they who have demonstrated the reality of physical Gestalten. Surely of all the critics none has before accused Gestalt theory of representing a point of view exactly the opposite of what it does maintain. It is certainly not the Gestalt theorists to whom the specific reproduction effects of wholes should seem inexplicable. On the contrary, the specific reality of structures is set forth by the Gestalt concept in a way not to be found in any other psychological theory.

396 *The role of attention.*—Gestalt theory, according to Müller, abandoned the path of science when it failed to envisage Gestalt perception in terms of attention. When a perceived figure appears now in one form, now another; when a part occurs now alone and again in a larger whole, even the Gestalt theory should admit that such processes are due to attention.

But such an admission cannot be made even for reversible figures since neither the place, time, nor degree of collective attention corresponds with the place, time, or firmness of figural articulation.[1]
To comply therefore with Müller's demand would require that we
397 place ourselves squarely against common experience. This does not mean, of course, that one cannot alter a perceived form by active interference. But we are compelled by common experience to recognize that such occurrences are extremely rare. We experience numberless closely knit Gestalten all day long; we do not, however, as normal human beings ordinarily reverse or disrupt these figural experiences. How does it happen, Müller asks, that upon seeing 10 I at one time say "ten" and at another time "one
398 and zero"? This is done by attention! But it would be utterly

[1] [This subject is treated in greater detail on p. 368 above. Very often one finds attention powerless when confronted by reversible figures. The design is first apprehended in a certain way, let us say, and one then tries to reverse it, but this may fail entirely; then suddenly, even though one may have abandoned the attempt, the reversed figure appears. Or conversely, though one tries to maintain the original apprehension, the other nevertheless appears after a time. Attention has little more to do than to follow along after the change has occurred.]

false to assume that a shift of this sort were an everyday occurrence. When I see a 10 on a clear background I either say nothing or I naturally say " *ten* ". But when one *does* disrupt a presented figure by means of active interference, then one can really appreciate the dominant properties of that figure itself even for the interference. Why is it that Müller finds 1 and 0 the possible alternatives of 10 when looking at the number 10? Why does he not see | | | in the 10? He does not even mention this possibility. The reason is because one's disruption of Gestalten follows along the lines laid down by the articulation of those figures. Otherwise, i.e., if one seeks to disrupt the figure in a way *opposed* to its own articulation, one discovers that the figure has, so to speak, " a will of its own." [1] This much seems undeniable: whatever the nature of the active interference may be, it does not create Gestalten; instead, where such interference is really effective, it merely establishes for the original Gestalt-process a new set of conditions to which it responds in terms of its *own* nature. From a clear grasp of these facts one can only conclude that active attention is merely an added condition for the development of Gestalt-processes.

399 Müller claims that we have failed to show how, in cases where we had to assume the influence of analytic attention on the disruption of whole patterns, a part of the excited neurones could be detached from its functional connection with the rest. To accomplish this, he says, attention would have to exert a most astonishing and incredible influence upon the electrical conduction resistances in the optic sector. One would naturally assume that the author of this criticism must himself have thought the problem through very carefully since he accuses us of negligence in this respect. But in searching for his own deliberations one finds only that attention sometimes combines large complexes, and sometimes singles out smaller units. This, however, is no answer to the question he has raised. At one place, it is true, Müller does refer to the influence of attention as a " reduction of resistances ". This is precisely the hypothesis which he attributes to Gestalt theory and rejects as extremely unsatisfactory.

[400: while not denying that past experience can exert an influence upon present experience (cf. *Selection* 5, p. 331, and *Selection* 4, pp. 518 f.)

[1] [An example given on p. 368 is the following. I look at the papers on my desk and concentrate all my attention on the corner of a paper-weight and the immediately adjacent paper. This region becomes more " lively " and a kind of unity between the two is established; but the unities of weight and paper themselves are certainly not lost. Indeed their unities are not at all comparable to the ineffectual unity of weight and paper which I had myself established.]

we are unwilling to speculate upon the nature of this influence (as Müller demands) until the facts have been properly established without the traditional associationistic bias.]

401 *Physiological theory.*—Müller also maintains that Gestalt theory is unable to account for form-blindness or for totalized whole-apprehensions. As regards the former, he can understand how "elementary sensation processes" may remain intact while the collective apprehension is disturbed, but he cannot see how a physiological whole-process could disappear while the individual cell-processes remained. This argument starts with an erroneous interpretation of the facts, for it is not true that "sensations" remain even when forms cannot be apprehended as such. Instead the processes which occur are degenerate in character (in the direction of chaos); the perceptions of these patients contain
402 not unconnected sensations but hazy and unstable forms. But normal people also experience dissolving, unclear structures as a positive attribute of certain perceptions: e.g. groups of objects seen in insufficient illumination, peripheral vision, tactual experiences where moving the hand is prohibited, etc. One certainly has no difficulty in distinguishing experiences such as these from the occurrence of an unconnected sensation-manifold. Dissolution, unclearness, etc., as the positive attributes of an amorphous region can no more be comprehended in terms of unconnected sensations than can well articulated forms. In addition to the opposites "piece-aggregate—whole-process" there is another dimension whose poles are "organized whole-process—unclarified whole-process".

403 It would be impossible, according to Müller's version of Gestalt theory, for the retinal image of a half-circle to yield the same whole-process as a full-circle would give.[1] If Müller were familiar with the theory of physical Gestalten, he would know that under certain circumstances a half-circle *must* become a full-circle. Totalized whole-apprehensions such as this will occur when it is the best possible, and most *prägnant* development of a perceived form from the competent side of the field towards its unstimulated half.

[404–407: many psychologists have so completely accepted the physiological assumptions of elementarism that they no longer think of them as constituting a physiological theory. Anyone proposing a frank and conscious inquiry into physiological principles is often admonished to abandon the attempt as unprofitable or dangerously confusing. Müller does not condemn an interest in physiology, but

[1] Cf. *Selection 29*, p. 11 f.

he does attack (from the traditional point of view) every effort by Gestalt theorists to treat these problems, without, however, working out a concrete and consistent physiological theory of his own. (405–406): Müller's criticism of Wertheimer's original theory is based on a confusion of Wertheimer's two concepts of short-circuit and concentric effect. (407): several of Müller's false interpretations of Köhler's book on the *Physische Gestalten* (cf. above, *Selection* 3) are corrected.]

408 Müller's principal attack against our functional theory is this: There is nothing new in Wertheimer's assumption of reciprocal effects between excitations in the optic sector. This theory has always been advanced to explain contrast phenomena, but surely no one has ever before sought to derive from their reciprocal effects a *unity* of these excitations. There are at first the independent excitations e_1, e_2, e_3, etc.; *after* their mutual influences these become $\acute{e}_1$, $\acute{e}_2$, $\acute{e}_3$, etc., and these are now just as independent as were the first because nothing more has been changed than the types of local excitation.

The facts are these: Like many others, Müller has seen that the purely mechanistic view of a constrained conduction of isolated excitations is futile. But he seems to have no idea of what will happen if transverse communications (and hence functional intercourse) occur in the conducting system. While by abandoning the assumption of perfect isolation he establishes the possibility of interaction, Müller treats the excitations at the same time as though
409 under the new assumption they *could* be independent. The interaction he is here suggesting may be illustrated in the following manner. Three men stand facing each other; each has in one hand a hat and in the other a piece of chalk. They are independent and constitute a mere total of unrelated parts. Suddenly each places a hat on one neighbour and makes a chalk mark on the sleeve of the other. After this all three are different but remain as independent of one another as before, i.e. they represent $\acute{e}_1$, $\acute{e}_2$, $\acute{e}_3$. The current in a conducting system (thermal, electrical, etc.) is never of this type. Müller seems to hold that after the " reciprocal effect " has occurred the excitations have nothing further to do with one another. But how, then, would this effect be initiated? What causes it? What stops it so suddenly? When does it really come to a stop? The principal theme of my book on the *Physische Gestalten* is a direct attack on these questions, yet Müller dismisses this as not worth considering.

[410: reasons are drawn from the argument contained in *Selection* 3 above why Müller *cannot* dismiss these questions as of no importance.]

411 One consequence of the general theory is that no theory of contrast can be set up in which " interaction " between colours would resemble the relations between the three men in our example. If the assumption of isolation between the individual nerve paths is set aside at all, it is set aside completely; the communication between different processes cannot be a " device " merely for the purpose of producing contrast. There can be contrast only in a whole whose local colour-processes are so determined (by the process as a whole) that the distribution of colours helps to maintain a stable
412 state of that whole. Our theoretical procedure in accordance with these principles seems to Müller, however, " crude " and he finds it incredible that we should hope in this way to discover the fundamental laws of perception. But is it not perhaps really " crude " completely to neglect in a contrast theory the rich functional relationships of our general theory? An adequate procedure in the investigation of such phenomena, far from being " crude ", imposes the utmost demands upon scientific method.

A dynamic whole such as we have described is a unit [*Einheit*] in a very real sense since it can only exist *as* a whole. But according to Müller's notions of " interaction " one can find nothing more than individual excitations plus *laws* of reciprocal influence and functional relationships: hence no physically real thing. The only psychophysical reality which Müller accepts is " the present state of a material system ". I maintain: the pervasive tension system by which such an extended state is sustained, is real. Gestalt theory has obviously never claimed that the general laws of interaction are real. Laplace's equation, for example, states the conditions every stationary electric current must satisfy. But who would argue that these laws create a unity in the current? The term " functional relations " must be very carefully examined, for it can have several meanings. There are undoubtedly functional relations which involve no reality in the sense just discussed even though we can demonstrate that in the given instance they "subsist" ["*bestehen*"].
413 Suppose, for example, that there are two pendulums, one 4 m. and the other 1 m. long. The relation of their frequencies is as 2 : 1, but between the two pendulums there is nothing real as representative of this functional relationship. If there were a relation such as this between two brain processes it would be false to designate it as the psychophysical correlate of a conscious state.

But the next example is quite different. If, of two plates in a plate

condenser, one is held, by a battery connection, at a constant potential and the other is grounded, the charges (opposite signs) will be the same and both will be equally distributed throughout. Between them there is something *real*: the electric field whose density can be measured, which varies with the character of the intervening space, which contains a quantity of energy, and therefore possesses mass. Its characteristic property is a "pull" at right angles to the plates. Here, as in all cases of a stationary electrical current and for all stationary distributions of current, there is more than a mere law of statistical relations between independent local
[414–416: omitted] states. And it is a reality such as this which I also assume for processes occurring in the optic sector.

Selection 34

REPLY TO EUGENIO RIGNANO

By Wolfgang Köhler

" Bemerkungen zur Gestalttheorie (in Anschluss an Rignanos Kritik)," *Psychol. Forsch.*, 1928, **11**, 188–234.

188 The purpose of this paper is to answer certain criticisms of Gestalt
theory which have been made by Eugenio Rignano.[1]

The concept " Gestalt ".—We hold (and to this Rignano also
subscribes) that perceptual space and time contain neither an
indifferent mosaic nor an indifferent continuity; instead it is
characteristic of seeing, hearing, etc., that they disclose compact
189 units [*Einheiten*] and groups relatively segregated from their
environment. Units and groups of this kind we call " Gestalten in
the narrower sense ".[2] They occur in different degrees of pronouncedness—from semi-" chaos " to completed, clear articulation
[*Durchbildung*].

Rignano, however, who believes that every whole is compounded
of independent elements, is at a loss to see how Gestalt psychology
can do other than begin with elementary sensations. Nor is he alone
in this, for many psychologists still hold that for compounding to
occur there must first be something to compound. This argument
rests on the assumption that a psychical compounding process is
constantly in progress. But it is precisely this which Gestalt theory
refuses to accept. That all organization [*Gestaltung*] comes about
as the result of a psychical process is an hypothesis which we reject
on the grounds of experience. Certainly every Gestalt psychologist
190 knows perfectly well that a beam of light falls on a certain retinal

[1] *Scientia*, 1927; also *Psychol. Forsch.*, 1928, **11**, 172–187; see also Rignano's article, " The psychological theory of form," *Psychol. Rev.*, 1928, **35**, 118–135.

[2] (P. 203): in a later publication (*Scientia*, 1928) Rignano claims that this use of the term " groups " proves that I consider wholes to be mere summations of parts and that these parts are precisely the elementary sensations which he also has designated. But in vain will anyone search in my writings for a definition of Gestalten as groups. The expression " units and groups " is used to indicate that some segregated wholes are continua, others (the groups) possess discrete members. The former sometimes, and the latter always, contain *genuine parts* (cf. *Selections 3* and *33*, 389 f.).

Grateful acknowledgment is hereby made to *Julius Springer*, *Verlagsbuchhandlung*, Berlin, for permission to reproduce the illustrations used in this Selection.

spot as if there were no other retinal points and no other light beams upon them.[1] But there is no proof that the physiological sequel of such stimulation is made up of local independent processes. Instead the local aspects of this physiological whole-process are dependent upon their dynamic relationships within that whole. And so, when Rignano asks what the psychical factor is which
191 unites sensory elements, we are quite ready to answer that we have no theory to offer because, as we see it, there are no antecedent sensations to which such a theory could refer.

193 *Rignano's empiristic interpretations.*—According to Rignano we have failed to see that it is the emotional significance [*Bedeutung*] of a sensation-manifold which constitutes the unity of that manifold and segregates it from its environment. In this way "*a* fruit" or "*a* stone" become segregated, individual things out of the chaos of "infinitely small and infinitely numerous" elements because of our affective tendencies (pleasure and displeasure). Later other sensation complexes more or less resembling such objects would associatively remind us of them and hence be also apprehended as wholes corresponding to those earlier ones: for example, the groups of dots and lines in Wertheimer's experiments.[2] But in no case does the unity itself have anything to do with *vision*.

Rignano has become so accustomed to his own hypotheses that he believes them to be established truths, and he therefore holds any deviating *interpretation* to be false. Rignano's mode of thinking (essentially empiristic in character) has indeed dominated psychology for a long time; *now*, however, a very different point of view has arisen. Gestalt theory holds that though past experience does often influence present experience-structures (including cases with emotional colouring), "autochtonic" sensory organization

[1] An opposite point of view has been attributed to us by Woodworth ("*Gestalt* psychology and the conception of reaction stages," *Am. J. Psychol.*, 1927, **39**, 62–69, esp. pp. 67 f.): "[The configurationists] point to the existence of real, dynamic, physical configurations. . . . Finding configuration to exist outside the organism, they suggest that it passes by some continuous flux into the organism. . . ." This misunderstanding may be avoided in the future if I express the issue even more radically: in no case of visual or auditory organization does the purely physical stimulus-manifold exhibit any whole-coherence worthy of practical consideration. At the same time, however, it is both possible and important for the sensory process which occurs in the nervous system to correspond in objective organization to the things or events from which the stimuli originate. When someone plays on the piano, organized processes take place within him, but the physical wave-progression brought about by his activity constitutes no organized whole. Nevertheless another person, if he "understands" the music to some degree, at least, hears processes organized similarly to those occurring in the pianist. But melodies are certainly not transported through the air to the second organism. (Cf. also *Selection 3*, p. 193, and original text of that Selection, p. 194.)

[2] *Selection 5*.

precedes, and indeed *must* precede this influence. Any contrary argument is sure to be circular. The value of empiristic interpretations in a theory of perception has been vastly over-estimated.
194 Nor is Rignano justified in accusing us of being unfamiliar with this point of view.[1] He himself fails to see that his theory of the *exclusively* affective nature of organization is unfounded in fact. Preceding the emotion one might have regarding a perceived object, that object itself must be experienced. The constellation of stars which we call the Dipper may remind one, say, of a "wagon", but this can occur only *after* one has experienced some organized form which then and *as such* is seen to resemble a wagon.

195 In Rignano's theory it is not necessary, however, for every unity arising from an aggregate of elementary sensations to depend upon an emotional organizing process. Some aggregates (e.g. the dots, etc.) in Wertheimer's experiment (*Selection* 5) will remind us of more or less similar objects in our earlier experience, and hence become wholes in present experience. The power of reproduction which Rignano thus ascribes to aggregates of elementary sensations would, by his own theory, be due to the reproductive influence of the several sensations acting independently—i.e. there would be merely a sum of separate reproductions each connected with a separate sensation. But one can make radical changes in the colour, size, and position of an object—i.e. in the "sensory elements" of Rignano's theory—yet the object will still appear as a whole of the same properties as before. If it is proposed that "relations" between the elements are responsible for the reproductive effect, one can ask: But which relations? There are so many relations, one as good as another, logically, yet many are of no importance for the
196 whole in question and can be changed without materially affecting it, while certain other, *special* relations are crucial for the whole. In order to distinguish between relations one must first have a principle of selection, and this can be obtained only from the whole itself. Thus, since wholes must *precede* the reproductive emotional experience, it would obviously be superfluous to inconvenience the emotions and their corresponding reproductive effects with this task—the hypothesis had all along to assume what it now seeks to derive.

197 But surprisingly enough Rignano himself raises an issue which makes his theory quite untenable. He claims that we confuse the meaning [*Sinn*] of objects with their organization since in

[1] See *Selection 5*, pp. 331–336, also *Selections 4*, *9a*, *9b*, and *33*, p. 400 f.

interpreting the meaning of an object we merely employ the word "Gestalt". In his opinion the "meaning" of an object is the reproduction of an affective tendency associated with the use (harmful or helpful) which that object has.

Let us first consider his criticism. It is clear from his examples what Rignano means by the term "*signification*" (his French translation of "*Sinn*"). Some things are nutritious, others poisonous; we live in one thing, wear another, upon a third one rests: these are their "significations". Rignano is dealing with the empiristic-practical functions of objects. But Gestalt theory certainly does not hold that these "*significations*" of things are to be explained by an appeal to the Gestalt concept. Although we do not believe that such acquired "*significations*" are purely arbitrary, we nevertheless agree perfectly with Rignano that they
198 are of empiristic origin. It is not true, as Rignano maintains, that we have simply overlooked the empiristic nature of such functional values.[1] He has observed that we look upon "meaningful coherences" as Gestalt-coherences, and further, that when we speak of "meaningful figures" we have their Gestalt properties in mind. This is perfectly true, but not in the sense that Rignano would interpret it. The following distinction will make this clear.

There are in German two uses of the word "*Sinn*". In one rather superficial use it has approximately the meaning of "signification." In this sense a design used symbolically might be spoken of as a "*sinnvolle Figur*"—meaning a figure which had by custom attained a certain empiristic significance as the symbol of some well-known thing. Gestalt psychology has no particular connection with this meaning of the word. The other use is much more important. If I can survey the structure of an entire situation and my behaviour therein yields a "solution" relevant to the intrinsic property of that situation as a whole, my behaviour is "meaningful" ["*sinnvoll*"]. On the other hand in clear cases of organization [*Gestaltung*] the whole-process is determined by intrinsic properties of a whole situation and therefore meaningful behaviour may be considered as a case of organization [*Gestaltung*]. This characterization applies also to certain perceptions. For the meaningfulness of either process, consciousness is only of secondary importance. It is

[1] See, for example, W. Köhler, "An Aspect of Gestalt Psychology," *Pedag. Seminary*, 1925, **32**, p. 702: "Most things are certainly *known* objects for the adult. This means, for instance, that when seeing a pipe we see it as something with a specific function in smoking, and of course this 'meaning' of that optical unit on our desk is brought into it by experience."

199 just as intrinsic to visual structures that they should strive towards
their own definite closure as it is for a human being that his
behaviour should proceed towards the intrinsically appropriate end
of a behaviour sequence. If the circumstances of a visual perception
permit such a closure, the presented object is said to be a " *sinnvolle* "
figure, organization, design, etc.

While discussing these points Rignano inadvertently refutes
his own theory of whole-formation. He holds, it will be remembered, that the unity of a sensation manifold is due to the affective
tendency which it arouses. If, therefore, *no* affective tendency were
aroused, whole formation should not occur. In his attempt to show
that " signification " cannot be accounted for by Gestalt theory
he cites pathological cases in which the patients have so far lost
all " affective reaction " to their environment that although they
perceive the *sensory form* (Rignano's own terms) of things, they
nevertheless fail to recognize the objects seen. Rignano does not
200 see that cases such as this constitute a conclusive argument against
his own theory. If these patients can experience visual objects
without even knowing what they are, it cannot be true, as he
would otherwise maintain, that affective processes are essential
for the unification of elements.

[201–218: here begins the second Part of this article. Part I was first
published in *Scientia*; Rignano's answer appeared in the May, 1928,
issue of the same journal. The discussion of pp. 202–212 takes up
the question of part-whole relationships (omitted here because a
similar discussion is given in *Selection* 33); on pp. 213–218 the
empiristic explanations upon which Rignano's second article also
relies are again criticized and their pertinence denied.]

219 *The segregation of wholes.*—Rignano asks why nervous processes
correspond so well in their Gestalt properties to the objects they
represent. A first answer to this question is that such correspondence
is by no means universal. That we experience certain groups of
stars, for example, does not mean that these stars themselves constitute groups. More generally: most groups (i.e. wholes with
discrete members) are wholes only in our own vision, whereas
among themselves the members have no physical connections.
220 And indeed the same holds also for many continua which are
experienced as wholes without there being any corresponding
physically unified object. The question therefore arises, how are
really unified things so often correctly seen as such—does this
occur only by virtue of some pre-established harmony between
events in our environment and the laws of sensory dynamics?

In order to answer this question we must consider the essential principles of segregation by visual objects.

The first of these principles is that whereby *one* continuous surface is separated from *another* (field) surface. If both are homogeneous but qualitatively different, the boundary between them will exhibit a sudden leap [*Sprung*] in quality, in keeping with the principles of physical chemistry. In the interior of a homogeneous solution, for example, there are strong inner forces; at its
221 boundaries forces of a different sort occur. Numerous instances in nature could be cited where homogeneously coloured objects are, by a leap in colour, set off from their environment: e.g. the trunk of a tree against the surrounding grass, etc. The results of sensory dynamics correspond in all such cases with the unities given by external nature. And again, a path or river seen in a landscape is a practical unity regardless of whether or not we so name it. The river reflects light differently from the way its banks do, and a road likewise differs from the fields which surround it. One needs here no past experience with the uses these things might serve in order to effect their segregation.

222 But colour alone is not the only factor involved in segregation. A rough area surrounded by a smooth surface will also yield a segregated unity, and vice versa. This relationship holds also for murky and clear, hazy and definite, confused and orderly. Indeed it is not necessary that the entire *surface* of an object differ in character from its environment; it usually happens that an area will be segregated if only its boundary exhibits a "leap in character". A pencil mark on a homogeneous surface will suffice to illustrate this. If a small area is enclosed by the mark, this enclosed area will be seen as a segregated whole even though its physical properties are exactly the same as those of the surrounding region.
223 And in general we may say that all physical objects will be seen as segregated things if there is at their visual *boundaries* a suitable leap in quality relative to their environment.

On the other hand not all boundaries are unequivocal: often there will be two or more competing possibilities. The following discussion (illustrated by Fig. 1) will make this clear. Why, for
224 example, does one see *abcda* and not *abefgda* as the segregated whole in this figure? There are four factors which contribute to this: (1) the "statistical" or average similarity of *surface* property is more uniform in *abcda* than in *abefgda*; (2) a leap in quality which is the *same* all along a contour has an advantage over one in which there are differences; (3) the more radical a leap is, the better will

it delimit the enclosed surface; (4) the contour whose course is "good" (or one might say "organic") will be stronger than another which lacks this property. The boundaries of stationary physical systems, for example, assume not just any arbitrary form; they are usually "simple" or "organic" and more often smooth than irregular.

Finally, another principle of segregation is that of motion. It is well known in optics that weak contours which would otherwise escape notice will suddenly become very pronounced when they are moved. And a physical object which formerly was indistinguishable from its background will, upon being moved, become
225 visually real and its boundaries immediately stand in contrast to the surroundings. This effect occurs quite irrespective of earlier experiences with the motion of objects.

It would naturally be quite unsatisfying if these principles only *chanced* to conform with the "correct" sensory wholes. But it is not chance, nor is there any reason to believe that the sensory processes of human beings (and higher animals) have gradually attained this appropriate capacity. As a matter of fact the behaviour of nervous substance in such cases is probably a fundamental characteristic of its physical-chemical functioning. And as regards the principle of "good" structure one can only say that if it did *not* hold, a genetic inquiry into the reasons for this certainly would be needed. And the same applies also to the principle of motion, for its occurrence can be traced much too far back into the fields of colloidal chemistry and even the physical chemistry of crystalloid systems for there to be any doubt but that it need not nor even could be bred into the human nervous system if it were not already present.

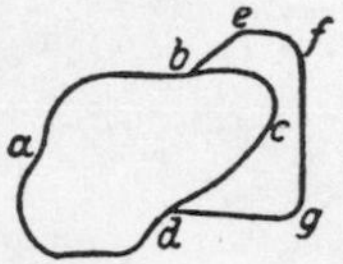

FIG. 1.

226 And so the correspondence between nervous processes and physical objects may be explained thus. The segregation of natural objects takes place or persists as a result of their physical-chemical nature. Their colour, texture, geometric form, and compactness of structure are due to physical-chemical forces. It is through the operation of forces exemplifying the same principles that segregation of whole processes occurs in the nervous system. There is here no more pre-established harmony than in the fact that spectroscopic analysis shows the stars to contain the same chemical elements as the earth.

[227–234: several problems discussed in Part I are here brought up again because Rignano, failing to account for them in terms of his own theory, has merely reasserted his original position. These include the definition of " *Sinn* ", the question of transposition of melodies and the issue of when the term " Gestalt " may properly be used.]

INDEX

Items preceded by an asterisk (*) are but *partially* indexed since references to them in the various *Selections* are so numerous as to make an adequate listing impossible.